THE HISTORICAL MUSEUM BASLE

Guide to the collections

MERRELL HOLBERTON
PUBLISHERS LONDON

Published by the Historisches Museum Basel
in association with Merrell Holberton Publishers
simultaneously in English, French and German editions

Authors:

AN Anne Nagel
BIS Benno Schubiger
BS Beatrice Schärli
EJB Eduard J. Belser
FE Franz Egger
IPM Irmgard Peter-Müller
JP Jacqueline Portmann
RCW Rahel C. Warburton
SF Sandra Fiechter
VG Veronika Gutmann
vR Burkard von Roda

Photographs: Historisches Museum Basel, Maurice Babey,
Allan Eaton
Plans: Hochbauamt Kanton Basel-Stadt, René Thiébaud
Bibliography prepared with the help of Therese Wollmann

Project administration: Lukas Hartmann
Editorial: Lukas Hartmann, Paul Holberton
English translation: Kim Schumann, Judith Hayward, Edmund
Jephcott
Editor of English edition: Kay Sutton

ISBN 1 85894 003 6

Printed in Switzerland

Production: Merrell Holberton Publishers
Axe & Bottle Court, 70 Newcomen Street, London SE1 1YT
Design: Karin Dunbar Design, London
Composition: August Filmsetting, St Helens
Reproduction: Columbia (UK), London
Printing: Gissler Druck AG, Basle

THE HISTORICAL MUSEUM BASLE

CONTENTS

Introduction

With the opening of the Historisches Museum Basel (the Basle Historical Museum) in the Barfüsserkirche on 21 April 1894 what was then the largest and most important public collection of its kind in Switzerland found a fitting home. On the occasion of its jubilee in 1994 the opportunity has been taken to look once more at the Museum, in its present state, in overview. In the hundred years that have passed the size of the collection has multiplied several times over; scholarship relating to it has advanced and its facilities have expanded to fill four buildings. The Museum's importance has increased. There can be no doubt of the desirability of presenting a whole picture of the Historisches Museum as it is today. Hence the present catalogue, for which 500 objects have been selected from the collection and discussed in the light of the latest scholarship.

Comparable publications, dealing with the whole collection, lie a long way in the past: *Offizieller Führer* [official guide] by Albert Burckhardt-Finsler, 1899, and *Historische Schätze Basels – eine Auswahl schöner Gegenstände* [historical treasures of Basle – a selection of fine objects] by Hans Reinhardt, Adolf Glaser and Robert Spreng, 1942). In now presenting a catalogue-handbook combining both precise information and attractive illustrations, the Museum is responding to the expectations of the museum-going public of today. The selection the different curators have made is designed to be representative of the full range of the Museum's holdings. The book's division into 21 sections is an appropriate one for a museum specialising in artistic and cultural history. Each section has an introduction outlining the total holding from which the selected items have been drawn. Information on the origin, scope and status of different groups of objects allows them to be compared to those in other collections. In order to achieve an overview of the Museum's very diverse material – something not so easily done when visiting the Museum itself – each section is arranged chronologically. It has been decided to abandon the method that hitherto has usually been followed, of grouping objects by their collection history or 'fonds' (the Münster treasury, the Amerbach Cabinet, the Faesch Museum – to which anyway special publications have already been devoted). To make it easier to use the catalogue as a guide, every item on permanent exhibition that features in it has been labelled in the Museum with its catalogue number in the book.

To introduce a collection as wide-ranging as that of the Historisches Museum, today numbering several hundred thousand objects, it will be helpful to explain the essential programme behind the Museum. The founding programme formulated towards the end of the C19 has been progressively adapted and supplemented as the institution has developed; nevertheless, over the last 100 years, during the period when the collection has experienced its greatest increase, the original conception has continued to determine the way in which the Museum has grown. At that time the institution's objectives were defined as follows:

"The interest of the collection is primarily local. The aim is to unite in it the historic antiquities of Basle and its region, and the products and utensils of its early indigenous arts,

Aerial view of the Barfüsserkirche (church of the Discalced Franciscans), the main building of the Historisches Museum since 1894 (for the church, see catalogue no. 224)

trades and crafts. However, the development of the collection has gone far beyond this circumscribed area: the collection has become an historical museum not only of Basle, but of the Upper Rhine region and the whole of Switzerland; many outstanding pieces have also come from abroad. At present the early Middle Ages and the end of the 18th century mark the limits of the collection" (*Katalog der Mittelalterlichen Sammlung zu Basel* [Catalogue of the Basle Medieval Collection], 1890). Four years later, after the Historisches Museum had been established in the Barfüsserkirche, important areas of the collection were listed and different areas distinguished: "In general, we have started out from the principle that our Museum should be especially concerned with those branches that are already well represented, and can therefore bear comparison with corresponding departments in larger institutions. Here we refer in the first place to goldsmiths' work, wood sculpture, furniture and joinery, weaving, and embroidery. Cultural history is another important aspect. In this respect our Museum is well on the way to becoming an increasingly complete illustration of the history of the Basle citizen's household over four centuries. A third aspect, finally, relates to arts and crafts, which has a decisive influence on the allocation of the Federal subsidy. In this respect the Historical Museum is also a craft museum… It hardly needs to be emphasized that despite all this the historical element is not overlooked…" (Annual report 1894). Finally, in 1899 it was stated: "First of all, all objects that have a historical significance, in the widest sense of that term, for the city of Basle and its surrounding area, shall be collected. Secondly, the Museum shall be a centre of stimulation and instruction regarding present-day crafts; and thirdly it intends to give a vivid picture of the domestic lives of our forbears" (*Offizieller Führer*, 1899). The opening of the Schweizerisches Landesmuseum in Zurich in 1898 relieved Basle of the additional task it had had to perform until then, of protecting the national cultural heritage "from oblivion or removal to other countries" (*Führer durch die Mittelalterliche Sammlungen* [guide to the Medieval Collections] 1880).

With their temporal limit extended to include the present, these programmes from the time of the institution's foundation still form the basis of the collecting carried out by the Historisches Museum Basel today. In general, the task consists of building on the Museum's existing strengths. The Museum is concerned, secondly, with the history and art of the city and its region, and, thirdly, with areas relating to Basle domestic life; these areas combine the history of everyday life, the history of furniture and decoration, and social history. Fourthly, it includes applied art in selected areas of western European decorative art.

An aspect peculiar to Basle, established by law in 1892, is that the collections of its great museums (the Historisches Museum, the public library, the Kunstsammlung [art museum] and the ethnographic collection) belong to the University. This status not only underlines the museums' important educational function, but ensures the proper maintenance of the collections. With the University they form "an inalienable property of the canton of Basel-Stadt, which is indissolubly linked to the physical location of the city of Basle and may never be divorced from the constitutions of the institutes of higher education" (decree of 1919).

As is well known, the origin of the Basle museums can be traced back to the Amerbach 'Cabinet', a collection containing mostly works of the late C15 and C16. The city owes its position in the forefront of museological history to this collection, originated by a Basle bourgeois family in the Renaissance period, acquired for the University in 1661/62 and open to the public since 1671. The Historisches Museum owns important parts of the Amerbach Cabinet – the effects of Erasmus, the coins collection that constituted the core of the Cabinet, the collection of goldsmiths' models. After 1856, when the Medieval Collection, the predecessor of the present Historisches Museum, was founded, following the example of the Germanisches Nationalmuseum founded in Nuremberg in 1852, its range was expanded and its modern development, in keeping with the general systematisation of museum scholarship, began. The Museum has continued to develop until the present day. As a result, individual areas not present in the original collection, such as musical instruments, coaches and sledges or, in the field of applied art, ceramics and clocks, have an importance in their own right equal to that of individual museums.

Today the Historisches Museum Basel deserves the title of the leading collection of cultural history in the Upper Rhine region, and boasts a number of specific collections of major international significance. It owes this position in large measure to a tradition of donation well established among Basle's citizens. In documenting this remarkable tradition through many examples, this publication is designed to express the Museum's thanks to those who have upheld and maintained it, and to encourage future benefactors.

Acknowledgements

This Guide to the Collections owes its existence to the recognition of the educational department of the canton of Basel-Stadt and of its chairman, Prof. Hans Rudolf Striebel, and the director of the cultural department, Dr. Susanne Imbach. The confidence in the project,

Aerial view of the Haus zum Kirschgarten, built 1775–80, with (right) the older annex of the Haus zum kleinen Kirschgarten, now housing the clocks collection

despite its being undertaken at short notice, of the Kommission zum Historischen Museum under its chairman Dr. Bernhard Christ has been supportive at every stage. Generous financial contributions have been made by the Berta Hess Cohn-Stiftung Basel under its chairman, Herr lic. iur. Martin Hug-Batschelet (printing costs), by the Stiftung für das Historische Museum under its chairman, Dr Alfred R. Weber-Oeri, by the Ulrich und Klara Huber-Reber-Stiftung under its chairman, Dr. Christoph Helbing, and by the Ceramica-Stiftung under its chairman, Dr Thomas Stähelin. Dr. Georges Segal helped in an advisory capacity. Our sincere thanks are due to all who have been involved, not least the committed staff of the Museum, the publisher, the translators and the printer, for enabling the Historisches Museum Basel to offer such a useful compendium of the treasures entrusted to it.

Who can doubt that such treasures make Basle rich!

Burkard von Roda
Director

Brief chronology of the Historisches Museum Basel

1536 The estate of Erasmus of Rotterdam was inherited by Bonifacius Amerbach (1495–1562) and, with his own coins collection and paintings by Holbein, formed the nucleus of the Amerbach Cabinet.

1585–87 Inventory D of the Amerbach Cabinet, drawn up by Basilius Amerbach (1533–1591), lists the collection according to the way it was installed in the private building housing the collection, the Haus Zum Kaiserstuhl, completed in 1580.

1661 The Basle town council decided to acquire the Amerbach collections for the University.

1671 The Amerbach Cabinet was made publicly accessible in the Mücke, the former meeting-house of the Basle nobility – the earliest public museum of a civic community.

1823 Substantial expansion of the collection by the addition of the holding of the Faesch Museum, formed during the C17.

1849 Opening of the Museum on the Augustinergasse in a building designed by the architect Melchior Berri – the first purpose-built museum in Basle. Here all the collections were united (the library, the art collection, the collection of antiquities and coins, the natural history collection).

1856 First division of the public collection with the founding of the Medieval Collection, the predecessor of the Historisches Museum, at the instigation of Wilhelm Wackernagel. The Medieval Collection was housed in ancillary buildings of the Münster in the Bischofshof.

1872 Foundation of the Verein für die Mittelalterliche Sammlung und für Erhaltung baslerischer Altertümer (Association for the Medieval Collection and for the Preservation of Basle Antiquities); since 1892 Verein für das Historische Museum.

1892 Amalgamation of the Medieval Collection and the antiquities collection (without ethnographic objects) and of the holdings of the Basle Zeughaus (armoury) under the new name of 'Historical Museum'. The new institution – the largest and most important of its kind in Switzerland – was endowed with two salaried posts, for a curator and an attendant.

1894 On 21 April the Historisches Museum Basel was opened in the greatly modified Barfüsserkirche (church of the Discalced Franciscans).

1899 Project for an enlargement of the Museum on the Steinenberg (not carried through).

1904 Part of the building at Steinenberg 4/6, built as a schoolhouse in 1822, was assigned to the Historisches Museum for administration, workshops and storage.

1923 The Museum received as a bequest from Marie Burckhardt the Segerhof, a merchant's house built in 1788–91, which was opened as the first 'Wohnmuseum' (museum of domestic life) in 1926.

1935 Demolition of the Segerhof. Allocation of the Haus zum Kirschgarten as a replacement (not opened until 1951).

1938 Installation of the Stadt- und Münstermuseum in the Kleines Klingental, with items from the Historisches Museum's collection and from the Reformed church of Basel-Stadt.

1943 Opening of the musical instrument collection at Leonhardskirchplatz 5 (in the music department of the University).

1951 Opening of the Haus zum Kirschgarten as a museum of domestic life in Basle in the C18. At the same time the following special collections were established: Greek and Roman antiquities (hence the name 'Griechischer Saal' [Greek room], still used), ceramics, sledges, clocks, toys.

1953–54 Closure of the Barfüsserkirche; replacement of the floor, rearrangement of the collections (caused by the refurbishment of the Haus zum Kirschgarten).

1956 Enlargement of the crypt of the chancel of the Barfüsserkirche to form the 'Untere Schatzkammer' (lower treasury).

1957 Opening of the collection of early musical instruments after its move to Leonhardsstrasse 8. Donation of the Lobeck collection by Dr. h.c. Paul Sacher.

1965 Closure of the antiquities collection of the Historisches Museum. Its objects (except for coins and gems) were transferred to the newly founded Antikenmuseum and excavation finds from Augst were moved to the Römermuseum located there.

1975 Re-erection of the Baroque garden pavilion from the Haus zum Hof, St. Albanvorstadt 36, in the garden of the Haus zum Kirschgarten (providing further space for display of the collection).

1977 Opening of the porcelain collection of the Pauls-Eisenbeiss-Stiftung (ca. 750 porcelain figures and tableware items from the factories at Meissen, Frankenthal, Hoechst and Ludwigsburg) in the Haus zum Kirschgarten.

1979 Acquisition of the Dr. Edith Stocker-Nolte-Stiftung (C19/20 house with complete contents).

1981 Re-opening of the renovated Barfüsserkirche. Alterations carried out included replacement of the nave pillars, repair to the west façade, reconstruction of the rood-screen demolished in 1843, demolition of the side-aisle galleries, enlargement of the crypt to create new display rooms and offices.

1981 Opening of the coach and sledge collection in Brüglingen.

1986 Re-opening of the musical instrument collection after renovations to the building.

1986 Opening of the Haus zum kleinen Kirschgarten, now annexed to the Haus zum Kirschgarten, with ten new exhibition rooms: clock collections of Carl and Lini Nathan-Rupp (242 clocks) and the Dr. Eugen Gschwind-Stiftung (208 clocks); residential rooms of the C19 and C20.

The winning design (by Gregor Höll of Basle) in the open competition for a poster for the Museum held in 1993–94

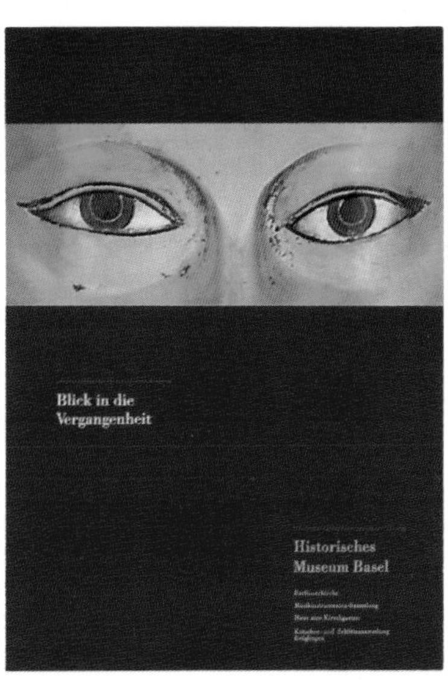

1987 Dissolution of the collection of the Gewerbemuseum Basel; its collections were taken over by the Historisches Museum until 1994 (ca. 20,000 objects).

1990–95 Reorganization of the storerooms.

1993 Enlargement of the administration building at Steinenberg 4.

The four buildings of the Museum

The Historisches Museum Basel is installed in four buildings with four permanent exhibitions, in a total exhibition area of ca. 8,000 m^2. All four buildings are historic; on the one hand they provide an environment conducive to the enjoyment of the collections, while on the other their fabric imposes practical limitations on their use as museums. The Barfüsserkirche and the Haus zum Kirschgarten contain objects from subject areas across the collections, while the musical instrument collection in the Haus Vorderer Rosengarten and the coach and sledge collection in the Botanical Garden at Brüglingen are specialist museums in the strict sense.

The Barfüsserkirche

The Barfüsserkirche, now a monument of national importance, is the most impressive church of the Franciscan order north of the Alps. It is an aisled basilica with a superb choir fully lit by 13 large windows, built in the first third of the C14, before the great earthquake of 1356. Its size and regular proportions are evidence of the important position held in Basle by the Franciscan order, established there from 1231 until the Reformation in 1529. The foundations of a preceding building to the south, consecrated in 1256, are exposed in the basement of the Museum. The other monastery buildings (see no. 224) were demolished after 1820.

After the Reformation of 1529 the church had mixed fortunes. Its furnishings, with the exception of the Peter Rot altarpiece (no. 180), were destroyed. The chancel was converted for use as a fruit loft by the addition of intermediate floors, while the nave was still being used for services as late as 1794. After its complete secularisation the space was used as a goods warehouse, and for more than 30 years from 1799, despite warnings from specialists about the decay of the stone, as a salt store. Work to convert it into the warehouse of a commercial firm began in 1843, but it served this function only until 1865. Public debate about its fate culminated in 1882 in the Regierung's recommendation that it be demolished to make way for a new private girls' school, a project narrowly defeated by 52:50 votes in the great council. After it had enjoyed temporary use as a pawnbroker's shop, a butter market and an auction room, the council decided in 1888 to use the church as a museum, and to offer it to the Federal parliament as the site for the Swiss National Museum which was being founded at that time. Despite the government's decision in favour of Zurich, the citizens of Basle held to their project of a museum church.

Hence in 1894 the Historisches Museum acquired for its site an imposing building in the city centre. In the exhibition plan of that time, the nave was used for the display of weapons, the chancel was reserved for religious antiquities, the sacristy became the treasury, while eleven historical rooms and the coins collection were laid out in the different bays of the side-aisles, with the musical instruments, the 'State and Law' antiquities, the domestic utensils and arts and crafts objects in the galleries above. The reconstruction completed in 1981 reinstated the Late Gothic structure, following extensive repair work to obviate the instability caused by salt damage. The Museum was redesigned and benefited from the addition of a basement floor which is used for a permanent exhibition devoted to Basle's history. It was now possible to represent the city's pre-medieval past with a large number of archaeological finds. vR

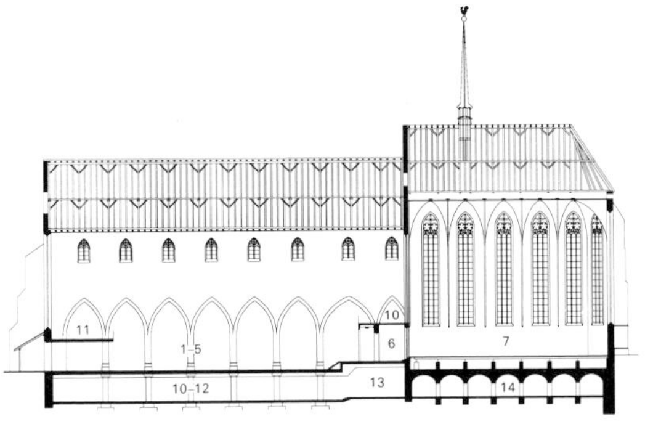

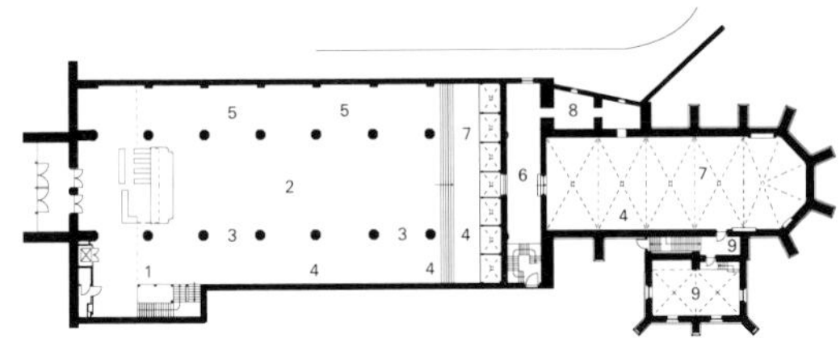

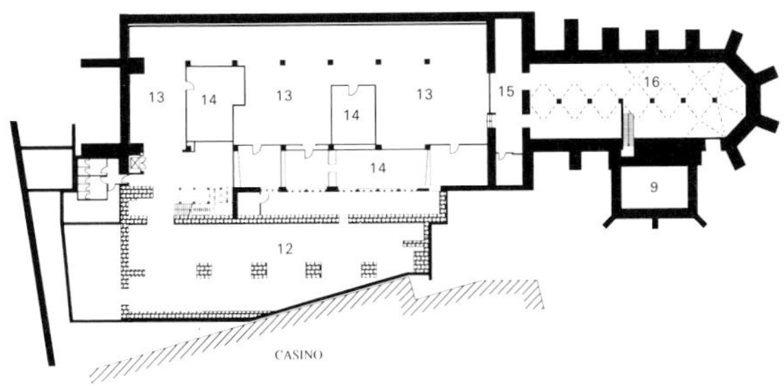

Ground floor
1 Basle bells
2 Basle fountains
3 Arts and crafts C15/16
4 Late medieval tapestries from Basle
5 Guilds and crafts
6 Basle *Dance of Death*
7 Altarpieces and church sculpture
8 Church plate
9 Treasury of Basle Münster
10 Religious art (rood-screen gallery)
11 Temporary exhibitions (west gallery)
Underchurch
12 History of the town up to 1200
Archaeological finds
from Celtic times
from Roman times
from the early and High Middle Ages
Special exhibitions: recent finds
13 Basle history since 1200
54 special themes, including:
Guilds and societies
Basle in the time of the Council of Basle
Warfare (Burgundian spoils)
Wettstein and his time
Council constitution and government 1529–1798
Ancien régime
Basle silk ribbon industry
Basle University
Carnival customs
14 Historical rooms
Glass painting/furniture/textiles
Gothic room (Haus zum Kardinal)
Rear Gothic room
Iselin room
Spiesshof room
Great Spiesshof room
Meyer zum Pfeil room
Gundeldinger room
15 Coin cabinet
16 Secular treasury with Amerbach Cabinet
Effects of Erasmus of Rotterdam
Faesch Museum
Goldsmiths' work, plaques, medals
Treasures of the Basle guilds

The Haus zum Kirschgarten

The Haus zum Kirschgarten, built in 1775–80, marks a high point of Neoclassical architecture in the Upper Rhine region. For a Basle merchant's house-cum-office it is unusually prestigious. It has a finely detailed sandstone façade, a blind portico in three bays, an entrance hall with coupled columns in the manner of the Palazzo Farnese, and above all a spacious stairway with an impressive landing preceding the main salon. The original owner was Johann Rudolf Burckhardt-de Bary (see no. 197), only 25 at the time he built it, a silk ribbon manufacturer and son-in-law of the mayor. In Ulrich Büchel-Fatio he found a Basle architect, even younger than himself, versed in the latest fashion.

In its present condition the visitor can gain only an incomplete picture of the original interior furnishings of this town residence. Admittedly, much of the fabric has been preserved: the main suite of rooms on the piano nobile with the staircase, the landing and the 'great salon', all with their stuccoed decoration; the former library on the ground floor (the so called Greek Room) and three rooms on the second floor, namely the green 'Täferstube', the Burckhardts' bedroom and the 'Rose Boudoir' dated 1780 (no. 389). But all the rooms are without their original movable furnishings, and these are not recorded. A matrimonial court case and a charge of treason had forced Johann Rudolf Burckhardt to abandon the new building in 1797. In the several changes of ownership before its designation as a museum in 1933 the former contents were lost and changes were made to the arrangement of the rooms.

Five floors of the building are used by the Museum with a total of ca. 2600 m^2 of exhibition space (including the earlier Haus zum kleinen Kirschgarten). Although since its opening in 1951 the emphasis of the permanent exhibition has shifted, as a result of important acquisitions, towards specialist collections (clocks, porcelain, faience), the Haus zum Kirschgarten is traditionally regarded as a museum of domestic life ('Wohnmuseum'). Of the ca. 50 exhibition rooms, half are devoted to domestic life in the city of Basle.

The exhibition plan preserves the idea of the first museum of domestic life in the Segerhof. This merchant's house, which Marie Burckhardt bequeathed to the city in 1923, with its contents going back to the late C18, was demolished in 1934. A virtually intact collection of furniture accumulated over time by a Basle family was thereby lost. However, in modified form, five rooms from the Segerhof have been transferred wholly or partly to the Haus zum Kirschgarten: the office (on the ground floor), the 'Visitenstube' or reception room, the dining room, the Grey Room and the kitchen (on the second floor).

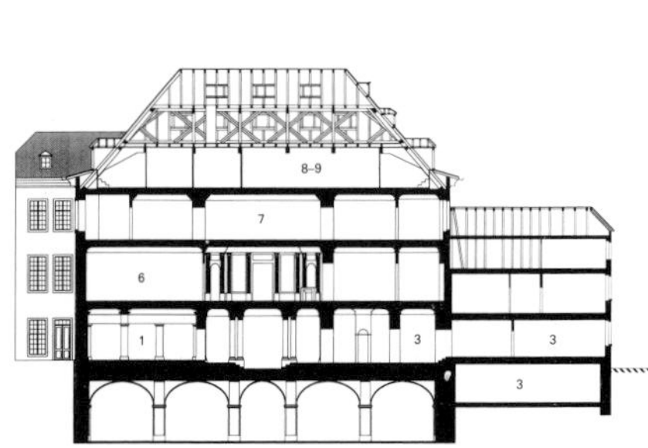

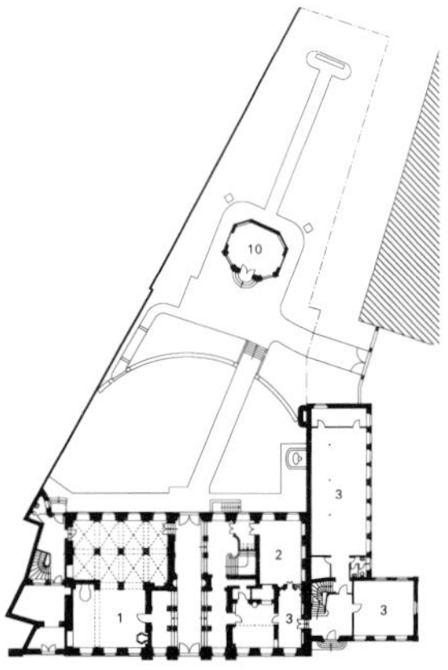

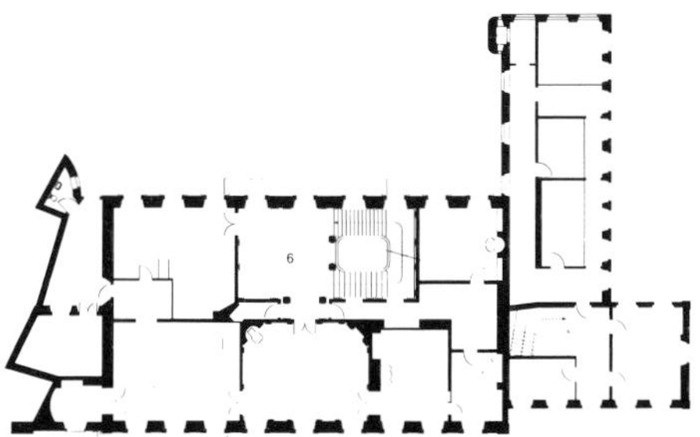

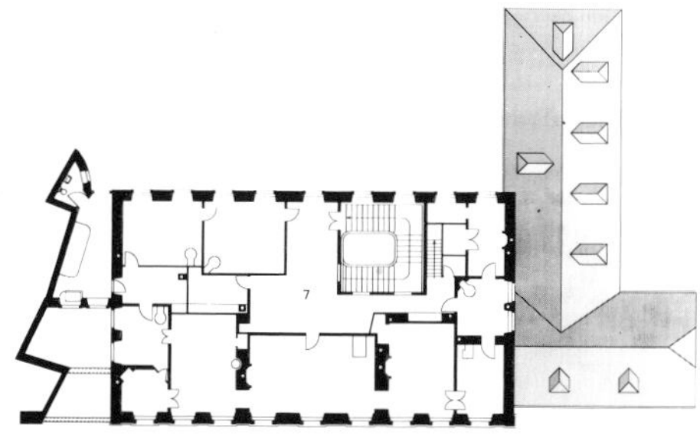

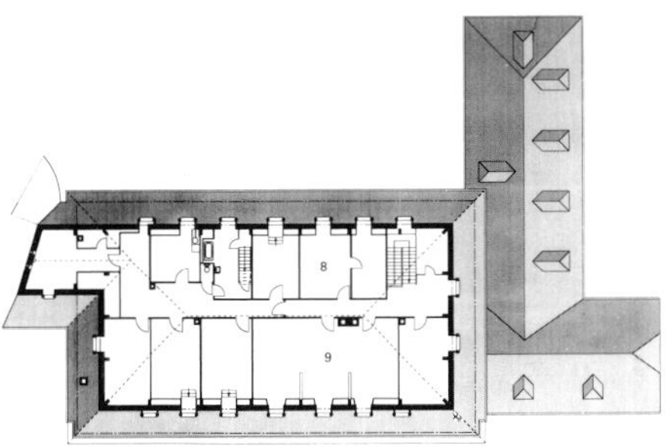

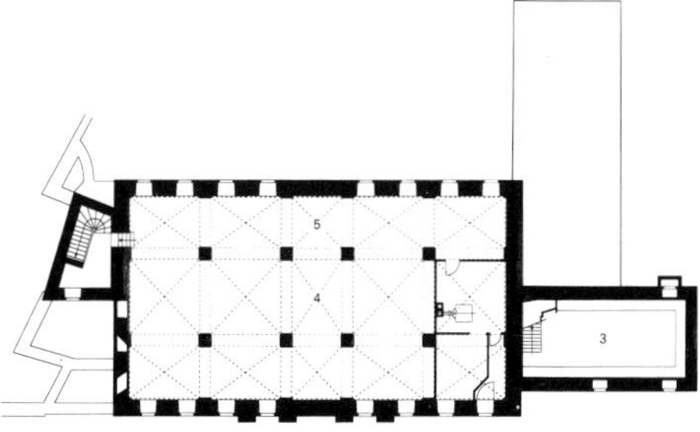

Ground floor
1 Porcelain
(Pauls-Eisenbeiss-Stiftung collection)
2 Griechischer Saal (Greek Room)
Temporary exhibitions
3 Clocks
Basle clocks
Clocks of the Nathan-Rupp collection
Non-mechanical clocks and science cabinet
Basement
3 Clocks
(Dr. Eugen Gschwind-Stiftung)
4 Faience and porcelain
Strasbourg faience
Other manufactories
5 Wrought iron
1st floor
6 Basle domestic life
Landing
Alcove room
Anteroom
Costume room (temporary exhibitions of dress and fashion)
Tapestry room
Family chapel
Large drawing room
Louis XV Salon
Louis XV closet
Box passage
Treasury (Basle table silver)

Haus zum kleinen Kirschgarten
Landing
Empire room
Biedermeier room
Christoph Merian room
Napoleon III room
Art Nouveau room
Corridor (history of the Christoph Merian Stiftung)
2nd floor
7 Basle domestic life
Summer-house
'Visitenstube' (Segerhof)
Dining room (Segerhof)
Parlour
Kitchen (Segerhof)
Zum Lichthof closet
Rose Boudoir
Burckhardts' bedroom
Grey Room (Segerhof)
Green 'Täferstube'
Corner room
Miniatures collection
Neustuck room
Passage (Zizenhausen figures)
Attic
8 Dolls' houses
9 Toys
Garden pavilion
10 Glass

Musikinstrumenten-Sammlung (Musical instruments collection)

The Historisches Museum Basel owns the largest collection of musical instruments in Switzerland. A separate building in the city centre, though still too small, has been made available to house a permanent exhibition of this collection since 1956. The late Neoclassical former residence of Councillor C. Burckhardt, the Vorderer Rosengarten, which is now the gatehouse of the neo-Baroque courtyard of the Musikakademie der Stadt Basel (the city academy of music), has space for only a quarter of the Museum's copious holdings. The exhibition is distributed over nine rooms on two floors (details of the collection on p.292).

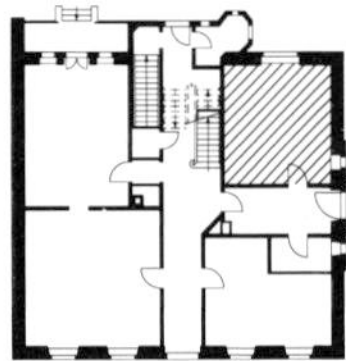

Ground floor
Woodwind instruments
Organs and mechanical instruments
Brass instruments

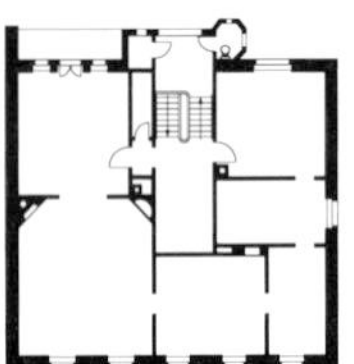

1st floor
Plucked instruments
Stringed keyboard instruments
Stringed instruments

Coach and sledge collection

The collection of coaches and sledges established on a site outside Basle in 1981 is the most recent addition to the Historisches Museum. The museum is situated about 3 km south-east of the city centre (municipality of Münchenstein, canton of Basel-Landschaft) in Brüglingen, an extensive park and leisure area. The former property of Vorder-Brüglingen was rebuilt in 1837–39 by the Basle architect Melchior Berri as a country residence for Christoph Merian. The imposing barn in which the collection is housed is a replacement building of 1906 (the original burned down in 1905). The building and site belong to the Christoph Merian Stiftung (details of the collection, p. 304).

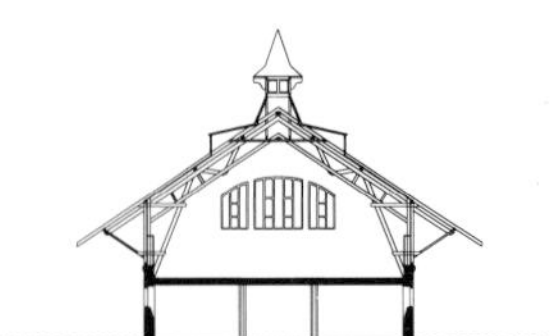

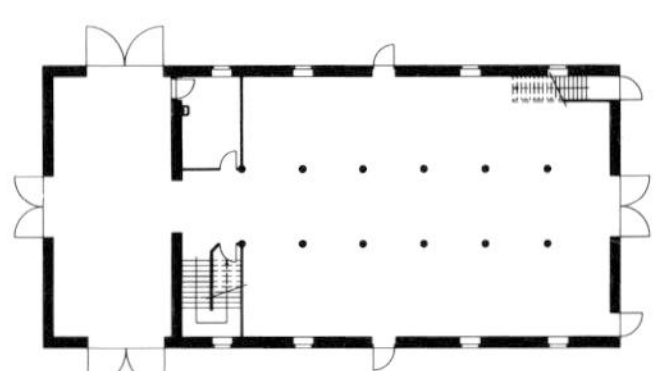

Ground floor
Luxury coaches
Children's coaches
Hunting sleighs
Commercial carts
Mail coaches

Archaeology

Interest in the archaeology of Basle goes back to the early C16. During the first systematic investigations (1582–85) of the ruins at Augst (now in the canton of Basel-Landschaft) Basilius Amerbach established that the remains were those of a Roman theatre. In 1763 Daniel Bruckner, in his book *Versuch einer Beschreibung historischer und natürlicher Merkwürdigkeiten der Landschaft Basels* [descriptive essay on the notable historical and natural features of the county of Basle], published all the discoveries and finds made at Augst until then. The Historisches Museum still holds some of these finds in the so called 'Alte Sammlungen' (old collections). In the C19, in parallel to the excavations at Augst, local scholars such as Wilhelm Vischer, Theophil Burckhardt-Biedermann and Karl Stehlin searched within the city for the origins of Basle. In 1898 the 'Delegation for old Basle' was set up by the Historische und Antiquarische Gesellschaft zu Basel (Basle historical and antiquarian society) and the Verein für das Historische Museum (Historical Museum society). Its task was to observe and preserve finds "of an archaeological nature of any kind". In 1961 Basel-Stadt was the first Swiss canton to create the post of a cantonal archaeologist with full civil service status. Today, while the Archäologische Bodenforschung (archaeological research department) is responsible for current excavations and their evaluation, the finds themselves are the responsibility of the Historisches Museum. Since 1981 the permanent exhibition 'Stadtgeschichte I' (city history 1) has documented the city's past with finds from a period extending from the second millennium BC through the Celtic and Roman eras to the High Middle Ages. JP

1
Barfüsserkirche

Axehead, ca. 1400–1300 BC
Found at St. Alban-Rheinweg, Basle
Cast bronze; length 18.7 cm
Inv. no. 1984/22.208.

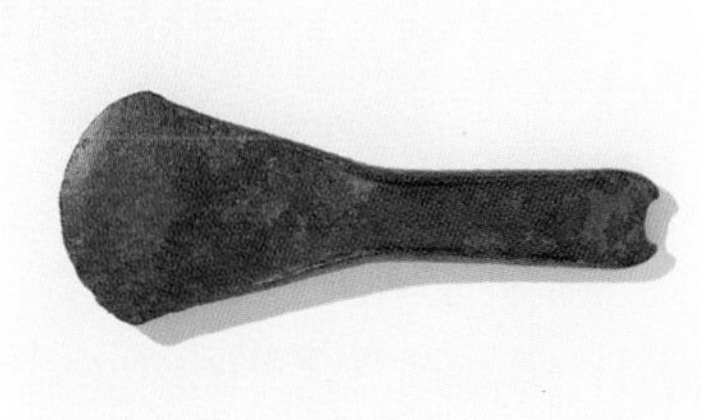

As early as the Bronze Age (2300–800 BC) there were prolonged, and perhaps continuous, human settlements along the bend of the Rhine at Basle. While most of the funerary deposits that have been found are of bronze, the objects found in the settlements are primarily ceramics. Most of the find sites are close to the Rhine, such as the settlements at the Rheingasse, in Kleinhüningen and near the St. Alban-Kirche. Protected on three sides by natural slopes and probably by a ditch on the fourth, there was a settlement near the present Martinskirche at the northern end of the Münsterhügel. In 1984, during excavation for a channel in the St. Alban-Rheinweg, this bronze axehead was unearthed at a depth of 9 m. It is in an excellent state of preservation and has a bell-shaped blade. Most bronze axes found in Europe were probably used for working wood; but they also served as weapons and prestige objects. JP

2
Barfüsserkirche

Five bracelets, 2nd half 2nd century/
1st half 1st century BC
Found at the Gasfabrik, Basle
Coloured glass and clear glass with inner layer of yellow foil; diameters 4–7 cm
Inv. nos. 1917.100.160.163.243.244.

In 1911, during construction work for a gasometer near the Voltaplatz, directly beside the Rhine, pits dug in the natural river gravel and filled with humus were discovered. They contained animal bones, ceramics and metal and glass objects from the late Celtic period. To date about 300 pits have been found, which had served as store-rooms or work places but had already been filled with refuse in the Celtic period. They were part of a settlement covering about 12 hectares founded in the middle of the C2 BC by a group of the Raurici and occupied for about 80 years. It is the oldest large settlement on the soil of Basle city. The five glass bracelets illustrated came to light in the burial ground attached to the settlement, containing about 120–30 graves. The glass used to make the bracelets was coloured by the admixture of metal oxides. A layer of yellow glass was fused inside the clear rings. The intense colours of the bracelets can only be seen when light shines through them. As well as bracelets small glass rings used as pendants have survived. JP

3
Barfüsserkirche

Spherical pot, 2nd half 2nd century/1st half 1st century BC
Found at the Gasfabrik, Basle
Clay, turned, painted, assembled from several pieces; height 37 cm
Inv. no. 1915.362.

In the roughly 300 pits discovered so far in the late Celtic settlement at the Gasfabrik (gasworks) in Basle, after animal bones ceramics are the most frequent finds. To date several tens of thousands of fragments have been retrieved. This spherical flask is an especially fine and rare example of Celtic pottery. The lower half of the vessel is unpainted. Above there is rich decoration, painted in brown pigment on a white ground. Four circular forms are surrounded by foliage and triangles and other decoration. The gently curved tendrils give an impression of movement. However, most Celtic vessels are decorated with geometrical patterns. The great variety of decoration on Celtic pottery provides important evidence of Celtic art, alongside that of metal, which was worked by sophisticated and complicated techniques to make prestige objects. JP

4
Barfüsserkirche

Pendant from a horse harness, 2nd half 1st century BC
Found at Rittergasse 4, Basle
Cast bronze; length 6.4 cm
Inv. no. 1991/19.3966.

The oldest continuously settled site in Basle is on the Münsterhügel, where a fortified Celtic settlement, the so called 'Basel-Münsterhügel' *oppidum*, stood from about the middle of the C1 BC. It had a *murus gallicus* ('Gallic' wall) and a defensive rampart behind a ditch. The settlement covered about five hectares and was inhabited by a group of the Raurici. This pendant came to light during recent excavations there. It is part of a horse harness made up of several pieces, and it can be imagined that such costly equipment would hardly have been used by a simple horseman: its owner was most likely a member of the Celtic upper class. It has an openwork whorl at the centre with three arms that seem to consist of stylised animal bodies. The motif is a common one in Celtic art. Underneath the pendant has an extension, also pierced. The object is the only one of its kind to have been discovered so far in the territory of present-day Switzerland. Parallels to it are rare, and are distributed in distant parts of Europe. JP

5
Barfüsserkirche

Bronze mount in the form of a human head, 2nd half 1st century BC
Found at Rittergasse 4, Basle
Cast bronze; length 3.5 cm
Inv. no. 1982/6.2611.

This bronze mount in the shape of a human head is the only anthropomorphic representation discovered so far in the late Celtic *oppidum* on the Basel-Münsterhügel. The chin is weak, the mouth seems to be open and the eyes are slightly slit-shaped with the lids half-closed. On the forehead a head covering is clearly delineated. It is probably a helmet with two horn-like extensions: such Celtic helmets are archaeologically well documented. The object was produced by the hollow casting process. This technique, in conjunction with the remnants of solder on it and its slightly concave back, suggests that it was mounted or appliquéd on a bronze vessel. It was part of an important piece owned by a member of the elevated and wealthy class. A second human representation, a knife with the handle end adorned by a male head, was found in the older late Celtic settlement at the Gasfabrik. JP

6
Barfüsserkirche

Campana dish, 3rd quarter 1st century BC
Found at Augustinergasse 2, Basle
Clay, turned, with red-brown coating, made good with added pieces; diameter 32 cm
Inv. no. 1968.1581.

The inner surface of the plate is decorated with concentric grooves and a riffled band; the russet coating is flecked with black-brown spots and stripes. It is a piece of so called Campana tableware. The name comes from the Italian province of Campagna south of Rome. However, the piece shown was imported from Lyons, France, as an analysis of the material has established. So far about 50 fragments of Campana pottery have been found in the two Celtic settlements at the Gasfabrik and the Münsterhügel in Basle; some of them come from Italy and some from Gaul, which was Romanised at an early date. Other imported articles which have come to light in the settlements are fragments of amphorae, originally used to transport wine from the Mediterranean region to Basle. Campana ware, amphorae filled with wine, and other imports such as glass were the luxury goods of their time. JP

7
Barfüsserkirche

Small pendant, last quarter 1st century BC
Found at the Münster, Basle
Splint of stag antler, sawn and carved; length 4.5 cm
Inv. no. 1974.A.9144.

At the beginning of the second decade before Christ Rome decided to advance across the Rhine against the Germanic peoples. In connection with these campaigns a Roman fortress was built on the Münsterhügel in Basle. The pendant with the inscription T.TORI is a typical find from a military zone: similar small plaques, generally of bronze, are known from numerous other Roman military bases. They were used to identify the property of an individual soldier or a detachment. There are two alternative interpretations of the letters scratched on the plate. The abbreviation T. may stand for *turma*, a mounted squadron of 30 men; it may be followed by the name of the detachment leader in the genitive. In the nominative his name can be assumed to be Torius. However, the inscription could also mean 'Titi Torii', the property of Titus Torius. In the first case the piece would be a label from a piece of luggage, perhaps a sack of supplies, belonging to the Torius squadron. In the second it would have marked Torius's personal equipment. JP

8
Barfüsserkirche

Terra sigillata bowl, 1st half 1st century AD
Found at Bäumleingasse 20, Basle
Clay, turned, with red coating and relief decoration, minor repairs; diameter 21.8 cm
Inv. no. 1960.516.

The bowl, decorated with flowers and foliage, bears the stamp of the potter Gabianus. In the Roman Empire special *terra sigillata*, or terracotta stamped by the potter or factory owner, was often used as tableware and crockery. A great variety of vessels were mass produced in large potteries, first in Italy, then in southern and central France, then from the C2 AD in Germany and from the C3 AD in Switzerland (for example, in Lausanne and Berne). In addition to the high-quality imported *sigillata* crockery, similar pottery was sold more cheaply as a local product in most areas. A dish of the quality of the one illustrated here cost about 20 *asses*, roughly equivalent to a day's wages for a soldier or a worker. JP

9
Barfüsserkirche

Warriors, 2nd century AD
Found behind the Domhof, Münsterplatz 12, Basle
Limestone carved in relief, originally painted; length 168 cm, height 43 cm, depth 93.5 cm
Inv. no. 1895.97.

The limestone block was found in the wall of the Late Roman fortress on the Münsterhügel. Large sections of this were made of spoils, incorporating reused parts of buildings, blocks from large burial monuments, and tombstones. The relief must originally have formed part of a victory monument. It is highly probable that it came, like the other spoils, from the Roman colonial town of Augusta Raurica. After it had fallen into decay in the C3 AD stones from it were transported to Basle by boat along the Rhine, despite prohibitions, and used as building material. The figures are shown in high relief, the ornament in low relief. Two Roman soldiers can be made out. The cupid flying from the left and the person on the right holding a tablet indicate a subject concerned with good fortune and victory. Two figures were represented on the left-hand side of the block but only their feet and the hems of their garments are visible. They seem to be linked to each other by a chain. JP

10
Barfüsserkirche

Mars, 2nd century AD
Found in Niederholzstrasse, Riehen bei Basel
Cast bronze with copper inlay; height 9.5 cm
Inv. no. 1922.61.

In the first half of the C1 AD the Basle Münsterhügel lost its importance as a military base securing the border, as the frontier of the Roman Empire had moved north. However, a street settlement or village (*vicus*) remained on the site, though overshadowed by the rising colonial town of nearby Augusta Raurica (Augst). In the country around Augusta there were numerous temples or sacred precincts, as well as villages and villas inhabited by a Romanised Celtic population. On the right bank of the Rhine stood a complex of Roman buildings which was settled in the C1 AD and which continued to be inhabited until the Late Roman era. This statuette of the Roman god of war, Mars, was found there. The bearded and helmeted god wears armour and leg guards. He once held a spear in his right hand and a shield or sword in his left. He may have stood, with other statuettes, in a *lararium*, or small domestic shrine made of stone or wood and about 50–100 cm high. JP

11
Barfüsserkirche

Fibula with a XP, 4th century AD
Found in the burial site in Aeschenvorstadt, grave 379, Basle
Bronze, gilt, with niello ornament, made of several pieces soldered together; length 7.7 cm
Inv. no. 1958.280.

When the Alemanni broke through the Roman *limes* or border in AD 259/60, the frontier of the Empire was moved back to the Rhine. Basle once again became a Roman fortress-town. In the C4 AD, in the graveyard attached to the town and used since the C1 AD, a belt and this clasp were interred with a corpse as burial offerings. The clasp is embellished with a monogram only 4 mm high, consisting of the first two letters of Christ's name in Greek (**X** = Ch, P = r). The four engraved medallions show male busts, wearing garments held at the shoulder by a round clasp. Fibulae such as this, with button-like projections, especially of gold, were sometimes given by the emperor to his officials on jubilees celebrating his accession. The sumptuous belt laid at the feet of the dead man also suggests that he had been a high state official, perhaps a Christian, for in Late Roman usage *cingulum dare,* to bestow the belt, meant to appoint someone a state official. JP

12
Barfüsserkirche

Pair of earrings, 1st half 4th century AD; **disc fibula and finger ring**, 7th century AD
Found at the burial sites at Kaiseraugst-Stalden, grave 24, Aargau and at Kaiseraugst, grave 21, Aargau
Earrings: gold, embellished with filigree, length 2.2 cm; clasp and ring: bronze overlaid in sheet gold, filigree inlay, coloured stones, clasp partly repaired; diameters 4.3 cm and 1.5 cm
Inv. nos. 1906/839.37 and 38
Inv. nos. 1906.839./33 and 34.

The Roman fortress of Castrum Rauracense, situated in present-day Kaiseraugst on the Rhine, was built soon after AD 300 for protection against the Alemanni. The burial offerings in the Kaiseraugst burial site to the south-east provide evidence that the *castrum* was inhabited continuously until the C7, even after the end of the Roman *imperium*. For a long time the *castrum* was the seat of the bishop, before he moved to Basle. The ornaments come from women's graves in two different cemeteries. The earrings, made in the first half of the C4 and found in the Late Roman burial ground of Kaiseraugst-Stalden, consist of a wire with hook fastener and a pendant in the form of a club of Hercules. Such pendants were popular, worn primarily by women and children as amulets, for Hercules could ward off evil and protect against misfortune, or as magic objects that could ensure growth and fertility. The richly embellished disc fibula represents a typical form of clasp for garments of the C7. JP

13
Barfüsserkirche

Sword (*spatha*) with gold hilt, ca. AD 500
Found at the burial site at Kleinhüningen, grave 63, Basle
Gold and gilt silver, with iron, wood, leather; length 99.7 cm
Inv. no. 1933.760.

The burial site of the Alemanni at Kleinhüningen was created about the middle of the C5 AD and was used until around 700. The settlement attached to it has not as yet been discovered. The man buried with the *spatha* (long sword) with a gold hilt died at about the age of 60. Besides this double-edged long sword, a sax (short sword), a lance, a shield, an axe, a belt and a pottery vessel were buried with him. They guaranteed him the entry to continued life in the realm of the dead that befitted his status. The contents of his grave reveal that the dead man must have held a leading place in the village community. The *spatha* is remarkable for its valuable gold hilt. Parts of the sheath of poplar and leather have been preserved. The two eyes through which a strap could be passed to attach the sword to it can be clearly seen. JP

14
Barfüsserkirche

Necklace, ca. AD 570
Found in the burial site at Bernerring, grave 27, Basle
58 glass beads, one amber bead and two gold pendants; length 33 cm
Necklace: inv. no. 1932.155.
Pendants: inv. no. 1932.156.a. and b.

The burial site belonged to a noble Frankish family, and the necklace was part of a richly furnished woman's tomb. The woman died between her 30th and 40th years and was buried in a wooden chamber. A gold coin, called an obolus, was placed in her mouth. According to the belief of the time it would enable her to pay for her journey to the realm of the dead. Other burial offerings were a bracelet of glass and amber beads, an ivory comb with a sheath, a weaving needle and a key of iron, a glass goblet and a small birchwood casket with a decorated sheet of bronze riveted to it. The necklace is remarkable for its two disc-shaped gold pendants. They are decorated with nine rings placed between two circles. The rings and circles are made of finely-grooved gold wire soldered to the gold discs. JP

15
Barfüsserkirche

Appliqué in the shape of a bust, 12th century AD
Found at the Rosshof site, Petersgraben 47–55, Basle
Cast bronze; length 19 mm, with spike 32 mm
Inv. no. 1983/15.1286.

In the late C11 bishop Burkhard of Fenis built a first city wall around Basle. In the first half of the C13 a second fortification was built, the so called 'inner town wall'. The present street called Petersgraben follows the line of the filled-in ditch of this inner town wall. After the earthquake of 1356 a longer wall was built, enclosing the suburbs as well. Near the inner town wall simple wooden houses were built on the so called Rosshof site. During excavations in 1983 remains of a wooden house from the latter part of the C12 came to light. The inner floor was lined with compacted clay, the walls were formed of double wattle layers woven over thin laths. This tiny bronze figure was found immediately beside the house. It shows the bust of a man with his hands resting beside him, emerging from a stepped base. The use of the figure is unknown; it may originally have embellished a wooden box. JP

16
Barfüsserkirche

Fragments of a painted cup, 3rd quarter 13th century
Found at Augustinergasse 2, Basle
Clear glass with enamel colours; maximum height of fragments 9 cm
Inv. no. 1968. 1514.

The enamel painting shows two capitals and four standing figures with nimbi beneath a pictorial frieze. Two figures are characterized as bishops by their crosiers, a third carries a palm frond. Between one of the bishop figures and the fourth figure, of which only parts of the nimbus and the hand survive, stands a small bird. The frieze has an inscription which can be completed to form: AVE MARIA GRACIA PLENA (Hail, Mary, full of grace). Medieval hollow glass vessels with enamel painting are so far known only in the form of conical cups widening from a smooth reeded foot. The division into picture zone and frieze, usually with an inscription, is a widespread decorative scheme. Saints, animals, mythological figures or coats of arms are often shown. Murano near Venice has been suggested as the place of production; cup painters are documented there from the C14. However, in view of the quantity of such finds north of the Alps, other such workshops are likely to have existed. JP

17
Barfüsserkirche

Stove tile, mid–14th century
Found at Rittergasse 5, Basle
Red-brown clay, side to view glazed brown; length 13 cm, height 13 cm
Inv. no. 1973.267.

The stove tile with a figure of a knight was produced at a time when tournaments were held on the Münsterplatz in Basle. The strong relief of the tile, which was pressed into a mould, permitted careful detailing. The knight wears a helmet with an eye-slit and a peacock-feather plume. The shield hung from his shoulder displays his coat of arms. In his raised hand he holds a sword ready to strike. His leg with a spur on the heel can be seen. The knight sits stiffly on the horse, which is somewhat ill proportioned and has too long a neck. Tiled stoves were built in the wealthier houses in Basle from the C11 at the latest; they first had unglazed earthenware tiles, then glazed and increasingly elaborate decorated tiles. This development gave rise to a new group of craftsmen who broke away from the potters proper in the mid-C14: the 'Hafner' or stove potters. JP

18
Barfüsserkirche

Fat catcher, 1st quarter 15th century
Found at Rittergasse 5, Basle
Red clay, glazed brown-green, part of handle missing; length 50 cm
Inv. no. 1972.3877.

The fat catcher has an eye at the side and a hollow handle. The inside of the vessel has a brown-green glaze. While the meat on the spit was slowly cooked in front of the fire, the fat catcher caught the fat dripping from it, and was used to pour it back over the meat. About 1300 the big-bellied, unglazed cooking pot was superseded, and more complex vessels with handles, three legs and glazing on the inside came into use (see no. 430). Kitchen equipment now also included metal pots of iron, bronze or brass. Cauldrons of beaten copper were hung over the open fire by the 'Häli', a chain with a hook. Kitchen utensils included serving and stirring ladles, knives, roasting spits, pots for dripping and preserves, strainers, mortars, bottles and spice jars. In upper-class kitchens an automatic roasting spit driven by hot air was used. In the C15 the cooking stove of table height replaced the hearth at floor level, allowing cooking to be done more comfortably. JP

Coins and medals

The coins and medals collection is known as the 'Münzkabinett' or 'coin cabinet', which evokes and preserves the venerable collecting tradition that lies behind it. Coins and medals ranging very widely in quality have come into Basle public ownership from private hands over centuries: as an element of the Amerbach Cabinet in 1661, of the Museum Faesch in 1823, in the diverse collection of one Colonel Brüderlin in 1917, from the comprehensive Schorndorff Cabinet in 1911 and 1943; or as the fruit of the labours of collectors who concentrated on one particular theme, including antiquaries and historians such as Daniel Bruckner (1778), Johann Jakob Schmid (1857), Wilhelm Vischer (1864), Auguste Quiquerez (1880), Johann Jakob Bachofen (1921), Andreas Alföldi (1982) and Leon Der Grigorian (1989); but also from connoisseurs of coins of Basle and its region such as Hieronymus Falkeisen (1815), Louis Ewig (1894 and 1917), Friedrich August Lichtensteiger (1957) and several other specialists. Every collection was a product of the numismatic interests of the original owner and his heirs and consequently in the 'coin cabinet' at present there are both individual rarities and complete series, but also noticeable gaps in the history of both coins and medals. The public coin collection used to be housed in the public library in Basle, as is still the case today in some other places. In 1849 it was transferred to the new museum in Augustinergasse as part of the Antiquarian Collection and finally to the Historisches Museum founded in 1892.

The Basle 'coin cabinet' comprises some 60,000 items dating from the C7 BC to the present day. It is universal in scope, and includes coins from every part of the world except the Far East. There are only a few examples of banknotes and written documents relating to the history of money. Models and designs for medals, plaques and games pieces dating from the Renaissance period, seals and insignia of orders and other such items traditionally kept in coin cabinets have been handed over to other departments of the Museum as belonging to the field of history or the history of art.

Within the coin collection proper, there are approximately 11,000 antique coins and 20,000 medieval and modern coins; coins struck in Basle, Roman and Renaissance coins and bracteates from the Alemannic-Swabian region are particularly well represented.

The topographical department consists of about 13,000 coins and numismatic objects with an identified provenance, particularly the canton of Basel-Stadt, or old finds from other parts of Switzerland and from abroad.

The medals collection numbers some 12,000 items, constituting a collection of international standing with superb examples from the Italian and German Renaissance as well as important works by later medallists.

About 500 dies for coins and medals from Basle mints have been preserved. These were supplemented in 1950 by about 350 dies made by the Basle medallist Hans Frei (1868–1948). Sixty examples of the most important kinds of balances in use between the C16 and C19 are present in the collection.

Carved stones, of which there are more than 600, about 60% antique, 40% modern, form another section of the 'coin cabinet'. A few private collections of plaster or sulphur casts after famous antique and modern gems attest to the flourishing interest in glyptics in the C18 and C19.

A representative selection (about 4% of the total collection) of coins and medals is on display in the 'Münzkabinett' and the 'Untere Schatzkammer' (lower treasury) in the Barfüsserkirche and provides a general survey of the history of European coins, and of Basle coinage in particular, since their inception. One case illustrates the variety of types of balances in use. Two others demonstrate the wide range of coins found in Augst and Basle. Finally five cases provide some idea of the important collection of C15 to C17 medals. The only coins to be found in other exhibition areas are those in the archaeological part of the history of the city of Basle and in the history of collecting section. BS

19
Barfüsserkirche

Caulonia (Bruttium)
Noummos, ca. 520 BC
Silver, struck; weight 8.185 g; diameter 29.6 mm
Inv. no. 1908.589. Wilhelm Vischer collection

The Archaic and Classical coins of the Greek colonies in southern Italy and Sicily represent an artistic peak in the design and striking of antique coins. This coin from Caulonia on the coast of southern Italy depicts Apollo, the patron god of the town, walking towards the right. He holds a branch in his raised right hand. A small backward-looking figure whose significance is not clear runs along his outstretched left arm. As for Apollo, is he depicted purifying himself before taking over the shrine and oracle of Delphi? A stag, emblem of the town of Caulonia, stands on a separate level with its head turned back. A guilloche border runs round the image. The reverse of the coin has the same image in reverse and incuse, but the small figure and the deer's antlers are in relief and there is no legend. Incuse strikings are typical of Magna Graecia from the mid-C6 BC until well into the C5. BS

20
Barfüsserkirche

Macedonia, Alexander (III) the Great
Alexandria, **stater**, ca. 312–310 BC
(minted posthumously)
Gold, struck; weight 8.537 g; diameter 18.8 mm
Inv. no. 1908.919. Alter Bestand

Alexander the Great required huge sums of money to conquer his empire. He introduced a new currency based on the Attic standard, in gold the stater, and in silver the tetradrachmon. On the obverse the stater bears the head of Athena, protrectress of Greek heroes. Alexander's whole campaign was dedicated to Athena, and avenging the destruction of her city of Athens and the sacking of her acropolis by the Persians in 480 BC. The reverse bears Nike, the winged goddess of victory, in a long flowing robe. In her right hand she holds a wreath, and a decorated 'stylis', the sternpost of a Greek ship, is supported in her left arm; a pennant and ribbons are hung on it as decorations. The stater bearing Nike enjoyed long-lived success, continuing to be struck into the C1 BC throughout the area that had been Alexander's empire. RCW

21
Münzkabinett

Roman Republic
Rome, **quadrans** (*aes grave*), 241–235 BC
Bronze, cast; weight 67.198 g; diameter 44.3 mm
Inv. no. 1921.747. Collection of Prof. Dr. iur. Johann Jakob Bachofen

In Italy bronze was used as barter, its exchange value corresponding to the weight of the metal. Even when bronze pieces were given images in the C3 BC, in Rome the twelve-ounce pound was determined by weight. From the C3 BC the Romans struck silver and small bronze coins of their own for trade with the Greek colonies. The images on Roman *aes grave* ('heavy money') included reflections of the daily life of an agrarian society with its patron gods. Here the right hand and the sickle together with two grains of wheat on the obverse symbolize harvest. The weight of the piece, a quarter of a pound or three ounces, is indicated on both sides by three balls. The example illustrated came from Bachofen's collection and may have appealed to him as a scholar of religions particularly interested in the meaning of the hand in relation to funerary symbolism. He equated the left hand with the female principle of motherhood and death, and the less frequently depicted right hand with the male principle of cognition and divinity. RCW

22
Barfüsserkirche

Carthaginian empire
Carthage or an Italic mint, **bronze coin**, ca. 221–202 BC
Bronze, struck; weight 17.975 g; diameter 32.6 mm
Inv. no. 1908.2580. Alter Bestand

With colonies in North Africa, Spain and Sicily as well as Sardinia and Corsica, the Phoenicians secured the whole of the western Mediterranean for their trading ships. Carthage, the most famous Phoenician colony, did not strike its own coins until near the end of the C4 BC, when they were used to pay its mercenaries fighting against the Greeks in Sicily. The imagery, a woman's head on the obverse and a horse on the reverse, was designed at the beginning of the C3 BC and remained on its coinage until Carthage was destroyed by the Romans in 146 BC. As a consequence of the second Punic War (218–201 BC) Carthage produced large amounts of bronze money in a great many mints. On this coin the proportions of the horse in front of the palm seem strangely distorted. The two Punic letters between its legs must indicate where the coin was minted. RCW

23
Barfüsserkirche

Parthian empire, Mithridates II
Rhagae, **drachma**, ca. 123–88 BC
Silver, struck; weight 4,127 g; diameter 19.8 mm
Inv. no. 1908.2282. Alter Bestand

In the Persian Empire the great king and his representatives, the satraps, occupied the supreme place, while in Greek territory it was the town divinity. In Asia Minor, at the meeting-point between Persians and Greeks, Persian satraps put their image on coins by the end of the C5 BC. Only with the altered concept of a sovereign associated with Alexander the Great and the rulers of the epigonous kingdoms did portraits become usual on coins in Greek territory. The Parthian great king Mithridates II (ca. 123–88 BC) consolidated a kingdom that would last for centuries – and its coinage, too. The first collision between the Parthians and the Romans also occurred in his era. His drachmae show his head squat, with his beard cut straight along the bottom in oriental style, and an extremely aquiline nose dominating his face. He wears a riding cloak slung over his shoulder. There is a diadem in his hair. This is the image of an oriental ruler adapted to the iconography of his Hellenized empire. RCW

24
Münzkabinett

Gem: *Donkey playing the lyre*
Roman empire, 1st century BC
Translucent orange cornelian; oval, height 13.6 mm, width 11.9 mm
Inv. no. 1987.252. Alter Bestand

It has only recently been possible to identify and interpret the gem illustrated here; the image on it, deeply cut in intaglio (the opposite of cameo), shows a left-facing donkey reared on his hind legs (dancing?). He is involved in a human activity, and despite his lack of musicality is playing an instrument, the lyre; a lion's skin is draped round him and he is trying to pass for a lion. However, his braying voice gives him away, he is unmasked and punished. This is a mixture of elements from various stories. Proverb and fable have been given an individual pictorial expression in the glyptic medium. The gem gives some indication of Roman humour. The donkey was regarded as stupid and was therefore frequently made fun of. BS

25
Barfüsserkirche

Roman Republic, gens Hostilia
Rome, **denarius**; mint-master L. Hostilius Saserna, 48 BC
Silver, struck; weight 3.874 g; diameter 19.7 mm
Inv. no. 1951.107. Schorndorff Cabinet

From the C3 BC a triumvirate was responsible for the minting of gold, silver and bronze coins in Rome; it was an office for young men, appointed yearly. The mint-masters signed the coins struck under their supervision. From the end of the C2 BC the officials were largely free in their choice of the coins' imagery, so they tended to allude to the heroic deeds of their own ancestors, or depict divinities particularly venerated in their own families; for no other visual medium was as widely distributed as a coin. Increasingly in the C1 BC there were references to the politics of the day, and images on coins could become statements of political allegiance. Thus the head of a long-haired Gaulish woman and the carnyx, a Celtic musical instrument, are a direct reference to Caesar's Gallic campaigns, and Saserna's allegiance to Caesar's party is clearly illustrated by his choice of image for this coin. RCW

26
Barfüsserkirche

Roman Republic, gens Munacia
Rome, **aureus**; mint-master L. Munatius Plancus, 45 BC
Gold, struck; weight 8.039 g; diameter 21.1 mm
Inv. no. 1911.116. Purchase

Julius Caesar while holding the office of *dictator* largely stripped the Senate of its powers. Alongside the official coinage special coins were struck in his honour. While Caesar was serving his third term as *dictator* the prefect of the city of Rome (*praefectus urbi*) Lucius Munatius Plancus struck this gold coin for him. The reverse bears the name and office of Plancus and the representation of a pitcher in which sacrificial drink was carried. This pitcher is special to Plancus and must allude to his membership of a college of priests. At the same time it is the pictorial representation of the virtue of *pietas*, devoutness, belief in the old Roman gods and observance of the sacrificial traditions handed down from olden times. After holding office as city prefect Plancus was appointed governor of Gaul – a very important province to Caesar. He founded Lugdunum (Lyons) in 44 BC and another colony in the territory of the Raurici on the site either of Basle or of Augst. Plancus survived the upheavals of the civil war that followed Caesar's assassination. In 27 BC in the Senate he put forward the proposal that Caesar's adopted son Octavian should be given the title Augustus. RCW

27
Münzkabinett

Celtic, Sequani
Bronze coin, 2nd half 1st century BC; found 1987 in the Deutschritterkapelle, Rittergasse 29, Basle
Bronze, struck; weight 3.83 g; diameter 15.5 mm
Inv. no. 1987/3.1766.

Following the example of the Greeks and Romans, the Celts produced their own gold, silver and bronze coins. Gradually the imagery on the coins altered to conform to the typically Celtic repertoire. The Celts also evolved new forms. Scholars often suppose that the various inscriptions refer to the name of a prince, for example TVRONOS on the obverse of this coin (not illustrated), inscribed before a left-facing head with long hair. The small coin was not large enough to accommodate on the reverse (shown) the rest of the legend, CANTORIX. The image of a horse is surrounded by symbols: an S-loop, a star, a rosette of beads and a stylised dagger-sheath. The fact that the surface of the coin has been filled in this way must be an expression of the *horror vacui* which is a feature of Celtic art. These coins were part of the currency circulating in the Augustan military camp on the site of Basle and, as this find proves, in the civilian settlement attached to it. BS

28
Münzkabinett

Roman Empire, Augustus
Nîmes, **dupondius**, ca. 10 BC – AD 10; found 1979 in Rittergasse, Basle
Bronze, struck; weight 13.232 g; diameter 31.4 mm
Inv. no. 1979/25.222

Augustus transferred some of the minting of coins to Lugdunum (Lyons) and Nemausus (Nîmes). The imagery on this coin must have been chosen with the army in mind. The obverse shows two heads facing away from one another, that of Agrippa, Augustus's great general who was by then dead, with the attribute of a mural crown, and that of Augustus as *imperator* and son of the deified Caesar. The crocodile chained to a wreathed palm on the reverse is a reminder of the conquest of Egypt in 30 BC, ending the civil war that followed Julius Caesar's assassination. The allusion to past victories is intended to conjure up new ones. By an oversight, when this coin was being minted it was turned and struck a second time: beneath the crocodile on the reverse the face and neck of Augustus as portrayed on the obverse can clearly be discerned, as can his description as son of the deified Caesar, DIVI F[ilius]. RCW

29
Barfüsserkirche

Roman Empire, Nero
Rome, **sestertius**, ca. 65 AD
Brass, struck; weight 26.168 g; diameter 35.6 mm
Inv. no. 1903.4771. Alter Bestand

Since the days of the Roman republic buildings had been very popular images on coins; the Romans' building activity and that of their forefathers in honour of the gods and in the service of the city of Rome could thus be publicised throughout the Empire. The Temple of Janus had a special significance: according to tradition it dated from the period of the legendary kings, and its doors were closed only when no war was being waged anywhere in the area ruled by Rome. Octavian had closed the temple at the end of the civil wars following Julius Caesar's assassination, thereby promising peace and well-being to the realm. Nero, too, announced peace throughout the Empire at land and sea, for after a war lasting for years he had succeeded in compelling the great king of Parthia to ask him, the Roman Emperor, for the crown of Armenia for his brother. Nero handed over the king's diadem in Rome, and celebrated this recognition of Roman primacy as a great victory. BS

30
Barfüsserkirche

Roman Empire, Marcus Aurelius and Lucius Verus
Silandos (Lydia), **bronze medallion**, AD 164; found at Augst, 1886
Bronze, struck; weight 52.246 g; diameter 43.1 mm
Inv. no. 1951.272. Alter Bestand

Many towns in the Greek eastern part of the Roman Empire produced coins for local use, and as in the west special pieces were also minted as gifts for special occasions. To judge from their size and weight these medallions were not used as currency. Their larger surface invited imagery with more detail. The medallion illustrated was made in Silandos in Asia Minor in the reign of the archon Attalianos in honour of Emperor Lucius Verus and his victory in Armenia in AD 163. As well as the names of the town and its highest official, the reverse bears an image of the Emperor riding down a barbarian in chains; he is marked as an eastern barbarian by his Phrygian cap. The medallion from Lydia is one of a small number of coins from remote parts of the Empire found in Augst. RCW

31
Barfüsserkirche

Roman Empire, Septimius Severus for his son Geta as Caesar
Rome, **denarius**, ca. AD 198–200
Silver, struck; weight 3.331 g; diameter 19.1 mm
Inv. no. 1903.3390. Alter Bestand

Septimius Severus, who was of North African origin, was a commander in Carnuntum on the Danube (about 40 km east of Vienna) when he was acclaimed Emperor in AD 193. With his Syrian wife Iulia Domna he founded the Severan dynasty, members of which held on to the throne with some interruptions until 235. When Caracalla was elevated to be joint ruler in 198 the young Geta became *caesar* (designated heir). The image on the coin shows him as a boy of about ten with his name and official title, L[ucius] SEPTIMIVS GETA CAES[ar], but no laurel wreath; that did not appear on images on coins until 209 when Geta was elevated to be joint ruler with the rank of Augustus. The reverse (not illustrated) shows Felicitas, the goddess of happiness, with a herald's staff and a horn of plenty: the young Caesar represented the happiness of the Empire. After his father's death Geta did not live long to enjoy his reign; the 22-year-old was murdered in Rome at the end of 211 and declared a non-person (*damnatio memoriae*). RCW

32
Barfüsserkirche

Roman Empire, Constantius I Chlorus as Caesar
Trier, **aureus** ca. AD 294–305
Gold, struck; weight 4.921 g; diameter 18.5 mm
Inv. no. 1903.2277. Museum Faesch

Diocletian (284–305) tried to save the Empire by introducing a new system of rule, tetrarchy, and economic and monetary reforms. Two *augusti* – Diocletian and Maximianus – each with a *caesar* with the right to succeed him shared the emperor's power and duties amongst themselves. Each of the four was responsible for one part of the Empire with its own capital city. The division was made on the basis of military achievement. Constantius Chlorus as *caesar* of the Western Empire was responsible for Gaul and Britain, and he also minted coins in his capital city of Trier. He took over some coin types from his *augustus* and adoptive father Maximianus Herculius: Hercules wrestling with the snake is a reference to his second name. In 305 the two *augusti* resigned, the two *caesares* were promoted, and two new *caesares* were appointed. However, as early as 306, following the death of Constantius Chlorus, the dynastic principle was reasserted, and the army elevated his son Constantine I (the Great) to be *augustus*. Civil wars broke out once again until Constantine could impose his rule over the whole Empire. RCW

33
Münzkabinett

Carolingian Empire, Lothar I
Location of mint not known, **denarius**, before 833(?); found 1987 in the Deutschritterkapelle, Rittergasse 29, Basle
Silver, struck; weight 0.899 g; diameter 20 mm
Inv. no. 1987/3.1341

The coins found in the Basle area reflect almost the whole history of coins and money in this region from the Middle Ages until the last century. One find of a late hoard and two individual finds are known from the Carolingian period. The *denarius* of Lothar (died 855), son of Louis the Pious (814–840) and joint ruler with him from 817, bears a right-facing head-and-shoulders image with completely distorted proportions. Probably struck in northern Italy, the coin is difficult to date. The hair of the upper part of the head stands on end, and two very long ribbons are hanging down from the loop in the wreath. Indicated by two semi-circular lines, a *paludamentum* (cloak) is laid round the powerful neck, and seems to be fixed on each side with a round fibula. The legend gives Lothar's name. The reverse (not illustrated) shows a temple façade intended to represent a church with the legend CHRISTIANA RELIGIO. BS

34
Barfüsserkirche

Grafschaft zu Freiburg, Konrad II
Freiburg im Breisgau, **penny**, ca. 1316–27; from a hoard of coins buried ca. 1320, found at Winterthur-Haldengut in 1930
Silver, struck; weight 0.301 g; height 15.1 mm, width 15.8 mm
Inv. no. 1957.441.265. Friedrich August Lichtensteiger collection

The image with the two letters F-R (= Freiburg) and the ball of feathers on the helmet matches the decoration on the coat of arms of Graf Konrad II of Freiburg. This *penny* may be ascribed to him and dated between 1316 and 1327. Konrad II succeeded his father in 1316, and in 1327 granted minting rights to the town of Freiburg. The *penny* is typical of coins produced in the Alemannic-Swabian region: round, cut or stamped blanks were not used for minting, but thin, rectangular pieces of sheet silver the corners of which were just roughly rounded off with a few hammer strokes. They were hammered into the image engraved on a die. In modern numismatics coins cheaply produced in this fashion and struck on one side only are called bracteates (from *bractea* = thin). BS

35
Barfüsserkirche

Undated medal celebrating the marriage of Mary of Burgundy and Maximilian of Habsburg on 20 August 1477
Unsigned, attributed to Giovanni Candida
Bronze, cast; weight 32.037 g; diameter 49.4 mm
Inv. no. 1905.998. Amerbach Cabinet

Giovanni Candida (before 1450-after 1504) came from the kingdom of Naples but worked as a secretary at the Burgundian court from 1472 to 1480. He was also a productive and influential medallist. He is presumed to have created this medal with the portraits of Mary of Burgundy (1457–1482) and Maximilian of Habsburg (1459–1519) on the occasion of their marriage. The young couple are both modelled in life-like busts facing right; Maximilian is wearing a cloak over a shirt, his head is adorned with a wreath and he has shoulder-length hair. Mary's hair is plaited and caught into a bun; the two Ms beneath a crown at her neck refer to the union of the couple. Maximilian survived his first wife by 37 years; his marriage to her brought him and the Habsburgs the Burgundian Netherlands, which would remain in their possession for centuries. As Emperor Maximilian I he bequeathed on his death in 1519 to Mary's and his grandson Charles V an empire on which the sun never set. Maximilian's heart is buried in Mary's coffin, while his body lies in Wiener Neustadt. BS

36
Barfüsserkirche

Duchy of Milan, Gian Galeazzo Maria Sforza, in ward of his mother Bona of Savoy
Milan, **double ducat**, undated, 1479(?)
Gold, struck; weight 6.963 g; diameter 23.9 mm
Inv. no. 1918.1724. Museum Faesch

In the C13 gold coins once again began to be issued successfully – in 1252 by Florence and Genoa and in 1284 by Venice. Before that the monetary system introduced by Charlemagne of silver currency divided into pounds, shillings and pence had been the accepted standard for centuries (although only pence were actually coined). When Galeazzo Maria Sforza was murdered in 1477 his widow took over as regent on behalf of her six-year-old son, Gian Galeazzo Maria, and portraits of her appear on several coins. Bona of Savoy, born in 1449, was the first woman since the days of imperial Rome to be depicted on an Italian coin, and her father-in-law Francesco Sforza (1450–1466) had been the first Renaissance prince since Antiquity to have himself depicted on the ducat he introduced in 1462. BS

37
Barfüsserkirche

Bishopric of Sion, Niklaus Schiner
Sion, **'Guldiner'**, 1498
Silver, struck; weight 29.23 g; diameter 42.2 mm
Inv. no. 1903.1662. Alter Bestand

In an innovative move important for the future Duke Sigismund of Tyrol (1446–1490) introduced gradually larger silver coins in his duchy. He minted first the equivalent value of the pound of account, the 'Pfundner', then the silver equivalent of the gold guilder, the 'Guldiner'. The new type of coin later came to be known as the '(Joachims-)Taler' after 'Guldiner' or 'Guldengroschen' had been produced in large numbers from 1520 in the Joachimstal in the Erzgebirge. Ambitious Swiss city authorities were quickly convinced by the new coin (Berne 1493, Sion 1498, Solothurn 1501, Zurich 1512, etc). Tyrolean precedent was followed even in the image: Duke Sigismund had figured in an equestrian portrait surrounded by the coats of arms of his territories; the reverse of the 1498 Sion 'Guldiner' (not shown) displays Niklaus Schiner's coat of arms surrounded by an armorial wreath. The Duke's portrait had been matched by those of local saints; on the Sion coin the temporal rule of the bishop is legitimated by reference to myth – Charlemagne enthroned endows with his feudal sword St Theodule, the bishop kneeling before him, with the rights of a count in Valais. BS

38
Münzkabinett

Uri-Schwyz-Nidwalden
Bellinzona, **half 'Dicken'**, undated, 1512/13
Silver, struck, gilded, traces of a rim; weight 4.938 g; diameter 28.3 mm
Inv. no. 1905.1499. Museum Faesch

The town and county of Bellinzona, Blenio and Riviera were subject to Uri, Schwyz and Nidwalden as shared territory for almost 300 years. Until about 1548 the so called 'Drei Orte' (the first three cantons) coined money in Bellinzona, separately or together, then they moved their mint to Altdorf north of the Alps. They had begun minting shortly after 1500 when Milan could no longer meet the need for coin because of the disputes over its dukedom. Current events were reflected in the imagery of their coin: following antique Roman models, reference was proudly made to the Pavia campaign in 1512 and the victory of Novara in 1513 – hence on the reverse of the half 'Dicken' the seated figure of Mars and the legend VICTORIA ELVETIORVM (victory of the Swiss). After Pope Julius II had honoured the Swiss Confederates for their prowess with titles and banners in late 1512, the 'Drei Orte' added the papal crossed keys to the imperial eagle and the coats of arms already figuring on their coin. BS

39
Barfüsserkirche

Medal of Maria Jakoba of Bavaria, 1534
Unsigned, Matthes Gebel
Bronze, cast; weight 26.932 g; diameter 41.4 mm
Inv. no. 1959.21. Gift from the Verein für das Historische Museum Basel

Maria Jakoba, the eldest daughter of Margrave Philipp I of Baden and Elisabeth of the Palatinate, married Duke Wilhelm IV of Bavaria (1493–1550, duke from 1508) in 1522 at the age of 15. In 1534 when she was 27 a portrait medal was made of her by the leading Nuremberg sculptor and medallist Matthes Gebel (ca. 1500–1574 Nuremberg). The bust portrait shows an elegant lady wearing a pleated bodice decked with necklaces; on her head she has a plumed hat and her hair is held in a net. The reverse of the medal shows two clasped hands holding a heart from which two twigs with buds are sprouting, with the triple coat of arms denoting the alliance of the Palatinate, Baden and Bavaria, supported by two lions. BS

40
Münzkabinett

Medal with an allegory of Fortune, 1554
Unsigned, Hans Jacob Stampfer I
Silver, cast; weight 19.833 g; diameter 47.3 mm
Inv. no. 1917.1050. Rudolf Brüderlin-Ronus bequest

Fortuna, the goddess of luck, rides high on a dolphin swimming towards the left, holding taut reins in her left hand and a cloth puffed up by the wind as a sail in her right. Another dolphin and a small ship are travelling behind her left leg, and there is a siren above the dolphin's head. A fortified town appears on the horizon. The eight-line text on the reverse of the medal admonishes the reader to take care of the good luck given and warns that in the end it is God's grace that determines our progress. The Zurich goldsmith, medallist and die-cutter Hans Jacob Stampfer I (1505–1579) and his workshop created many portraits of famous contemporaries (scholars, leaders of the Reformation) and medals with biblical and allegorical motifs, but also cut coin dies – for foreign clients as well – and produced important goldsmiths' work. BS

41
Münzkabinett

Basle, half 'Guldentaler', 1565: obverse die and gold coin struck from it
Basle, unsigned, Urs Schweiger
Die: height 36 mm, diameter 35.4 mm; coin: gold; weight 14.24 g (= 4 ducats); diameter 35.4 mm
Inv. no. 1905.3619. Alter Bestand
Inv. no. 1903.603. Hieronymus Falkeisen collection

In Basle as elsewhere, goldsmiths often engraved coining dies. The die illustrated is for a silver coin, a half 'Guldentaler' dated 1565 with the Basle coat of arms in a quatrefoil, and was made by Urs Schweiger (died 1574/75) who had worked as a die engraver for the members of the Rappenmünzbund (currency federation of Habsburg-Austria, Basle, Freiburg-in-Breisgau, Colmar and Breisach). The short cylindrical obverse die with its broken-off grip shows very clearly the marks left by powerful hammering. Between 1564 and 1584 the town of Basle produced whole and half 'Guldentalers' worth 60 and 30 'Kreuzers' respectively in accordance with the 1559 decree on imperial coinage. Surprisingly enough not a single reverse die for these coins (imperial eagle and the legend DOMINE CONSERVA NOS IN PACE [Lord, preserve us in peace]) has survived. BS

42
Barfüsserkirche

Medal of Nicolas Brulart, Marquis de Sillery, 1613
Signed Guillaume Dupré
Bronze, cast, gilded; weight 100.521 g; diameter 72.6 mm
Inv. no. 1917.1115. Rudolf Brüderlin-Ronus bequest

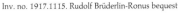

Guillaume Dupré (Sissonne ca. 1576–1640 Charenton) represented the diplomat Nicolas Brulart de Sillery in this medal of 1613 as chancellor of Navarre (from 1605) and France (from 1607). He also made a large bronze medallion of Brulart for the Louvre. The famous sculptor, medallist, die-cutter, gem-cutter and mint-master was a leading artist of the French school and one of the first artists to apply a sculptural relief style to medals. As the French ambassador in Solothurn (1587–95) Brulart intervened actively in the policies of the Confederates and the 'Drei Bünde'. He finally asked to be recalled because he could not satisfy the ever increasing demands being made by the many creditors of the French crown. In spite of this in 1601 and 1602 he led the French negotiations with the Swiss for a renewed alliance. BS

43
Münzkabinett

Medal commemorating the 1619 Synod of Dordrecht

Gold, struck, with a ring and eye; weight 124.167 g (= 36 ducats); diameter 58.2 mm
Inv. no. 1905.2103. Alter Bestand

The first and only general synod of the Reformed churches was held from 13 November 1618 to 9 May 1619 in the town of Dordrecht in southern Holland. As well as representatives from the seven northern provinces of the Netherlands and the Walloon churches of Holland, Zeeland and Drenthe, those taking part included envoys from the English crown, the Palatinate, the Landgrave of Hessen, the four Confederate cities of Zurich, Berne, Basle and Schaffhausen, the united counts of the Wetterau, and the cities and republics of Geneva, Bremen and Emden. As a leaving present the delegates were given a gold chain with a medal. The one given to the Basle envoy, Professor Dr. theol. Sebastian Beck (1583–1654), turned up in 1775 in the coin collection of the Öffentliche Bibliothek (public library) of Basle in 1775. Today it is in the 'coin cabinet' of the Historisches Museum – without its chain. One side of the unsigned medal shows the delegates gathered in the assembly hall, the other (not shown) the temple flooded with celestial light and battered by the four winds on Mount Zion. BS

44
Münzkabinett

Basle presentation medal

Gabriel Le Clerc, undated, 1691
Gold, struck; weight 208.678 g (= 60 ducats); diameter 67.9 mm
Inv. no. 1905.851. Alter Bestand

This medal is not only the largest, but also one of the most valuable presentation medals of the city of Basle: in 1691 and even later it was presented to Swiss ambassadors and other eminent men in versions weighing 30, 60 or even 100 ducats. It was struck using an obverse die with a view of the town engraved and signed in 1685 by Le Clerc (active in Basle 1683–94) for another medal, and a new reverse die made shortly afterwards, not signed. A boy holds by the jaws a lion moving towards him while a snake between the lion's legs darts its tongue at him; but the Lord protects both him and the city of Basle from enemy attacks (DOMINVS CVSTODIT ME). The medal illustrated is also a splendid example of the dedicated acquisition policy of the C19: aware of its rarity, the Antiquarian Collection of Basle Museum purchased the gold medal in 1867, working on the principle that they should "make the collection of Basle coins and medals as complete as possible". BS

45
Münzkabinett

City of Nuremberg
Nuremberg, Thaler, commemorating the 1697 Peace of Ryswick, 1698
Gold; weight 17.379 g (= 5 ducats); diameter 43.6 mm
Inv. no. 1928.1018. Rudolf Nötzlin-Werthemann bequest

Ducats were struck in Nuremberg from 1632 and from the very beginning the images on them illustrated the deep longing for peace during the Thirty Years' War. In a similar vein peace treaties were also celebrated with gold and silver coins. The 1698 thaler shows Pax (the goddess of peace) in antique style with two genii at her feet supporting the two coats of arms of the city. The legend refers to the Treaty of Ryswick, concluded in 1697 and briefly successful in creating a balance of power in Europe. The year 1697 appears as a chronogram: in the legend letters picked out in a larger typeface combine to form the Roman numerals. Its thaler, multiples of the thaler and gold struck to the value of ducats as well as actual ducats attest to the self-confidence of the free imperial city of Nuremberg: it produced not only ordinary coins, but also sought-after presentation coins. BS

46
Münzkabinett

Venice, Alvise Mocenigo II
Osella, 1702
Gold, struck; weight 13.906 g (= 4 ducats); diameter 36.5 mm
Inv. no. 1917.1003. Rudolf Brüderlin-Ronus bequest

According to an old custom dating from the C13 the doges of Venice used to give each member of the Great Council five wild ducks as a New Year present. New Year money was introduced to replace the game birds in 1521. These silver *oselle* (from *uccelli* = birds), each worth a quarter of a ducat, could also be used as currency. Until 1796, the year before the end of the Venetian Republic, new *oselle* were produced every year. Gold *oselle* had no official role; private individuals commissioned their coining, and they always corresponded to a multiple of the sequin in value. Historical and allegorical references often served as motifs on *oselle*. This 1702 *osella* alludes to Venice's neutrality in the War of the Spanish Succession: the lion (of St Mark) protects the sea of Venice with the strength (FORTITVDO) of the sword and the prudence (PRVDENTIA) of the snake. BS

47
Münzkabinett

City of Basle
Basle, **double thaler**, signed Johann Jakob Handmann I
Gold, struck (= 24 ducats); weight 84.044 g; diameter 49 mm
Inv. no. 1903.445. Alter Bestand

Merovingian (ca. 600), Carolingian (ca. 910) and Burgundian (937–93) rulers and the kings and emperors of the Holy Roman Empire (1429–1509) had coins struck in Basle; the bishops of Basle (ca. 1000–1373), the city of Basle (1373–1796), the Helvetic Republic (1798–1803) and lastly the canton of Basle (1803–1848) had minting rights and exercised them in Basle for differing lengths of time. From about 1680 Basle followed the example of other Protestant republics in illustrating a view of the city on its coins. Eminent die-cutters were often commissioned to produce the design. Basle first struck gold impressions with the new dies for silver coins. The denomination "THALER" first appeared on a Swiss coin on the Basle thaler of 1765. To prevent coins from being clipped for their precious metal the edges were decorated – in Basle from 1740. Alternatively, on larger coins, a legend such as "CONCORDIA FIRMAT VIRES" (agreement brings strength) was printed round them. BS

48
Münzkabinett

Cast-iron plaquette of Susanne Maria Schorndorff-Iselin, 1823
Berlin, after a wax model by Johann Carl Hedlinger of ca. 1742
Iron, cast, bronze finish, in contemporary frame made of pressed sheet brass; diameter with frame 105.2 mm
Inv. no. 1983.444. Purchase

Johann Carl Hedlinger (Seewen [Schwyz] 1691–1771 Schwyz) became medallist to the royal Swedish court and achieved renown for his finely characterized, life-like portraits of contemporaries. About 1742 he produced a wax portrait of Susanne Maria Schorndorff-Iselin which was replicated as a plaquette decades later – in 1823 – by the Königliche Eisengiesserei (royal iron-casting works) in Berlin. A native of Basle, depicted here in a lace dress with her hair pinned up, in 1740 she became the wife of Johann Schorndorff (1705–1769), who when he was secretary at the embassy in Stockholm had befriended Hedlinger. From 1741 Schorndorff, now postmaster general in Basle, received many works by Hedlinger which formed the basis of his own cabinet of medals. This was extended – to include coins as well – by his descendants, some of whom were keenly interested in Hedlinger, and finally in the C20 it was absorbed into the Basle coin collection as the Schorndorff Cabinet. BS

49
Barfüsserkirche

Money balance of Master Johann Friedrich Mayer, with incomplete date "ao 17"

Nuremberg, late 18th century

In the scales box: beam scale, 15 money weights, 9-part nest of weights and 10 counterweights; scales and weights: brass; box: walnut; length 20 cm, width 12 cm

Inv. no. 1893.284. Gift of Ulrich Sauter (father or son)

After a resurgence of trade and the circulation of a wide variety of different currencies associated with it, from the C14 money balances – originally the property only of money-changers – became an indispensable aid for travelling merchants. As well as checking the amount and the genuineness of what they received they needed to verify that the weight of the coins conformed to the law, using calibrated weights marked with a set nominal value by a named issuing authority. The great demand for money balances that arose from the C16 onwards was met by manufacturers working in important centres of trade. Thus in the C18 and C19, for instance, many balances were brought to Switzerland from Nuremberg. In the C19, with the improvement of minting techniques, the reduction of currencies in circulation to a small number of international standards and the emergence of paper money, balances became less important. BS

50
Barfüsserkirche

City of Lucerne
Lucerne, 10 francs, 1804
Gold, struck; weight 4.778 g; diameter 21.7 mm
Inv. no. 1903.1062. Alter Bestand

In the small area covered by modern Switzerland prior to 1798 there were on occasion more than 20 mints striking coins at the same time, each making their contribution to a very wide range of coinage. The unitary state created by the French (the Helvetic Republic) then centralised the mint briefly for the first time. With the Mediation constitution (1803–13) the rights of coinage were transferred to the individual cantons, then 19 in number, with certain guidelines that had to be observed by all. Only when the Federal constitution was introduced in 1848 was the prerogative of coinage established as the sole right of the Swiss Confederacy. The canton of Lucerne, where coins had been struck since 1422, was one of the few to issue gold coins. On the 10-franc piece the "Alter Schweizer" (old Swiss) sits in a relaxed pose holding a halberd in his right hand and leaning his left arm on the shield inscribed XIX/CANT. The obverse of the coin (not shown) shows the Lucerne coat of arms with a crown above it, and gives the name of the issuing authority, the value and the year. BS

51
Münzkabinett

Medal commemorating the 'Eidgenössisches Schützenfest' (Federal shooting festival) **held 1979 in Lucerne**
Signed Hans Erni
Silver, struck; weight, 20.071 g; diameter 33 mm
Inv. no. 1979.234. Purchase

Shooting festivals are part of a very old tradition in Switzerland, and they enjoyed renewed popularity in the C19. The first Federal shooting match was held in Aarau in 1824 and then they were repeated at short intervals, developing not just into national occasions, but increasingly taking on a political significance. After 1848 they became politically neutral events and have continued to be held at intervals up to the present day. From the C16 onwards tokens and medals (often given as prizes) tended to be popular at such festivals. If they corresponded to legal coins in weight and material, the 'Schützentaler' were accepted as currency during the festivals. Hans Erni (born Lucerne 1909) was commissioned to design the jubilee medal commemorating the 50th 'Eidgenössisches Schützenfest' held in Lucerne. His medal alludes to the story of Wilhelm Tell: the obverse (illustrated) shows the apple pierced by the arrow on the Swiss cross, and the reverse a crouching archer. Erni, well known as a painter, graphic artist, draughtsman, potter and sculptor, designed several superb high-relief medals which were struck at the federal mint in Berne. BS

State and Law

The section 'State and Law' comprises objects which were used by the authorities and administration in the course of their public duties or for state ceremonial. Most of the collection dates from the period between the Reformation and the French Revolution, a period notable for an increase in the tasks undertaken by the administration and for a pronounced love of ceremonial. The civic development of Basle was a slow process extending over several centuries. In 1373 the bishop as lord of the town accorded the people of Basle the right to levy customs, a mint and a mayoral office – an important milestone on the road to independence; the establishment of a 'Landvogt' or governor there in 1386 meant that a fourth important office was located in the town. The first official recognition of Basle as a free city came in 1385 and from then on the council had full sovereign powers with the same rights as those enjoyed by a lord or an imperial authority.

The section 'State and Law' is unusually varied as it is categorised not by the material of which the items in the collection are made, but by their function. For example, antiquities relating to the state or to the law may include official signs or notices, executioners' swords, seals, boundary stones or measuring vessels. The holding is divided into the following sub-sections: signets and seals (state seals, ecclesiastical seals, guild seals, seal impressions, etc); items relating to state and law in the narrower sense (official shields, maces, city hall furnishings); boundary stones and the like; the administration of justice (executioners' swords, instruments of torture); weights and measures (with numerous subdivisions); genealogy, documents and records; city plans and maps; heraldry and armorial books, finance (in particular money boxes); miscellaneous (emblems, mementoes of revolutions, famines and so on); and historical curiosities (entrance tickets, rationing coupons, etc). FE

52
Study collection

Seal matrix from St. Katharinenthal (canton of Thurgau)
Probably Constance, ca. 1260/70 (first definite record: 15/23 August 1277)
Brass; marginal inscription in Gothic capitals: *S'CONVENT.SOR'.VALLIS SCE.KATHARINE. PPE.DIEZENHOVEN; height 6.3 cm, width 4.3 cm
Inv. no. 1903.239. Purchase

The former Dominican convent of St. Katharinenthal, a jewel of Baroque architecture, lies nestling in the peaceful Rhine valley between Lake Constance and Schaffhausen. Founded between 1242 and 1246, the convent was dissolved in 1869 by the canton of Thurgau. St. Katharinenthal, a centre of mysticism in the Upper Rhine and the owner of works of art of outstanding quality (graduals, a famous image of Christ and St John), experienced a late heyday in the Baroque period. The dissolution of the convent resulted in its movable art treasures being scattered to the corners of the world. In 1903 the Museum bought several seals, including this superb matrix. The picture on the seal shows the Virgin and Child, St Dominic and a female saint, most probably the patron saint of the convent, St Catherine. The three figures are standing on pedestals, with the two saints set a little farther back, so appearing smaller than the Virgin. The bodies are slightly curved, so fitting into the vesica shape of the seal. In spite of the rich drapery and the play between falling and gathered folds, the figures have a sense of corporeality. The seal-engraver, who almost certainly came from Constance, must have been familiar with contemporary sculpture in French cathedrals. FE

53
Barfüsserkirche

Town seal of Kleinbasel
Probably Basle, ca. 1275 (first record: 19 March 1278)
Bronze; holder broken off; marginal inscription in Gothic capitals: + S' : CIUIVM : MINORIS : BASILIE :; diameter 5.12 cm
Inv. no. 1936.123. On deposit from the Staatsarchiv

Kleinbasel is the name given to the smaller part of the town on the right bank of the Rhine which was united with Basle politically in 1392. The original village settlement expanded into a small town after the bridge was built over the Rhine in 1225–26. Its legal status was very complicated: the feudal lord of the manor was the prior of the St. Alban monastery in Basle proper, the temporal ruler was the bishop of Basle, ecclesiastically Kleinbasel was a dependency of the bishop of Constance, and the monasteries of Wettingen and St. Blasien were important landowners. The population consisted of peasants, craftsmen and tradesmen; there were no nobles or merchants. A mayor appointed by the bishop ran the town and administered justice. From 1270 a board of magistrates is documented as well as the mayor; they also acted as a council fulfilling the duties of a parish council, including the sealing of documents. Citizens as such were also mentioned for the first time in the same year. The town seal of Kleinbasel shows a façade framed by twin towers; a bishop's head appears in the main doorway. The picture on the seal symbolizes the bishop of Basle's temporal rule over Kleinbasel. The seal continued to be used until 1392 when the bishop sold Kleinbasel to the city of Basle and its development as an independent entity came to an end. FE

54
Barfüsserkirche

Matrix of the seal of the Zunft zu Brotbecken (bakers' guild)
Probably Basle, ca. 1300
Brass; marginal inscription in Gothic capitals: + S' PISTORVM DE BASILEA; diameter 3.5 cm
Inv. no. 1892.44. Gift of Wilhelm Deck-Sandreuter

The guild of 'Brotbecken' (bread bakers) included not only bakers who sold their wares in bread shops, but also home-bakers who were paid for baking bread for people who provided their own flour, and the grain-measurers. It is not known when their trade association was formally elevated into a guild as no document registering its foundation has been preserved, but its origins certainly go back to the C13. There were sales kiosks – selling pretzels, rolls and other baked goods as well as bread – all over the town. However, because of the risk of fire, baking was allowed only on the outskirts. Regulations of this type led to the interesting phenomenon of streets and districts given over to a particular trade or profession. As the guilds became more powerful they, too, began to have their own coats of arms and seals, in imitation of the nobility and church dignitaries. The elegant seal of the bread-baking guild bears the guild's arms, a triangular shield with a pretzel and two rolls before sexfoil tracery. Two beaded circles form the wide ring containing the Latin inscription, which means "seal of the bakers of Basle". FE

55
Barfüsserkirche

Seal of the city of Basle
Probably Basle, ca. 1360 (first definite record: 27 April 1361)
Silver, parcel-gilt; marginal inscription in Gothic capitals: * SIGILLVM * CIVIVM * BASILIENSIVM *; diameter 8.22 cm
Inv. no. 1936.125. On deposit from the Staatsarchiv

The first decades of the C13 were a period of political and economic improvement for Basle. In 1225–26 the townspeople and bishop constructed a bridge over the Rhine, establishing the town for centuries as an important centre for trade. A toll was charged on through traffic and trades and crafts flourished. It was in these decades that the guilds were founded and the Münster rebuilt. Mendicant orders established themselves in Basle. The council administration, community life and civic self-confidence strengthened. A town seal was mentioned for the first time in 1225; it was probably lost in the 1356 earthquake (oldest impression 1256). The oldest surviving seal matrix of the town shows the choir of a church, almost certainly that of Basle Münster, with the first and last letters of the Greek alphabet above it, referring to Christ's words "I am the Alpha and the Omega, the beginning and the end" (Revelations 21:6). The Latin legend expressly names the signet as the "seal of the citizens of Basle". The same seal picture remained in use with some modifications in style until the C17. There is an impression of it on the 1501 document of Basle's joining the Confederation. FE

56
Barfüsserkirche

Matrix of the seal of the Basle Charterhouse
Probably Basle, ca. 1455 (first record: 24 May 1458)

Bronze; marginal inscription in Gothic minuscule: s·poris + 9uent9 . uallis btē. mar|garete ī basilea ord^{9}. cartusien̄; height 6.3 cm, width 3.8 cm
Inv. no. 1936.129. On deposit from the Staatsarchiv

The Carthusian order founded in 1084 by St Bruno combined a strict solitary life with monastic community. This is reflected in the layout of all Carthusian monasteries: the monks' cells consist of tiny individual houses with a garden, but the church, the cells and the few communal areas are linked. The St. Margarethental Charterhouse in Kleinbasel provided accommodation for 16 monks. It had been founded in 1401 by a rich guild chief warden, Jakob Zibol, and though it continually received further endowments was always in financial difficulties. During the long tenure (1459–80) of Prior Arnold von Alfeld there was some consolidation. He was also responsible for promoting the cult of St Margaret in the monastery. The charterhouse celebrated the feast of its patron saint, St Margaret of Antioch, on 15 July. The vesica-shaped monastery seal shows St Margaret with a crosier, palm branch and dragon beneath a canopy with slim pillars and small Gothic turrets. The saint reputedly overpowered a dragon by making the sign of the cross. A separate field in the lower point of the seal shows a kneeling monk at prayer, no doubt St Bruno. FE

57
Barfüsserkirche

Matrix of the seal of the Faculty of Arts
Probably Basle, 1460

Silver, new brass head, marginal inscription in Gothic minuscule: S facultatis : artium : studij : basiliensis; diameter 4.8 cm
Inv. no. 1973.228. On deposit from Universität Basel

The main difference between the medieval and the modern university was the existence of a faculty of arts, later replaced by the faculty of philosophy and history and the faculty of natural philosophy. The faculty of arts (covering the seven *artes liberales* or liberal arts) was not on the same level as the other three faculties of law, medicine and theology, but served as a preliminary stage to them. Every student was first obliged to study the seven liberal arts before being able to enter one of the other three faculties. The seal – the only one dating from the foundation of the University to have been preserved – shows St Catherine with three pagan scholars in a Late Gothic building. According to legend the patron saint of the arts converted to Christianity 50 philosophers in all (here reduced to three) through her scholarship and steadfast faith. The coat of arms of Basle proclaims the town's authority over the University. The seal has been cut so deeply in places that good impressions can be achieved only on paper or on a wafer; wax and sealing wax stick in the grooves. FE

58
Barfüsserkirche

Matrix of the great seal of the Faculty of Law
Probably Basle, end 15th century; holder new
Silver; inscription in Gothic minuscule: *f* : S : *f* facultatis *f* iuridice *f* [coat of arms] *f* studij *f* basiliēn; diameter 4.85 cm
Inv. no. 1973.224. On deposit from Universität Basel

The seal was used by the Dean of the Faculty of Law to authenticate official documents. In the C17 and C18 this seal was used almost exclusively for important and ceremonial documents while a smaller seal was kept for everyday use. The keys and triple crown identify the right-hand figure as the pope; in his left hand he is holding a book, either the Bible or the codex of canon law. Facing the pope is a bearded emperor, depicted with crown, imperial orb and sword of justice. The figures are turned slightly towards one another and are wearing long loose robes. Their crowns extend into the inscription band, touching the outer beaded rim. The field of the image is set with five-pointed stars. The Basle coat of arms indicates that the city is the highest authority to which the university can appeal. Pope and emperor embody spiritual and secular law, the two great branches of medieval law; they are not actual individuals. This seal depicting the pope and emperor continued to be used even after the Reformation and Switzerland's independence from the Holy Roman Empire. FE

59
Barfüsserkirche

Matrix of the great seal of Basle University, dated 1516
Probably Basle
Silver, holder new; inscription in Late Gothic minuscule: *S*alme*universitatis*Study*basiliensis*1516*; diameter 5.15 cm
Inv. no. 1973.218. On deposit from Universität Basel

This matrix replaced an older one with the same motif dating from the time of the University's foundation. After being used for over 50 years the old signet was perhaps worn or it may have been lost. Our Lady in an aureole stands on a sickle moon and carries a sceptre in her left hand. The Christchild, holding out an open book, sits on her right arm. Five-pointed stars are scattered between the radiating flames. An inscription band with scrolled ends at the top frames the image. Her sceptre, crown and the sea of stars identify Mary as the Queen of Heaven. The religious motif is indicative of the links between the University, opened in 1460, and the Church. Medieval universities were perceived essentially as places where the doctrine of salvation was taught. The Basle coat of arms at Mary's feet indicates that the city had authority over the University; it had created the University, and the University's rights stemmed from it. The seal with the Madonna continued to be used even after the Reformation and right up until the C20, and the motif of the Madonna in an aureole still appears on the University's official documents today. FE

60
Barfüsserkirche

Matrix of the later seal of the Faculty of Medicine
Probably Basle, 1570/71

Silver, steel holder; inscription in Baroque capitals: * SIGIL : * FACVLTAT * MEDICAE BASILIENSIS *; diameter 4.05 cm
Inv. no. 1973.277. On deposit from Universität Basel

Between 1450 and 1459 twenty-seven citizens of Basle had studied at Erfurt, and when Basle University opened in 1460 five of the lecturers teaching there were graduates of Erfurt. These personal links explain why the organization of Basle University was largely modelled on Erfurt; in places the statutes of Basle repeat those of Erfurt word for word. Basle's dependency on Erfurt is evident even in the choice of imagery for its seals. As in Erfurt, the ox of St Luke (without the Evangelist himself) was chosen for the seal of the Faculty of Medicine. According to a passage in St Paul Luke had been a doctor (Colossians 4:14). The ox as the symbol of Luke was therefore also used as a symbol of the medical profession. The earlier seal of the Faculty of Medicine also had the ox of Luke on it. In this more recent matrix – there is documentary evidence that it was made in 1570/71 – the ox is holding an open book with its front legs containing the inscription LV/KAS//ME/DI/CVS. It is not clear why the faculty had this seal made in 1570/71 as a very similar one dating from the C15 is still in existence; perhaps the older matrix had been mislaid for a short period. FE

61
Barfüsserkirche

Ceremonial mace from the treasury of Basle Münster
Basle(?), probably C14

Wood painted black, strip of silver, gilded copper, cut rock crystal; length 21 cm
Inv. no. 1870.624.

Fifteenth-century inventories of the treasure of Basle Münster list several ceremonial maces, but none of the descriptions matches this one, for which there is a counterpart only in inventories dating from 1511 and 1525: "Item ein steckhen mit silber strichen umbwunden, pro pedello in magnis processionibus" (a stick with a silver strip wound round it to be carried by the 'Pedell' in large processions). The 'Pedell' was the beadle. It was his duty to arrange prayer meetings and the celebration of the Mass, to see that the order of the Mass was observed, to prepare the liturgical instruments and to collect the offerings. The beadle of the chapter of Basle cathedral was a priest. He walked in front of processions with a mace as the symbol of the dignity of his office. Depending on the occasion he carried a simple staff or a more lavish mace. This ceremonial mace consists of a wooden stick painted black with a strip of silver wound round it in a spiral. The top end of the stick is encased in a plain gilded copper ferrule, and the decorative top consists of a whorl-shaped knob with a cone-shaped tip made of rock crystal in a gilded copper mount. FE

62
Barfüsserkirche

Sceptre of the University of Basle
Master Andres (Ueberlinger?), Basle, 1460/61; coat of arms 17th century
Silver, beaten, parcel-gilt; length 92 cm
Inv. no. 1942.533. On deposit from Universität Basel

The sceptre of the University was and is a symbol of the high esteem accorded to scholarship and the honour due to the University or its rector, a token of the University's self-governing status, an emblem of its powers to administer justice and control discipline, and the visible sign of the maintenance of law and order in accordance with its constitution. The costly materials used and its high artistic quality emphasize the great importance attached to the sceptre. It was presented to the University shortly after it had been opened in 1460 by the inner council of the city of Basle. The head of the sceptre is formed by two exquisitely executed garlands of beaten leaves and a gilded pomegranate held by five flame-shaped sepals. With its simple form, clear construction and harmonious proportions the Basle sceptre is one of the most important surviving university sceptres. Not only is it a rare example of late medieval secular goldsmiths' work, it is also an important legal memento. Master Andres, rejecting the typical Late Gothic tabernacle with figures, created instead a delightful wealth of decoration of timeless elegance. FE

63
Barfüsserkirche

Badge of the 'Bannwart' (field warden) **of the 'Gescheid'** (land court) **of Grossbasel**
Basle, ca. 1500
Silver, parcel-gilt, wildman figures cast in the round; diameter 15.2 cm
Inv. no. 1875.78. Gift of the Gescheid Grossbasel

The escutcheon of Basle supported by male and female woodhouses is set in a strongly profiled, raised sexfoil surround. The wildman pair fit neatly into the lateral lobes, and acanthus leaves fill the top and bottom ones. The Basle crosier, originally enamelled in black, lies on the surface of the escutcheon which is engraved with fine tendrils. The small, charming figures give the escutcheon a monumental appearance. The foliage, the surface of the escutcheon and the uncovered parts of the wildman and wild woman in silver stand out from the gilt work. The goldsmith is unknown. The 'Bannwart' (field warden) of the Grossbasel land court wore the badge on the left side of his chest. On the back there are two bars and a hinge with a long pin and a protruding eye so that it could be fixed to his clothing; the badge was therefore known as a 'Fürspanne' (something to be pinned on in front). Many of those who wore the badge have scratched their initials and various years on the back of it. Made about 1500, the badge reflects the self-confidence of the politically independent citizenry and expresses their sense of worth and desire to impress; it is also a rare example of late medieval secular goldsmiths' work. The badge was copied with slight modifications by the goldsmiths Andreas Koch and Theodor Merian in 1561. FE

64
Barfüsserkirche

Basle messenger's box, 1553
Possibly Hans Meyer I, known as Stempfer, Basle
Silver, parcel-gilt, engraved; Basle crosier of black cement; height 9.4 cm, depth 3.8 cm, length with chain and rosette 26 cm
Inv. no. 1870.891.

A small stone figure in the inner court of the Basle town hall shows us what a C16 Basle runner or messenger looked like. He wore a doublet over his shirt and tight-fitting leggings, with a bag for letters on his hip and on the left side of his chest a small messenger's box displaying the Basle coat of arms. A runner's most important external emblem was the messenger's box or chest badge with the arms of the local lord. These boxes should not be understood as containers – they are too small; rather, they were symbols legitimating the messengers and making them recognisable. Initially the badges and boxes were made of wood or leather; it was only with political emancipation, the extension of the administration and the greater need for show that these symbols came to be made in precious metals. Silver or silver-gilt badges conferred distinction not only on the sender, but also on the recipient. Thus in 1499 the Swiss Confederacy complained that the Basle runners had delivered letters wearing wooden messengers' boxes rather than silver ones; the Basle council replied that up till then only wooden boxes had been in use. FE

65
Barfüsserkirche

Mace of the mayor of Grossbasel
Johann Ulrich Fechter III, Basle, between 1755 and 1762; figure of Justice and pedestal probably late C16
Silver, cast, gilt and engraved, with ebony; overall length 151 cm, length of top 40 cm
Inv. no. 1870.1151. Gift of the Stadtrat

During his period of office 'Oberstknecht' (chief magistrate) Isaak Merian (1700–1762, in office 1755–62) had this mace made by the Basle goldsmith Johann Ulrich Fechter III (1709–1765, guild member 1741) at his own expense. A silver angel holding an escutcheon featuring the Basle crosier originally crowned the mace, but Merian did not like it; he had the angel replaced by the figure of Justitia (Justice), also at his own expense. He had the angel set on another mace which has not survived. The Roman goddess Justitia had been very widely used as a motif personifying the virtue of justice and as an allegory of law and jurisprudence in state and legal symbolism since the Renaissance. Nevertheless the composite mace lacks stylistic unity. The style and form of the handle, ferrule and lower part of the top with its twisting baluster point to the mid-C18; the elongated, small-headed standing figure and its pedestal are the products of C16 late Mannerism. The goddess of justice has her usual attributes – the scales as a symbol of the balance between right and wrong and the sword as the emblem of punishment – but the blindfold betokening impartiality is missing. FE

66
Barfüsserkirche

Basle death-sentence staff
Basle, before 1763

Carved ivory, ebony(?); overall length 125 cm, length of ivory top 9 cm
Inv. no. 1876.13. Gift of the Staatskanzlei Basel

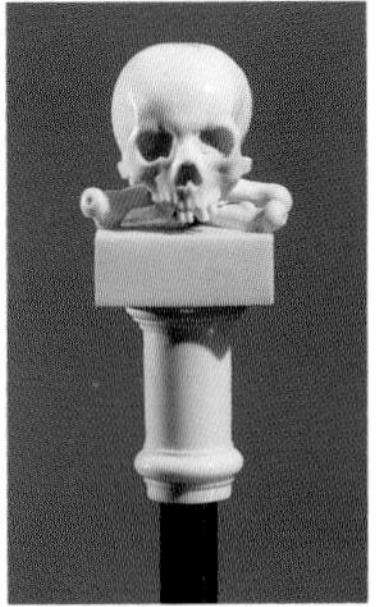

Staffs or maces were widely used in state and legal symbolism in early Switzerland, and are still used by ushers in the Federal, cantonal and town administration today. Staffs were particularly popular in courts, as is evident from panels depicting court proceedings or in Swiss picture chronicles, and from the dozens of legal maces that have survived. They are generally fairly long wooden sticks tapering towards the top, with a metal knob at both ends; the top often finishes in a sphere with a figure mounted on it (St George, Justitia, etc). The top of the Basle death-sentence staff has an age-old symbol of death on it, the skull and crossbones. The white, ivory top contrasts with the black stem. This staff was not made about 1800, as is often stated, for it is already listed in an inventory made in 1763. The presumption that the staff was carried in front of criminals who had been condemned to death on their way to their place of execution is probably incorrect, too, or at least not the whole story, as the inventory mentioned states that the 'Oberstknecht' (chief magistrate) used it when announcing the death sentence. FE

67
Barfüsserkirche

Badge of a Basle 'Weibel' (usher)
Abel Handmann, Basle

Silver, chased; height 14 cm, width 10.5 cm
Inv. no. 1891.85. Gift of the Staatskanzlei

The impressive collection of old official insignia from Basle ends with three silver badges of 'Weibeln' or ushers made in 1770 by Abel Handmann (1715–1788), a goldsmith, jeweller and mint-master from Basle. The three identical badges, each an oval framed by rocaille work, display the symbol of Basle's sovereignty, a black enamelled Basle crosier. On the reverse side the badges have the mark "Handman", the year 1770 and the numbers 2 to 4, so there must originally have been four badges in existence. They were worn by ushers on the left side of the chest. A 'Weibel' or usher is a person who escorts the authorities on official occasions. He wears the insignia of the town, canton or Federation. The office of 'Weibel' is a Swiss tradition still in existence today. FE

68
Barfüsserkirche

Stone marked with a cross
Basle, 14th/15th century
Red sandstone (top corners broken off); height above ground 140 cm, width 54 cm, depth 36 cm
Inv. no. 1900.49. Gift of the Baudepartement

In judgements issued by the city of Basle up to the end of the Middle Ages there are frequent references to people expelled from Basle because of behaviour that broke the peace having to "serve [their time] outside the crosses". The duration of the penalty was laid down, and in the most extreme cases consisted of a lifelong ban. Stones with a cross engraved on them arranged more or less in a circle round the town delimited the area which the miscreants were no longer allowed to enter. Although these stones are often mentioned in written sources our knowledge of how many there were and where they stood is hazy; obviously the people of the time were so conversant with their whereabouts that they kept no records of them. Presumably there were stones marked with crosses on every road leading into Basle. This particularly fine specimen was found in the courtyard of the 'Bannwart' or field warden's house near the bridge over the Wiese (built in 1432); it must originally have stood near where it was found. An event that took place in January 1563 confirms that the Wiese river was the boundary of an old legal district: a delegation from the Basle city council received Emperor Ferdinand I and his courtiers there and escorted their distinguished guest to the Bläsitor leading into the town. FE

69
Barfüsserkirche

Three blazes
Basle, C16/17
Fired clay; length 12.5–15.5 cm
Inv. nos. 1920.308/309. and 1921.36. Gift of the Baudepartement

Because of the city's geographical location at the intersection of established trade routes, its political position at the meeting-point of three countries and the proximity of powerful noble families, Basle watched over its boundaries with especial vigilance. As in other places the boundary lines were marked with stones. Boundary offences and the moving of boundary stones were quite severely punished. Several 'Gescheide' (land courts) supervised the boundary markings and had to adjudicate in disputes relating to them; 'Bannwarte' (field wardens) were employed by them. Boundary stones, generally rectangular blocks from local quarries, stood about 50 to 80 cm above the ground. Usually the coat of arms of the ruling authority was chiselled on the face, and the date of the year in which they were set up. As boundary stones could easily be moved, 'Lohen' (blazes) were laid beneath them as a secret sign in the form of clay cones, clay disks or simple pebbles. In boundary disputes only the blazes counted as legally valid; they were thus the binding symbol of legal surveys. FE

70
Barfüsserkirche

Boundary stone, dated 1779
Basle
Red sandstone; height above ground 90 cm, width 48 cm, depth 33 cm
Inv. no. 1949.300. Gift of the Wohnbaugenossenschaft 'Uff eigenem Bode'

Although boundaries were marked with stones as far back as the late Middle Ages, many boundaries were rather approximately defined. As a rule old boundary records, maps and plans were also imprecise, which explains the strikingly high number of boundary disputes. Many parish boundaries were not finally established until the C18, and most older boundary stones also date from then. Obviously in the Age of Enlightenment people felt a great need for clear-cut boundary distinctions. As the date still legible beneath the cartouche indicates, this stone was set up in 1779. It marked the parish boundary between Kleinbasel and the village of Kleinhüningen. On both sides there is a deeply engraved cartouche emblazoned with the Basle crosier along with the year the stone was set up and the letters KHB or BKH for Kleinhüningen 'Bann' (jurisdiction). When the parish of Kleinhüningen was incorporated into Basle in 1908 the boundary between the parishes disappeared. When the stone was removed from Kleinhüningerstrasse 137, three greywacke stones were found buried underneath as blazes (secret boundary signs). FE

71
Barfüsserkirche

Counting table from the Basle town hall
Basle, 16th century
Table top: walnut; supports and cross-rail: beech; length 208 cm, width 84 cm
Inv. no. 1870.893.

Three tables of Roman figures have been inlaid on the surface of the table; they have the following significance: M = 1000, C = 100, X = 10; lib = libra = pounds, s = solidus = shillings, d = denarius = pennies. Tokens rather than real money were used for counting, and their position on the table gave them the value marked on the left-hand side. There is a raised rim round the table top to prevent the counters falling over the edge. The supports and cross rail are decorated with Gothic foliage. The table was probably used as a counting table by what was known as the 'Dreieramt', an office created in 1453 consisting of three members of the inner council. It was responsible for overseeing all transactions relating to income and expenditure and had a key role in the administration. The counting table would have gone out of use about 1600, when Basle went over from Roman numerals to Arabic figures. Although counting tables of this kind were once in widespread use in government offices and among merchants and bankers, only some half dozen have survived in Europe. FE

72
Barfüsserkirche

Four notched sticks, one dated 8 March [15]94
Basle
Probably maple; length 15.5–20 cm
Inv. no. 1870.895.a.-d. Gift of the Staatsarchiv Basel

Notched sticks fulfilled a function similar to that of written receipts in transactions involving payments today. Debtors and creditors each received one half of a small stick which had been split lengthwise. When interest was paid by the debtor the two halves were laid side by side, and a notch cut through both. The custom of receipting payments in this way must have been very old, going back to a time when many people were unable to write. It became so widespread that it was used even by the literate, and it continued in use long after the average town-dweller knew how to write. A few notched sticks carry the date and the name of the former bearer written in ink on the back. These notched sticks belonged to Georg Wildysen (1556–1602), a pastor, to Lux Just (1573–1633), a doctor, to a certain Doktor Jacob and to Professor Heinrich Just (1561–1610). FE

73
Barfüsserkirche

Alms box
Basle, 17th century
Oak with iron mounts; height 22.6 cm, diameter at base 12.8 cm
Inv. no. 1875.31.b. Gift of the Staatskanzlei Basel

Social welfare and the care of the sick were undertaken mainly by the Church in the Middle Ages. The rapid development of the towns in the C13 led to the provision of new forms of care for the poor and sick. The towns started running hospitals of their own, providing accommodation and care not just for the sick, but also for the poor and elderly. When the Reformation was established in Basle in 1529, religious good works fell into abeyance, and ecclesiastic social welfare also disappeared. In taking over welfare provision the town assumed new social and political responsibilities.

As well as the hospital the town ran two important welfare agencies: the 'Elendenherberge', providing shelter for poor people from outside the town, and the 'Almosen', which did not take anybody in, but distributed clothes, food and money to the needy. The cross of St Anthony, the two pilgrim's staffs and the Basle crosiers burnt on to this box indicate that it was used as an official alms box. Like those of modern collecting boxes its opening is constructed in such a way that money may be put in, but cannot be taken out. FE

74
Barfüsserkirche

'Lällenkönig'
Probably Daniel Neuberger, Basle, ca. 1640
Copper, chased and painted; height 31 cm
Inv. no. 1870.1262. Alter Bestand

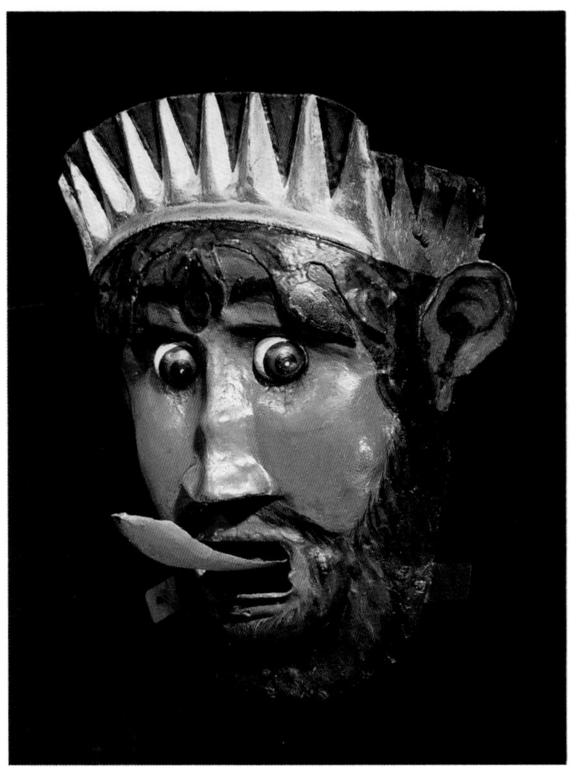

The 'Lällenkönig' (buffoon king) – first recorded in 1658 – was affixed to the Rheintor which guarded the approach to the Rhine bridge on the Grossbasel side. For nearly three centuries the larger-than-life bearded head with its protruding ears, prominent nose, hair falling over its forehead in acanthus fronds and a jagged crown on top greeted all those who entered Grossbasel across the bridge. The eyes and tongue were attached to a clockwork motor so that the mask stuck out its tongue and rolled its eyes in time with the ticking. The original meaning of this peculiar watchman – apotropaic magic, a mocking gesture or simply a joke – is unclear. The figure was subsequently elevated into a symbol of the city, and endowed with local historical significance. After the French Revolution the crowned mask was at one time regarded as a symbol of bondage, at another as an expression of rivalry between Grossbasel and Kleinbasel, and was therefore removed for political reasons. In 1839 the gate guarding the bridge was demolished; since 1870 the 'Lällenkönig' has stuck out his tongue at museum visitors. FE

75
Barfüsserkirche

Paraphernalia used in Basle for the election of city, university and guild officials in accordance with the Ballot Order of 1688 (amended 1718 and 1740)
Basle, 17th/18th century
Box: walnut; balls: ivory, ebony and silver; bags: leather and cloth; height of box 20.4 cm, length 26.1 cm, depth 26 cm
Inv. no. 1880.103. Gift of the Staatskanzlei

In 1691 the people of Basle rose up in an attempt to break the power of the oligarchy of council families. The so called 'Einundneunzigerwesen' (events of '91) was the only political revolution in a Swiss city state in the period of the Ancien régime to have been at least partially successful. The domination of a clique of a few families – furthered by electoral bribery and nepotism – was curtailed. The power exercised by the inner council ('Kleiner Rat') was reduced and that of the great council ('Grosser Rat') extended so that henceforward the latter had the ultimate say in government. The complicated electoral system introduced in 1688, supplemented in 1718 and refined in 1740 was a product of this wider political context. The so called ballot of 1688 – votes were cast secretly using balls – was intended to prevent the use of undue influence and bribes. As there was even more corruption under this electoral system than before, the 'Losordnung' was introduced in 1718. This brought in a very complicated system for choosing by lot between three candidates; in 1740 the number of possible nominees was enlarged to six. FE

76
Barfüsserkirche

Liberty hat
Basle, end 18th century
Sheet metal painted in colour; length 100 cm, height 90 cm
Inv. no. 1894.38. Gift of the Zeughaus

At the end of the C18 the constitution introduced at the time of the Reformation was still in force in Basle. Country people were excluded from all higher political offices and theoretically were the chattels of the town. A few families had controlled Basle and the surrounding countryside for generations. The Declaration of Independence and the constitution of the United States of America in 1776 heralded a new form of society; then the French Revolution provided the external impetus for the overthrow of the existing system in Switzerland. In the canton of Basle the country people demanded equality with the townspeople, and the recognition of human rights. The town conceded to these demands on 20 January 1798. On 22 January a festival of fraternity was held in Basle. The new red, white and black flag symbolizing the new relationship between Liestal and Basle flew above the town hall, and a large liberty pole with a three-coloured tin hat on top was erected on the Münsterplatz. Coloured pictures of the festival, the fact that this hat came from the armoury and the red, white and blue colouring of the feathers and cockade suggest that this is in fact the liberty hat from that festival. FE

77
Barfüsserkirche

Basle wine measure, dated 1356
(escutcheon added later)
Basle

Cast bronze; height 42 cm, diameter at base 59 cm
Inv. no. 1884.168. On loan from E.E. Zunft zu Weinleuten

In 1356 Basle experienced the worst natural catastrophe in its history. On 18 October, St Luke's day, there was an earthquake; the fires and epidemics resulting from it had a devastating effect. The Latin inscription on the wine measure also mentions the earthquake: "Ulrich wrote these lines as best he could, may God and the Virgin save him. In the year of the great earthquake – my report is true – I was cast in Basle by the townspeople". Wine was not just a means of enjoyment, but also of sustenance and of income. The council imposed taxes on wine at a very early date and for centuries they were an important source of revenue for the town, as well as a frequent cause of disputes between the citizens and the authorities. The fact that a new wine measure was produced in the year of the earthquake attests to the financial importance of wine to the town's coffers. In fact the town's finances recovered very quickly after the earthquake. Basle was able to repay fairly large loans taken out earlier, build the outer city walls, and in 1363 marked the end of the reconstruction with the consecration of the rebuilt high altar in the Münster. FE

78
Barfüsserkirche

Five Basle weights
Basle, ca. 1600

Cast bronze; largest weight: height 11.2 cm, width 9.6 cm, depth 9.6 cm
Inv. no. 1905.1364. Alter Bestand

A variety of pound weights were in use in old Basle. Chemists used the apothecary's pound weighing 357.78 g. The brass pound weighing 480.23 g was used for dealings in spices, drugs, confectionery and wool. Goldsmiths and silversmiths used the silver pound weighing 468.58 g. In the 'Kaufhaus' (warehouse and customs) goods were weighed using the heavy iron pound which weighed 493.24 g. The light iron pound weighing 486.17 g, subdivided into a half pound, a quarter, a 'Loth' and a 'Quint', was in widespread use in shops. While overall supervision of weights and measures was a council responsibility, the weights had to be calibrated and checked by the different guilds. The Safranzunft (merchants' guild) was the guild with the greatest powers: it calibrated the brass pound, the light iron pound and the heavy iron pound, appointing an official to carry out these duties. The five weights illustrated come from a series of 13 weights of the Basle light iron pound. The tops of the weights feature the Basle coat of arms, and the bigger ones also show a basilisk supporting it. It is uncertain whether these weights were used by the Safranzunft as master weights for calibration purposes or whether they were normal weights for everyday use. However, the highly visible Basle coat of arms suggests that they were used officially as master weights. FE

79
Barfüsserkirche

Nest of cup weights
Basle, 17th century (the smallest weight does not belong to the set)
Cast bronze; height with handle 13 cm; diameter of lid 8.4 cm
Inv. no. 1905.365. Alter Bestand

Nests such as this consist of cup-shaped weights usually made of bronze or brass that fit inside one another. The largest weight is also a container and can be closed with a lid. For centuries in Basle there were five different pounds in use, each with a different weight: the apothecary's pound, the silver pound, the light and the heavy iron pound, and the brass pound (see no. 78). The weight of this set is 1925 g, i.e. four times the weight of a Basle brass pound (=480.23 g), and this is indicated by the figure 4 on the lid. The empty container at 963 g weighs exactly half as much, that is, 2 Basle brass pounds. The largest nesting cup is 480.75 g, one Basle brass pound. With each cup the weight reduces by half. Because the brass pound was calibrated by the Safranzunft (merchants' guild), on the bottom of the cup there is the lily of the Safranzunft alongside the impression of the Basle crosier. The brass pound was used by silk merchants, button-makers and sellers of wool and sewing thread as well as confectioners and spice-sellers. FE

80
Barfüsserkirche

Two Basle dry measures, dated 1669
Basle
Turned, carved walnut (probably darkened later); larger vessel: height 11 cm, diameter across top 9.5 cm; smaller vessel: height 8.5 cm, diameter across top 8.3 cm
Inv. no. 1877.23.a.b. Gift of the Bürgerrat

These two tumbler-shaped dry measures were for measuring grain, flour or dried fruit. When the vessels were calibrated, the Basle crosier and the year 1669 were carved on the sides to show that they were legally tested measuring vessels. In Basle most dry measures were calibrated by the Gartnernzunft (growers and grocers). A notice in the guild documents for 1527 explains how the calibration was carried out: "When weights and vessels are tested at the guild, the masters must have a little beechwood tub with water in the big room and on behalf of the guild weigh and measure with all the pails and everything belonging to it, thus calibrating old and new vessels". The larger container holds 0.54 l, the smaller one 0.27 l. In Basle the measuring units were called 'Mässlein' or 'halbes Mässlein' or 'Gäzlein' – the capacity of a 'Gäzlein' is not known, but is thought to be 0.25 l. As the inscription beside the Basle crosier says, "Nota ist abszustreichen" (remember to level off), the measures were not heaped but level ones. FE

81
Barfüsserkirche

Express scales from the Basle armoury, dated 1687
Reinhard Siegfried, Basle
Forged iron; cast brass, scale painted on; length 440 cm
Inv. no. 1874.124. Gift of the Zeughausverwaltung

The longer arm is marked with the scale and the running weight can be pushed to and fro along it. The load is suspended from the hook on the shorter arm, and the running weight on the longer arm pushed along until the balance beam lies horizontal; then the weight is read off the scale. Loads of up to four and a half tons could be weighed on these scales. They were purchased in October 1687 by the inner council from Reinhard Siegfried (guild member from 1662), a master toolmaker specialising in such scales, and were set up in the Basle armoury where they were used for weighing particularly heavy objects. According to the armoury inventory of 1711 they hung at the entrance under a wooden roof. There are two impressions of the Basle coat of arms and the year 1687 on the bell-shaped brass running weight. The brass cap placed on the shorter arm also carries the Basle coat of arms accompanied by a basilisk supporter. These emblems indicate that the scales were officially commissioned, but they also reflect the strong civic self-confidence of Basle in the Baroque period. FE

82
Barfüsserkirche

Two dry cereal measures from Basle
Basle, 16th/17th century
Cast bronze; larger vessel: height 20 cm, diameter 37 cm; smaller vessel: height 10 cm, diameter 27 cm
Inv. nos. 1906.2838 and 1906.2839. Alter Bestand

Cereals – always referred to in Basle sources up until 1798 as 'Frucht' (fruit) – were the most important human foodstuff up until very recent times. Until the second half of the C19 cereals were not weighed, but measured, as were leguminous vegetables, berries, salt, honey, etc. Measuring was simpler than weighing which required weights and scales. In spite of local diversity in systems of weights and measures in old Switzerland the comparable dry measure units tended to be about 20 litres. The basic measure in central Switzerland was known as a 'Viertel' (quarter), but in Basle people talked of the 'Sester', which had a capacity of 17.08 l. The two bronze measuring vessels of one 'Sester' (17.08 l) and a half 'Sester' (8.54 l) almost certainly came originally from different sets. Because of their heavy weight we can assume that they were not intended for everyday commercial use. Both were probably used by the authorities as master measures to calibrate other less cumbersome dry measures; the escutcheons with the Basle crosier also suggest this. FE

83
Barfüsserkirche

Basle wine measure, dated 1753
Basle
Cast bronze; height 56 cm, diameter at widest part 40 cm, diameter at neck 14 cm
Inv. no. 1906.2851. Alter Bestand

Since the Middle Ages wine had been subject to several taxes, two of which were especially important to the town, the 'Pfundzoll' and the 'Ungeld'. The 'Pfundzoll' was an import duty levied on all goods intended for resale. The 'Ungeld' was a tax on consumption, and the wine 'Ungeld' was one of the city's most lucrative sources of income; in accounts of weekly income it regularly headed the list. As the taxes were reckoned by fluid quantity, great importance was attached to measuring and checking the measures. The town had acquired the right to calibrate wine measures from the bishop around the mid-C14. The Weinleutenzunft (vintners' guild) was entrusted with carrying out the measuring and checking it. The calibration of barrels was known as 'sinnen', and that of smaller containers as 'fechten'. Two 'Fechtmeister' from the Weinleutenzunft had to calibrate all the vessels used for selling wine once a year. If the vessels had passed inspection, they were marked with the Basle crosier and the coat of arms of the guild, a measuring pail. This round-bellied jug was probably used by the guild as a master measure. It holds 16 'Mass' (= 22.72 l) or a half 'Ohm' (awm). FE

84
Barfüsserkirche

Two weights from the Basle 'Fronwaage', dated 1781
Basle
Cast bronze; heights with ring socket 35 and 28 cm, diameters 19 and 14 cm
Inv. no. 1877.20. Gift of the Bürgerrat

When on 12 March 1373 the bishop accorded the town the right to levy tolls and to control the 'Fronwaage' (weighing scales), the mint and the office of local mayor, the citizenry acquired much more power – it was a milestone in Basle's development towards independence. The council immediately built a 'Kaufhaus' which served as a warehouse and customs office. Since the right to exact customs is linked with the control of weights and measures – goods have to be counted, measured and weighed before customs duty can be charged on them – the council installed the so called 'Fronwaage' in the 'Kaufhaus'. For centuries imported goods had first to be taken to the 'Kaufhaus' and placed on the 'Fronwaage' so that the 'Pfundzoll' (import duty) could be levied on them. Two weights dating from 1781 have been preserved. The Basle coat of arms in a laurel wreath indicates that the city was responsible for the laws relating to weights and measures. The letters F W stand for 'Fronwaage'. The weights weigh 49.28 kg and 24.64 kg respectively, so are based on the pound weight which for these scales was set at 493.24 g. FE

85
Barfüsserkirche

Basle dry measure
Basle, 18th century
Cast bronze, turned oak; height 7 cm, diameter of opening 7.5 cm
Inv. no. 1906.2848. Alter Bestand

Up until the C19 there were dozens of different counting systems in use for weights and measures even within the small state of Switzerland; while these were of course adequate for local trade links, they involved a complicated conversion into different systems when trading with other regions. When it acquired important sovereign rights around 1400 the city of Basle had also gained control of weights and measures, but by and large the old plurality continued unchanged until the C19. The diversity and confusion were not ended until the advent of industrialisation and the increase in international trade. The Federal constitution unified the weights and measures used on Swiss territory only in 1874, converting to the international metric system. The C18 measure illustrated here holds 0.355 l, corresponding to a very small unit known in Basle as a 'Schüssel'. Made of bronze, with the Basle escutcheon supported by a basilisk on its side, and weighing 1263 g, it is disproportionately heavy. It would almost certainly not have been for everyday use, and more probably was a master measure used by the authorities to calibrate other vessels. FE

86
Barfüsserkirche

Dry measure for cereals
North-west Switzerland, 18th century
Beech, iron; height 11 cm, diameter 20 cm
Inv. no. 1898.294. Purchase

The right to determine and oversee weights and measures was closely linked with sovereignty and the right to hold markets. The local lord – in free cities the council – put a 'Fechtmeister' (calibration officer), or sometimes the guilds, in charge of overseeing weights and measures. From time to time the 'Fechtmeister' would check all implements used for weighing and measuring goods against master weights and measures. By contrast to today, it used to be more common for goods such as cereals, salt, berries, etc, to be measured rather than weighed. The units used in measuring varied from one small political and economic sovereignty to another. Simple tub-shaped wooden vessels with sides reinforced by iron bands were used to measure cereals, and were also calibrated by the 'Fechtmeister'. If they passed inspection they were generally marked with the coat of arms of the ruling authority and a year number indicating when they had been checked. The dry measure for cereals illustrated here displays the coat of arms of Prince Bishop Johann Conrad von Reinach-Hirtzbach of Basle who was in office from 1705 to 1737. The year 1711 burnt on to the vessel records the year of calibration; it was calibrated for a second time in 1756. FE

87
Study collection

Bird's-eye view of the city of Basle from the north-east, signed and dated 1615
Matthäus Merian, Basle
Pen and ink drawing on paper (later mounted on linen), coloured; height 116 cm, width 164 cm
Inv. no. 1880.201. Gift of the Regierungsrat

As well as a great many town views created as pictures there was a widespread demand for legible views or plans based on surveys, combining ground-plan and elevation in a bird's-eye perspective. The view from above provides an instant grasp of the whole town but closer inspection of the detail is also possible. This bird's-eye view by Matthäus Merian is undoubtedly the best attempt ever made to provide a true-to-life, topographically correct picture of the city of Basle. Merian, who was only 22 years old in 1615, could not have carried out the necessary surveying himself, and must have used the work done earlier by Hans Bock. The plan is a wonderful source for knowledge of Basle as it was in the C17, besides being more narrowly the most important available source for the city's historical topography. In 1615 Basle still had the appearance of a medieval town. The thinly settled suburbs provided adequate room for the slowly expanding population until the mid-C19. The drawing was probably a preliminary for the copper engraving printed in 1617 using four plates.
FE

88
Barfüsserkirche

Bird's-eye view of the city of Basle from the north-east, signed and dated 1847
Friedrich Mähly, Basle
Coloured lithography; height 61.7 cm, width 84 cm
Inv. no. 1901.108. Purchase

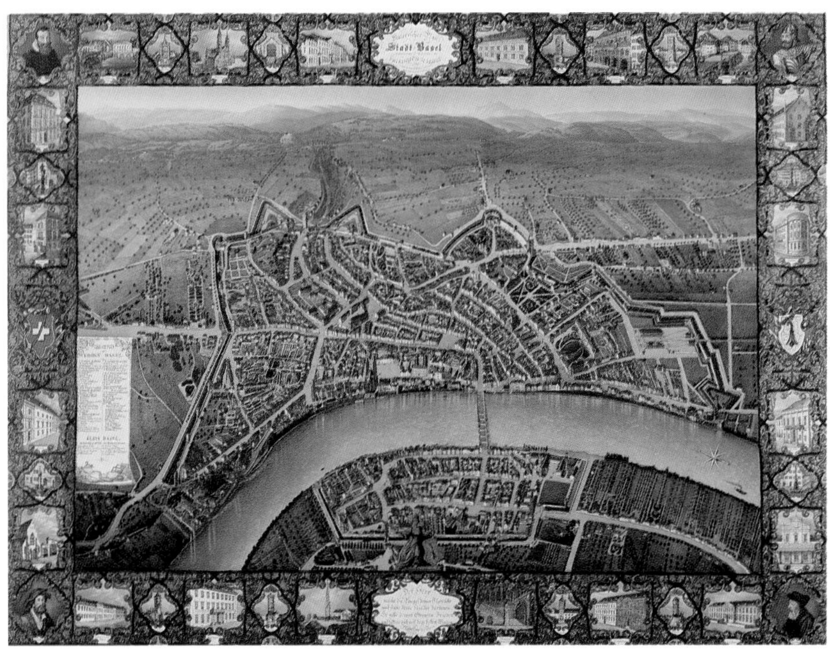

Mähly's plan is topographically correct, but also has the merit of following the ground-plan of the bird's-eye view by Matthäus Merian (no. 87). Comparing the two plans gives us an insight into the continuity and changes in the city of Basle over a period of 230 years. Although not a great deal of building work was undertaken in the private or the public sector between 1615 and 1847, there are quite a few changes in detail. By 1847 not only had the outworks of several city gates disappeared, but the fortifications along the Rhine and a great many towers and chapels as well. The Stadthaus, the Haus zum Kirschgarten, St. Jakobsdenkmal, the Botanical Garden and the city hospital were new. The projecting outlines of the first factories and the Elsässerbahnhof (railway station) are the precursors of a new era. The picture of the town nestling round a bend of the Rhine like some Biedermeier idyll idealises the image of old Basle. The reality was different: one has only to visualise, where Falknerstrasse now is, the open Birsigbach, a foul-smelling sewer running through the middle of the town that was the source of devastating epidemics. FE

Crafts and trades

In the C13 and C14 the ruler of the city of Basle, the bishop, established the guilds as a political counterweight to the nobility. The original number of 15 guilds was not exceeded until the demise of the guild system in the C19. To exercise his profession, every independent craftsman and trader had to join a guild. In Basle the guilds were particularly important not only as professional associations but as a political force: for centuries the inner council was made up of 15 councillors and 15 guild masters (one guild master for every councillor); Basle was regarded as ruled by its guilds. The memory of the old guild rule was still very much alive when the Historisches Museum was founded at the end of the C19.

The 'Crafts and Trades' section is chiefly devoted to the traditional professions of past centuries. It includes both the craft tools of particular professions – and whole workshops in exceptional cases – and semi-finished and finished products. Trade signs or boards, including an extensive collection of inn signs, some items of furniture from guildhouses (plaques with coats of arms, guild chests etc) and masters' and journeymen's certificates are also included. The collection is very heterogeneous. Unfortunately, it has been little developed. Few objects reflecting the industrial and technical achievements of recent decades are present, so that the modern development of Basle into a centre of services and, above all, of industry, with its its three chemical firms of worldwide reputation, Ciba-Geigy, Hoffmann-La Roche and Sandoz, is only sparsely documented. FE

89
Study collection

Touchstone for gold assay, dated 1546
Slate, brass gilt and engraved; length with ring 33 cm
Inv. no. 1890.86. Gift of Hegetschweiler-Schaub

The cost of gold constantly gave occasion for forgery or mis-statement of the gold content of gold products. The scraping test is an old and simple method of testing gold content, and is used by goldsmiths even now. The gold to be tested is rubbed on a black slate touchstone so as to leave a mark. The colour of the mark is compared to that of needles of precisely known gold content. The assay with acid is somewhat more exact. The mark on the touchstone is dabbed with several acids calibrated against the usual gold alloys. The acid that dissolves the mark indicates the fineness of the gold alloy. For very exact measurements the fire test (which cannot here be described in detail) is used. It has, however, the major drawback that a sample must be cut out of the object, involving a considerable intrusion. The touchstone shown here is a particularly finely made goldsmith's instrument from the mid-C16. The gilt brass ferrule fitted to one end of the touchstone has two unidentified escutcheons on its narrow sides. On the wide sides floral ornament and the date 1546 are engraved. The narrow sides of the stone have relief decoration. FE

90
Barfüsserkirche

Guild chest of the Steinmetzen (stonemasons), dated 1592
Probably Basle
Oil painting on wood (pine and cherry); height 17 cm, width 45.2 cm, depth 28.4 cm
Inv. no. 1870.898. Gift of the Handwerk der Steinmetzen und Maurer

Guild chests were used by guilds for storing important documents and other valuables. While many chests have a rich architectural articulation, that of the Basle stonemasons is remarkable for its painting. The four sides are painted with illusionistic architecture with round arched niches. Two escutcheons occupy the two niches on the front. Their significance is not known, although the one on the right with stonemasons' tools resembles the coat of arms of the Breiter family. The date 1592 is painted above the heart-shaped keyhole plate. In the niches at the sides stand four crowned figures, who have stonemasons' tools such as compasses, setsquare, ruler and plane as attributes. They are fairly exact copies of four paintings formerly set into the panelling of the guildroom of the Spinnwettern (building trade workers' guild). The four crowned figures are the patron saints of stonemasons, four brothers, all stonemasons, who suffered martyrs' deaths during the persecution of Emperor Diocletian (284–305): as Christians they had refused to carve statues of the pagan gods. They wear crowns instead of haloes, recalling the crowns of thorns placed on them during their martyrdom. The chest is interesting evidence of the long persistence of the cult of saints in Protestant Basle. FE

91
Haus zum Kirschgarten

Sign of the inn 'Zum wilden Mann', Freiestrasse, Basle
Basle, ca. 1600
Oak, carved, painted; height 171 cm
Inv. no. 1870.1202. Alter Bestand

Wildmen were a very popular motif in the Middle Ages; the term 'wild' embraced a wide spectrum of behaviour and could include anything alien or unusual. Wildmen appear in many embroidered tapestries of the Upper Rhine, on 'Minnekästchen' (courtly love caskets) and in drawings and engravings, as well as in Basle glass paintings. On the feast of the Epiphany in 1435 wildmen performed a dance before the civic nobility of Basle and guests of the council. They had a human body covered by a thick coat of hair or hide, and the male usually carried a club or a tree trunk with roots. A figment of the urban patriciate and court society, they originally had a moralising significance, but it was largely lost with their popularisation in the Renaissance and the Baroque. This wildman sculpted fully in the round about 1600 is no longer intended to instruct, although with his garlands of fur, leaves and fruits around his head and loins and a tree trunk in his right hand, he is based on traditional medieval models. Even now the wildman plays an important role in the Basle carnival. FE

92
Study collection

Ornamental hammer, dated 1649
Head of cast bronze, engraved; iron mount on the face; strips of engraved brass, handle of turned boxwood; length 38 cm
Inv. no. 1930.214. Purchase

To judge from its appearance and the engraved motifs the small hammer might have been used by a blacksmith. When shoeing a horse the nails were struck with the face; the forked pane was used to extract them. Images of blacksmith's tools such as pliers and hammer, shoes and nails are engraved on it. Other tools such as a wooden mallet and a circle cutter are more likely to have been used by saddlers. But the little hammer could hardly have been used as a craft tool, as it is too light and the material (bronze) too weak. The split pane is blunt and the shape of the notch is ill-suited to pulling out nails. It is much more likely to have been part of the lore of lovers or married couples, and some of the engraved depictions support this interpretation. Both sides of the forked pane show a pair of lovers. Horseshoes have since ancient times been a popular sign of good luck. The cut-out hearts in the brass strips are to be interpreted as love symbols. The hammer is not a practical tool but an instrument of the power of luck over love and marriage. FE

93
Barfüsserkirche

Drinking vessel of the Basle Schuhmacherzunft (shoemakers' guild), dated 1661

Leather, silver-gilt mouthpiece; height 16.4 cm
Inv. no. 1894.304. Gift of the E.E. Zunft zu Schuhmachern

Drinking vessels in the shape of humans, animals, boats, tools and implements of all kinds were very popular in the Baroque age, with its love of surprise effects. These vessels, known as 'Trinkspiele' (drinking toys), were used to embellish a banquet and could be purely for show as well as for use. On special occasions they were sometimes filled with wine and passed round among the guests. Some of them had a clockwork mechanism in the base. The figure could be set in motion; the guest it pointed to when it stopped had to empty it. Other vessels were designed to surprise or even frighten the drinker for the amusement of the revellers. The 'game' embodied in the leather shoe of the Basle shoemakers' guild lay in the fact that the raised dolphin's head caused a sudden surge of wine into the unsuspecting drinker's face. FE

94
Barfüsserkirche

Two carved nogs for barrels, *Rhenus and Basilea*
Attributed to Johann Christian Frisch, Basle, ca. 1680

Carved walnut; *Rhenus*: height 21 cm, width 40.5 cm; *Basilea*: height 24.5 cm, width 37.5 cm
Inv. nos. 1932.1042 and 1932.1043. Acquired by exchange

The two carved nogs are a matching pair and come from the Basle Waisenhaus (orphanage). The first nog shows a bust of a bearded man with a pointed crown, carrying two crossed, fleshy dolphins on his shoulders. He is a personification of the Rhine. On the other piece a female bust has two horns of plenty crossed behind her neck, from which pour crowns, Basle coins and fruit. Here the city of Basle is personified as Basilea. The two nogs are outstanding examples of Basle sculpture in the C17. As they bear a close resemblance to his figures on the carved council table (no. 379), they are attributed to Johann Christian Frisch. In 1675 this wood carver from Linz had produced a superb draw-table as his masterpiece, in order to be able to marry a Basle cabinetmaker's widow and run her business. In 1676 he presented the table to the council, whereupon his admission fee as a citizen was waived. FE

95
Barfüsserkirche

Pile driver, signed and dated 1757
Basle, Johann Friedrich Weitnauer
Cast bronze; height 165 cm, width 39 cm, depth 39 cm
Inv. no. 1921.183. Gift of the Baudepartement Basel

The building of the Rhine bridge at Basle, completed in 1226, was an important precondition of the city's commercial and political rise in the late Middle Ages. The citizens always lavished great care on the structure. In 1457 six stone piers were added to the wooden bridge on the Kleinbasel side. On the Grossbasel side the water was too deep and fast-flowing to be dammed with the technology of the time; here, up to the C20, the bridge was supported on seven wooden stilts made of oak piles. This part of the bridge had to be renewed very frequently. The pile driver was used to drive the piles into the river bed. A model, exhibited beside the pile driver, explains the procedure. The driver is signed IOHANN FRIDRICH/WEITNAVER GOSS/MICH IN BASSEL/ANNO DOMINI MDCCLVII (Johann Friedrich Weitnauer cast me in Basle AD 1757), and is richly embellished with foliage and animals. In the centre two basilisks hold a Basle shield. Below them is a strip with dolphin, lizard, frog and stag-beetle, creatures that are also to be found on church bells; in pre-Christian times they were thought to offer protection against charms. At the foot of the pile driver at the front a stork with a snake in its beak can be read as a symbol of Christ. FE

96
Mühlemuseum Brüglingen

'Kleiekotzer' (bran puker)
Reportedly from Murten (Fribourg), ca. 1770
Oak carved and painted (not original), mounted on an oak board, initials JSH HR at the top edge; height with board 60 cm, width 45.5 cm
Inv. no. 1896.197.b. Purchase

The 'Kleiekotzer' or bran puker – a wooden mask with wide open mouth – is a decorative feature of many grain mills. Above the two millstones there is an inverted wooden box to guide the grain and prevent it from being scattered around the stones. To obtain white flour the ground product, consisting of flour, semolina and bran (outer skin of the grain with valuable vitamins and trace elements) has to be sieved, to separate the flour from the bran. Up to the C16 this laborious task was done by hand, and white flour was therefore an expensive product not widely used. About 1500 the bolt mechanism was invented, whereby the sieving was done mechanically by the mill. The flour was fed into a tubular inclined bag of very fine material (flour silk). Through constant shaking of the bag the fine flour fell into a wooden box, while the coarse bran was ejected from the end of the bag through the mouth of the bran puker into the bran trough. According to popular belief the grimacing face could drive away evil spirits. FE

97
Haus zum Kirschgarten

Inn sign
Switzerland, 19th century
Iron, tin coated, embossed, painted (present paint not original); diameter of hat 102 cm, length of arm 220 cm
Inv. no. 1895.166. Gift of Aktienbrauerei Kardinal

Within an iron ring below a cardinal's hat with cords hanging down at both sides, each with 15 tassels, are brewing implements such as a ladle and a malt scoop, as well as a wreath of hops, a sheaf of barley ears and a tankard of beer. The six-pointed star on the tankard has been a sign of inns which brewed their own beer since the Middle Ages. In C19 it became the symbol of breweries. Beer only became a national drink in the last century, when railways made possible the transportation of the grain and the quick distribution of the beer over long distances; the brewing industry expanded rapidly. About 1880 there were more than five hundred breweries in Switzerland. Most of them were small household breweries which served beer in their own inns. The sign was probably made for such a brewery; the inn may have been called 'Zum Kardinal'. From about 1840 to 1895 the sign was displayed outside the Basle 'Kardinal' brewery. It is said to have come originally from the village of Eiken in Aargau, where, however, no inn called 'Zum Kardinal' and no brewery of that name can be traced. FE

98
Haus zum Kirschgarten

Inn sign
Basle, ca. 1850
Iron, tin coated, embossed, painted (present paint not original); length of ship 150 cm
Inv. no. 1889.102. Gift of Charles Schielé-Lorenz

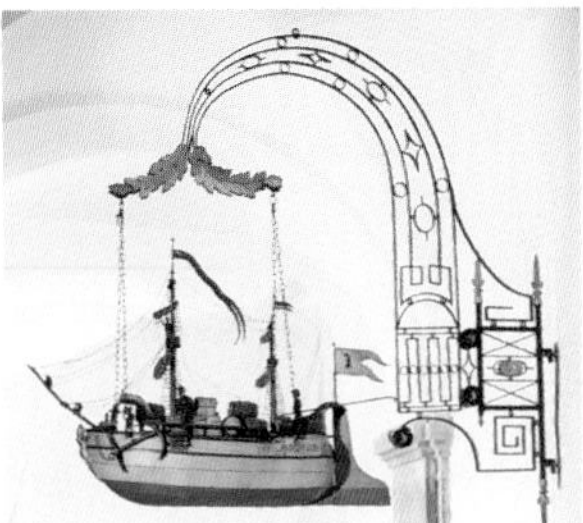

In the extensive collection of more than 80 trade signs 'Das Schiff' (the ship) is certainly among the finest. The splendid freighter of sheet iron is probably the work of a tinsmith. The ship as a whole is an imaginary model, although details are authentically reproduced, corresponding to contemporary shipbuilding practice and obviously based on observation. The tall masts with five and four shrouds respectively (with thick ropes to stabilise the masts), and the names of distant destinations such as St Louis, Havana and Constantinople on the cargo, indicate a ship of the high seas. However, the overlapping clinker construction of the hull, the small cabin windows in the stern, the exceptionally wide rudder and the loading of cargo on deck instead of in the hold are signs of a river-going boat. Until 1888 the sign was outside the 'Zum Schiff' inn at Barfüsserplatz 3, one of the oldest inns in Basle. In 1888 the model ship was repainted, probably by a certain J. Vogt, as is suggested by the date and name on a barrel in the cargo. FE

Metals

The 'Metals' section is extremely extensive, embracing the sub-groups iron, copper, brass, bronze and tin (but not gold and silver, which form part of the art historical sections). The metals mentioned were for centuries the main materials for producing numerous objects, especially for daily use; one need only think of the almost unlimited possible uses of iron. The great importance of metals as a material in former times is reflected not only in their quantity – this section comprises thousands of objects – but also in their variety. Categories deserving special mention are the collection of bells, including one of the oldest in existence; the extensive holding of works of the blacksmith's and locksmith's art (keys, locks, mounts, railings, gargoyles, wind vanes, weathercocks, etc); the collection of about 80 stove plates from the high period of ornamental iron casting in the C16; the pewter collection comprising roughly 600 objects, among them the outstanding sacred pewter vessels from the Basle Münster treasury. The 'Metals' section is a source of the first importance for research into the arts and crafts of the Upper Rhine and in particular Basle in earlier centuries; it provides scholars with important information on the cultural and economic history of the region. FE

99
Barfüsserkirche

Tower bell
9th century (crown and crown plate not original, clapper missing)
Cast bronze; diameter 41 cm; pitch cannot be determined as the bell has as yet no pure tones
Inv. no. 1907.289. Alter Bestand

The bell is a member of the famous 'Theophilus' group of bells, having the characteristics of cast bells as described by Theophilus Presbyter in the early C12. The main feature is three triangular 'sound holes' in the shoulder, which, according to Theophilus, accentuated the overtones. The most recent experiments demonstrate, however, that the openings do not influence the tone. Another feature of most Theophilus bells is their cylindrical shape. The Basle example has almost no narrowing towards the top. Theophilus bells, cast by the lost-wax process, have a somewhat rough surface and sometimes residues of casting faults. The almost complete absence of decoration and inscriptions concentrates attention on the well proportioned shape. The Basle Theophilus bell is one of the finest of its kind and one of the oldest bells in existence. It comes from the Basle Münster and probably hung in the Martinsturm (St Martin's tower). It may be the bell called in later centuries the 'Pfaffenglöcklein' (little papist bell) that was 'without clapper' even in the C18 and was moved to the Zeughaus or the Werkhof in 1734. FE

100
Barfüsserkirche

Pot for holy oil, from the Basle Münster treasury
Basle, Meister H, 2nd half 14th century
Cast pewter, soldered, engraved; height 27 cm
Inv. no. 1870. 443.c. Gift of the Regierung Kanton Basel-Stadt

This pot and two others of the same shape and with a similar spout form a trio of international importance. These 'Tüllenkannen', so called after their long spout ('Tülle'), are mentioned in the inventory of Basle Münster as early as 1477: "Item iii zinnen kannen pro oleo sacro" (three pewter pots for holy oil). According to the book of ceremonies of the Basle Münster for 1517, they contained holy oil that was consecrated by the bishop of Basle for the whole diocese each year on Maundy Thursday. Gothic capitals chased on the hinged lids describe the liturgical use of the vessels. The pitcher illustrated was reserved for oil used for the sick (I/S O INFIRMOR) while its companions were used for baptismal oil (P/S O PVERORVM) and for consecrated oil or chrism (C/S CRISMA). Impressed on the handles of the pots is the mark of the Basle Master H (ca. 1375), while the bottom of the vessel is marked with a relief medallion signifying ownership by the bishop of Basle, Jean de Vienne (1366–82). These pitchers are therefore not only the oldest dated objects in the Basle pewter collection, but are among the oldest pewter vessels in the world. SF

101
Barfüsserkirche

Fragment of the papal bell ('Pabstglocke') of Basle Münster
Jörg von Guntheim, Basle, 1493
Cast bronze; height 31.6 cm, width 16.3 cm, depth 5 cm
Inv. no. 1873.55. Gift of the Baukollegium

On 25 June 1439 the Council of Basle deposed Pope Eugene IV and on 5 November of the same year elected pope Duke Amadeus of Savoy. He called himself Felix V. The new pope arrived at Basle in the summer of 1440 and was crowned on the Münsterplatz on 24 July. No doubt to commemorate the occasion he donated a bell to the Münster; it was cast by Hans Peier on 5 September 1442. While sounding a storm warning in June 1489 it disintegrated. In 1490 the cathedral chapter and representatives of the council commissioned Ludwig Peier to cast a new bell; for reasons unknown this commission was never carried out. It was not until 17 October 1493 that the gun founder Jörg von Guntheim, who worked in Strasbourg, cast the new bell on the Münsterplatz. Together with a four-line verse by Sebastian Brant it bore the inscription: "Christus, König der Herrlichkeit, komm zu uns mit Frieden, 1493" (Christ, king of glory, come to us in peace, 1493). The fragment comes from this second papal bell. Above the coat of arms of Savoy it shows a Basle 'Rappen' coin, and above that the crossed keys of St Peter with the three-tiered crown (tiara) as papal symbols, also a 'Stebler' (half a Basle 'Rappen'). The fragment was drilled out of the papal bell in 1873, before the Münster bells were recast. FE

102
Barfüsserkirche

Pot with handle
Berne(?), without marks, ca. 1500
Cast pewter, soldered; height without handle 44 cm
Inv. no. 1885.118. Purchase

Pitchers accounted for most of the output of the pewterer's trade. Evidence of this is the earlier name of the trade, 'Kannengiesser' (pitcher casters), and it is reflected in the pewter collection, made up mostly of pots. The Museum's holding, including types known as 'Stizen', 'Rundelen' and 'Stegkannen', and examples with prismatic, bell-shaped or big-bellied bodies, gives a representative overview of Swiss pitcher production. This bow-handled pot dating from about 1500 is the oldest secular pewter pot in the collection. With other pieces of similar shape – the Schweizerisches Landesmuseum in Zurich, for example, owns an identical pitcher – it is among the oldest surviving examples of Swiss secular pewter. The weighty vessel has a thick conical foot and a dome-shaped hinged lid. A spout with an animal's head at its tip curves up from the vessel's belly. Two opposed bridges projecting up from the belly serve as mounts for the iron handle. On each side of the body are relief coats of arms of the Bubenberg family of Berne and of Spiez (canton of Berne). SF

103
Barfüsserkirche

Brass dish
1st half 16th century
Brass, hammered, embossed and punched; diameter 27.5 cm
Inv. no. 1870.998. Gift of Prof. Wilhelm Wackernagel

The oldest brass dishes are without ornament. Only when they were used as baptism or collection plates in church or to embellish citizens' rooms in the C15 did they begin to be decorated, usually with religious imagery. The craft reached its peak at the end of the Middle Ages; the second half of the C16 brought its decline. On the dish shown *Samson and the Lion* is the principal motif. Samson's fight with the lion was understood in medieval theology as prefiguring Christ's Passion. The image was made by hammering into a negative form from the back. Only the scale decoration at the base of the rim is embossed without the use of a pattern; it serves to reinforce the dish where the metal is thinnest. The ornamental wreaths around the bottom and the rim were impressed with two different punches from the upper side. It is thought that the men who carried out this work were merely artisans, as they would hardly themselves have made the brass sheet, the punches and the negative forms. The relatively small number of motifs on surviving brass dishes indicates that the craftsmen worked with only a few negative forms for centuries. FE

104
Barfüsserkirche

Stove plate, dated 1516
Master G.F.(?), Alsace
Cast iron; height 81 cm, width 91.5 cm
Inv. no. 1875.75. Gift of the Baukollegium

The plate has an important place in research due to the initials G.F. on the banderole. They are assumed to be the initials of a mould-maker working in the early C16 in Alsace, to whom more than two dozen stove plates in museums in the Upper Rhine region have been attributed. Characteristic of this master is the depiction of individual people or statuesque groups; he avoids scenes in motion. Almost all the figures are surmounted by a round arch with dogtooth-like tracery along its lower edge. The spandrels are filled with foliage linking to the rectangular frame. The apex is surmounted by a bird or a fabulous creature. Master G.F. stands at the transition from Late Gothic to Renaissance, not only stylistically but in subject-matter. Apart from traditional religious subjects, figures from ancient history and mythology appear increasingly in his work. The left half of the plate shows Thisbe over the corpse of Pyramus. The lovers had met in a wood because of their parents' hostility. A lion tore Thisbe's dress to pieces, and Pyramus, believing his beloved dead, committed suicide, as did Thisbe on her return (Ovid, *Metamorphoses* 4,55). The half-length male figure in the right field has not been identified. FE

105
Barfüsserkirche

Stove plate, dated 1519
Meister G.F.(?), Alsace
Cast iron; height 81 cm, width 91.5 cm
Inv. no. 1965.34. Gift of Hans Peter His-Miescher

Usually richly decorated, cast-iron plates were a necessary part of the iron stoves that before 1500 were in widespread use in town halls, monasteries, guildhalls, and later in the houses of the upper middle classes, and that continued to be produced until the Baroque period. A centre nearby Basle was Kandern in the Black Forest, where an iron foundry is documented from 1512. The plates were often decorated with reliefs showing coats of arms, single figures or sequences of scenes. While saints predominated before the Reformation, during the Renaissance motifs from ancient history, literature and mythology became very popular. Phyllis riding on Aristotle is one of a series of moralising stories that originated in the late Middle Ages, then found their way into literature and later into visual art. The moral of the tale was that even Aristotle, the greatest sage of antiquity, was conquered by female wiles. This plate is dated 1519 and is attributed to the Alsatian Master G.F. (see no. 104). The motto, probably only added when the plate was painted in the C18, announces: "Wie wohl er doch / kein Pferde was / Ein Wyb im denocht ybersass" (though he never was a steed, yet a woman on him rode). The Augustinermuseum in Freiburg owns an almost identical plate. FE

106
Barfüsserkirche

Stove plate
Signed Philipp Soldan zum Frankenburg, Hessen, ca. 1550
Cast iron; height 71.5 cm, width 85 cm
Inv. no. 1930.137. Purchased with Federal subsidy

Patterns for the reliefs on stove plates were made by cutters ('Formschneider') or carvers ('Schnitzer'), as they were also called by contemporaries. They carved the wooden form with which the founder impressed a mould into a sandbox and then cast the plate in an open furnace. This procedure made undercutting impossible and cast-iron stove plates are always in a flat, low relief. The frame was produced using separate forms. The foundries kept the wooden forms sometimes for centuries, and used them in different combinations. The form-cutters were far from being court artists, usually living and working near the foundries in remote valleys, and like the founders almost always remained anonymous. One of the few identifiable carvers is Philipp Soldan zum Frankenberg (ca. 1500–1569). Better than almost any other form-cutter he understood the requirements of cast-iron relief and took great care with the technical execution of his work. Under him stove-plate casting reached an apogee. This plate, signed PHILIPS SOLDA FO[RM]SCHNIDER, shows a scene of *The Return of the Prodigal Son* after an engraving by Hans Sebald Beham, published in 1540. FE

107
Barfüsserkirche

Lock for a chest
Ca. 1600

Iron, punched, blued; height 22.5 cm, width 28.3 cm, depth 4.6 cm
Inv. no. 1914. 154. Alter Bestand

In the C14 and C15 the urban artisanate and middle class enjoyed a rise in their economic and political status that was reflected in many aspects of everyday living. In the ironworking sector, for example, the locksmith's craft developed in the C15 into an important small trade, because the locks for gates and doors, chests and boxes were no longer made of wood, as earlier, but of metal. In addition, fittings and locks were elaborated more and more by cutting, engraving, etching and blueing. Contemporary engravings gave considerable impetus to this ornamentation. Numerous engravers disseminated the Renaissance idiom emanating from Italy. Fabulous beasts, animal masks, intertwined foliage, arabesques and grotesques were very popular ornamental forms in the late C16. This chest lock is likely to have been produced about 1600. The lock case is screwed to the punched mount with nine rivets (two are missing). The trefoil extension is necessitated by the lock mechanism. The cover plate shows a mermaid with entwined scrolls ending in grotesque faces. The lock has three latches that can be operated with a single key. FE

108
Barfüsserkirche

Padlock
17th century

Forged iron, blued; cast brass, cut, engraved; height with shackle 15 cm, width 8.5 cm, depth 4.5 cm
Inv. no. 1883.50. Gift of the Erben Hauser-Ober

Locks not fixed to a base and including a shackle are called padlocks; their great advantage is that they can be removed and used elsewhere. This example is distinguished by especially fine workmanship, a rather rare combination of materials (brass and blued iron), and a sophisticated mechanism. Pierced, engraved brass plates are attached to the front and back of the lock case. A cast-brass bust conceals the keyhole. The dark blue ground of the case sets off the sheen of the brass. To open the lock a small brass ornament (near the hair of the bust) must be moved aside, giving access to a small hole. A pin inserted in the hole will release a device that holds the bust in place on the other side. By turning the bust the keyhole is exposed. The key releases the locking mechanism of the shackle, which can be swivelled up to open the lock. FE

109
Barfüsserkirche

Water tank with tap and handbasin
Indistinct marks, 17th century(?)

Cast pewter, soldered; tank height 28.3 cm, width 25 cm, depth 16 cm; washbasin height 20.5 cm, width 31 cm, depth 24.3 cm
Inv. no. 1906.2875. Alter Bestand

Pewter water containers in the form of casks with handbasins were almost indispensable items of household equipment until the C19, when water mains were laid in towns. They were installed against walls, on corbels, in niches or as part of buffets, and show considerable richness of form. Illustrated is a polygonal water tank with handbasin incorporated in a Renaissance buffet. The tank is mounted above the basin on two dolphin brackets at the sides; the lid surmounted by two dolphin handles can be removed when filling the tank with water. The water flows out through the lion mask and a brass tap (the top is missing) that is soldered to the bottom of the tank. The water collects in the handbasin, the high back of which protects the buffet from splashing. The caryatid handles at each side of the basin facilitate emptying. The unity of tank and basin is emphasized by common decorative edging strips. SF

110
Barfüsserkirche

Bottle belonging to the Basle inner council
Johannes Linder I, Basle, 1638

Cast pewter, soldered; height 42 cm
Inv. no. 1875.29. Gift of the Staatskanzlei Basel

The guild and corporation vessels documented since the C15 can be classified neither as ostentatious display pieces, like, for example, pewter with relief decoration, nor as mere decorative showpieces in the nature of honorary or commemorative gifts, nor again as simple utility ware. Rather, they combine show and use functions. The flat flask illustrated, for example, was used functionally for serving wine but only on solemn and festive occasions. It has a lenticular body, an angular foot and a cylindrical neck; the neck is closed by a hinged lid. The relief medallion on the body consists of a foliage wreath enclosing two basilisks with the Basle coat of arms. Concentric rings, ridges and punched acanthus friezes enrich the decoration. Two basilisk figures form hooks for the pewter chain. This is one of a series of 12 flat bottles ordered by the council of Basle in 1638 from the Basle pewterer Johannes Linder I (1611–1678). SF

111
Barfüsserkirche

Mortar, dated 1650
Hans Heinrich Weitnauer I, Basle
Cast bronze, turned, punched; height 26.5 cm, diameter of top 31.8 cm
Inv. no. 1879.19. Gift of the Erbengemeinschaft Pfarrer Respinger

Although the mortar was known in antiquity, none made north of the Alps is known until the C13. Mortars remained important for housewives and apothecaries for centuries. They were produced by three different groups of craftsmen: gun, bell and boiler founders. Since each trade applied specific elements of their craft to them, most mortars can be assigned to one group or another. When this tall, tapering, cylindrical mortar is turned upside down, its origin in a bell foundry is immediately revealed. Not only the form but the inscription and ornamental bands point to a bell founder. The pure, unbroken profile typical of bells is disturbed on the mortar only by the two handles in the form of dolphins. The named maker, Hans Heinrich Weitnauer I (Basle 1613–1673 Basle), was a bell founder and ancestor of an important Basle family of bell founders. The bell bears his somewhat gloomy motto, ALLES MIT SORG MYE VND ARBEIT (everything with care, pains and labour). FE

112
Barfüsserkirche

Plate with an allegory of Temperance
Mould: Caspar Enderlein; cast: Hans Sigmund Geisser, Nuremberg, 2nd half 17th century
Cast pewter; diameter 46.5 cm
Inv. no. 1899.195. Purchase

The plate shown is an important example of the relief pewter production concentrated in Nuremberg in the C16 and C17. The mould for the plate, dated 1611, pattern no. 2 for an allegory of Temperance, is one of the chief works by Caspar Enderlein (1560–1633), the leading form-cutter in Nuremberg. On the back the plate has a medallion of him with an inscription running round it. However, this particular piece was cast, as the mark states, in the workshop of the Nuremberg master Hans Sigmund Geisser (1626–1682, guild member 1652). The plate displays an ambitious figurative programme indebted to international Mannerism. Its raised centre is occupied by an allegorical figure of TEMPERANTIA. A ring of four cartouches with allegories of the Four Elements (TERRA, IGNIS, AER, AQUA) with luxuriant scrollwork between herms surrounds the centre. The rim is filled by eight cartouches with allegories of the Seven liberal arts (ARITHMETIQVA, MVSICA, RHETORICA, DIALECTICA, GRAMATIC, ASTROLOGI, GEOMETRIA) and of the goddess of wisdom MINERVA amid scrollwork with masks, animals and bunches of fruit. SF

113
Barfüsserkirche

Tower bell, dated 1685
Jakob Roth and Hans Heinrich Weitnauer II, Basle
Cast bronze; diameter 95 cm, height 82 cm; pitches G + 27; + 4; + 7; + 27; $B^{\flat}$ + 20; D″ + 1; + 28
Inv. no. 1962.63. Purchase

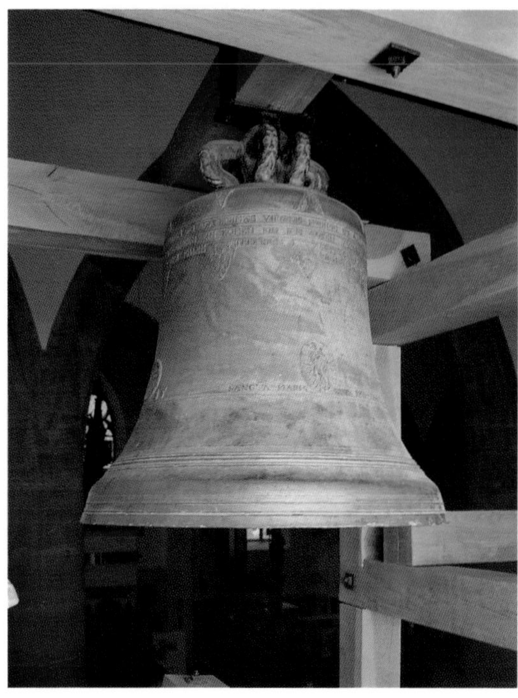

In the first half of the C16 the output of Basle bell founders was relatively small; it increased only after the middle of the century. In C17, with the bell-founder families of Roth and Weitnauer, quality and quantity reached their peak. This bell, with all its inscriptions and relief images, was cast in 1685 by Jakob Roth (Basle 1631-ca. 1687 Basle) and Hans Heinrich Weitnauer II (Basle 1649–1722 Basle), who were brothers-in-law. It comes from the Catholic parish church of St. Leodegar in Schliengen (Germany). The inscriptions record the founders, the year it was cast, the names of the spiritual and secular authorities in the parish of Schliengen and the delivery of the bell. The alphabet in small letters below the relief image of the crucifix signifies the beginning and end of all things. There is also an oval plaque showing the mother of God in a nimbus, and a relief image of St. Leodegar, the tutelary saint of Schliengen, with drill, book and sceptre. The hanging and standing acanthus palmettes near the shoulder of the bell are a typical feature of Basle bells cast in these years. Bearded male heads form the six shackles crowning the bell. The bell hung in the church tower at Schliengen until 1951, when it was sold to a bell foundry to be melted down. FE

114
Barfüsserkirche

Cooling bucket, dated 1689
Probably Basle
Beaten copper; height 34 cm, length 67 cm, width 34 cm
Inv. no. 1904.2331. Alter Bestand

Guild members' duties went far beyond the activity specific to their trade. The guilds in Basle were obliged to organize and carry out the keeping of the watch and fire-fighting, and in times of war every guild had to provide soldiers properly equipped. For centuries the system of administration depended on the guilds. The centre for every guild was its guildhouse. In it the guild meetings and elections, as well as numerous festivities, were held. In some respects the guildhouses played the role of present-day pubs or inns. In the Baroque age, with its fondness for ostentation and festivity, even simple craft guilds set much store by accoutrements such as furniture, paintings, cutlery, crockery, etc. The Zunft zu Webern (weavers' guild), in the Middle Ages a poor artisans' body, attained a leading role among the craft guilds during the guild regime of the C16 and C17. As an outward sign of its prestige during this period, the guild building was renovated, enlarged and enriched with stained glass and a large collection of goblets, cups and cutlery. Only isolated pieces of these once copious furnishings have survived, such as this copper cooling bucket. On the side is blazoned the emblem of the guild, documented from 1378, a griffin holding a yardstick in its claws. FE

115
Barfüsserkirche

'Ohrenschüssel'
Niklaus Übelin II, Basle, 1st half 18th century
Cast pewter, soldered, engraved; height 8.8 cm, diameter 19.7 cm
Inv. no. 1907.381. Purchase

From the C17 to the C19 pewter dishes and bowls of various shapes were in common use in middle-class households for serving and preparing meals. The dish shown – known in German as an 'Ohrenschüssel' (ear dish) on account of its opposed, ear-like volute handles – was likewise used for food. This one is unusually small. Its lid, with claw feet, can be used upside-down as a plate. The 'ear-dish' was especially handy for serving sick and bedridden people – it was frequently also called a 'childbed dish' or 'Wöchnerinnenschüssel'. This dish is identifiable by the marks on the inside of the lid and on the underside of the dish as a product of the Basle master Niklaus Übelin II (1682–1756; guild member 1705). In addition, the coat of arms engraved on the top of the lid identifies its former owners as the Wettstein family of Basle. SF

116
Barfüsserkirche

Cruet from the monastery of Olsberg
Unknown master, 18th century
Cast pewter, soldered, engraved; height 34 cm
Inv. no. 1893.336. Purchase

The Church always preferred sacred vessels made of precious metals, but approved the used of pewter cruets as early as the Middle Ages. Church pewter has never attained the status and importance of secular pewter, even though it is the earliest medieval pewter of any kind to have survived. Pewter was not widely produced again for church use until the C17 and C18. Most of the sacred pewter in the Museum dates from this period, including this cruet from the monastery at Olsberg (canton of Aargau), made in the C18 by an unknown Basle pewterer. It has a beak-shaped spout typical of the kind generally used in German-speaking Switzerland. Just like a secular pot in form, the vessel reveals its religious function only in its decoration: the body is embellished with an engraved Christ crucified between the Virgin and St John the Evangelist. SF

117
Barfüsserkirche

Railing
Basle(?), 1st half 18th century
Wrought iron; height 97 cm, width 242 cm
Inv. no. 1880.172. Purchase

For centuries iron was the most widely used metal – for all kinds of fittings, inn signs, grave crosses, spire tops, weathercocks, gratings, railings and household utensils of all kinds, such as door-knockers, door-handles, andirons, torch-holders, candelabra, locks, chests, clockwork, etc. The art of wrought iron enjoyed a flowering all over Europe in the C15 and C16, but the Thirty Years' War (1618–48) brought about a rapid decline. However, French architects in particular made deliberate use of iron gratings, railings, gates and window guards as decorative elements in the surge of building activity fostered by princes, prelates and patricians in the Baroque age. In Basle the art of wrought iron attained its highest quality in the C18 – the golden age of Basle architecture. This railing, said to come from the Rebhaus at Riehentorstrasse 11, is likely to have been made in the first decades of the C18. Five upright rectangular panels are infilled with volutes, tendrils and foliage. The delicate play of forms within the fields is reminiscent of contemporary patterns for lace. There is no hint of the weight and rigidity of the material. FE

118
Barfüsserkirche

Stove plate, dated 1745
Cast iron; height 135.5 cm, width 124.5 cm
Inv. no. 1896.100.a. Gift of the Baudepartement Basel

The stove plate was given to the Museum with a second, identical plate by the Basle city building department in 1896. As is shown in a drawing in the state archive of 1824, the plates were part of an iron stove standing on slender legs that was used for rapid heating of the Hintere Kanzlei (inner chancery) of the Basle town hall. The iconography of the plates, too, indicates that they were made for the state: two opposed basilisks hold a Basle coat of arms. These fabulous creatures had been popular and widespread supporters of the Basle coat of arms since the Middle Ages, alternating with angels, wildmen and lions. The large, almost square field of the plates is broken up by ornament in French Regency style. Although the plates were probably officially commissioned, neither the form-maker nor the founder is known. Their artistic quality is high and the execution of a good standard; they are evidence that even two centuries after the heyday of stove-plate casting in the C16 significant cast-iron works were being produced. FE

119
Barfüsserkirche

Mould, dated 1766, **and plate**
Mould: Johann Jakob Scholer, Basle; plate: Johann Konrad Zinck, Lörrach (Germany), last third 18th century
Cast bronze, diameter 29.5 cm; cast pewter, diameter 26.7 cm
Inv. no. 1932.1118. Gift of Emma Huber-Klein
Inv. no. 1976.155. Esther Thurneysen bequest

According to the statutes of the pewterers' guild, only holders of the title of master were allowed to run an independent pewterer's workshop. A Basle statute of 1563 laid down that a master's examination should require the production of moulds for a pitcher, a platter and a bottle, the casting of these from the moulds, and the presentation of the moulds. This regulation remained in force until the C18. Moulds might be produced of clay, plaster, stone, bronze and other metals. Here a bronze mould from the workshop of the Basle master Johann Jakob Scholer (Basle 1739–1815 Basle) is shown with its corresponding pewter plate with a typically Baroque profile. SF

120
Barfüsserkirche

Key of the Zeughaus (armoury), **Basle**
Probably Basle, ca. 1820/30
Forged iron, cast bronze; length 17.5 cm
Inv. no. 1909.257. Gift of the Zeughausverwaltung

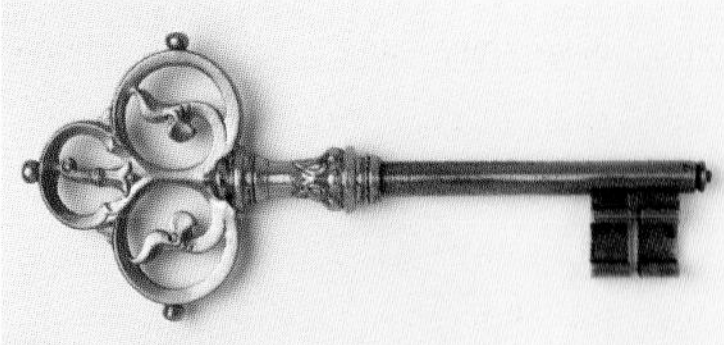

Keys are not merely instruments for locking, but often also symbolic. To have the key is to have power to rule; this applies in both the sacred and the secular spheres. For instance, the handing over of a town's key signifies recognition of its ruler. The relinquishment of keys after a lost war means subjection and abdication of sovereignty to the enemy. In popular belief the key has protective powers. It is a defence against the evil eye, sickness, witches, fire, etc. Not only a real key, but a key amulet worn on the body can work miracles. In the imagery of love, finally, the key embodies the phallus, the lock the womb. The Basle crosier on the key of the Basle Zeughaus designates the city state of Basle as sovereign over the armoury and the army. In its imitation of Gothic idiom the key is also a revealing example of the Romantic age's enthusiasm for the Middle Ages. The handle imitates Gothic trefoil tracery. The two larger lobes are traversed by foliage; the small lobe contains the Basle crosier. The stem has a knop and the bit is in two parts. FE

121
Barfüsserkirche

Relief plate, dated 1938
Hans Frei, Basle
Cast pewter; diameter 28.8 cm
Inv. no. 1939.926. Purchase

Pewter ware for display purposes is now the most familiar form in which tin appears. Modern display pewter – presentation pieces and trophies awarded at sporting events and special occasions – is also to be found in the Museum, especially the works of the Basle medallist and pewterer Hans Frei (Zunzgen 1868–1947 Basle); it complements the Museum's holding of older showpieces of the guilds and corporations. This relief plate is a particularly splendid modern piece. In the centre are a round medallion showing two basilisks with the Basle coat of arms, and the inscriptions INCLYTA BASILEA (famous Basle) and HANS FREI 1938. The rim of the plate shows medallion portraits of Basle personages accompanied by decorative inscriptions: H. HOLBEIN 1497 1543 / ERASMUS. R. 1466 1536 / L. EVLER 1707 1783 / A. BOECKLIN 1827 1901 / J. BVRCKHARDT 1818 1891 / J. BACHOFEN 1815 1887 / WETTSTEIN 1594 1666. SF

Militaria

The weapons in the Historisches Museum can be divided into three groups (excluding archaeological finds) according to origin. First in time is the small but very important group of weapons from the Burgundian spoils. In the battles of Grandson and Murten against Duke Charles the Bold in 1476, the victorious Swiss and their allies captured vast booty, including, besides traditional trophies such as flags and weapons, a ducal treasury, a ducal chancery and even a ducal sacristy. Of the part of the booty received by Basle only the weapons have been preserved. The weapons displayed in the armoury retained their commemorative value over the centuries, whereas that of the jewellery faded rapidly – indeed, the jewels were soon sold. Even hundreds of years after the event foreign visitors were shown the trophies that had been won, by now augmented by spurious additions. Preserved for symbolic and commemorative reasons, these weapons are today among the most precious items in the collection. Other weapons, too, had great memorial value attached to them: the dagger of Erasmus of Rotterdam recalled the humanist who died in Basle in 1536, and the dagger of Johannes Amerbach kept alive the memory of one of the founders of book printing in Basle.

A second group in the present collection – incomparably larger with about 3500 items – comprises the former holding of the Zeughaus or armoury. It was assigned to the Museum at the end of the C19. As the weapons held by the Zeughaus were kept more or less up to date with the current conditions of warfare – outmoded weapons being removed – the great majority of them date from the C17 to the early C19. The stock of weapons, therefore, is that of a civic armoury from the pre-revolutionary era, not one accumulated from several periods. It contains chiefly firearms. However, it happened in Basle, as elsewhere, that keepers of the armoury from the C16 onwards deliberately put aside obsolete weapons that were of interest to them. This is the only possible explanation of the fact that certain weapons from the Middle Ages and the Early Modern period were preserved there. The Basle Zeughaus must have had an 'historic' store since the C16.

A third, numerically very small group is made up of weapons donated or purchased by the Museum since its inception. It includes, for example, two crossbows and three precious Swiss daggers that would never have entered the Zeughaus, since such weapons were worn only by rich and distinguished citizens.

The Museum's weapons collection cannot bear comparison with a princely collection. Its significance is chiefly that it was the stock of the old city armoury. Nevertheless, there are several pieces that are important from the historical, art historical or cultural point of view and these add some lustre to the collection. FE

122
Barfüsserkirche

Sword of justice
14th century, hilt 16th century
Forged steel; overall length 123.5 cm, length of blade 93.5 cm, width of root of blade 7.1 cm
Inv. no. 1870.529. Alter Bestand

In the Middle Ages supreme secular jurisdiction was wielded by the king or the emperor, although jurisdiction was usually delegated to bailiffs or local rulers. In many places the symbol of judicial authority and sign of sovereignty was a sword of justice (not to be confused with an executioner's sword). The present example can be assigned to the judicial sphere on account of the engravings on the blade. On the front the imperial eagle and a sequence of letters not yet interpreted – probably the first letters of a biblical quotation – are engraved and inlaid with brass. The back shows a lion and another series of letters. The lion may be understood either as a symbol of judicial authority or as the Habsburg lion. The sword very probably dates from the time of the Habsburg imperial governors who exercised supreme judicial power in Basle from 1286 to 1382. After the battle of Sempach king Wenzel in Prague permitted judicial authority to pass from the Empire to the Basle town council. Basle thereby acquired the key offices that led to the city's independence. It remains uncertain whether this sword fulfilled a strictly symbolic function as a sword of justice, or was used by the executioner for beheading. FE

123
Barfüsserkirche

Mail shirt
Basle, 14th century
Iron and brass rings, welded and riveted, length 68 cm
Inv. no. 1874.104. Gift of the Zeughausverwaltung

The chain-mail shirt, a mesh of welded, riveted or stamped wire rings, was a form of protective armour already known in antiquity. In the Middle Ages makers of armour became a separate professional group, mentioned for the first time in Basle in 1280. The mail shirt, also known as a habergeon, was worn over a leather tunic; a capuche-like chain-mesh hood protected the head and neck. Horses, too, were often protected with chain mail. In the C15 the mail shirt was gradually replaced by plate armour, but was still worn for decades by foot-soldiers. Of the coats of mail listed in the inventories of the Basle armoury, once numbering more than 160, five examples have survived; the others were cut up and used for scouring pots and pans, or incorporated in money boxes or toll boxes. On this particular coat a number of brass rings on the front left stand out from the iron rings and form a Basle crosier. FE

124
Barfüsserkirche

Cannon from the Burgundian spoils
(left)
Burgundy, Mons(?), 2nd quarter 15th century
Forged iron, length 273 cm, calibre 34.5 cm
Inv. no. 1874.93. Gift of the Zeughausverwaltung

In the battles of Murten and Grandson against Charles the Bold in 1476, enormous quantities of valuables and weapons fell into the hands of the victorious Swiss as spoils of war. As an ally of the Swiss – Basle joined the Confederation only in 1501 – Basle had a share of the spoils. Most was lost in the course of the centuries: in 1504 the council sold various jewels to the Fugger brothers in Augsburg; in 1529 the flags hung as trophies of victory in the Münster fell victim to the iconoclastic 'Bildersturm'; almost all of the captured Burgundian cannon was melted down when the Basle artillery was recast from time to time. These two large cannon, among others, have survived. The bigger gun is a masterpiece of forging: twenty longitudinal rails welded together are held together by rings of various thicknesses welded close together. The triangular plate mounted in front of the touch hole shows the coat of arms of the Flemish family of d'Auxy. Jean d'Auxy IV supplied cannon from Flanders to Charles the Bold in Vaud, after the duke had lost his artillery at Grandson. The cannon on the right is described under no. 126. FE

125
Barfüsserkirche

Late Gothic crossbow with laminated horn bow
Switzerland or South Germany, ca. 1460
Wood, bone, animal tendon, birch bark, hemp cord, leather, iron and horn; length of shaft 78.5 cm, length of bow 70 cm
Inv. no. 1990.370. Purchase with special credit from the Basler Regierung

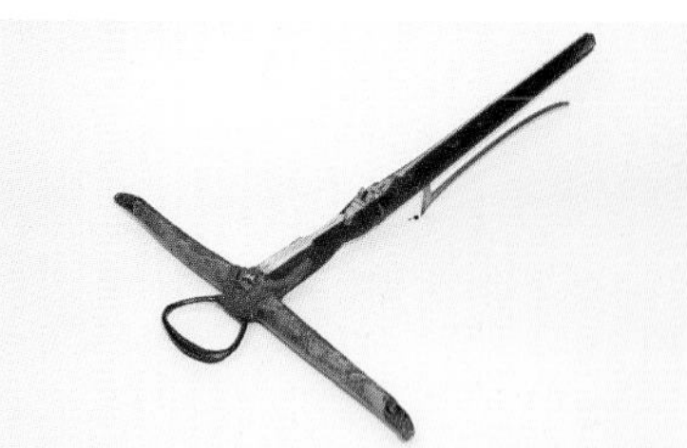

The crossbow was the most important long-range weapon in the late Middle Ages. The inventory of the Basle armoury in 1361 names as many as 143 crossbows owned by the city. But despite technical improvements the crossbow had been superseded by firearms as a military weapon by 1500, and from then on it was used only for hunting and sport. This Late Gothic crossbow still has a horn bow, unlike later examples with a steel bow. The core of the bow is made up of several layers of horn glued together. On the back of the bow (target side) a number of layers of animal tendon are applied; birch bark is used to protect the costly bow bar from drying out. The shaft, of fruitwood, is partly faced in bone. On both sides of the shaft, at the front, a small Basle crosier (facing left) is burnt in. This type of crossbow with a large stirrup had to be drawn with a hook. The bowman knelt on one knee, put his other foot in the stirrup, engaged the hook attached to the strap on the string and bent the bow by standing up. When Wilhelm Tell performed his famous shot with a crossbow the weapon took on symbolic value in Switzerland; today a crossbow is often stamped as a sign of quality on Swiss products. FE

126
Barfüsserkirche

Cannon from the Burgundian spoils (detail), dated 1474
Jean de Malines, Mechelen
Cast bronze; length 255.5 cm, calibre 22.8 cm
Inv. no. 1874.95. Gift of the Zeughausverwaltung

The Basle chronicler Johannes Knebel reports that on 14 March 1476 the Basle troops brought back from the battlefield at Grandson two large bombards with the Burgundian coat of arms. One was melted down about 1790, while the other has been preserved as being particularly precious. The barrel is cast in one piece and is the oldest dated gun barrel with trunnions. On the first section near the mouth, which is superbly made, the gunsmith gives his name in embossed lower-case Gothic script: "iehan de malines ma fayt lan MCCCCLXXIIII" (Jean de Malines made me in the year 1474). On the second barrel section is the coat of arms of Charles the Bold, its former owner, and on each side of the coat of arms the insignia of the Golden Fleece. The invention of trunnions, which made aiming easier and improved accuracy, should probably be credited to the gun founder Jean de Malines, who had been in the service of the Burgundian dukes since 1466. The cannon was among the most modern of its time; it was later depicted in the cannon book of Emperor Maximilian. An inscription formerly attached to it in the Basle Zeughaus read: "Burgund bin ich genandt / Brich Maur und Want" (The Burgundian they me call / Breaker of brick and wall). FE

127
Barfüsserkirche

Plate mail jacket
Italy(?), 2nd half 15th century
Iron plates on canvas, riveted, remnants of red half-silk; length 56 cm
Inv. no. 1874.102. Gift of the Zeughausverwaltung

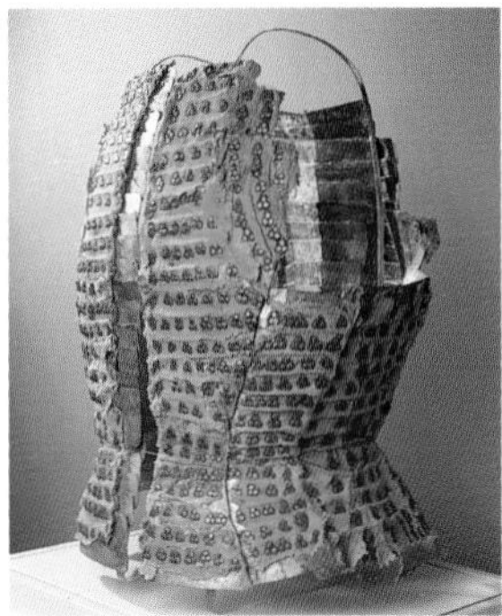

The mail jacket or brigantine consists of a system of tin-coated iron plates overlapping like the tiles of a roof, fixed in groups of three to a canvas base by rivets with fluted heads. The jacket was originally lined in red half-silk; remains of it were found under the rivet heads. The brigantine thus survives only in part, since of the three layers, iron plates, fabric base and lining, the last is missing. On the back of the plates is stamped a Lamb of God, which may have been either a protective sign for the wearer or the mark of the producer. Like Florentine costume of the time the jacket fits closely around the waist and is opened at the front; it may come from Italy, as Milan was a centre of production of such mail jackets. The brigantine was not only used for protection, but was favoured by the nobility as a ceremonial garment. The jacket was preserved in the Basle armoury in the C18 as the "armour of Duke Charles of Burgundy" – an attribution that probably saved it from oblivion. FE

128
Barfüsserkirche

Helmet
North Italy, ca. 1485/95
Forged steel, riveted; height 24 cm
Inv. no. 1874.29. Purchase

At the end of the C14 a new form of helmet emerged and was in widespread use in the C15: in German it was called the 'Schaller', as its shell fitted tightly around the head. Forged in one piece, this 'Schaller' is embellished with 16 brass nail rivets. The visor has a narrow slot for vision, the lower edge of which projects slightly, so that a thrust cannot enter the eye. The front has a reinforcement, the point of which leads into the strong central ridge of the helmet. The projecting cowl at the back of the neck, giving the wearer great freedom of movement, is characteristic of the 'Schaller'. The attachable bib joined to the front of the armour and protecting the chin is missing. The shape of the helmet and the mark indicate a North Italian origin; it may have come from the workshop of the Missaglia family in Milan. The helmet was not part of the original holding of the Basle armoury, but was acquired by the Museum in 1874 from a private owner in Lucerne. The smooth, closed profile, the lustrous surface and the hemispherical rivet heads of contrasting colour endow the helmet with a special elegance. FE

129
Barfüsserkirche

Cannon, dated 1514
Jörg von Guntheim, Basle
Cast bronze; length 493 cm, calibre 12.5 cm
Inv. no. 1874.94. Gift of the Zeughausverwaltung

The gun is a work by the Strasbourg bell and gun founder Jörg von Guntheim of unique artistic quality. The bronze casting is decorated with Late Gothic ornamentation and finely chased. The middle section bears the Basle coat of arms held by a lion. The date of production is given by the figure 1514 on the chamber. An inscription in Gothic miniscule on the front section runs: "ich bin der track ungehir was ich schis das duon ich mit fir meister ierg zu strosburg gos mich" (I am the monstrous dragon dire, what I shoot I do with fire. Master Jörg of Strasbourg cast me). A fearsome dragon's head holds the mouth of the barrel in its open jaws. A Late Gothic frieze running round the barrel forms the transition from the smooth tube to the strong, octagonal mouth flange. The renowned founder from Strasbourg worked for Emperor Maximilian and the kings of Aragon and England among others. On 17 December 1513 the council of Basle commissioned him to cast several guns, the city providing the bronze from obsolete and broken guns and also making available the assistants and tools. 'The dragon' was cast in 1514 in the workshop of the Basle armoury. FE

130
Barfüsserkirche

Shaffron
Early 16th century
Iron embossed, riveted; height 50 cm, length 65 cm, width 40 cm
Inv. no. 1874.112. Gift of the Zeughausverwaltung

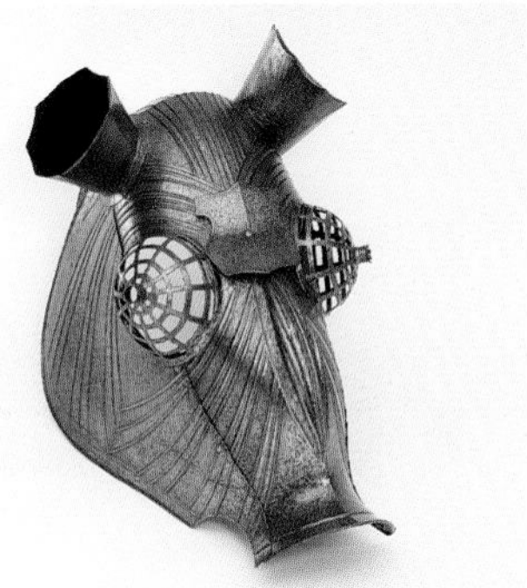

The shaffron or headpiece, part of a horse's armour, is hammered from four iron plates and riveted together. Tubular, octagonal cups protect the ears, projecting grilles the eyes. At the front centre a blank, laterally folded targe is riveted to the headpiece. Groups of three ridges radiate from under the targe and from the central ridge. A broad, recessed strip runs round the edges. Technically remarkable features are the low number of rivets and the fact that the side pieces fit over, not under the centre piece, which would prove a drawback in battle since the rivets could easily be broken. As the shaffron was a unique item in the Basle armoury – it is mentioned for the first time in the inventory of 1591 – the legend came into being that it was part of the personal armour of Duke Charles the Bold of Burgundy. The piece probably owes its survival to the attribution. The fluting and the rough hammered finish argue against its being a Burgundian work of the C15; it was probably produced by an armourer in the early C16. FE

131
Barfüsserkirche

Halberd
Switzerland, 2nd half 16th century
Forged iron, etched; overall length 250 cm, length of point with blades 119 cm
Inv. no. 1903. 139. Purchase

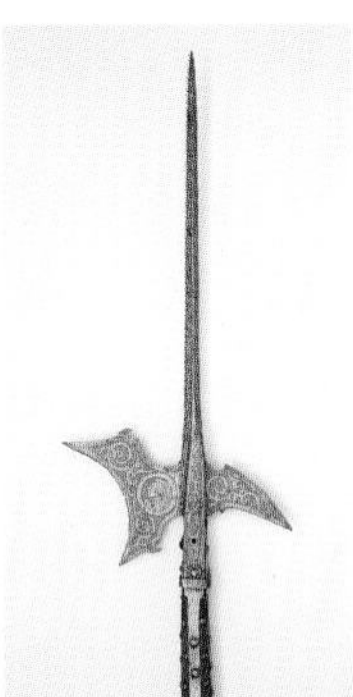

The victorious battles of the Swiss against the Habsburgs at Morgarten in 1315 and at Sempach in 1386 founded the halberd's reputation, and since the emergence of a Swiss national consciousness in the C16 it has been used as a symbol of Swiss military prowess. Although the halberd gradually lost its military significance in the C16, large numbers of 'Sempach halberds' were still produced in the C17. The earlier halberd resembled an axe with blade and head; but on top the blade narrowed to a point. The thrusting point and the hook emerged in the C15 and C16. The weapon was used for swinging and thrusting, and was suited both to defence and to attack. When the halberd became obsolete in the C16, its form was elaborated decoratively. The halberd illustrated represents this late stage: the blade is crescent-shaped, with hooks and teeth at the sides, the point is very long, and the flat hook also has teeth. It is covered in etched interlacing, and is enlivened on the axe-blades by medallions with a female bust and a warrior. The octagonal shaft is studded with numerous brass nails. FE

132
Barfüsserkirche

Crossbow with steel bow and rack and pinion winch, dated 1565
Switzerland or South Germany
Steel, wood, ivory, hemp cord; length of bow 60 cm, length of shaft 63 cm
Inv. nos. 1888.99. and 1888.99.a. Gift of the Schweizerische Eidgenossenschaft

In the late C15 steel bows replaced those made of laminated horn. The innovation brought many advantages: the power of the crossbow was significantly increased, and the steel bow bar suffered no damage from wet or dry conditions, nor did it lose its elasticity if kept drawn for a long time. Its disadvantage was that it could only be drawn using a rack and pinion winch, which slowed the firing rate. Despite technical improvements the crossbow had reached the end of its useful life as a weapon by about 1500. By then soldiers with firearms could shoot at archers from beyond the effective range of the crossbow. But as a hunting and sporting weapon for the upper classes the crossbow held its place for a long time afterwards. The wooden shaft of this crossbow has rich ivory inlays. The underside shows at the front St Mary Magdalene with a skull and the date 1565, and at the back the Roman heroine Lucretia. Hunting scenes are shown on the sides of the shaft. The juxtaposition of the virtuous Roman and the repentant Christian sinner is typical of the age of humanism and suggests that the crossbow was ordered by a cultured buyer. FE

133
Barfüsserkirche

Swiss dagger, dated 1572
Probably Basle
Blade in cast brass, gilt; length of dagger 37.9 cm, length of sheath 30.8 cm
Inv. no. 1882.107. Gift of Johann Jakob Handmann

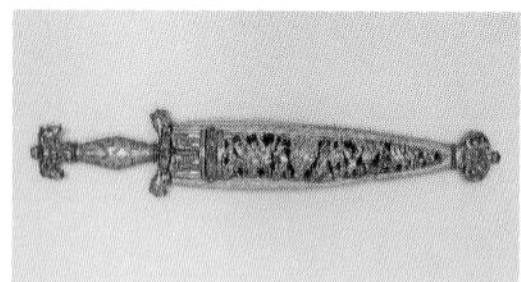

Display weapons were seldom made in Switzerland, since for both economic and political reasons the circle of patrons was small; theoretically at least, the emphasis was on cooperative confederation. But the Swiss dagger was an important exception; developing from a simple functional instrument into a richly decorated ornamental weapon, it became a distinguishing mark of a whole social class in the C16. Officers, high officials and wealthy citizens ordered these luxurious products; the Museum holds three especially costly examples. The 'Swiss' dagger, as it was already known by contemporaries, is distinguished from daggers from other countries by the shape of the handle and blade. Subjects from biblical, ancient and Swiss history served as motifs for the richly worked and sometimes gilt sheaths. The sheath of the Swiss dagger shown here is cast in brass and gilt; it shows scenes from a Dance of Death. The date 1572 is engraved on the back of the sheath. The Museum owns contemporary lead models from Basle goldsmiths' workshops for various parts of this display weapon. FE

134
Barfüsserkirche

Half suit of armour
Austria or South Germany, 1st half 17th century
Forged iron, riveted, cast brass, gilt; height 110 cm
Inv. no. 1874.108. Gift of the Zeughausverwaltung

From the many pieces of armour that the Basle armoury donated to the Historisches Museum in the C19, three half-suits of armour in all can be assembled. This small number reflects not only the sometimes rather fortuitous way in which items were preserved at the Zeughaus, but also Basle's political fortunes in the C19. When Basle was divided into the two cantons of Basle-Stadt and Basle-Landschaft in 1833, the armoury was also divided. It should be borne in mind that many suits of armour were not even originally made as a unity, and armour had to be individually fitted to the wearer. Existing pieces were combined – not least for reasons of cost – with new ones. The finest piece in the collection is the so called Russinger armour. It is a horseman's armour consisting of a battle helm with barred visor with neck protector, collar, arm plates, gauntlets, breastplate, backplate and tassets. As a special decorative element, two gilt-brass lion's heads with a ring in their jaws secure the pallettes on the arms. The initials T.R. in a heart-shaped frame on the breastplate gave rise to the suggestion that the armour belonged to the Basle councillor Theodor Russinger (died 1610). FE

135
Barfüsserkirche

Model cannon, muzzle-loading
Before 1675
Bronze gilt, carriage of wood with enamelled plates; length of barrel 45.5 cm, calibre 15 mm
Inv. no. 1894.119. Gift of the Zeughausverwaltung

The model cannon recalls an affair that turned out unpleasantly for Basle in the C17. It is first listed, with a second, identical piece that went to Liestal when the canton was split in the C19, in the armoury inventory of 1709. During the Dutch war of 1675–76, a certain Count di Broglio was staying in Basle. Giving up his incognito, he led the life of a great lord as an imperial and Spanish envoy without mission, moving in the best circles and donating two model guns to the council. During a ride in the surrounding country he was captured by the French and unmasked as an imperial spy, a certain Simon de Breuil. The French demanded that his papers be handed over and threatened economic reprisals. Many of Broglio's creditors made claims on Basle, so that after numerous court cases the council had to liquidate his property. It was decided to consign his papers "to Vulcan" (the fire). The French took de Breuil to Paris, where he probably ended his days in the Bastille. FE

136
Barfüsserkirche

Muzzle-loading needle gun for guncotton cartridges
Valentin Sauerbrey, Basle, 1846

Wood, steel, brass, leather; overall length 144.5 cm, barrel length 96.5 cm
Inv. no. 1949.62.a. On deposit from the Institut für Organische Chemie

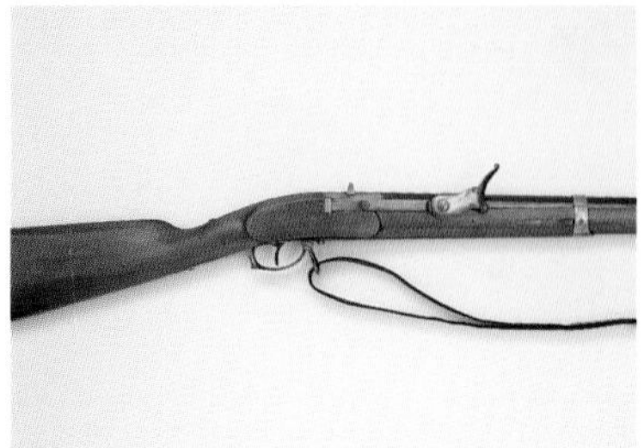

In 1846 Christian Friedrich Schönbein was responsible for a discovery in Basle that had a major influence on the development of modern explosives. The guncotton he invented, a mixture of cotton fibre soaked in sulphuric and nitric acid, produced a greater explosive force than the black powder previously used. Guncotton also had the advantage of burning without residue or smoke. The custodian of the Basle armoury, Valentin Sauerbrey, constructed a needle gun for guncotton cartridges – the first firearm that could be fired without smoke. In 1849, in the presence of the Federal Councillor Ulrich Ochsenbein and General Henri Dufour, shooting tests were carried out in Berne. However, the new explosive met with little success, as it was prone to spontaneous combustion and was unstable when stored. Sauerbrey donated the gun (signed on the barrel "V. SAUERBREY IN BASEL") with cartridges and a box of guncotton to the Institut für Organische Chemie in 1877. Smokeless nitrocellulose powder was not produced successfully until 1886, by the Frenchman Paul Vieille. FE

137
Barfüsserkirche

Basle uniforms and various military items from the 18th and 19th centuries
From left to right: Uniform of the Basle war commissioner Johann David La Roche (1817–31); uniform of a mounted 'Jaeger' patrolman, ca. 1830; uniform of an officer of the volunteer company, late 18th century; uniform jacket of an officer of the Helvetian Republic, ca. 1800; uniform jacket of a grenadier of the 1st Basle Regiment, ca. 1810
Inv. no. 1893.70. Gift of A.C. La Roche-Merian
Inv. no. 1905.5586. Gift of Emanuel Weitnauer
Inv. no. 1927.210. Gift of F. Buxtorf-Schilling
Inv. no. 1894.131.b. Gift of Albert Merian
Inv. nos. 1905.5591. 1917.72. 1896.208. 1913.561. Gift of Albert Vischer

Compulsory uniform dress for soldiers is a relatively recent phenomenon, of the C18. Until well into the C19 the uniform's role had more to do with display and appearance than with practical function. The earliest written evidence of Basle troops wearing uniform dates from 1719. The appearance and development of uniforms have in most cases been ascertained by study of the ordinances, as few uniforms have survived; only one service coat from the C18 has been preserved, for example. With the creation of the federal Swiss state in 1848 the military sovereignty of the cantons was transferred to the Federation; since then the uniform has been decided by parliament. FE

138
Barfüsserkirche

The oldest city banner of Basle

Basle, 2nd half 15th century

White Italian silk damask with pomegranate pattern, the black Basle crosier sewn on; height 100 cm, width 122 cm
Inv. no. 1905.5559. Transferred from the Staatsarchiv in 1862

The coat of arms of the city of Basle and of the present canton of Basle-Stadt consists of a black, curled staff with crossbar and three downward-pointing spines on a white ground. As is apparent from coins and seals, this was the insignia of the Basle bishops in the C12 and C13, although their crosier was red, as the Zurich roll of escutcheons shows. The rising citizenry of Basle took over the bishop's coat of arms before 1400, but changed its colour. This large city banner is the oldest evidence of the black colour of the city's emblem. It may be the banner produced in 1476–77, for the council's expense book for that year records a major outlay "for silk for the new city banner and for making it". After the Pavia campaign of 1512 Pope Julius II granted Basle an enhancement of their coat of arms, the right to bear a golden crosier. After the Reformation of 1529 the papal privilege was rejected and the black crosier reinstated. The direction of the crook – left or right – was an arbitrary matter for centuries. FE

139
Barfüsserkirche

Banner of the Zunft zu Weinleuten

(vintners' guild)
Basle, ca. 1500

Tempera on canvas; height 95 cm, width 95 cm
Inv. no. 1875.84. On deposit from E.E. Zunft zu Weinleuten

For centuries the 15 guilds, which were more exactly professional associations, exerted great influence in Basle, indeed up until the C19 they were the pillars of the state: the 30-strong council was made up of 15 councillors and the 15 guild masters. The four prestigious major guilds of 'Schlüssel' (literally key[makers]), 'Hausgenossen' (house-companions), 'Weinleute' (vintners) and 'Safran' (saffron [merchants]) represented the merchant and manufacturing class, while the eleven other guilds embraced the artisans. The vintners' guild, which was also called the 'Geltenzunft' (bucket guild) because of the measuring pail in its coat of arms, is mentioned for the first time in 1357. It comprised wine merchants, owners of wine taverns, wine transporters, wine measurers and 'Weinrufer', who publicly called out the arriving wine. Apart from duties relating to their trade and from political tasks, the guilds also had a religious role. The flag reflects the religious side of the Weinleute, as it shows not the guild coat of arms but the patron saint of vintners, Pope Urban I (222–30) who stands in front of a trellis wreathed in vines and holds up a bunch of grapes. St Urban's day (25 May), which coincided with the flowering of the vines, was especially associated with religious customs such as pilgrimages and processions in the wine-rich region of the Upper Rhine. FE

Sculpture

The ecclesiastical wood sculpture owned by the Historisches Museum consists of 280 individual figures of Christ, the Madonna and 60 different saints. The origin of about half of these can be traced, whether to the place of their acquisition, to the locality or workshop where they were produced, or to their original location. The main emphasis of the collection is centred on Basle, its surrounding region, the cantons of Innerschweiz and the area along the upper Rhine from Chur along Lake Constance and on to Baden-Baden. Most of the sculpture dates from the C15 and early C16, that is from the period before the Reformation. Nonetheless, the display of six winged altarpieces and about 70 separate wood sculptures in the choir of the Barfüsserkirche cannot adequately represent the rich decorations and furnishings of Basle churches that were destroyed by iconoclasts in the 'Bildersturm' of 1529. The acquisition of wooden religious sculpture for the Medieval Collection began in 1856. But, because of the shortage of works with a Basle provenance and in view of the city's application to be the location of the Swiss national museum, until the end of the C19 the collection took on a more supra-regional role. In 1887, when the winged altarpiece by Ivo Strigel from the Calanca valley (no. 156) was acquired, Basle was still the only museum in Switzerland capable of housing such monumental altarpieces.

Large stone sculptures in the collection consist mainly of works made for tombs and fountains in Basle. The Romanesque, Gothic, Renaissance and early Baroque styles are all represented.

Small-scale secular sculpture from the C15 to the C17 forms a third important category of the collection. Through these works and through other objects from the Amerbach Cabinet and the Faesch Museum the tradition of collecting can be traced back to the bourgeois 'Kunstkammer'. Italian Renaissance bronzes, small-scale southern German sculpture, as well as single pieces of French and Netherlandish provenance determined an international orientation from a very early stage. Among the small-scale sculptures the collection of several hundred plaquettes must be regarded as a category in its own right. It is one of the most significant of its kind because it includes entire collections that were already being acquired as such in the C16 and C17. The small-scale sculpture is remarkably heterogeneous, not least because of the diversity of materials used – stone, wood, bronze, copper, ivory, mother of pearl, lead, wax, plaster and clay. The collection is completed by several works made by two renowned artists of the C18, Aubert Parent of France (no. 173) and Valentin Sonnenschein from Württemberg (no. 175). vR

140
Barfüsserkirche

Head of a bearded man
Basle(?), late 12th century, Romanesque
Red sandstone, height 24 cm
Inv. no. 1956.10. Alter Bestand

This head of a man with a beard, a fragment from a stone relief, was discovered in store in the Museum in 1956 and recognised to be of high quality. Its original location is unknown. The obvious hypothesis that it had come to light during excavations carried out in the C19 or C20 around Basle Cathedral cannot yet be verified, in the absence of any comparable material. With its masterly treatment of surface and great precision of line, the head can be attributed to the master mason of a Late Romanesque workshop. It resembles contemporary Burgundian sculpture; characteristic features are the large pupils and the refined treatment of the beard which curls into little rolls around the cheeks. vR

141
Barfüsserkirche

The Madonna enthroned with the Christchild
South-west Germany, ca. 1370
Limewood, painted in polychrome, height 96 cm, width 40 cm, depth 17 cm
Inv. no. 1913.104. Purchase

It had been standard practice since Early Christian times to represent the Mother of God seated on a throne, and only rarely were other saints venerated in this way.
In this variation on the theme, which was widely diffused in German-speaking countries during the C14, she is represented with the Christchild half-seated, half-standing and clothed (in contrast to his appearance naked in the C15). The bird he plays with in his hands has symbolic meaning: according to one of the apocryphal Gospels, Christ made a clay bird which he threw into the air and so brought to life – an analogy for the Redemption of the soul. Originally the Madonna, as Queen of Heaven, wore a crown over her veil and held a sceptre in her right hand. The figure is carved in very flat relief, measuring only 17 cm in depth. It was acquired in the Freiburg-Breisgau region and is closely akin to a seated Madonna in Rottweil in the Black Forest, which in the C14 was a flourishing free city of Swabia. On the borders of the Upper Rhine region, Rottweil evolved a local style of sculpture with which this very early piece in the Museum's collection must clearly be associated. vR

142
Barfüsserkirche

Fountain (now lacking basin) from the Basle Fischmarkt
Basle, ca. 1380
Red sandstone, originally painted, overall height 10.6 m, height of Madonna 128 cm
Inv. no. 1910.104.

The fountain at the Fischmarkt (fish market) in Basle was commissioned at approximately the same time as the oldest and most famous of Gothic city fountains, the Schöner Brunnen in Nuremberg. Its early date, its size and the quality of its sculpture reflect the self-confidence of the up-and-coming civic community of Basle. Rising more than 10 metres, the pinnacled column together with its figures was moved into the Museum in 1910 and was replaced at the Fischmarkt by a copy. The column develops from a round base to a square to bold interlocking triangles, crowned by tracery canopies over the main figures. These are the Madonna, St John the Evangelist and St Peter. On a smaller scale, Sts Agnes, Barbara and Catharine are set above the columns supporting the canopies. Prophets and angels playing musical instruments complete the sculptural programme. In architectural and sculptural form the fountain represents a South-west German version of the Parler style (the style of the Parler family of stone-masons); comparable examples can be found in Thann, Strasbourg and elsewhere in Basle. We owe the oldest description of the fountain to the Venetian Andrea Gattaro, visitor to the Council of Basle (1431–48): he mentions "the very big fountain with Our Lady and two saints on it, in which the fishermen put their boxes when it is their market day". A spring in the nearby grounds of the Haus zum Sessel provided the water supply. vR

143
Barfüsserkirche

The Madonna from the Basle Spalentor
Basle, ca. 1398
Red sandstone, height 218 cm
Inv. no. 1934.580. On deposit from the Baudepartement Basel

Together with the Christchild she holds, the Madonna, the city's patron saint, watched over the outer façade of the Spalentor (Spalen Gate). Set above the coat of arms of the city and between two Prophets on a corbel decorated with figures, she was sheltered by a canopy and surrounded by the rays of a halo. The Spalentor was part of the third and outermost wall of the town's fortifications, enlarged in the C14 to a length of 4 km, and architecturally and iconographically it marked the main entrance to the city. The Madonna itself is an outstanding work of sculpture of the period around 1400, though its author is unknown. He introduced innovations from the 'Weicher Stil' or 'soft' style of International Gothic, for example the motif of the crescent moon beneath the Madonna's feet, and was not afraid to endow her with pigtails, fashionable among noble ladies at the time. Stylistically this monumental work is comparable to the figures on the tower of the Charles bridge in Prague. It represents the last phase of the 'Parler' style (see no. 142) and illustrates the influence of this tradition in Basle, which dates back to the great earthquake of 1356 when Johann Parler III was called to Basle from Prague in order to direct the reconstruction of the cathedral. vR

144
Barfüsserkirche

St Ursula, four Virgin Martyrs and St Pantalus
Upper Rhine, ca. 1450 or 1472
Limewood, painted in polychrome, height 30 cm
Inv. no. 1976.100. Purchase

Popular veneration of St Ursula reached a high point in the C15 with the production of numerous pictorial cycles in Spain, Italy and the Netherlands. According to legend, the English princess, accompanied by 11,000 virgins, had disembarked and continued her pilgrimage to Rome by road from Basle. On the expedition's return to Cologne they were martyred. In the statuette, a bishop, probably St Pantalus, stands next to St Ursula, and a group of four virgins represents the whole company. The gestures of some members of the group show their expectation of imminent martyrdom. The small carving originates from the Dominican nuns' house of Klingenthal near Basle, where the cult of St Ursula had special importance because the convent housed the relics of St Euphrosyne, one of Ursula's companions. It is not clear whether the group, which has not survived complete, would have stood on the altar of St Euphrosyne's chapel. Stylistically the statuette appears to date from about 1450, but may also be associated with a payment for a statue of St Euphrosyne and several images documented in the accounts book of the convent for 1472. vR

145
Barfüsserkirche

Winged altarpiece with the patron saints of the diocese of Würzburg

Franconia, ca. 1470–80

Limewood, carved and painted, outer sides of wing panels painted; height 184 cm, width (open) 212.5 cm
Inv. no. 1886.88. Purchase

The altarpiece was purchased in 1886 even before the Historisches Museum had moved into the Barfüsserkirche. Although the predella is missing it was at the time the most complete example of a Late Gothic carved altarpiece in the collection. Its original location – it was bought from a castle in the Pinzgau by the collector Soiter and was last kept in the Museum at Augsburg – is unknown. However, the sculptural programme gives some clear indications. The deacons Kolonat and Totnan are represented on the exterior of the wing panels, and inside in the central position stands the missionary bishop St Kylian; these three suffered martyrdom in Würzburg, and St Kylian is accompanied on his right by St Burkhard, the first bishop of Würzburg. The other saints are Jerome, Christopher and Dorothy. A more precise location within the see of Würzburg is difficult to establish, since the cult of St Kylian was common and no less than 126 churches were dedicated to him. The altarpiece's date is partially preserved on the frame and in style it belongs to the period immediately before the career of the influential sculptor Tilman Riemenschneider. vR

146
Barfüsserkirche

Shieldbearer from the Basle Spalentor
Basle, ca. 1475
Red sandstone, height 115 cm, width 83 cm
Inv. no. 1906.3617. Alter Bestand

The armour-clad man with a sword in his left hand and a shield in his right belonged, together with a counterpart, to the sculptural decoration of the late medieval Spalentor (Spalen gate) in Basle (see no. 143). The two reliefs were set about 5 m above the outer portal on the central merlons of the battlements of the gate's barbican, which was added in 1473–74. The remaining four merlons on the entrance front and those on the flanks were equipped with complicated embrasures. These sculptures were detached and replaced by copies in 1893. vR

147
Barfüsserkirche

Mary, Queen of Heaven
Basle, ca. 1480
Limewood, originally painted; height 96 cm
Inv. no. 1910.44. Purchase

This Madonna with the crescent moon at her feet is attributed to the Guntersumer family workshop, which produced the lost high altar of the Predigerkirche (Dominican church) in Basle in 1504. Before it was bought for the Museum, it stood on the altar of the church in Warmbach near Rheinfelden together with the accompanying figures of Sts Odilia and Barbara. The Christchild the Madonna once held is missing and unfortunately the colour has been stripped off. Jos and Dominicus Guntersumer, father and son, represent, together with Heinrich Isenhut, the most important of the 13 Late Gothic workshops active in Basle between 1450 and the beginning of the C16. With her characteristic motif of drapery lifted up above her right knee as if caught by a gust of wind, this Madonna is considered to be an early work of the Guntersumers; she has a close resemblance to the Madonna from Hellikon which is also in the Museum. vR

148
Barfüsserkirche

St Lawrence
St Lawrence Master, Basle, ca. 1480
Limewood, with original paint; height 142 cm
Inv. no. 1910.117

In 1910 at the time of its purchase the statue of the youthful deacon was the first wooden sculpture to be recognised as the work of a Late Gothic Basle workshop. The figure is indicative of the enormous losses of works of art in churches in Basle caused by the Reformation, and the scratches on its expressive face are themselves a document of the iconoclastic 'Bildersturm' of 1529. It can be assumed that the statue's original location was the Andreaskapelle (St Andrew's chapel) of the Safranzunft (merchants' guild), which was demolished in 1792. The lean, deeply undercut figure is the principal and eponymous work of a master carver and his workshop to whom six further statues of saints can be attributed. The sober expression of the face, permitting no overt emotion, is characteristic of the sculpture of Basle of the time. The lively, yet dry manner of the drapery folds is typical of the St Lawrence Master. vR

149
Barfüsserkirche

Domestic altar, dated 1484
Upper Rhine area
Limewood, shrine with figures carved and painted, wings painted on both sides; height 36 cm, width (open) 56 cm
Inv. no. 1977.256. Gift of Dr. h.c. Robert von Hirsch

This shrine, which is dated 1484 on the base, is a miniature version of a full-scale winged church altarpiece and functioned as such for private worship at home. With the wings closed it shows the Annunciation with a detailed representation of a Late Gothic chamber. Open, the shrine depicts the Passion of Christ, centred on the carved group of the dead Christ held by an angel between the Virgin and St John. On the inside of the wings, the suffering of Christ in the Flagellation and the Crowning with Thorns is dramatically represented. For these scenes the unknown painter used two engravings by Martin Schongauer as models. vR

150
Barfüsserkirche

St Dorothy
Ulrich Bruder, Basle, ca. 1500
Limewood, originally painted in polychrome; height 78.5 cm
Inv. no. 1919.488. Purchase

According to legend the Roman virgin Dorothea refused to marry the city prefect Fabricius, as she claimed to be the bride of Christ. At her execution – Dorothy was boiled, beaten, burnt and decapitated – a heavenly messenger arrived with a basket filled with apples and roses even though it was winter, thus confounding the clerk of the tribunal who had mockingly asked the accused to send flowers from the garden of her groom. This Late Gothic wooden *St Dorothy* is a rare example showing her accompanied by a little boy. His appearance is particularly interesting since he has been copied from an engraving made by the Upper Rhine Master E.S., the *New Year's greeting with Christchild.* After the mid-C15 engravings from the Upper Rhine area contributed greatly to the circulation of new iconography, often of single motifs, as in this case. With a provenance from Arlesheim, the figure is attributable to a Basle master craftsman of repute, namely the cabinetmaker Ulrich Bruder from Otwyl on Lake Constance (see no. 365), who signed the choir stalls of the church of St Peter in Basle in 1494. vR

151
Barfüsserkirche

Palmesel (Palm Sunday ass)
Lake Constance, ca. 1500
Limewood, painted, height 190 cm
Inv. no. 1898.225. Purchase

The Museum holds the astonishing number of five Late Gothic *Palmesel*, or wooden donkeys for the reenactment of Christ's entry into Jerusalem. Three originate from the Upper Rhine area, but this example, outstanding both for its artistic quality and for its survival intact, comes from Kreuzlingen on Lake Constance. The Rosgarten Museum in Constance preserves a comparable example originating either in the same workshop or under its influence. The figure of Christ blessing as he rides on the ass is detachable. Traces of painted palm branches can be distinguished on the base board. This is the only example of the five in the collection still to have its wheels. The tradition of commemorating the entry of Christ into Jerusalem on the Sunday before Easter by pulling a 'Palmesel' in procession is first recorded in the *Vita* of St Ulrich about 982–92. In pre-Reformation Basle Palm Sunday processions without a 'Palmesel' were customary; however in Ammerschwihr in Alsace, for example, the C16th 'Palmesel' is still in use today. vR

152
Barfüsserkirche

St Catherine of Alexandria
Strasbourg, ca. 1500
Carved and painted limewood, height 127.5 cm, width 39.5 cm, depth 39 cm
Inv. no. 1977.240. Gift of Prof. Dr. Edgar Heibronner

Together with St Maurice, St Barbara and a saintly pope, and with the Madonna in the centre, this statue of the youthful princess Catherine formed part of the high altar of the St. Mauritiuskirche in Kippenheim near Offenburg. The fate of this Late Gothic altarpiece, the figures of which are dispersed in four locations (Basle, Breisach, New York, Kippenheim), is typical of many such ecclesiastical sculptures preserved in museums. In this case the altarpiece was replaced by a more modern one in 1714–15 and so lost its liturgical function; it was being stored in the attic of the priest's house in 1872, when permission was granted for its dismemberment; it was sold in 1874, then again for 10DM in 1902–03; in 1990 its original location was identified. It can be assumed that the figure originated from an important workshop in Strasbourg around 1500. In its forceful, fluent drapery it shows reminiscences of the Upper Rhine style of around 1460; the deeply undercut folds and the voluptuous face surrounded by flowing hair are highly characteristic elements. vR

153
Barfüsserkirche

Three crucifixes (two unfinished)
Basle(?) or Upper Rhine area, ca. 1500
Carved boxwood, partially painted, and carved limewood, heights 20, 18.1 and 18.2 cm
Inv. nos. 1870.1185., 1870.947., 1870.948. Amerbach Cabinet

The three small crucifixes belonged to the collection of the Basle jurist Basilius Amerbach, who purchased them between 1578 and 1582. In their varying degrees of completion – also the main reason for the interest in them of the universal polymath Amerbach – they are unique illustrations of the working method of a carver of the Late Gothic period. It is uncertain whether they were left incomplete by chance, or even because they were rejects, or whether they were workshop models for the guidance of journeymen producing a larger number of replicas. The presence of these three crucifixes and two other small unfinished figures in the Amerbach Cabinet documents the change in connoisseurship during the Renaissance. vR

154
Barfüsserkirche

Venus
Padua(?), ca. 1500
Bronze, height 26.5 cm
Inv. no. 1909.234. Amerbach Cabinet

The graceful figure, probably deriving from an antique model, represents the naked Venus looking in a mirror, a motif often interpreted in the Renaissance as a symbol of transience. Her gaze is emphasized by the counterfeiting of the eyes in silver and copper. To the Basle jurist and collector Basilius Amerbach, who had bought it from his friend Demoulin de Rochefort in 1578, this piece had special importance as he displayed it on an alabaster base (lost) in the central niche of his coin cabinet (no. 369), between the copper statuettes of Jupiter and Mercury. The gilt belt with the hanging pearl was added by the Basle goldsmith Christoph Kumberger. It enabled the statuette to be secured from behind. vR

155
Barfüsserkirche

Adam and Eve
Hans Weiditz the Elder, Upper Rhine area, ca. 1505/10
Carved boxwood on a limewood base, height with base 21.8 cm
Inv. no. 1870.942. Amerbach Cabinet

A parallel to Dürer's famous engraving of *Adam and Eve* of 1504, Weiditz's group marks the beginning of German Renaissance small-scale sculpture. Although in style the figures still conform to Late Gothic conventions, the decisive moment of the Fall is now represented more from a psychological than from a moralising point of view. The sculptor can be identified as Hans Weiditz (Wydyz) by the initials H and W on the inset bases on which the figures stand. Weiditz, who came originally from Strasbourg, is documented as active in the Freiburg-Breisgau region between 1497 and 1510. One of the most influential patrons there was the imperial chancellor Konrad Stürzel, for whose private chapel Weiditz created an altarpiece representing the three Magi. This statuette group is to be associated with the humanistically inclined circles in Freiburg, where the Imperial Diet of 1498 had taken place and a residence for Emperor Maximilian I was built in 1516. The *Adam and Eve* statuette was in the collection of Basilius Amerbach in Basle by 1578. vR

156
Barfüsserkirche

Large winged altarpiece from the church in Santa Maria in Calanca (Grisons), dated 1512
Workshop of Ivo Strigel, Christoph Zeller and other masters, Memmingen
Carved and painted limewood, with painted panels, height 375 cm, width 567 cm (open)
Inv. no. 1887.95. Purchase

Above the predella with Christ and the twelve Apostles the opened altarpiece displays the statue of the Virgin flanked by four scenes from her life carved in the round and, on the wings, eight scenes carved in relief. On the back of the altarpiece and the outer sides of the wings are painted panels of the four Evangelists and eight saints. With its original painting intact, this Late Gothic altarpiece from the leading town of the Calanca valley is an impressive demonstration the importance of the south Swabian workshop of Ivo Strigel, which exported such large altarpieces all over the Alps as far as the Italian-language border.

Different parts of this multiple work were produced by various craftsmen. The Virgin is an outstanding work by Christoph Zeller, a pupil of Hans Herlin. In 1887, when the altarpiece was acquired from the church of Sta Maria for the Medieval Collection in Basle, at the time the largest public collection of such objects in Switzerland, it received the highest praise: "After the high altar in Chur cathedral, [this is] the most ambitious and iconographically important altarpiece on Swiss soil". vR

157
Barfüsserkirche

'Anna Selbdritt'
Basle, ca. 1520
Carved limewood, with remnants of painting, height 115 cm
Inv. no. 1927.217. Purchase

The medieval image known as *Anna Selbdritt*, or *zu dritt* (in a group of three) as it would be in modern German, represented Mary's mother St Anne, the Virgin herself and the Christchild. This group differs from older representations in which Mary was a tiny attribute of St Anne since all the figures have relatively realistic proportions. The group came to the Museum from a pilgrimage church near Bad Burg in the upper Birsigtal, but it was probably moved to this location, perhaps from Basle as a consequence of the 1529 Reformation. With two accompanying figures of St Agnes and St Barbara, also in the Museum, this *Anna Selbdritt* is attributed to a Basle woodcarver who combined influence from the Upper Rhine Master H.L. with older Basle traditions. His works are diffused in a wide area around Basle, into Alsace, the region around Baden and in Switzerland. vR

158
Barfüsserkirche

Christ crucified
Martin Hoffmann, Basle, ca. 1525
Carved hornbeam, height 43 cm
Inv. no. 1927.94. Purchase

In its moving expression of suffering this representation of the dead Christ ranks among the finest of Basle's Late Gothic sculptures to survive. The original cross and the arms of Christ, which were fixed to the torso with dowels, are lacking. The original location of the crucifix was the church of Courrendlin near Delémont in the Swiss Jura. A number of comparable works, including two busts of Prophets in Basle town hall, support the attribution to the woodcarver and joiner Martin Hoffmann. Having come from Stollberg in Thuringia, Hoffmann became a guild member in Basle in 1507 and lived in the city until his death in 1530. During the years before the Reformation, the likely date of the crucifix, he suffered from shortage of commissions. In 1526 he petitioned the town council of Basle against the stricter guild regulations which, for reasons of competition, forbade woodcarvers to follow their earlier practice of employing journeymen joiners. vR

159
Barfüsserkirche

The Last Supper
Circle of the Master of Ottobeuren, Upper Swabia, ca. 1525
Carved and painted limewood, height 70 cm, width 105 cm, depth 10 cm
Inv. No. 1877.56. Purchase

This carved panel belongs to a series of five reliefs of the Passion of Christ believed to have come from the cathedral in Chur. The other scenes depicted are: *Christ in the Garden of Gethsemane*, the *Betrayal* and *St Peter with Malchus*, *Pilate washing his hands* with Christ being led away, and the *Crowning with Thorns*. Their original arrangement is unknown. The *Last Supper* is a realistic representation of the twelve disciples dining with Christ; particular attention is paid to such details as the lamb served on a pewter platter, the lidded wine vessel in the foreground, the sleeping figure of Christ's favourite disciple, John, and Judas who is shown with the thirty pieces of silver hanging in a purse around his neck, in allusion to the rope of his suicide. Stylistically the relief is an example of the 'parallel fold style' that is associated with the Master of Ottobeuren (Hans Thoman) and Jörg Kendel of Biberach. This style became widespread during the first third of the C16 in southern Swabia. vR

160
Barfüsserkirche

Erasmus of Rotterdam
Basle, after 1536
Alabaster on red marble, diameter 27.5 cm
Inv. no. 1894.75. Alter Bestand

The profile portrait, encircled with the inscription ERASMUS ROTTERDAM[US], corresponds in form and size with the bust-length portraits after antique models found in Renaissance tomb sculpture. There is, however, no evidence that links this tondo either to an unfinished project, or to the memorial of Erasmus in the Basle Münster that was made by the stonemason Hans Mentzinger in 1538 and was the first funerary monument erected in Basle after the Reformation (the cult of the dead had been abolished there from 1529). In this context it is worth remembering the memorial to Erasmus erected by the city of Freiburg im Breisgau in 1537, and that the only two portrait memorials to be made in Basle at the end of the C16 commemorated prominent scholars, who, like Erasmus, came from outside the city. The anonymous sculptor of this certainly posthumous portrait (Erasmus died in 1536) drew on the small woodcut by Hans Holbein the Younger that appeared in Froben's 1533 edition of Erasmus's *Adagia*. vR

161
Barfüsserkirche

The Holbein fountain
Basle, ca. 1545
Sandstone with paint,
height 497 cm
Inv. no. 1910.132.

162
Barfüsserkirche

***Samson and Delilah*, from the Stäblins fountain, Freiestrasse**
Basle, 2nd half 16th century
Red sandstone, height 84 cm, width 52 cm, depth 35 cm
Inv. no. 1914.481.

The design of this fountain is related to the contemporary Pfeilerbrunnen in Berne made by the Fribourg sculptor Hans Gieng. The Holbein fountain, also known as the Sackpfeiferbrunnen (bagpiper fountain), owes its popular epithets to the figures which decorate it. The unknown artist has made precise transpositions into sculpture of compositions invented by two famous painters and graphic artists who had connections with Basle. The three pairs of peasants cheerfully dancing around the centre of the column are taken from a woodcut titlepage by Holbein of 1523 and the bagpaper crowning the fountain is taken from an engraving by Dürer of 1514. The fountain originally stood at the Spalen-Schwibbogen, then from 1859 nearby in the Spalenvorstadt, where a copy has now replaced it. vR

The Old Testament (Judges 16:4) tells of the enormous strength of Samson who in battle with the Philistines killed 1000 men with the jawbone of an ass. Delilah, beloved by Samson, was bribed by the Philistine nobles to find out and betray the secret of his strength. After several attempts she discovered that Samson would lose his might if seven locks of his hair were shorn. The group shows this happening, while Samson sleeps in Delilah's lap. Both figures are in Renaissance dress. The subject symbolized the all-conquering power of women and served as an example of female cunning, as do scenes with other couples such as Adam and Eve, Aristotle and Phyllis and Judith and Holofernes. The Basle fountain was recorded by Theodor Zwinger in 1577. The sculptor is unknown. The fountain was illustrated in the guide-book *Voyage pittoresque en Alsace* (Mulhouse, 1844), where it was characterized as 'un monument d'une naiveté charmante'. There is a copy on the Barfüsserplatz. vR

163
Barfüsserkirche

Minos and Scylla, dated 1569
Hans Jamnitzer, Nuremberg
Cast lead plaquette, diameter 18.2 cm
Inv. no. 1904.1044. Amerbach Cabinet

The centre of German plaquette-making in the C16 was Nuremberg, where the carver Peter Flötner had introduced a new form of decorative art by producing relief moulds for multiple duplication and sale. The original models were made of wood, stone or wax, or rarely of metal, and the final plaquettes, in contrast to the Italian use of bronze, were cast mostly in lead. Increasingly goldsmiths, who had usually copied others' designs, themselves became the designers of the moulds. This was the case with Hans Jamnitzer (ca. 1538–1602), son of the famous Wentzel Jamnitzer, whose designs often show the influence of Franco-Flemish prints. This roundel shows a scene from Ovid's *Metamorphoses* (8, 6–151): Minos gallops towards the fortified town of Alcathoe looking up at the figure of Scylla waving from the battlements. A tree stump carries the date 1569 and the monogram HG (Hans Gamitzer). More than a dozen replicas are known. Plaquettes were produced as independent small-scale art objects and were highly sought-after collectors' items. vR

164
Barfüsserkirche

***The Elector Johann Georg of Brandenburg and his wife Elisabeth von Anhalt*, double portrait in a case**, dated 1578
Heinrich Rappusch, Berlin
Modelled wax in copper-gilt engraved and lidded case, diameter 10.5 cm
Inv. no. 1874.66. Faesch Museum

The art of making wax portraits flourished in the late C16 and was highly valued by noble collectors for the impression they gave of being lifelike while evoking the preciousness of carved gemstones. The wax portrait in medallion form derived from portrait medals and Antonio Abondio was the most important exponent of the art. Six outstanding examples of wax sculpture from Brandenburg-Saxony came to the Museum from the collection of the Basle goldsmith and natural scientist Leonhard Thurneysser (1531–1596). For 14 years he was the Elector's personal physician and was in close contact with the portrayed couple. He is recorded as wearing golden 'favour pennies' ('Gnadenpfennige'), or portrait-coins, around his neck. The double portrait, of which a variant of 1579 is known, was probably made by Heinrich Rappusch in the year before his appointment as court goldsmith. Rappusch came to Berlin from Nuremberg. The minute description of the precious armour of the Elector and the jewels of his wife are noteworthy, as is the contrast in the sitters' complexions. vR

165
Barfüsserkirche

Jupiter
Hans Michel, Basle, ca. 1582
Alabaster, height 17.2 cm
Inv. no. 1906.28. Amerbach Cabinet

The Basle collector Basilius Amerbach recorded in 1585 that the sculptor Hans Michel had copied the torso of Jupiter from a bronze statuette. The bronze original showing Jupiter crowned and holding bolts of lightning in his right hand was believed to be antique, but in reality it was a Renaissance work. The bronze and the wax model, which documents the transformation from the original to the torso, both survive in the Museum. A comparison of the works provides an insight into the late Renaissance understanding of the antique. It also illustrates the personal style of the sculptor, whose other known works are all large-scale. Hans Michel was originally from Strasbourg and was granted citizenship in Basle in 1574. In 1580 he made the monumental stone figure of *Munatius Plancus* in the courtyard of the town hall. Architectural sculptures, fountains and tombs by him survive in Delémont, Ribeauvillé and Säckingen. Next to Daniel Heintz he was the most important sculptor in Basle at the end of the C16. vR

166
Barfüsserkirche

Grape-harvester, drinking vessel
Bartholomäus Paxmann (woodcarver) and Stephan Aberli (goldsmith), Zurich, ca. 1620
Pearwood and silver, height 29 cm
Inv. no. 1920.10. Purchase

Drinking vessels in the shape of grape harvesters were common during the Renaissance and Baroque periods, especially in the wine-producing areas of southern Germany, Alsace and Switzerland. In contrast to the stiffer figures produced in Basle this striding grape harvester has an individualised and animated appearance and it can be attributed to the Zurich carver Bartholomäus Paxmann on the basis of its similarity to a signed work. The silver mount, the lizard, crayfish and fly on the pedestal, and the pannier, were made by the Zurich goldsmith Stephan Aberli (guild member 1612, died 1663). The 16 silver shields attached to the gold-plated bands of the pannier carry the coats of arms of families resident in Schaffhausen (von Mandach, Hurter, Schwarz, Veith, Mäder, Seiler and Abegg) and the emblem of the coopers, who were incorporated in the tanners' guild. This suggests that the figure was used in Schaffhausen. Thirteen of the shields are dated 1679, and one 1710. vR

167
Barfüsserkirche

***The Crucifixion* (after Grünewald)**
'FE', southern Germany, 1627(?)
Carved walnut, height 59 cm, width 29 cm
Inv. no. 1870.950. Faesch Museum

The technical virtuosity of this carving is characteristic of a 'Kunstkammer' object. It is an example of the so called 'Dürer Renaissance', the stylistic trend in the early Baroque period in which, in contrast to the far more important classical revival, Late Gothic works were drawn upon as artistic prototypes. In this case the source was the Small *Crucifixion* by Mathias Grünewald (died 1528), copied from an engraving of 1605 by Raphael Sadeler. This is the only known transposition of this composition into relief. The unidentified sculptor carved the monogram FE and the date beneath the feet of St John the Baptist. The coat of arms on the base of the cross is that of the Zurlauben from Lucerne, and the relief is likely to have been commissioned for a member of that family, perhaps Konrad Zurlauben III (1571–1629). vR

168
Barfüsserkirche

A gentleman with the arms of the Zurlauben family
Switzerland, ca. 1625/30
Limewood, height 23.5 cm, width 15 cm
Inv. no. 1870.1192. Faesch Museum

In the early C16 relief portraits of persons of rank had already incorporated motifs of *memento mori* and this portrait's resemblance to a funerary monument is part of that tradition. In front of Gothic tracery on a red background, two angels hold a rich hanging with openwork borders. In front of this the three-quarters-length figure of a nobleman armed with a sword almost steps out of the frame. He is dressed in the fashion of ca. 1625, has scars on his forehead, and his right hand is decorated with rings on his thumb and little finger. The coat of arms to the left of his head belongs to the Zurlauben family, residents of Zug who made careers for themselves in foreign service. He is perhaps Konrad Zurlauben III (1571–1629). The relief, including the frame, was carved from a single piece of wood: the unknown artist's display of technical skill was a response to an appreciation, typical of 'Kunstkammer' collectors, for the virtuoso and intricate as an end in itself. vR

169
Barfüsserkirche

Mercury abducts Psyche
Melchior Barthel(?), Ulm(?), ca. 1650/51(?)
Ivory, height 28 cm (with plinth 58cm)
Inv. no. 1894.421. Faesch Museum

Towards the end of the C16, partly as a result of increasing trade with the East Indies, ivory came into fashion as a favourite material for small sculpture in the flourishing lathe-turning workshops. Collectors valued representations in the nude of mythological figures, such as this abduction of a woman from the collection of Remigius Faesch (died 1667). Mercury carrying Psyche off to Mount Olympus was a popular subject at the court of Rudolf II: the most outstanding interpretation was probably the over-life-size bronze that Adriaen de Vries made for the Emperor in Prague in 1592. The Basle group shows the same concern with its appearance from all angles: in this it reflects Florentine prototypes from the circle of Giambologna. It is attributed to the Dresden artist Melchior Barthel (1625–1672), who trained in Ulm with David Heschler the Elder ca. 1647–50, and worked as an ivory carver in Venice for 17 years. Consequently this group may play a key role in relating the sculpture of Ulm to Italy, northern and middle Germany. There are comparable objects in Dresden, Florence and New York. vR

170
Barfüsserkirche

Bacchic group
Netherlands, 1st half 18th century
Cast lead, height 12 cm
Inv. no. 1906.2015. Daniel Bruckner collection

This small group showing two fauns and two nymphs entwined in a bacchanalian dance translates a pictorial invention of Rubens into a statuette. The motif is taken from the painting known as *The Feast of Venus* in the Kunsthistorisches Museum in Vienna. The immediate model for the lead cast was a boxwood sculpture in the Kunstgewerbemuseum, Berlin, that is attributed to an artist in Rubens's circle, Lucas Faidherbe of Mechelen (1617–1697). The Basle collector Daniel Bruckner (1707–1781) mistakenly associated the prototype of the group with the Roman excavations in Augst and commented in 1763: "With regard to artistic value, this is the most noble piece to have been found among the sculptures in Augst, as, when making it, the artist forgot all sense of shame". The version in his collection, however, would only have been a cast after the original, which had by then been sold to a collection in England. vR

171
Barfüsserkirche

Memorial to Maria Magdalena Langhans, copy of the gravestone in the parish church of Hindelbank near Berne
Valentin Sonnenschein after Johann August Nahl, after 1775
Terracotta, height 37.7 cm, width 25 cm, depth 9 cm
Inv. no. 1904.619. Gift of Dr. Ludwig Sieber-Bischoff

In 1751 on the day before Easter, nine months after her marriage, Maria Magdalena Langhans, the 28-year-old wife of the parish priest of Hindelbank, died giving birth to a still-born child. The tragic death of this young woman, who was famed for her beauty, was witnessed by the Prussian court sculptor, Johann August Nahl, who was a guest in the priest's house. In the same year Nahl gave his experience artistic expression in a famous monument in which he interpreted the promise of Resurrection by showing the gravestone breaking open. The inscription was provided by Albrecht von Haller. Twenty to 30 years later miniature copies of the sandstone monument were produced in several versions: they were made of wax, terracotta or biscuit-ware by factories in Nyon and Niederweiler. These replicas, which were distributed as far afield as England, not only served as souvenirs for travellers, but were also used for the consolation of the bereaved. vR

172
Barfüsserkirche

Count Cagliostro
Strasbourg, ca. 1780/86
Plaster, height 31.8 cm, width 19.2 cm, depth 13.4 cm
Inv. no. 1983.527. Purchase

The inscription on the underside of the base provides incomplete information on the origins of the bust: it states that it was made by a certain Ja... de Viller, who lived with the goldsmith Büttner in the rue des halles Bardes, opposite the bookshop le Roux in Strasbourg. The sitter bears a close resemblance to the man portrayed in an engraving made by Christophe Guérin in Strasbourg in 1781, and so may be identified as a Sicilian named Giuseppe Balsamo but known as Count Cagliostro (1743–1795). Cagliostro was both infamous as a charlatan and admired as a clairvoyant and faith healer (see also no. 423). He had a staunch supporter in the Basle ribbon manufacturer Jakob Sarasin of the Weisses Haus (see also no. 388). In 1781 Johann Kaspar Lavater arranged for Cagliostro to undertake the apparently hopeless case of Sarasin's wife, Gertrude. His success in curing her brought him widespread fame and popularity. A visitor to the Sarasins described his encounter with this extraordinary character in 1787: "He is a small, very fat man, whose most astounding feature is his head: it is exactly like a marble bust of him that Sarasin had displayed in a small cabinet. Should I paint a magician, I would take his head as a model. His glance is threatening, devouring and fleeting". Cagliostro founded a lodge of Freemasons following the Egyptian rites in Basle (see no. 388). They met in the Glöcklihof in Riehen bei Basel. vR

173
Barfüsserkirche

'Unis à jamais', dated 1795
Aubert Joseph Parent, Neuchâtel
Limewood, diameter (with frame) 33.5 cm
Inv. no. 1931.25. Purchase

A scroll on the relief has the inscription "Unis à jamais" (joined forever) and the date 1795, and the mount bears the artist's dedication of this wedding present to the Basle couple Dietrich Forcart and Gertrud Merian. Their marriage is symbolized by the coats of arms of the two families chained together on the altar on which two flaming hearts are set, with a pair of billing and cooing doves fluttering above. The painter, sculptor and architect Aubert Joseph Parent (1753–1835), originally from Cambrai, specialised in the design of interior decoration and furniture. In 1792, as a refugee from the French Revolution, he had been commissioned by the Forcart family to furnish the Württemberger Hof and to design its garden. His success had begun in 1777 when a beautifully carved flower basket caught the attention of Louis XVI and was placed in the King's apartment in Versailles. The almost untreated surface of the limewood, relying for its life-like effect on the technical perfection of the carving, corresponded to the taste of the period and gave perfect expression to the contemporary call for a return to nature. The presence in the Museum of eight works by Parent and two by his imitator, Jean Démontreuil, all with a provenance from Basle collectors, demonstrates their popularity. vR

174
Barfüsserkirche

***Symbol of Concord,* cabinet for beakers**, dated 1807
Franz Abart, Innerschweiz
Limewood, height 137 cm
Inv. no. 1903.312. Gift of the Öffentliche Kunstsammlung

This Symbol of Concord, as it is identified by the inscription on the rock, is a departure from the usual classical female personification, drawing instead upon the iconography of two heroes of the Swiss Confederation. The bundle of spears refers to Arnold von Winkelried and his statue on the fountain bearing his name that was made by the sculptor Franz Abart in 1724 and was erected near his home town, in Stans. It also alludes to Wilhelm Tell, as he appeared in contemporary representations, with fasces with the 'Freiheitshut' (freedom hat) stuck on top. The sculpture was designed as a monument for a room. It fulfilled a highly individual function: an accompanying document records that the retiring commander of the 1st Regiment of the canton of Basle-Stadt, Oberstleutnant Rudolf Emanuel Wettstein, dedicated it as a token of friendship to his officers. The comradeship of the men was symbolized by the bundle of 17 spears. The initials of the friends are engraved on the beakers contained inside. vR

175
Barfüsserkirche

Memorial for Ludwig Rudolf von Jenner,
dated 1808
Valentin Sonnenschein, Berne
Terracotta, height 47 cm, width 45 cm
Inv. no. 1918.214. Purchase

The 33-year-old artillery captain, Ludwig Rudolf von Jenner, was among the 457 victims of the landslide at Goldau in Innerschweiz on 2 September 1806. He had been making an excursion with seven colleagues to the Rigi, a mountain near the Vierwaldstättersee popular for its panoramic views. His friend F.L. von May commissioned Valentin Sonnenschein, the celebrated sculptor from Berne, to model a memorial. The victim leans against a split rock, while at its foot a grieving spirit of death sits with an extinguished torch. vR

176
Barfüsserkirche

Ferdinand Stadler
Johann Ludwig Keiser, Zurich/Basle, 1871
Marble, height 48 cm, width 51 cm, depth 27 cm
Inv. no. 1991.69. Gift of the Evangelisch-reformierter Kirchenrat Basel-Stadt

In 1856 the architect Ferdinand Stadler (1813–1871), who was born in Zurich and educated in Karlsruhe, won the national competition to design the Basle parish church of St. Elisabeth. The commission for the building of the first Protestant church in Basle after the Reformation aroused great interest, and Christoph and Margarethe Merian-Burckhardt, the two very rich private donors, wanted it to be a memorial to themselves. The church's construction from 1857 to 1865 under the direction of Christoph Riggenbach led to the establishment of a masons' workshop following the example set in Cologne. It was to serve many future Swiss architects as a training ground. Material and furnishings for the church were obtained from Frankfurt (the copper roof), Paris (sculpture), Strasbourg (the tower clock), Mainz (metal candelabra), Zurich (bells) and Munich (stained glass). The building is Stadler's principal work and is regarded as the most important neo-Gothic church in Switzerland. The sculptor Ludwig Keiser from Zug, a pupil of Ludwig Schwanthaler in Munich and his assistant on the monumental *Bavaria*, created the bust in 1871, the year of the architect's death. vR

Painting and graphic art

Paintings, drawings and prints, the areas in which the Öffentliche Kunstsammlung Basel is acknowledged as outstanding, are also well represented in the Historisches Museum. The main emphasis in the Historisches Museum collection is on the city of Basle and its region, and on the following categories and themes: Late Gothic panel painting (winged altarpieces), portrait and miniature painting, paintings from buildings in Basle (murals, wallpaper, furnishings), and images of the city, its buildings, its life and customs, and of particular events in the city's history and of its trades. In addition, there are special collections of family records and of designs and cartoons for stained-glass windows. These works make use of a great variety of materials and techniques, including painting on panel, canvas, metal, glass, parchment and paper; pastels, gouache, silverpoint drawings and various printing techniques including early photography are also represented. Criteria for collection, apart from artistic quality, include subject-matter, value as historical evidence, and original use and provenance.

About one third of the roughly 450 paintings (in oil on panel or canvas) are permanently exhibited in the Haus zum Kirschgarten and the Barfüsserkirche. Some 350 of the paintings are portraits, primarily of Basle citizens, from the C17 to the early C20. The collection constitutes a gallery of ancestral portraits representing the history of the city republic and its leading families and personages. The captured presence of its former citizens gives continued life to the city's past. The predominance of portraiture in the collection, as compared to genre, landscape or religious painting, manifests the general demand for this kind of art among the Protestant citizens, and the lack of commissions from the Church or secular institutions for other subjects. The quality of the portraits is uneven, reflecting the judgement of a contemporary (C.G. Küttner) of 1779, that Basle was a splendid place for portrait painters, since "they all found work, from the good to the mediocre to the very worst". In the portrait collection alone – excluding 'Kleinmeister' engravings and miniatures – about 90 different painters of Swiss, German, Bohemian, Netherlandish and Italian origin are represented. In this way the collection's emphasis on local people is supplemented by an international dimension, though not one that bears comparison with that of portrait painting in Basle in the time of Holbein.

In the graphic art collection the illustrations of lost or fragmented art treasures of Basle have special documentary value – for example, those of the Burgundian spoils sold in 1504 (no. 181), or of the Basle *Dance of Death*, destroyed in 1805 (no. 178), or of the Münster treasure, partly auctioned in 1836. vR

177
Barfüsserkirche

Altar cross from the convent of St. Katharinental
Lake Constance region (Constance?), ca. 1250–70
Beechwood, parchment, plaster with gilding, rock crystal, two gems, blue glass; Christ's body in tempera on chalk ground over canvas; 99.3 × 67 cm
Inv. no. 1905.70. Gift of Karl Bachofen-Burckhardt

The altar cross comes from the Dominican convent of St. Katharinenthal near Diessenhofen in the Swiss Thurgau. It is particularly important for the way in which Christ is depicted: it is one of the very few crucifixes from the German Late Romanesque in which His nude body is painted. Its early dating is based on the year of the convent's foundation in 1251 on the one hand, and on parallels with book illumination on the other. For example, the figure of Christ can be compared to a *Crucifixion* in the Psalter of Besançon, ca. 1260; in type it can be related to examples in Thuringian-Saxon book illumination and to the *Crucifixion* on the retable of the Marienkirche in Soest. The form of the cross, resembling a piece of goldsmith's work, has parallels in miniatures in the Psalter of the Benedictine abbey of Rheinau on Lake Constance, produced before 1241.vR

178
Barfüsserkirche

The Basle *Dance of Death*: fragment of a *Herald*
Konrad Witz or his circle, Basle, ca. 1435/40
Tempera on plaster; 56.5 × 45.5 cm
Inv. no. 1870.692. Gift of the heirs of Dorothea Burckhardt-Iselin

The Basle *Dance of Death*, famous since the C16, came into being at the time of the Council of Basle (1431–48), perhaps under the impact of the plague of 1439. Nineteen fragments retrieved when it was demolished in 1805 have been preserved in the Museum. The sequence of paintings on the inside of the cemetery wall of the Dominican convent in Basle originally presented, over some 60 metres, 40 figures of people doomed to death, all of different classes, professions, ages and attitudes. In a *danse macabre* with death they advanced, or processed, along the wall towards the charnel house. The herald is depicted as the servant of many lords, with the coats of arms of Austria, France, England and Burgundy. In view of its early dating and attribution to the painter Konrad Witz (though this is disputed), the Basle *Dance of Death* is a particularly important example of these *memento mori* images, found throughout Europe from the C15 particularly in the convents of the mendicant orders. vR

179
Barfüsserkirche

***The Crucifixion* on the inside of the lid of a burse, from the treasury of Basle Münster**
Follower of Stefan Lochner, style of Cologne, ca. 1456/60
Painting on silk; 18.5 × 19.4 cm
Inv. no. 1905.3947. Alter Bestand

The painting, applied directly, without priming, to the silk and unvarnished, decorates the inside of the lid of a casket which formerly contained a corporal, the cloth on which the host, chalice and paten were placed during mass. The subject of the Crucifixion obviously has a bearing on the Eucharist with which the casket was associated. Against a blue starry sky – alluding to the eclipse of the sun at the time of the Crucifixion – the Virgin, St John the Evangelist and Mary Magdalene mourn at the foot of the cross. The attribution of the work in 1959 not to a painter in Basle but to a Cologne follower of Stefan Lochner has recently been confirmed by technical investigation. It is related to the Darmstadt *Crucifixion* on cloth and to the small *Crucifixion* by the Master of 1456 in the Hessisches Landesmuseum Darmstadt. In addition, the small format and the reductive style have affinities to Cologne book illumination. vR

180
Barfüsserkirche

The Peter Rot altar (closed)
Circle of Bartholomäus Ruthenzweig, Basle, ca. 1476/84
Tempera on pinewood panel; 109.5 × 96 cm (closed)
Inv. no. 1978.322. Purchase

From the furnishings of the Basle Barfüsserkirche only one work, the Late Gothic winged altar bearing the name of its donor, Peter Rot, a mayor of Basle, has survived the Reformation and the iconoclasm of 1529. Its programme of imagery gives pride of place, in the Franciscan tradition, to the Virgin and specifically reflects the debate being carried on at the time it was painted over the dogma of the Immaculate Conception; the coats of arms of the two donors, Rot and his wife of the Rümlang family, allude to it even in their heraldic devices, the rose and the unicorn. The Virgin in her aureole, between the archangels Gabriel and Michael – symbolizing the gate of paradise – occupies the centre panel, flanked by 30 saints on the insides of the wings. On the outside panels (shown) the miracle of the Resurrection follows Schongauer's engraving produced about 1475; nevertheless Christ's having risen through a closed tomb slab is a symbolic allusion to His incarnation in the Virgin's womb. This rare example of Late Gothic panel painting from Basle illustrates not only the direct influence of Schongauer from nearby Colmar, but also – in the 'borrowing' of the Archangel Michael from a work by Colijn de Coter – the assimilation of Netherlandish models by a Basle workshop. vR

181
Barfüsserkirche

The 'Federlin' (feather) **from the Burgundian spoils**
Basle, before 1504
Watercolour on parchment; 34.2 × 25.9 cm
Inv. no. 1916.476. Alter Bestand

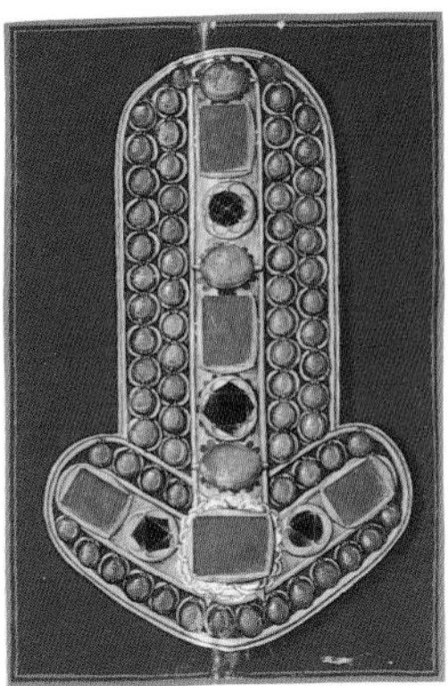

The drawing documents a piece of Burgundian jewellery, called a "feather" and intended to be worn on a hat, produced about 1460/65. Mounted on it to form an arrow head were five pale rubies, four diamonds and three large and 70 small beads. With three other precious objects from the possessions of Charles the Bold of Burgundy, also recorded in watercolours in the Museum's collection, it formed part of the spoils won at the battle of Grandson in 1476. It did not go to Lucerne like the rest of the general spoils, but, illicitly concealed from the Allies, was taken directly to Basle, where it was hidden for nearly 30 years. According to the deed of sale, dated 1504, the city sold the 'Federlin', the 'Gürtelin' (little belt), the 'Drei Brüder' (three brothers) and the 'Rose' to Jakob Fugger in Augsburg to pay off debts of around 40,200 guilders. The subsequent fate of the jewels is not known, but it may be surmised that they were reworked into new jewellery for the Emperor. vR

182
Studiensammlung

View of the Rhine at Basle (detail)
Basle, ca. 1520/30
Pen drawing on paper, with watercolour wash; 9 × 40 cm
Inv. no. 1870.924. Amerbach Cabinet

The unknown artist shows the stately extension of the city, then numbering about 10,000 inhabitants, along the left bank of the Rhine, looking upstream. In contrast to the schematic depiction of 1493 in Hartmann Schedel's *Weltchronik*, here, for the first time, an artist shows topographical and architectural details of Basle within a coherent overall perspective. The embankment frontage, still impressive today in its unbroken sweep over more than 2 km, is punctuated by the towers of the medieval fortifications. The Kleinbasel side, without significant buildings except for the monastery of Klingenthal, projects into the foreground. The two parts of the city are linked by the old Rhine bridge in front of the towering Münster. An indication of the nearby Jura mountains with Mt Gempen places the city in its surroundings. The draughtsman may have known engravings by Albrecht Altdorfer; former attributions to Conrad Morand and Ambrosius Holbein have recently been questioned. vR

183
Musikinstrumenten-Sammlung

Allegory of Music
South Germany, ca. 1540
Oil on canvas, 160 × 270 cm
Inv. no. 1906.2901. Alter Bestand

This large painting, said to originate from the collection of the Basle physician Felix Platter (1536–1614), is one of the few documents of its time showing in encyclopaedic detail the musical practices of the Renaissance period. It includes all the instruments known at that time. As the inscriptions "Delphi die Statt" (the town of Delphi), "Parnas der Berg" (Mount Parnassus) and "Castalius der Brunn" (the Castalian spring) indicate, the scene is ostensibly drawn from Greek antiquity, although the buildings and costumes are contemporary and the sacred spring at Delphi has the form of a Renaissance fountain. The nine Muses are dressed as patrician ladies of the C16, with the god of the arts, Apollo, standing a little apart. Antique tradition is combined with Old Testament history by the depiction of Bathsheba bathing in the fountain and observed by King David from the palace. The basis of their combination is the medieval Christian notion of the 'fountain of love'. A second version, identical except in not being cut down on all sides as this is, exists in private ownership; it preserves a concert of angels in the sky, which adds a further important element to the depiction of Music. vR

184
Barfüsserkirche

Portrait of the goldsmith Wentzel Jamnitzer
Nuremberg, 1562/63
Oil on canvas, 91.5 × 79 cm
Inv. no. 1920.143. Gift of Carl Siebenmann

Goldsmiths' work in Germany in the C16 was profoundly influenced by Wenzel Jamnitzer, who died in Nuremberg in 1585. As a master he ranks beside his famous Italian predecessor Benvenuto Cellini. His fame soon reached Basle, and the cast of the lost silver saddle that he made for the coronation of Maximilian II came to Basle even during his lifetime, together with several lead casts of small pieces (goldsmith's models). The 55-year-old goldsmith holds a gauging rod of his own construction for determining the specific gravity of seven metals, and a pair of reducing compasses – two aids needed to calculate the amount of material required to cast an object such as the as yet ungilt silver statuette in front of him. A speciality of Jamnitzer's were delicate garlands of silver flowers, cast after nature, like that in the background. The painting is an exact copy of the portrait commissioned by Jamnitzer from the Netherlandish artist Nicolas Neufchâtel, removed by Napoleon from the Nuremberg town hall and now in the Musée d'art et histoire in Geneva. vR

185
Barfüsserkirche

Marriage portraits of Bernhard Brand II and Dorothea Müller, dated 1620
Circle of Bartholomäus Sarburgh, Basle
Oil on panel, 112 × 82 cm
Inv. no. 1987.988. Purchase
Inv. no. 1887.103. Gift of Julius Gottfried Mende

This typical Basle portrait of a married couple of the early C17 shows husband and wife turned towards each other in three-quarters length. Following the practice usual since the C15, the left side, favoured in heraldic convention, was reserved for the husband. On both portraits the age of the sitter and the date of the painting is announced at head height – in the husband's case, emphasized by a motif of classical architecture, his four-year tenure of the rank of senator is also indicated. As senator he officiated beside the representatives of the 15 guilds in the inner council. Bernhard Brand II (1588–1650) had studied both branches of law at Basle and Bourges and in 1608 had made a long study tour through France, England, the Netherlands, Germany, Italy and as far as Malta. After his return he married Dorothea Müller (1584–1638), the daughter of a Basle spice and gunpowder trader. His further career as governor of Waldenburg (1625–35) and Kleinhüningen (1641–44) brought him the office of chief guildmaster, the second most powerful man in the city, in 1644. The costumes and attributes of the couple display a modest luxury in conformity with the strict sumptuary laws, and show them to belong to the educated and wealthy ruling class. Bartholomäus Sarburgh (born ca. 1590) successfully propagated not only in Basle but also among the patriciate of Berne this type of portrait, established in the Netherlands by Jan Antonisz. van Ravesteyn of The Hague, who is thought to have been his teacher. vR

186
Barfüsserkirche

Interior view of Basle Münster looking towards the chancel, dated 1650
Johann Sixt Ringle, Basle
Oil on canvas, 110 × 87 cm
Inv. no. 1906.3238. On deposit from the Evangelisch-Reformierter Kirchenrat Basel-Stadt

Such interior views of cathedral churches differ from those produced in the C17 by Netherlandish architectural painters in that their aim was documentary rather than artistic. They were commissioned, for example, by a synod (Augsburg) or were painted as a gift of the artist to the bishop (Bamberg). Although the actual occasion for this painting of 1650 is not known, the minute detail of its unsophisticated depiction of Basle Münster full of worshippers even in the side-aisles makes it an important pictorial document. The 'Häuptergestühle' or choir stalls for the city's authorities are seen in the foreground – the one preserved in the Museum on the left (no. 374) – with the council members in their proper seating order. On the left wall of the nave opposite the pulpit is the organ with wings painted by Hans Holbein in 1528 (now in the Kunstmuseum); the rood screen was demolished about 1850. The mayor, Johann Rudolf Wettstein, sitting in the Häuptergestühl, and the chief pastor, Theodor Zwinger, preaching, are two prominent personages shown present. vR

187
Barfüsserkirche

Portrait of the architect Jacob Meyer, dated 1654
Joseph Werner the Younger, Basle
Oil on copper, 30 × 24.5 cm
Inv. no. 1990.341. Purchase

With this small portrait of his Basle teacher Jacob Meyer the 17-year-old Berne painter Joseph Werner (1637–1710) gave early evidence of the talents that were to make him the first director of the Berlin Akademie der Künste und mechanischen Wissenschaften (academy of fine arts and mechanical sciences). The sitter taught mathematics and surveying from 1641 to 1659 at the Schule zu Barfüssern in Basle, and made a name for himself as a surveyor, cartographer, engraver and writer of textbooks. He left behind numerous plans and maps of the city of Basle and its surroundings, some also illustrated with elevated views of the town. In 1668 he was appointed to the important office of municipal paymaster, who supervised building. The plan in his right hand alludes to his involvement in the largest building project of the city since the Middle Ages, the enlargement, repair and maintenance of the fortifications in 1622–28. vR

188
Barfüsserkirche

Portrait of an unknown Basle woman
Basle, ca. 1680
Oil on canvas, 79.5 × 66.7 cm
Inv. no. 1990.344. Purchase

The Museum acquired this half-length portrait of a Basle woman, perhaps 30 years old, from the auction of the Vischer collection from Schloss Wildenstein in London in 1990. Probably it was once accompanied by a now lost pendant of her husband. The portrait is striking for the presence of the subject and her beauty, emphasized by the omission of the usual background accessories by the painter – perhaps Gregor Brandmüller, who was much in demand in Basle in the later C17. "La belle Baloise", as one might call her in imitation of Nicolas de Largillières's portrait, "La belle Strasbourgeoise" of 1703, is shown wearing the costume befitting her class, which was strictly controlled by sumptuary laws. Typical elements are the wide hat, called a "Schifflein" (little boat), commonly worn from about 1680 to 1700; the ample use of furs at the collar and sleeves – only marten was permitted, not sable – and the gold necklace with several strands. Comparisons enable the portrait to be dated about 1680. vR

189
Study collection

Page from the family record of the Basle goldsmith Johann Heinrich Schrotberger,
dated 1696
Entry by a member of the Blankenberg family, Cölln an der Spree, Berlin
Brush drawing over lead pencil, 11.2 × 17 cm
Inv. no. 1926.77. Purchase

Among the 30 or so family registers dating from the C16 to C18 in the Museum's collection are three rare journeyman's books. This one, made by the Basle journeyman goldsmith Johann Heinrich Schrotberger (1670–1748), contains entries by 22 friends and colleagues spread over the years 1694–1726. Most pages are adorned by a drawing and a dedication, and are particularly interesting as records of the goldsmith's contacts during his time in Berlin in 1694–98. These contacts included the journeyman goldsmith from Schaffhausen, Mattheus Schalch, the Zurich engraver Johann Melchior Fuesli, the Hamburg goldsmith Niclaus Jorden, the Berlin die-cutter Johann Sebastian Dattler, the painter Gregorius Schünemann, the Bremen journeyman goldsmith Johann Klump, the goldsmith Christian Fischer from Lindau and the Berlin goldsmith Otto Thiele. The drawing of a pipe-smoker is accompanied by a reference to a smoking and drinking club frequented at that time by the journeyman's circle. vR

190
Haus zum Kirschgarten

Quodlibet, dated 1716
Johann Rudolf Loutherburg, Basle
Oil on panel, 60.5 × 43.8 cm
Inv. no. 1935.20. Purchase

Among the many *quodlibets* (as you like it) or *trompe l'oeils* widespread in the C17 and C18 is the 'letter-board', a wooden surface fictively painted with stretched tapes to hold letters and newsletters. This example by a Basle painter shows a wall calendar in a black, ornately curved wooden frame with the current date, 15 May 1716. On the calendar page for the merry month can be seen a couple strolling in a Baroque garden. Attached to the board along with three letters and two newsletters is a calendar-diary of a kind widely used in Basle at the time and sometimes called a 'Rosius calendar' after its publisher, Jakob Rosius (1598–1676). The painter has signed the 12 May copy of the "Post- und Ordinari Nachrichten" with the words "Johann Rudolph Luterburg Basiliensis pinxit". Born in Basle in 1652 and dying there in 1727, he was the first of three generations of painters in this family, and worked primarily as a portrait painter. vR

191
Haus zum Kirschgarten

Portrait of the mathematician Johannes Bernoulli-Falkner I, dated 1725
G.(?) Stauder, Basle(?)
Oil on canvas, 92 × 75 cm
Inv. no. 1991.154. Legacy of Dr. h.c. Wilhelm Bernoulli-Preiswerk

Johann Bernoulli (1667–1748), from 1705 the leading mathematician on the Continent, appears in the pose of a Baroque ruler and is dressed in the court fashion. His science is evoked by the books and by the celestial globe in the background, an attribute which alludes to the ancient association of mathematics with astrology. For several generations the Bernoulli family, originating in Antwerp and settling in Basle in 1622, produced important scholars who attained renown especially in the mathematical sciences. The sitter taught mathematics at Basle University from 1705 and was a member of the academies in Paris, Berlin, London, Bologna and, from 1725 when the portrait was painted, St Petersburg. He was a successful protagonist of Leibniz's calculus, and with his brother worked on differential and integral mathematics. His collected works and his correspondence with Leibniz were published in 1742 and 1745. vR

192
Haus zum Kirschgarten

Landscape with ruins
Hubert Robert, Paris, ca. 1770
Oil on canvas, 137 × 156 cm
Inv. no. 1950.467.a. Gift of Sandoz AG

The celebrated landscape painter Hubert Robert (1733–1808) is represented in the Museum by two Roman paintings with ruins and pastoral staffage. They exemplify the aspiration of wealthy Basle families of the Ancien régime to participate in the contemporary style of Paris, which dictated fashions at that time. The works by this French painter trained by Piranesi reflect a reawakened interest in the buildings of Roman antiquity – one should also think of the Roman town of Augst near Basle in this connection. The contrasts cultivated in Robert's ruin paintings between dilapidated architecture and natural life also contain the idea of transience. The two paintings were ordered from the artist by the silk ribbon manufacturer Achilles Weiss-Ochs for his town residence in Basle, the Württembergerhof. His agent was the Basle engraver and art dealer Christian von Mechel, who was in contact with artists such as Fragonard, Van Loo and Boucher and helped to propagate the 'goût antique' in his own works. vR

193
Studiensammlung

Portrait of Philipp Matthäus Hahn
Johann Philipp Weisbrod, Kornwestheim, 1773
Pencil drawing, 12.6 × 11.5 cm
Inv. no. 1913.94.1. Alter Bestand

This small pencil drawing is the only known portrait of Philipp Matthäus Hahn (1739–1790), famous in his own lifetime as a pastor, astronomer, engineer and entrepreneur. All engravings, lithographs and oil paintings of the versatile inventor who lived from 1770 to 1781 in Kornwestheim near Stuttgart are based on this drawing. Weisbrod, a Ludwigsburg professor of art, succeeded in persuading Hahn to sit for him when Lavater needed a portrait for his *Physiognomic Fragments*. The subject himself records in his diary: "Weisbrod came to take my likeness for Lavater. I accepted this chalice of my own flesh in patience; I endured the sitting reluctantly". It is not known whether the drawing reached Basle through Lavater or through the Basle silk ribbon manufacturer Wilhelm Brenner. The latter ordered an astronomical longcase clock, also owned by the Museum (no. 318), from Hahn in 1775. vR

194
Haus zum Kirschgarten

Portrait of Peter Burckhardt-Forcart and family, dated 1775
J.J. Kaufmann, Basle
Oil on canvas, 76 × 108.7 cm
Inv. no. 1991.174. Dr. h.c. Wilhelm Bernoulli-Preiswerk bequest

Few images from the C18 record a Basle family in its domestic setting as vividly as this portrait of Peter and Anna Burckhardt-Forcart with their five children. The interior shows curtains and furniture, household utensils and crockery typical of the Louis XVI period. The spinet on the right even exactly matches a Basle instrument of 1775 in the Museum. The silk ribbon manufacturer Peter Burckhardt, later mayor and Swiss 'Landamman', was a member of wealthy Basle society. In a travel guide of 1782 he is mentioned among the 50 most prominent citizens of Basle. Although the painter has faithfully reproduced people and objects, the place cannot be determined with certainty. Some features suggest that the scene of the family idyll is not the family's town residence but their country seat at Maienfels in Pratteln. vR

195
Haus zum Kirschgarten

Portrait of Councillor Johann Jakob Thurneysen-Schweighauser, dated 1781
Anton Hickel, Basle
Oil on canvas, 120 × 89 cm
Inv. no. 1969.374. On deposit from Jean Alexandre Mendoza-Haug

The portrait, painted shortly before the end of the Ancien régime, is a representative image of the upper stratum of Basle's commercial aristocracy. It is at the same time a state portrait, commemorating the administration of the city by this group. The ribbon manufacturer Johann Jakob Thurneysen (1729–1784) was 'Sechser zu Gartnern' (guild official) in 1767, master of the same guild in 1771 and a council member in 1784. In 1768–70 he was director of the merchants' association and from 1777–83 he was in charge of the postal service – influential posts to which the ornate upper part of the frame, sumptuous by Basle standards, bears witness. The sitter wears the black habit prescribed for councillors, clerics and professors, with frilled ruff, lace cuffs, gloves and sword. A jewelled ring and furniture upholstered in silk damask are further attributes of his elevated status. The pretensions attached to the portrait are also expressed in the award of the commission to the Bohemian Anton Hickel, who painted princely and imperial subjects in Mannheim, Munich and Vienna. vR

196
Haus zum Kirschgarten

Shipwreck on a rocky coast, dated 1782
Jean Pillement, Basle
Pencil, chalk and opaque paint on paper; 72 × 105 cm
Inv. no. 1920.140. Gift of Carl Siebenmann

This large work drawn predominantly in pastel is one of four such overdoor landscapes produced probably in Basle in 1782. Two others are in the Kupferstichkabinett of the Öffentliche Kunstsammlung Basel. The Lyons painter's stay in Basle in 1786 is documented in a drawing by the Basle art collector Daniel Burckhardt-Wildt portraying the 58-year-old artist at work. Pillement, a landscape, marine, genre and flower painter but above all a designer of ornament and an engraver, had travelled throughout Europe; he was in Madrid and Lisbon about 1745, settled in London about 1750, worked at the imperial court in Vienna in 1763 and at the court in Warsaw in 1766, and finally became court painter to Marie Antoinette in Paris in 1778. In this work, in contrast to his pastoral landscapes in the manner of Boucher, he dramatically renders the natural violence of a storm at sea. vR

197
Haus zum Kirschgarten

Portrait of Johann Rudolf Burckhardt
Anton Graff, Basle, ca. 1795
Oil on canvas, 114.5 × 84 cm
Inv. no. 1976.175. Gift of M.J. von Wyss-Burckhardt and A. Feer-Burckhardt

J.R. Burckhardt (1750–1813) was by profession a silk ribbon manufacturer and from 1777 held the influential office of director of the merchants' association. Here, however, he appears as a private citizen. The statuette of Apollo and the books as attributes in the background recall the *Gedanken über den Stand eines Kaufmanns* (Thoughts on a merchant's station) by his Basle contemporary Jakob Sarasin, in which the merchant, too, is expected to have an understanding of the fine arts, "... for without them what use are knowledge of languages, grace and wit in life?" Burckhardt was a friend of Gessner, Lavater, Pestalozzi and Goethe. In Basle he has left his mark as an ambitious patron of architecture: his town residence, the Haus zum Kirschgarten (built 1775–80), is a high point of early Neoclassical secular architecture in the Upper Rhine region. In this portrait, Anton Graff justifies his high reputation as a portraitist and especially as a pioneer of the naturalistic portrait. vR

198
Haus zum Kirschgarten

Double portrait of Johann Peter Hebel and Elisabeth Baustlicher, dated 1814
Carl Joseph Alois Agricola, Karlsruhe
Brush drawing with body colour, 21.8 × 27.4 cm
Inv. no. 1953.436. Gift of Freiwilliger Museumsverein Basel

The miniature portrait, probably a study for a lithograph, shows the 54-year-old vernacular poet, theologian and educator in didactic discussion with the 19-year-old Elisabeth Baustlicher of Langendenzlingen. The newly built Catholic church of St. Stephan in the background locates the scene in Karlsruhe, where Hebel was director of the secondary school for girls from 1808. Hebel's parents, who came from the environs of Basle, were employed in the household of the Iselin family in the city. There the poet, orphaned at an early age, spent a part of his childhood. His *Alemanische Gedichte* (Alemannian poems), written in Baden dialect and published anonymously in 1803, induced one reviewer, Goethe, to predict a place for Hebel and his vernacular poetry on the German Parnassus. His contributions published in 1811 as the *Schatzkästlein des Rheinischen Hausfreundes* (The Rhineland lover's casket) were also celebrated and made Hebel popular far beyond the borders of his native country. vR

199
Haus zum Kirschgarten

Portrait of Johann Ludwig Burckhardt, called Sheik Ibrahim
Sebastian Gutzwiller, Basle, ca. 1830
Oil on canvas, 105.5 × 89 cm
Inv. no. 1947.221. Gift of Dr. Charlotte Burckhardt-Passavant

The sitter, in oriental dress, was a member of the well known Basle family of scholars. As the son of the builder of the Haus zum Kirschgarten he has a special relationship to the Museum building. Under the name Sheik Ibrahim, Johann Ludwig Burckhardt (1784–1817) travelled on behalf of the London African Society in Syria, Egypt and Nubia. He discovered the temple of Abu Simbel and the Jordanian rock-cut city of Petra. His accounts of his travels in the Middle East were published from 1819. He died of food poisoning aged 33 and is buried in Cairo. The posthumous honour bestowed on him in 1992, when the Queen of Jordan conferred an order on him, has recently drawn attention to his achievements in the land where he made his discoveries. vR

200
Haus zum Kirschgarten

Double portrait of Johannes and Wilhelm Leonhard Bernoulli as children
Giovanni Moriggia, Basle, ca. 1840
Oil on canvas, 86.5 × 70.2 cm
Inv. no. 1991.162. Legacy of Dr. h.c. Wilhelm Bernoulli

Several portraits in the collection document the work of the Italian painter from Caravaggio, Giovanni Moriggia (1796–1878), for the prominent Bernoulli, Merian and Sarasin families in 1836–40. The Bernoulli brothers pose as butterfly hunters, a popular motif at that time. Johannes (1826–1895), already in young man's dress, puts his arm protectively around Wilhelm Leonhard (1833–1919). A preparatory study for the careful treatment of the heads has been preserved. The swallowtail butterfly poised on the elder boy's hand in a snapshot effect cannot disguise the artifice of the pose. The brothers' interest in natural history goes beyond contemporary fashion, for the Bernoulli family's natural history collection had been an essential constituent of the Naturhistorisches Museum founded in 1830. Their father was the son of an apothecary and from 1840 owned the drugs, pharmaceuticals and paints firm of Geigy & Bernoulli, which soon became the leading drugs company in Switzerland and southern Germany. The firm was inherited and carried on by the subjects of this portrait. vR

201
Barfüsserkirche

View of the old French railway station in Basle, 1847
Signed G.L.
Oil on canvas, 56 × 75 cm
Inv. no. 1934.504. Purchase

The French railway line, having advanced as far as St Louis by 1839, began its service to Basle on 15 June 1844. Five trains ran daily between Strasbourg or Colmar and Basle. The view illustrates the fascination the epoch-making innovation exerted on contemporaries, one of whom reported: "The citizens of Basle and its surroundings frequently take advantage of the railway, especially on Sundays, and are finding much pleasure in it". The view from the city wall towards the north-west shows two trains, the covered platforms, and the station building of the Elsässerbahnhof, the completion of which in 1846/47 provided the occasion for the painting. As elsewhere, the decision to take the track inside the city walls had been preceded by heated debate in the city parliament, its supporters proclaiming the economic benefits and its opponents the danger of a decline in morals. vR

202
Barfüsserkirche

Poster for the Historisches Museum Basel, 1894/95
Design by Emil Beurmann; printed by Wassermann und Schäublin, Basle
Colour lithograph; height 101 cm, width 72 cm
Inv. no. 1990.588. Alter Bestand

On 21 April 1894 the Barfüsserkirche was officially opened as the main building of the Historisches Museum Basel. In the first year 13,000 tickets were sold, and on average 2000 visitors were counted on Sundays, when admission was free. The Museum's first poster does not focus on any particular object in the collection, but shows the public it aimed to attract, making a visit to the Museum into a social event. The eye is caught by a young lady accompanied by an older gentleman against a shadowy background of the nave of the Barfüsserkirche hung with flags. The contents of the museum are suggested symbolically by the heraldic colours, black and red, of the divided cantons of Basle-Stadt and Basel-Landschaft. More distinctly the 'Martinsreiter' (St Martin on horseback) from the façade of the Basle Münster (transferred to the Stadt- und Münstermuseum in 1939) can be made out. The poster indicates that the opening hours were from 8 am to 6 pm and that the cost of admission was 50 'Rappen'. The design, by the Basle artist Emil Beurmann (1862–1951), trained in Karlsruhe, Munich and at the Académie Julian in Paris, and strongly influenced by cosmopolitan Parisian taste, is in an avantgarde style and aimed at an international public. vR

Stained glass

Stained glass is a branch of art which in Switzerland has national importance; the city of Basle was not only formerly a flourishing centre of display glass, but also still has *in situ* a considerable amount of religious and secular stained glass from more modern times (ca. 1830–1930). Therefore stained glass is a field of particular interest to the Historisches Museum. In 1901 a complete catalogue of the Museum's 220 stained-glass items – a considerable holding already at that date – was published. In the intervening time the Museum has amassed about 600 glass-paintings and fragments of windows from a period covering eight centuries, more than a third of which have been incorporated into the permanent exhibition in the Barfüsserkirche.

The Museum's glass can be divided into four main categories: ecclesiastical stained glass from the C13 to the C16; display glass consisting predominantly of secular panels, beginning in the pre-Reformation period, very well represented for the C16 and C17, and including examples of the resurgence of the genre in Basle from about 1830; the large homogeneous group of 107 newly made armorial panels donated by Basle families on the occasion of the opening of the Museum in 1894; and finally a fourth group of 100 specimen panels produced by apprentice glass-painters and copies made in the C19 and early C20 (from Königsfelden, Freiburg in Breisgau, Eichstätt, Tiefenbronn), which were taken over from the Gewerbemuseum (arts and crafts museum) in 1989 – these, on long-term loan to the Musée Suisse du Vitrail in Romont, are useful for research into questions relating to craft techniques and conservation.

Among the early items are fragments from large-scale ecclesiastical stained-glass programmes not made in Basle, including two roundels from Chartres cathedral (C13; no. 203), two windows from the pilgrimage church in Bourguillon/Fribourg im Uechtland (C15; no. 205), parts of a window from St. Leonhard in Murau, Styria (ca. 1440) and infill panels for the tracery of the chapterhouse of the Constance Münster (ca. 1480; no. 207). Unfortunately, since the choir windows of the Barfüsserkirche were draped over in 1990 to protect objects on display from excessive light, the eight large stained-glass figures of about 1520 from the Charterhouse in Freiburg in Breisgau purchased from the Douglas stained glass collection (no. 217) are among items that it is no longer possible to exhibit permanently.

The secular stained glass, closely connected with the custom prevalent in Switzerland of donating windows and panels, represents the major part of the collection. These small glass pictures were intended to be viewed at close quarters; they were used to furnish castles, town halls, guildhalls, shooting-club houses and private living rooms, and consequently come in the form of official glass, glass relating to guilds and societies, and glass bearing the coats of arms of the principal families of the city. Special attention should be drawn to early examples such as the Zug panel from the council chamber in Baden (ca. 1501; no. 210), four windows from the Late Gothic town hall of Basle (1514; no. 213) or the armorial panel of the abbot of Murbach from the Dominican convent in Basle (1520; no. 215). About 100 items in the collection can be attributed to Basle masters from the period between 1550 and 1650, a flourishing era when 55 glaziers and glass-painters can be shown to have been working in the town. Individual items in the collection prove that the genre was at a peak in Basle in the C16, influenced by Hans Holbein the Younger, and underwent a remarkable resurgence in the early C19 in the person of the glass-painter Hieronymus Hess.

The collection is completed by drawings and designs for windows in the Museum's graphic art department. vR

203
Barfüsserkirche

Majestas Domini from Chartres Cathedral
France, 1st half 13th century
Diameter 82 cm
Inv. no. 1978.222. Gift of the Regierung Kanton Basel-Stadt

The stained glass collection of the Historisches Museum was enormously enriched by the purchase in 1978 of two Gothic roundels of French origin. Both were originally fragments of a window in Chartres cathedral which has now disappeared. They owe their round shape to modern additions. While one of them depicts the Easter scene described in St John's Gospel, Sts Peter, John and Mary Magdalene at the tomb of the risen Christ, the other shows a 'Majestas Domini': Christ accompanied by two angels sits enthroned as the ruler of the world holding a cross and an orb in a mandorla. Elements of modelling are introduced in black over the coloured panes, which are held together with strips of lead. AN

204
Barfüsserkirche

Christ Pantokrator, from the church of Nendaz
Switzerland, ca. 1300
Height 62 cm, width 67 cm
Inv. no. 1881.87. Gift of Eugen Rüsch

The trefoil window with Christ enthroned as the Pantokrator from Nendaz parish church in the Valais region is one of the few surviving pieces documenting Swiss glass-painting in the C13. Originally serving as infill in tracery, the glass found its way into the Historisches Museum from the Bürki collection in Berne, which was auctioned in 1880; the town of Solothurn bought two lancet window panels depicting bishops by the same artist and from the same source. In front of an uncoloured ground with foliate decoration, Christ sits in a strictly frontal position with His arms outspread showing the wounds in His hands. Originally the Redeemer was flanked in a Deesis group by the Virgin Mary and John the Baptist, interceding in adjacent panels now lost. Comparison with contemporary glass-paintings such as the *Madonna enthroned* in the monastery of Wettingen highlights the provincial character of this piece, which must have been the work of a local artist. AN

205
Barfüsserkirche

The Death of Mary, from Notre-Dame-de-la-Visitation, Bourguillon
Attributed to Michel Glaser, mid–15th century
Height 149 cm, width 76.5 cm
Inv. no. 1888.43.a. Purchase

The museum has two tall rectangular windows from the lepers' and pilgrims' church of Notre-Dame in Bourguillon near Fribourg, one depicting *The Crucifixion* and this one *The Death of Mary* or 'Dormition'. Like its counterpart, the scene is framed by a Gothic canopy. In the lower half of the picture the twelve Apostles surround the Virgin's death-bed in sorrow and devotion; in the upper zone Christ, hovering encircled by a nimbus of angels, receives the soul of Mary in the form of a child. Stylistic links to panel paintings and prints from the Upper Rhine, the sculptural conception of the figures, the expressive heads and the style of the drapery indicating the influence of Konrad Witz's workshop in Basle – these elements suggest the attribution to Michel Glaser, a glass-painter from Basle whose presence in Fribourg is documented. AN

206
Barfüsserkirche

***St Christopher*, from Läufelfingen church**
Basle, ca. 1470
Height 59 cm, width 41 cm
Inv. no. 1881.77. Purchase

The St Christopher panel, created by an unknown master ca. 1470, is a choice example of stained glass from Basle in the Late Gothic period. It came into the possession of the Historisches Museum from a private collection as early as 1881. In its original location in Läufelfingen church in the upper Basle region this window representing the patron saint of travellers presented an opportunity for prayer before ascending the Jura pass over the Hauenstein. Brilliant, contrasting colours and a formal vocabulary derived from contemporary prints are significant features. The red cloak tossed about by the storm contrasts with the calm determination of the colossal saint as he tries to reach the safety of the bank under the ever increasing burden of the Christchild. AN

207
Barfüsserkirche

***Angel with a monochord*, from the chapterhouse of the Münster, Constance**
Workshop of Peter Hemmel von Andlau, Strasbourg, ca. 1480
Height 62 cm, width 36 cm
Inv. no. 1891.106. Purchase

The two curved tracery infill panels with musician angels which the Museum bought in 1891 from the Vincent collection were once part of the splendid stained-glass decoration of the so called chapterhouse used as the cathedral library in the Münster of Constance. In 1480 the room was furnished with a cycle of 81 glass panels made by the Strasbourg workshop of Peter Hemmel. The Hemmel workshop, founded in 1477, had demonstrated its capabilities by providing stained glass for the Stiftskirche in Tübingen, the Marienkirche in Salzburg, the Münster in Ulm, the Liebfrauenkirche in Munich and elsewhere. The angel in a carmine-red dalmatic surrounded by dense foliage bows the string of a monochord, accompanying the angel playing an organ in another tracery panel. AN

208
Barfüsserkirche

Armorial panel of Johannes Gebwiler, dated 1497
Upper Rhine region
Height 45 cm, width 32 cm
Inv. no. 1958.19. On deposit from Dr A.L. Vischer von Bonstetten

The subject of the glass-painting, which according to the inscription was donated by Magister Johannes Gebwiler, is St Jerome: he was venerated as the patron saint of teachers, theologians and universities. Gebwiler came from Colmar and was educated as a theologian at Basle and Freiburg in Breisgau; nothing is known of his career in the last two decades of the C15, but in 1507 he became a canon at St. Peter in Basle. His academic career as a professor of theology, dean and three times rector at Basle University came to an end in 1523 because of his opposition to the Reformation. The repentant St Jerome with the features of a young monk is kneeling in his undergarment, having laid aside his red cardinal's robe, in front of the entrance to his cave, beating his breast with stones as he is tormented by temptations. In their present form his constant companion, the lion, and the coat of arms beneath it are later additions. Between the rocks the view opens out on to the landscape with a town in the background. The donor himself is depicted as a canon, recognisable by his fur, at the bottom left by the pedestal of the framing Gothic arch. AN

209
Barfüsserkirche

Armorial panel of the Counts of Thierstein
Basle, ca. 1500
Height 47 cm, width 32 cm
Inv. no. 1947.17. On deposit from the Gottfried Keller-Stiftung

This well preserved glass-painting displays the coat of arms of the old Thierstein dynasty from the Upper Rhine in front of a light damascene background surrounded by an arch of filigree acanthus leaves. The helm of the Pfeffingen branch of the family, a female torso with a crown and a pair of antlers adorned with roses, surmounts the escutcheon of a red hind on a triple peak. This powerful noble family had a final period of glory in the reign of Graf Oswald I of Thierstein who as Austrian 'Landvogt' in Alsace, Sundgau and Breisgau held the office of imperial councillor. In 1480 Oswald I transferred the family seat from Pfeffingen to Haut-Koenigsbourg which had been granted to him as an imperial fief by Emperor Frederick III. The family died out in 1519 on the death of his son Henry, the putative donor of this panel, whose possessions were divided between the cities of Basle and Solothurn and the bishop of Basle. AN

210
Barfüsserkirche

Armorial panel of Zug from the council chamber at Baden
Lukas Zeiner, Zurich, 1500–01
Height 50 cm, width 35 cm
Inv. no. 1870.1272. Purchase

The panel of Zug belongs to a cycle of armorial panels conceived as a whole and presented by the ten Confederated states at the instance of Baden town council to furnish the council chamber at Baden (canton of Aargau) in 1500. All the panels have been preserved. The states commissioned Lukas Zeiner, an important stained-glass artist from Zurich, to undertake the task. The Baden series of panels is an early example of the custom, widespread in Switzerland from the C15, of donating windows and coats of arms as an expression of political unity. The Zug panel is typical of the kind of glass Zeiner made, following a compositional schema which was extremely common in official C16th stained glass. Beneath a framing arch with figures in the spandrels – here wildmen – two shield-bearers are standing in front of a red damask background in the attitude of Confederates confident of themselves and of victory. They flank a pyramid formed by coats of arms, the Zug coat of arms, the imperial coat of arms and above them the German crown, and carry two Zug banners, the one on the left showing St Oswald, the patron saint of Zug. AN

211
Barfüsserkirche

St Gotman, dated 1508
Basle
Height 72 cm, width 50 cm
Inv. no. 1870.1277. Gift of E.E. Zunft zu Schneidern

Basle's medieval guilds were originally not just craft associations, but religious brotherhoods too, with charitable and welfare responsibilities. The so called spiritual guilds had close links with the city's churches; thus the altar of the confraternity of tailors and furriers had been in the Spitalkirche since 1352. The alms-giving St Homobonus on the display panel of the Basle tailors' guild embodies the economic morality and lay piety of the guild brothers. His German name of Gotman (Goodman) is here attested for the first time. The cult of the pious 'good man' from Cremona who according to legend had been a well-to-do tailor and cloth merchant was confined to the area of Lombardy and Venice until the beginning of the C16, when it reached Basle through the Cremona trade in fustian cloth. The Basle tailors' guild soon adopted him as their patron saint. AN

212
Barfüsserkirche

Armorial panel of Basle
Basle, 1512/20
Height 46 cm, width 32 cm
Inv. no. 1904.328. On deposit from the Schweizerische Gesellschaft für die Erhaltung historischer Kunstdenkmäler

The proliferation in the late Middle Ages of legends involving the basilisk in the foundation of the city of Basle resulted in the inclusion of the fabulous beast, part cock part snake, among the more established bearers of its escutcheon: the angel, the lion and the wildman. The unknown Basle stained-glass artist who created this panel succeeded in giving a striking picture of these fabulous creatures, feared for their poison-emitting beaks and their deadly stare. The basilisks hold not only the city coat of arms but also the banner of honour awarded to each of the Confederate councils in 1512 by Pope Julius II in gratitude for the conquest of Pavia – the gold-fringed 'Julius banner' which carries in its upper-left corner a representation of the Annunciation (see no. 238). The figures in the spandrel illustrate an element of the legend of the foundation of Basle: an armed man holds a mirror up to the basilisk so that the monster will succumb to its own annihilating stare. AN

213
Barfüsserkirche

Armorial panel of Basle with associated panel above from the Basle town hall,
dated 1514
Basle
Height 50.5 cm, width 49 cm; height 24 cm, width 55 cm
Inv. no. 1925.62. Purchase
Inv. no. 1925.179. Gift of Dr. R.F. Burckhardt

The armorial panel with angels and the richly figured panel above it were originally part of a set of four panels, of which the remainder are now lost, made for the small council room at the rear of Basle town hall by a Basle glass-painter in 1514. The main picture, which was completed by columns or pilasters on each side, depicts two angels splendidly dressed as deacons with the escutcheon of the episcopal city. The top panel, painted in grisaille with black and silver stain, relates the legend of Herkinbald, which Rogier van der Weyden had earlier illustrated in his picture cycle for the council chamber of Brussels town hall. Like the fresco cycle by Hans Holbein the Younger in the great council chamber in Basle, painted after 1521, the top panels were exemplary illustrations of justice of the type commonly found in council chambers and courtrooms in the Middle Ages. The writing on the curlicued Gothic banner contains the first of four maxims: "von dem recht nit wich" (do not deviate from justice). The others read: "richt glich arm und rich" (judge rich and poor equally), "bisz nit ze fast grim" (be not too severe) and "hör auch des andre stim" (listen to the other's point of view). AN

214

Barfüsserkirche

Armorial panel of Basle with the Virgin, dated 1519
Basle
Height 60.5 cm, width 35.5 cm
Inv. no. 1930.93. Gift of the Basler Kunstverein

Early Renaissance glass painting in Basle received powerful and lasting inspiration from Hans Holbein the Younger, who settled in the city in 1519: his drawings for glass panels were used as cartoons and frequently copied by Basle artists in the C16. The armorial panel of Basle with the haloed Madonna is redolent of the influence of Holbein in composition, draughtsmanship and colouring. Many motifs such as the powerfully articulated baluster columns, the arch of foliage springing from them, the putti romping amidst flowers and leaves and the escutcheon of Basle in the form of a shield are parallelled in the prints and drawings produced by Holbein at the same period. The self-absorbed Queen of Heaven with her divine son, an extremely tender and lovely figure, is similar to the Brunswick Madonna of 1520. The glass, which is believed to come from a country church in the canton of Berne, came into the hands of the Basle Kunstverein from a private collection; in 1882 they made it available to the Museum for display, and in 1930 presented it to the Museum. AN

215

Barfüsserkirche

Armorial panel of Georg von Massmünster, dated 1520
Basle
Height 61.5 cm, width 53 cm
Inv. no. 1935.479. Purchased with the assistance of the Gottfried Keller-Stiftung

The armorial panel of Georg von Massmünster is the only surviving glass-painting of the series of four panels executed after designs by Hans Holbein the Younger which were donated for the newly built refectory of the Dominican convent of St. Maria Magdalena an den Steinen in Basle, probably in 1520. An expansive Renaissance-style architectural backdrop, enlivened by putti dancing and making music, frames the donor's coat of arms. The lunette frieze below the coffered barrel vaulting depicts a triumphal procession. The quartered escutcheon with a mitre and two abbot's staffs above shows the coat of arms of the von Massmünster family along with the rampant dog of the monastery of Murbach in Upper Alsace and the blessing hand of Lure Abbey; Georg von Massmünster had been abbot of both monasteries since 1513. AN

216
Barfüsserkirche

Armorial panel of the town of Breisach,
dated 1521
Upper Rhine
Height 42 cm, width 31 cm
Inv. no. 1923.246. On deposit from the Gottfried Keller-Stiftung

The armorial panel of Breisach depicts the brothers St Gervasius and St Protasius whose bones had supposedly been brought to Breisach on the Upper Rhine from Milan in 1162 by Rainald von Dassel, archbishop of Cologne and chancellor to Emperor Frederick I. Veneration of the brothers as patron saints of Breisach reached a peak towards the end of the Middle Ages, and a large number of images of them were created in the region. Like the figures on the high altar of Breisach Münster executed a few years later by Master H.L., the saints are represented in princely attire holding the implements indicating their martyrs' death, the scourge and the sword. There is an unmistakable stylistic link with drawings by Hans Baldung Grien, who worked in Strasbourg and Freiburg in Breisgau. The picture above with a cheerful bathing and fishing scene also reveals his influence. AN

217
Study collection

***Our Lady of Sorrows*, from the Charterhouse, Freiburg in Breisgau**
Ropstein workshop, Freiburg in Breisgau, 1st quarter 16th century
Height 146.5 cm, width 54.5 cm
Inv. no. 1901.270. Purchase

The Mater Dolorosa is one of the set of 25 large figure panels of which eight were purchased for Basle at the spectacular auction of the Graf Douglas stained glass collection in 1897. When it was dissolved in 1782, the cycle made for the Charterhouse in Freiburg in Breisgau about 1520 was reused in the newly built early Neoclassical church of the Benedictine abbey of St. Blasien in the Black Forest. The transfer of the Late Gothic stained-glass windows, subsequently supplemented by other appropriate contemporary pieces, represents a unique example of the return to religious use of large-scale ecclesiastical stained glass in the C18. Our Lady of Sorrows, wrapped in a blue cloak and with a countenance expressive of grief, was presumably the counterpart of an Ecce Homo. The grape-vine forming an arch above her head also points, as a symbol of the Eucharist, to the death of Christ. The donor figure at her feet has hitherto been taken to be Canon Johann Wanner from Constance. AN

218
Barfüsserkirche

***Charity*, from the Niklaus Chapel, St. Peter, Basle**
Ascribed to David Joris, Basle, ca. 1545
Monopartite panel, diameter 20 cm
Inv. no. 1905.498. Valerie Socin bequest

It is difficult to fit the series of small roundels of the Christian virtues, originally seven but now six, which according to oral tradition came from the Niklaus chapel in the Basle canonical foundation of St. Peter, into the Basle tradition of glass-painting of the post-Reformation period. The style of the roundels, painted in soft black and silver stain, is Netherlandish. An attribution to David Joris, a glass-painter from Delft who lived in Basle from 1544, has therefore been suggested. The personification of Love, with Latin ("Charitas") and Dutch ("liefde") identifications beside her, stands dressed in a lavish robe in front of a broad river landscape. She is carrying the nest of a pelican which feeds its young with its own blood, a common symbol also of the sacrificial death of Christ. AN

219
Study collection

Standard-bearer of the Zunft zu Webern
(weavers' guild), dated 1560
Attributed to Ludwig Ringler, Basle
Height 102.5 cm, width 54.5 cm
Inv. no. 1894.64. On deposit from E.E. Zunft zu Webern

The large panel with the gonfalonier of the Basle guild of wool and linen weavers is a superb example of Basle glass-painting from the second half of the C16. Though unsigned, the work is assigned to the important Basle glass-painter Ludwig Ringler on the grounds of style. It was donated in 1560 for the renovated guildhall by the members of the guild committee. Since 1989 the Museum has also been in possession of the full-size cartoon, showing the panel, which has been cut down on the shorter sides, as it was originally designed. The representation of the splendidly attired and armed standard-bearer in a confident, victorious pose before the field of battle evokes the glorious period around 1500 when the citizens marched into battle under their guild banners. The battle scene, delicately painted in silver, the landscape and the busy and rather flat architecture of the frame reveal the influence of Netherlandish Mannerism. AN

220
Study collection

Basle troops marching out through the Spalentor
Basle, 2nd half 16th century
Height 15 cm, width 38.5 cm
Inv. no. 1895.69. Gift of the heirs of Sensal Buxtorf

Originally set above a glass-painting that is now missing, this small stained-glass picture, delicately painted in silver stain and black, depicts Basle troops marching out through the Spalentor. Fired by the fanfare blasts of the town trumpeter, the infantry leave the town in their armour with halberds, crossbows and pikes, led by a standard-bearer and a vanguard of armed horsemen. The detailed reproduction of the external façade of the city gate with the date of building shown as 1398 and of its rich sculptural decoration (including a Madonna flanked by two Prophets; see no. 143) makes the fragment an important early source for architectural research. While the soldiers' armour and weapons and the absence of the buildings that were added in front of the gate in 1474 suggest an early dating, the year 1510 displayed on a banner, alluding to the Chiasso campaign, and the style of the painting indicate the second half of the C16. Probably a picture dating from the mid-C15 was used as a model for the historicising scene. AN

221
Study collection

Armorial panel of Andreas Ryff and Daniel Burckhardt, dated 1595
Attributed to Jakob Plepp, Basle
Height 55 cm, width 37.5 cm
Inv. no. 1991.257. On deposit from Pierre Chiesa-Burckhardt

After his successful mediation in the 1594 rebellion of the subjects of the Basle region, thereby bringing the so called 'Rappenkrieg' to a peaceful end, the name of Andreas Ryff (1550–1603) was bound to go down in history. This panel with the coats of arms of Andreas Ryff and his son-in-law Daniel Burckhardt dated 1595 already records his diplomatic mission. The upper part of the picture shows the memorable meeting between the town's delegates and the peasants under the leadership of Hans Siegrist on the meadow before Schloss Wildenstein. An oval medallion forms the centre of the panel, depicting a crane holding a stone as a symbol of watchfulness and bearing the motto: "Trotz Hochmut und Rebellion / Macht gutte Policey zergon" (Good policy makes disappear defiance, haughtiness and rebellion). The allegories of Rebellion, War, Conciliation and Peace, symbolizing the course of events, accompany the central cartouche and coats of arms. AN

222
Barfüsserkirche

The ropemakers' banquet, dated 1615
Attributed to Hieronymus Vischer, Basle
Height 55.5 cm, width 56 cm
Inv. no. 1901.42. On deposit from the E.E. Zunft zu Gartnern

Every Basle guild had a drinking-room in its guildhall which was specially provided for festive occasions and convivial gatherings of guild brothers and their fellow tradesmen. From the C16, drinking and eating round the table became a popular theme in stained glass, especially in panels made for guilds and societies. This panel dated 1615 provides a glimpse into the drinking-room of the Zunfthaus zu Gartnern, showing 14 rope-makers belonging to the corporation in traditional Swiss dress with feathers in their hats and with Swiss daggers sitting round a lavishly decked table. Beneath the main scene are the 14 coats of arms of the donors; two herm figures appear at the sides. Above there is a picture in grisaille, showing a rope-making workshop: exhaustively illustrating its progress from the breaking of the hemp to the twisting of the rope, it is an important pictorial source for the history of the craft. AN

223
Barfüsserkirche

Armorial panel of Johann Konrad von Roggenbach, dated 1660
Wolfgang Spengler, Constance
Height 45 cm, width 42 cm
Inv. no. 1877.9. Purchase

The armorial panel, a signed work by the Constance glass-painter Wolfgang Spengler dated 1660, has been broken several times and is criss-crossed by repairs in lead. It commemorates Johann Konrad von Roggenbach, Prince Bishop of Basle (1656–93). Roggenbach was very active politically and in the Counter-Reformation, and his tenure of office meant for his bishopric a period of peace and reconstruction after the devastation caused by the Thirty Years' War. Besides founding several monasteries in Pruntrut where he had his official residence, in 1681 Roggenbach consecrated the new cathedral church of the diocese, financed by himself, in Arlesheim; the cathedral chapter had returned there from exile in Freiburg-im-Breisgau in 1678. The Madonna as the patron saint of Basle appears above the armorial cartouche decorated with an infula, a sword and a bishop's staff. The founder of Basle Münster, Emperor Henry II, and St Pantalus, a legendary bishop and patron saint of the bishopric of Basle, stand on either side of the escutcheon. AN

224
Study collection

Detail of the bird's-eye view of the city of Basle, from the inner council chamber of Basle town hall
Basle, 1663/64
Monopartite panel, height 36 cm, width 39 cm
Inv. no. 1870.1290

In 1663 the mayors Niklaus Rippel and Rudolf Wettstein and the master guildsmen Benedict Socin and Andreas Burckhardt commissioned a monopartite glass painting after the bird's-eye-view plan of the city of Basle made by Matthäus Merian in 1642. The city, depicted in a warm grey colour, is seen from the north. The section illustrated here shows the area adjoining the inner city wall formerly occupied by the convent of the Barfüsserkirche, the upkeep of which had been the responsibility of the neighbouring hospital (marked 12) since the Reformation. Although in the C17 the nave of the Barfüsserkirche continued to be used for worship, the choir was used as a grain store and the city mental asylum and alms office were housed in the cloister and other former convent buildings. The convent of St. Maria-Magdalena an den Steinen (10), located just outside the city walls, had also been secularised and was at that time uninhabited. AN

225
Barfüsserkirche

Titus Manlius
End 17th/beginning 18th century
Monopartite panel, height 37 cm, width 24.5 cm
Inv. no. 1971.226. Alter Bestand

The Museum owns four tall rectangular monopartite panels depicting Roman heroes after a series of copper engravings published by the Dutch artist Hendrick Goltzius (1558–1617) in 1586. The figure of the horseman Titus Manlius viewed from behind and from below is placed in the immediate foreground and occupies the whole surface of the picture. The vigorous muscular bodies and the sculptural depiction of their anatomy dominate the picture. In the middle distance the basis of the hero's legendary fame, his victorious duel on horseback, is reproduced on a small scale in the landscape almost as an attribute. AN

226
Study collection

Allegory of Transience, dated 1731
Johann Rudolf Huber(?), Basle
Monopartite panel, height 14.5 cm, width 14.5 cm
Inv. no. 1888.95. Purchase

The small octagonal panel shows Chronos, the personification of Time, as an old bearded man with his most usual attribute, the scythe, and with wings. He holds a cloak marked with the numbers and the lines of the hours (as on a sundial) spread out in front of him to conceal the nakedness of his body; death in the form of a skeleton peeps out from behind it. Two designs by Johann Rudolf Huber (1668–1748) for a sundial which are close to the glass-painting suggest that this panel is also his work, and that he was a glass-painter as well as a painter. However, the illogical arrangement of the numbers in the panel rules out its use as a glass sundial. The main message of the glass-painting is that of vanitas, the triumph of time and death over life: the inscription reads, "die Zeit get hin / här kombt der Tod / O Mensch betrachts / und ferchte Gott. / 1731." (Time goes by / death draws near / Oh man take note / and fear God). AN

227
Haus zum Kirschgarten

Memorial panel for Matthäus Merian
Designed by Hieronymus Hess, Basle, 1849; executed by Ferdinand Beck, Schaffhausen, 1852
Height 77 cm, width 47 cm
Inv. no. 1981.28. Purchase

In 1849 Eduard Merian-Bischoff had four glass-paintings commemorating illustrious members of his family made for his newly built neo-Gothic castle of Teufen in the canton of Zurich. No less a person than the Basle history painter Hieronymus Hess who had contributed substantially to the revival of glass-painting in Basle since 1833 designed the memorial panels. The final picture in the series shows the most distinguished of these ancestors, the engraver and art critic Matthäus Merian the Elder, who died in 1650. He is shown in his studio, surrounded by three of his children who were also practising artists. The portrait medallions in the framing pillars testify to Hess's personal admiration for the landscape painter Gaspard Poussin and his own teacher, Joseph Anton Koch. AN

228
Study collection

Armorial panel of the Drei Ehrengesellschaften Kleinbasels (three honourable societies of Kleinbasel), dated 1854
Adolf Mieg, Basle
Height 71 cm, width 60.5 cm
Inv. no. 1964.21. On deposit from the Drei Ehrengesellschaften

From 1841 the three 'honourable societies' of Kleinbasel, 'zum Rebhaus', 'zur Hären' and 'zum Greifen', historic associations which carried out mainly political and economic functions (see also no. 281), owned a joint club house on the right bank of the Rhine by the bridgehead. There was a banquetting room on the first floor of this late Neoclassical building constructed to designs by the city surveyor, Amadeus Merian, and this glass-painting was part of the original decor. The glass-painter Adolf Mieg arranged the honorary symbols of the corporations, the lion (Rebhaus), the wildman (Hären) and the griffin (Greifen), who took part in the 'Vogel Gryff' procession held in Kleinbasel at the beginning of each year, in a harmonious group beneath a trefoil arch. The slender trellis frame is reminiscent of the Byzantine-Moorish façade of the new building designed by Merian, and the panorama shown through a triple arcade entwined with a vine keeps more or less to the view which could be seen through the window of their banquetting room by the members of the societies sitting at their table. AN

229
Barfüsserkirche

Armorial panel of the von Bärenfels family
Basle or Winterthur, ca. 1895
Height 87 cm, width 58 cm
Inv. no. 1979.115. Alter Bestand

The opening of the Historisches Museum in the Barfüsserkirche in 1894 gave many Basle families an opportunity to express their support by donating a stained-glass panel. More than a hundred armorial panels were made by the Basle glass-painters Franz Joseph Merzenich and Heinrich Drenckhahn and the Meyner & Booser glass-painting studio in Winterthur between 1893 and 1897. Originally they decorated the choir windows of the Barfüsserkirche, but when the Museum was renovated in 1980 the 107 armorial pictures were placed in the south and west windows of the nave, arranged according to the year in which the donors' families obtained citizenship. The heraldic panel of the von Bärenfels family, who had been settled in Basle since about 1294, opens the series. In composition and in the details of the helmet, it imitates the armorial panel of Adelberg von Bärenfels dated 1533 in the town hall at Rheinfelden. AN

230
Study collection

Armorial panel of the Forcart-Bachofens, dated 1899
W.V., Basle
Height 59 cm, width 47.5 cm
Inv. no. 1990.562. Dr. Lothar Forcart-Müller bequest

The historicist armorial panel shows the young married couple Rudolf and Anita Forcart-Bachofen dressed in Renaissance costume, respectively as a warrior and a fashionable lady, acting as standard-bearers and supporters of the escutcheons; the artist signing himself with the monogram W.V. thus created a glass-painting reminiscent in composition and style of the civic armorial panels common in the C16. The portraits of the couple who commissioned the work, painted after photographs, are typical of this type of late C19th panel. In the pictures at the top above the framing candelabra-like columns, one can recognise Basle Münster and the building site of the villa in neo-Renaissance style which Rudolf Forcart had built for himself on St. Jakobs-Strasse in 1898 by the architects Vischer & Fueter. AN

Textiles

The fifteen tapestries and three smaller fragments of tapestries from the C15 in the Historisches Museum Basel count among its most precious possessions, because not only are they rare, but also they are of very high artistic quality and excellent condition. Of these wall-hangings, antependiums, cushion-covers and fragments 16 were made in Basle; two originated in Strasbourg. The Basle tapestries have a characteristic imagery, peculiar to the city, of a secular realm peopled by wildmen, fabulous beasts and idealised courtly lovers, embodying allegorical messages of virtue and passion. Three tapestries show religious scenes, from the life of Christ. All of them, including several from the early C16, are exhibited in the Barfüsserkirche.

The Museum holds important examples of embroidery in coloured wool or silk worked in Basle or elsewhere in Switzerland during the C16 and C17; these are exhibited in the historical rooms of the Barfüsserkirche. The three large pieces embroidered in white on white that are on permanent exhibition represent a larger collection of figurative linen embroidery from eastern Switzerland. Special mention must be made of an early example, a C14th tablecloth from the monastery of Feldbach (canton of Thurgau), and of several C16th embroideries with imagery deriving from contemporary bible illustrations or drawn from folklore. These, and a wealth of other items in the collection, can be seen for study purposes by appointment – including both European and non-European silks from the C12 to the C14, recovered from graves in the Basle Münster or preserved as part of the liturgical apparatus of churches.

The silk ribbon industry, which was the mainspring of Basle's economic prosperity in the C18 and C19, is represented in the Museum by the archives of three firms that have since closed down and by a great deal of other material from the C18 to the C20. About 900 pattern books, each with several hundred samples, around 6000 designs, more than 1500 ribbons and about 1600 textbooks, handbooks, documents, manuscripts and sample cards are preserved in the Basler Seidenband collection, established in 1981. It can be visited by appointment. Three Swiss firms that produce decorative ribbons today annually deposit their latest creations in the Museum, in order to keep the permanent display in the Barfüsserkirche, arranged around a preserved silk ribbon loom of 1776 (no. 244), up to date.

The textile holdings of the Basle Gewerbemuseum (now Museum für Gestaltung), which constitutes a separate study collection, consists of more than 5000 items, accumulated since the end of the C19. It is a good, well maintained collection spanning from the Middle Ages to modern times, and including particular items of outstanding quality and provenance (the Iklé collection, the Meyer am Rhyn collection). IPM

231
Barfüsserkirche

The Sion tapestry (detail)
Northern Italy(?), 14th century
Linen, block printed with black and red, height 106 cm, width 264 cm
Inv. no. 1897.48. Purchase

This fragment of a wall-hanging found its way into the specialist literature in 1857 as the 'Sittener Tapete' (tapestry from Sion). It is one of the most striking printed textiles of the C14, and no comparable work is known. Despite its frequent discussion, it has not been possible to establish either the place of its manufacture or its provenance. The tradition that it decorated a room in the episcopal palace in Sion (canton of Valais) has not been authenticated. Two further fragments, one in the Schweizerisches Landesmuseum in Zurich, the other in the Historisches Museum in Berne, exist but they are small and provide no additional information. The scenes are arranged in three registers: in the upper band a frieze of men and women dance hand in hand; in the middle groups of Christian knights are fired upon by oriental archers; the scenes in the lower band are unconventional interpretations of the Oedipus legend with identifying inscriptions. IPM

232
Barfüsserkirche

***Six lords and ladies with fabulous beasts*, fragment of a wall-hanging**
Basle, ca. 1410/20
Wool tapestry, three pieces, of height 70 cm, width 207 cm; height 77.5 cm, width 206 cm; height 75 cm, width 75.5 cm; original overall length ca. 630 cm
Inv. no. 1880.61. Auguste Quiquerez collection

The survival of this tapestry is due to the historian Auguste Quiquerez, who discovered the three fragments in 1880 on the wagon of a roadworker in the canton of Jura. Against a dark background interwoven with magical, blue-blossoming periwinkle, gentle human figures are dramatically juxtaposed with menacing monsters. These are led on chains attached to lavishly decorated collars by the slender youths and maidens in courtly dress. The magical powers of the sprays of blossom enable the couples to subdue the ferocity of the fabulous beasts. The theme of the taming of savage nature by courtly manners recurs in various forms in tapestries from Basle, and often had metaphorical significance. IPM

233
Barfüsserkirche

Altar frontal with three scenes from the Life of Christ
Basle, ca. 1440/50
Wool tapestry, height 104 cm, width 298 cm
Inv. no. 1920.107. Purchase

The scenes from the Life of Christ in the middle section of the frontal are flanked by Sts Agnes, John the Baptist, Elisabeth and Cecilia(?) on the left, and the Dominican saints Margaret of Hungary, Dominic, Peter Martyr and Thomas Aquinas or Vincent Ferrer on the right. In the first scene, the *Presentation in the Temple,* the wriggling Christchild is presented for circumcision to Simeon who receives him tenderly. In the background St Anne steps forward holding the dove and candle that signify the feast of Candlemas. The *Noli me tangere* follows, in which the resurrected Christ appears to Mary Magdalene. The third scene, representing the *Entry into Jerusalem,* shows Christ entering the city seated on an ass, followed by St Peter; both make gestures of blessing. A pious man spreads his cloak under the hooves of Christ's mount and a spectator watches these events from high in the branches of a palm-tree. The coats of arms of the families Schönkind of Basle and Am Rhyn of Lucerne indicate the patronage. The small figure of a woman donor dressed in Dominican habit on the right, as well as the reference to Candlemas, suggest a link to the Dominican convent of Klingenthal near Basle. This house had the privilege of celebrating the feast of Candlemas, and from ca. 1293 till 1460 the seal of the abbess bore an image of the Presentation in the Temple.
IPM

234
Barfüsserkirche

***Wildmen on a staghunt*, wall-hanging**
Basle, ca. 1468
Wool tapestry, two sections each height 123–128.5 cm, width 253 cm
Inv. no. 1981.88. Purchase

The purchase of this tapestry from a South German collection for the 1981 reopening of the Historisches Museum was funded by public and private donations. It is one of the most valuable textiles in the Basle collection. The sequence of images shows wildmen out hunting in the manner of noblemen. A hunter equipped with a boar-spear, sword and hunting horn bids farewell to his wife who waves a cooking spoon. He follows his dogs who chase a stag towards a net. In the second section, the setting of a further net by two other wildmen is followed by the group of a hunter flirting with a female falconer. Another huntress hands a quail to her companion and, in the scroll, makes the ambiguous promise of giving him more of the "tame and wild" ('Zahmem und Wildem'). The tapestry was made around 1468 for the marriage of Hans von Flachslanden to Barbara von Breitenlandenberg from St Gall. Hans von Flachslanden had been mayor of Basle from 1454 to 1463. Their coats of arms occupy the corners of the wall-hanging. In accordance with the occasion of the commission the subject-matter should be understood as a metaphor for the pursuit of the favours of the other sex. IPM

235
Barfüsserkirche

***Garden of love with a pavilion*, wall-hanging**

Basle, ca. 1490

Wool tapestry, three fragments, of height 95 cm, width 50–51 cm; height 103 cm, width 131 cm; height 98 cm, width 78 cm
Inv. no. 1870.741. Alter Bestand

The central scene of the tapestry shows the summertime pursuits of people in courtly dress in a sumptuous garden setting. The flowers are botanically recognisable and have symbolic meanings linked with love and thereby sorrow. A pavilion provides shade. The pennants and awning carry the coats of arms of the Basle families zem Lufft and Meyer zum Pfeil. Inside a noble couple sit on a wooden bench and play cards on a stone table. A youth tends to their bodily well-being by pouring a drink into a beaker. A precious goblet stands on the table next to a fruit basket and a radish. Yet the tranquillity of summer is deceptive: there is an erotic tension which is reinforced by the figures on the damaged fragments to either side. Playing his last card the young man surrenders himself to the lady with the words, "den. us. wurf. hand. ihr. wohl. besunnen." (That last play of yours was well considered), and she proudly confirms, "Do. mit. han. ich. das. spil. gewunnen." (Herewith I have won the game). IPM

236
Barfüsserkirche

***Allegorical animals*, fragment of a wall-hanging**
Basle, ca. 1500
Wool tapestry, height 112 cm, width 182 cm
Inv. no. 1870.745. Purchase

Four mighty allegorical animals stand in front of a dense background of interlaced tendrils. By means of the inscriptions on the scrolls emanating from them, the animals put forward Christian maxims. The gentle elephant says: "[*In Frieden wollen wir*] *stehen*" (Let us stay in peace); the king of beasts, the lion: "*Leid bringt Himmels Lohn*" (Suffering brings heavenly reward); the unicorn: "*Gott mus alles erschaffen haben*" (God must have created everything), and finally the stag: "*Deshalb loben wir seine Dreieinigkeit*" (Therefore we praise His Trinity). Shabragues and harness-bells identify the animals as the mounts for personifications of virtues. On a similar tapestry (private collection) based on the same design, and where the scrolls are complete, the animals are flanked by a young wildwoman and a wildman who represent the peaceful children of nature. IPM

237
Barfüsserkirche

***Wildwoman with unicorn*, cushion-cover**
Strasbourg, ca. 1500/10
Wool tapestry with silk and gold thread in parts, height 75 cm, width 63 cm
Inv. no. 1926.40. Purchase

A melancholy-looking young wildwoman sits in a landscape densely inhabited by plants and animals. Her garland of flowers is a redundant reminder of a now sorely missed past experience. The scroll reads, "Ich habe meine Zeit der Welt gegeben, nun muss ich hier im Elend leben" (I have given the world my time, now I must live here in misery). While all the paired animals have turned away from her and romp about the landscape, her sole remaining companion is the unicorn, who has found refuge on her lap from the hunters (of virtue perhaps). She lovingly consoles him, as he too gazes into the distance – an allegory of the yearning for love. IPM

238
Barfüsserkirche

The Annunciation, corner bearing of the Julius II banner of Basle

Basle, ca. 1513

Relief embroidery, gold thread and coloured silks, spangles and pearls on silk damask; sceptre and rosettes of goldsmith's work; two pieces, back to back, representing the same scene (in reverse); each height 38 cm, width 37 cm

Inv. no. 1882.92. Alter Bestand

After their success in the Swabian and Burgundian Wars Swiss mercenaries had acquired a high reputation. In 1512 a troop of 18,000 of them, an autonomous military force known as the 'grosse Pavierzug' (great Pavian troop), fought victoriously on the side of the Holy League in the conflict of the European powers in the Wars of Italy. In recognition of their "protection of the freedom of the Church and the whole of Italy" Pope Julius II conferred on them two papal banners. Further, every canton that had contributed soldiers to the campaign received a rectangular bearing with a scene from the New Testament or the Lives of the Saints; the city of Basle chose the Annunciation. The bearing was either swiftly embroidered in Milan at the Church's expense, or it may have already existed, for within the year the new banner with its charge was received in Basle with great public celebration. The Milanese original has been lost, and the present embroidery is a copy that was made in Basle for use in 1513 by an unknown, "foreign" embroiderer. It is a work of outstanding quality and richness; the composition of the Annunciation follows a design from the area of the Upper Rhine. IPM

239
Barfüsserkirche

Crucifix for a chasuble(?)

Basle(?), ca. 1521/22

Embroidery, gold thread and coloured silks on linen, height 125.5 cm, width 54 cm

Inv. no. 1917.684. Amerbach Cabinet

The crucifix embroidered in fine needlework is believed to have come from the Amerbach Cabinet. It may be either the "crucifix embroidered in gold" in inventory G of 1602, or that "in a single golden piece" on a chasuble of blue velvet, which Ritter Hans Kilchmann, a close friend of the Amerbach family, donated to the Carthusian monastery of St. Theodor in Basle. It belongs to the type known as 'Christus am Astkreuz' (Christ on the cross with branches): the Latin cross with stumps of branches recalls the Tree of Life and is a symbol of immortality. Needlework in which gradations of colour are achieved by the intermeshing of yellow, red and light blue silks, and which is couched with gold and silver threads, is typical of liturgical embroideries of the Late Gothic and Renaissance periods. IPM

240
Barfüsserkirche

The Bischofszell tapestry (detail)
Eastern Switzerland, 1st third 16th century
Embroidery, wool on woollen cloth, height 117 cm, width 285 cm
Inv. no. 1873.6. Purchase

The richly detailed pictorial chronicle was created by the subtle combination of different types of stitches in coloured wool threads on a pieced-together woollen cloth. It is a realistic portrayal of the town of Bischofszell (canton of Thurgau), lying on the slope of the Bischofsberg, and the landscape around the confluence of the rivers Sitter and Thur. The keep of the castle carries the coat of arms of the Bishop of Sonnenberg. The scenes in the rural landscape, enlivened with all kinds of livestock, are of particular historical interest. A rider whose saddlecloth is decorated with the coat of arms of the bishop, preceded by a gaily costumed entourage, makes his way towards a welcoming drink. A bather jumps from the other bridge and peasants joke with one another around a harvest wagon. Pedlars hurry to the castle, a woodcutter wields his axe, and even a priest is included in the vivid hustle and bustle. IPM

241
Barfüsserkirche

Tablecloth, dated 1563
Eastern Switzerland
Embroidery, linen, cotton and wool threads and metal cord on linen, height 144 cm, width 168 cm, diameter of medallion 64 cm
Inv. no. 1874.41. Purchase

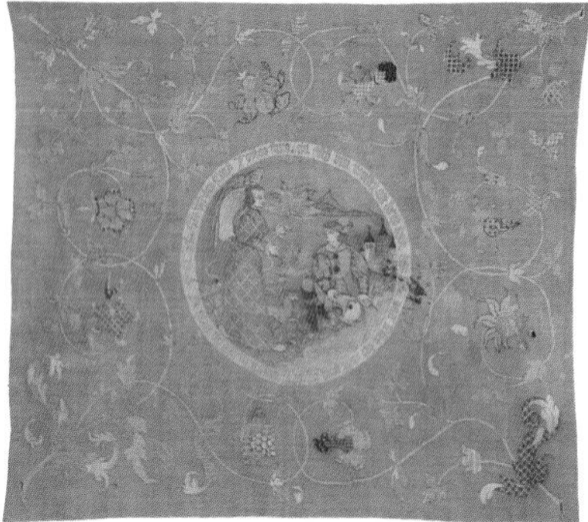

The area surrounding Lake Constance was a centre of production of large-scale figurative white embroidery on linen. The oldest extant example dates from the first half of the C13; next is a tablecloth from the C14 that came from the monastery in Feldbach (canton of Thurgau) and is now in the Historisches Museum. The peak of production of these pictorial embroideries was in the C16. Numerous examples are held by the larger museums of Switzerland and they are regarded as typically Swiss, although some probably originated in neighbouring areas of Germany. The scenes are usually taken from woodcuts or book illustrations, although some are fresh compositions. They are set within a field of interlaced tendrils, often within a medallion, and are sparingly outlined in blue and red wool thread, also occasionally picked out with silk or metal thread. They are frequently dated and have coats of arms to identify their place of origin. Here, the scene is of Tobias with the fish from which the archangel Raphael ordered him to extract the liver, gall and heart to cure his father's blindness (Tobias 6). The design is based on an illustration by Hans Holbein the Younger in the 1540 Bible printed by Froschauer in Zurich. IPM

242
Barfüsserkirche

Wall-hanging, dated 1598
Basle(?)
Embroidery, wool and metal thread on linen, height 75 cm, width 230 cm
Inv. no. 1910.225. Purchased with a contribution from the Verein für das Historische Museum

This tapestry, formerly owned by an old Basle family, documents the life of an otherwise unknown Basle woman named Charitas, who stands in the middle of her brood of 13 children. Seven of them are the children of her first husband, who, before he died, had entrusted mother and offspring to God. Six further children, five girls and an infant, are from her second husband, shown on the right, who expresses the hope that God may grant him good fortune in this life as well as the joys of the next. She confirms that through God's grace she gave birth to 13 children in two marriages. All stand in a row in front of a pattern of loose interlaced foliage, the children on the left absorbed in play, the girls on the right demurely stiff. The older children are dressed as small adults according to the contemporary fashion of wealthy bourgeois. Details show their toys (a hobby-horse and windmill), as well as fashionable accessories such as the belt with purse and cutlery, the decorative aprons, headgear and the rare depiction of an umbrella. IPM

243
Study collection

'Coffetuch', tablecloth
Silesia, ca. 1760/70
Silk damask in two colours, height 110.5 cm, width 89 cm
Inv. no. 1968.163. Gift of Beatrice Goppelsroeder-Sarasin

The term damask evokes the idea of white table linen with a delicate white design. The design is produced by varying the method of the weaving so that the smooth ground contrasts with the textured surfaces. This technique was employed in Europe from the C15 for linen damask in a wide variety of designs. In western Europe two-coloured designs using dyed weft threads were produced only in Silesia and Saxony where the production of damask had flourished increasingly from the second half of the C17. In these regions two-coloured damask, of either half silk or pure silk with a coloured weft, was produced in the same style and technique as white linen damask. The gallant or allegorical subject-matter of the pictorial pieces is sometimes comparable to motifs used in engraved glass from the same area. Vivid hunting scenes run around the borders of the 'Coffetuch' and the centre contains a scene of two elegant couples dining at a sumptuously laid table beneath a canopy, while two dogs wait for scraps and two hunters blow their horns. IPM

244
Barfüsserkirche

Silk ribbon loom, dated 1776
Basle
Framework wood, height 200 cm, width 240 cm, depth 140 cm
Inv. no. 1881.166. Gift of Emanuel Hoffmann-Eglin

The silk ribbon industry was founded in Basle at the beginning of the C17 by refugees from the Netherlands and France. By copying a loom that the weaver Emanuel Hoffmann had imported from Haarlem around 1670, on which several ribbons could be woven simultaneously, Basle weavers were soon able to outstrip their French competitors decisively. The mechanism of these looms, which were operated by outworkers in the country, resembled that illustrated in Diderot and d'Alembert's *Encyclopédie* of 1751 and remained much the same until the C20. The only modifications were electrification and the lateral attachment of a small Jacquard mechanism for weaving patterns. The manufacture of ribbons – formerly the most important industry in Basle – was superseded around the end of the C19 by the chemical industry, which for the most part was founded on the production and trade of dyes for silk threads. IPM

245
Barfüsserkirche

Pattern book of the Emanuel Hoffmann silk ribbon factory
Basle, ca. 1770/80
Bound in morocco leather, height 19 cm, width 11.5 cm
Inv. no. 1880.170. Gift of Emanuel Hoffmann-Eglin

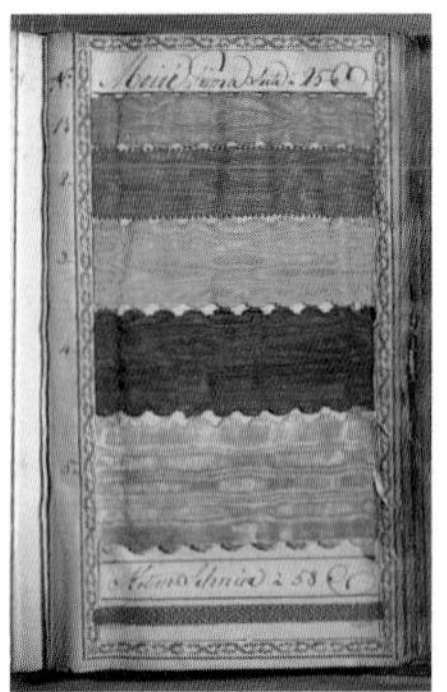

The pattern books which the producers of silk ribbons took to show customers or at trade fairs provide important evidence of contemporary fashion and of the technical level of achievement in the Basle textile industry. This small book, carefully bound in kidskin, is one of the rare examples extant from the C18. The page displayed shows taffeta ribbons of the highest quality, with richly decorated edges of 'picots' or 'dents de rats'. The shiny, iridescent wave-like patterns are produced by 'watering' the ribbons after weaving, a finishing process already being applied as early as the C13 on Islamic silk fabrics. The ribbon is run in a steamy atmosphere over wooden profiles which crush and facet the ribbed surface of the fabric so that it reflects the light like glittering water. Several hundred pattern books and more than a thousand collections are kept in the Seidenband-Studio of the Historisches Museum, where they can be viewed by appointment. IPM

47

udy collection

ouis XVI of France, dated 1795

ance (Paris?)

nbroidery of coloured silks on paper; diameters of
nage 10.5 × 8.5 cm; of frame 14 × 12.3 cm
v. no. 1893.372. Gift of the Universitätsbibliothek
asle

This embroidery was made in 1795, two years after the execution of Louis and Marie Antoinette, by an "ardent admirer of the Queen", la comtesse Antoinette Le Groing, "now citizen". She sent it to her French correspondent, Senator Falkner, with a handwritten dedication on the reverse. His addition to this dedication reveals that he thought highly of the embroidery, the "imaginem acu pictam", as a work worthy of Minerva. He parted with it in 1797, however, in order to give it to the Museum of the Fatherland ("Patriae Museo") "in eternal remembrance of him" (Louis XVI). It is not known from which museum or through what channels the portrait finally found its way into the Basle University Library. IPM

248

Study collection

Two silk ribbon samples

Basle, ca. 1913

Silk warp threads, printed with coloured inks, width 22.5 cm each, in a pattern book, height 48 cm, width 36 cm, depth 8.5 cm
Inv. no. 1981.539.109. On deposit from the Basler Bandfabrik, formerly Trüdinger & Cie

After the collapse of traditional silk ribbon weaving, only a few Basle ribbon manufacturers experimented with silk ribbons in unconventional techniques. Silk thread, which was often as expensive as gold, could not, for reasons of cost, be added on to the main weft to make a pattern in the brocading method. But in the first 30 years of the C20 successful experiments were made in which multi-coloured designs were printed on to the unwoven, provisionally secured warp threads. When these were woven a watercolour-like effect was achieved. At the same time, by this means, the manufacturers were able to avoid sinking to the level of printing on white ribbon, a method despised in Basle. Sometimes the designs reflected modern art, provoking the cry: "Cubist! Cubist!", as has been written beside these two samples. IPM

246
Haus zum Kirschgarten

Les Adieux du Fermier, wall-hanging
Aubusson, after Jean-Baptiste Huet, ca. 1790
Wool tapestry, height 236 cm, width 444 cm
Inv. no. 1923.320.a.1. Marie Burckhardt bequest

In the C18 it was fashionable in bourgeois houses in Basle – as it sometimes still is today – to furnish and decorate the reception rooms in the French style. The 'Visitenstube' (small reception room) of the Segerhof, a Basle residence of the Burckhardt family, which has been incorporated in its entirety into the Haus zum Kirschgarten, is a particularly complete and consistent example. Integrated in the oak panelling are three tapestries woven from cartoons by Jean-Baptiste Huet: *La Cueillette des cerises* (Picking cherries), *Les Adieux du fermier* (The farmer's goodbye), and *L'Arrivée de la fermière* (The arrival of the farmer's wife). The oak furniture in late Louis XVI style, which comprises a sofa, four armchairs, six chairs and four *tabourets* or stools (see no. 392), was produced in Basle and is also covered with tapestries; these show pastoral scenes and episodes from La Fontaine's *Fables*. The owners of the Segerhof placed a single order for all the tapestries from Grellet in Aubusson in 1790.
IPM

Goldsmiths' work

Basle's history as the centre of a bishopric, a city republic, and the capital of a canton is reflected in the Museum's rich store of objects made of precious metals. Together the sacred instruments and vessels of the Basle Münster and the silverware of 28 of the city's guilds and corporations constitute a remarkable treasury of ecclesiastical and secular metalwork, and form the core of the Historisches Museum's particularly important collection of goldsmiths' work. In 1944, on the occasion of the Museum's 50th anniversary, the curator Emil Major averred that of the four areas of collecting for which the Historisches Museum had an international reputation, goldsmiths' work was the foremost, surpassing even its medieval wood sculpture, its stained glass from the Upper Rhine and its C15 tapestries.

The collection of goldsmiths' work comprises three main groups: church silver, secular silverware and a third large group, which is unique to the Basle collection and is unrivalled even in Munich or Berlin: the goldsmiths' models from the Amerbach Cabinet.

The Gothic goldsmiths' work from the treasury of Basle Münster is not only the earliest of the major groups of precious metalwork in the collection, but also the most valuable. Other significant church treasuries survive in Switzerland – those of Chur, Sion, Beromünster and St. Maurice – but the treasury of Basle Münster is the richest. It is the imposing residue of a stock of reliquaries and liturgical instruments that were acquired over a period of 500 years by one of the oldest sees north of the Alps. The list of surviving treasures begins with the gifts made in 1019 by its especial benefactor the Emperor Henry II on the occasion of the Münster's consecration. These included the Golden Altar (now Musée de Cluny, Paris) and the Heinrichskreuz (Henry Cross) (now Kunstgewerbemuseum, Berlin). Even after the Reformation in 1529 the treasure of the Münster remained intact, until the partition of the canton in 1833 necessitated its division and auctioning. Today a little more than half of the original 70 or so objects are assembled in the Barfüsserkirche. The rest are dispersed throughout the world, in museums in Amsterdam, Berlin, St Petersburg, London, Munich, New York, Paris, Vienna and Zurich.

Besides the Münster treasure, Late Gothic and Baroque church plate and copper-gilt vessels with other provenances form a small, heterogeneous part of the collection. These include the remarkable works produced in Basle after the Reformation for use in Catholic worship. The liturgical vessels used in the Reformed church are not represented in the collection, as they are still in use today.

The collection of secular goldsmiths' work, including the important loans of silver from the city guilds, consists of about 1,000 objects. Around two thirds of these were made in Basle, the remainder having been produced in other centres of the goldsmith's art in southern and south-western Germany, the Upper Rhine and Switzerland. The cities of Augsburg, Nuremberg, Strasbourg and Zurich are well represented and individual pieces originated in Berne, Lausanne, Schaffhausen, Dresden, Frankfurt, Worms, Besançon, Lille, Paris, Vienna,

London and St Petersburg. The proportion of secular silver made in Basle workshops from the C15 to the C20 gives an idea of the importance of the goldsmith's craft in the city. It has been practised continuously from at least 1267, the date of the first document of a Basle goldsmith, until today, amounting to a total register of 720 master craftsmen. Both the C15 and C17, during which time there were approximately 30 masters active in the city, can be considered Golden Ages for Basle's goldsmiths' work.

If the silver insignia of office (university sceptres, staffs of office and badges) are assigned to the 'State and Law' section of the collection, the remaining silver objects can be classed into three larger groups: the silverware of the guilds, with the main emphasis on objects of the C17, such as the floral crowns of the guild masters, armorial books with covers of embossed silver, drinking vessels in the shape of animals or objects, goblets and table decorations; secondly the assorted drinking vessels and ornaments, toilet silver and jewellery from the C16 to the C18; and finally bourgeois table silver, consisting of cutlery, drinking vessels, containers for salt and sugar, vinegar and oil, candelabra and candlesticks, tea-kettles, teapots, coffeepots and *chocolatières* – objects that well represent the general development of C18th society.

The last of the three major groups within the collection of goldsmiths' work, the goldsmiths' models, consists of around 700 objects. The majority of these came from the Amerbach Cabinet and had been purchased from the estates of goldsmiths in the C16. These lead casts of small ornamental or figurative pieces for decoration and embellishment are duplicates that were used as intermediate models and patterns. The original designs can be traced back to workshops in Basle, Nuremberg and Augsburg. They allow an insight into workshop practices and, considered together with extant goldsmiths' work, assist the investigation of connections between the different workshops; they are an invaluable source material for research into Late Gothic and Renaissance goldsmiths' work. vR

249
Barfüsserkirche

Two censers from the treasury of Basle Münster

Upper Rhine, probably Basle, ca. 1200
Silver, embossed, height 13 cm
Inv. no. 1882.82. Alter Bestand
Inv. no. 1916.516. Gift of Frau Prof. C. Chr. Burckhardt-Schazmann

The use of incense at divine service and during processions had led to the development of the censer by Carolingian times at the latest. Under a cover that can be lifted lies a container for glowing coals, upon which can be sprinkled grains of resin to produce fragrant clouds of incense as the censer is swung back and forth on its chains. Whereas censers made of cast bronze are quite common from the C11 on, Romanesque examples made of beaten silver, and surviving in a pair, are of the greatest rarity. These examples stand on foot-rings and have an overall profile that is almost spherical, but they are quatrefoil in section. The outer surface is patterned with scale-like tiles. The cover is given an architectural form, resembling a Greek-cross-plan Byzantine church with domes, corner towers and window openings from which the incense could escape. It symbolizes the Heavenly Jerusalem. BIS

250
Barfüsserkirche

The Eptingen chalice, from the treasury of Basle Münster

Upper Rhine, probably Basle, after 1213
Silver, embossed, engraved, punched and gilded, height (without lid) 18 cm, diameter 15.5 cm
Inv. no. 1882.84. Alter Bestand

+ CALICEM·ISTVM·DEDIT·GOTFRIDVS·DE·EPTINGEN·BEATE·MARIE· + (this chalice is dedicated to the blessed Mary by Gottfried von Eptingen): both this inscription, engraved around the edge of the foot, and the style of the cup suggest that this Romanesque silver chalice was made about 1213 as a substitute for the golden chalice which Bishop Lüthold von Aarburg had had to sell in that year to cover debts. Gottfried von Eptingen's gift to the Münster is a somewhat squat goblet decorated in various techniques. The round foot bears four embossed medallions with the symbols of the Evangelists. These roundels and the leaf ornament between them are riveted on to the base. The supporting stem is almost entirely concealed by the massive knop of openwork filigree. This contrasts with the smooth cupa (bowl), which is simply decorated with a punched border of semicircles from which hang lilies. In 1467 the chalice was converted into a ciborium by remodelling the original paten: it was provided with a finial and knob to form a lid that could be closed over the consecrated host after the mass. BIS

251
Barfüsserkirche

Bust reliquary of St Pantalus from the treasury of Basle Münster
Basle, after 1270
Silver and copper, embossed, engraved, gilded, height 49 cm
Inv. no. 1882.87. Alter Bestand

Of all the different forms of reliquary, the head or bust reliquary is particularly impressive, as it required the artist to portray the human face. This head of St Pantalus, the legendary first bishop of Basle, was probably created by a local goldsmith, after the relic of the saint's skull was donated by the city of Cologne in 1270. Four lions support the shoulders and bearded head of the mitred bishop. The forceful delineation of the features and the fixed stare of the painted eyes give the image a hieratic presence. The head must have appeared even more removed from reality originally, when the decorative bands of leaf-sprays and precious stones on the shoulders and mitre were intact. The materials were carefully selected: the shoulders and supports and the bands of the mitre were made only of copper, while the head and the mitre, as the focus of the reliquary, were made of silver. After the dispersal of the treasury of the Münster in 1834, the relic of St Pantalus's skull in the reliquary, along with other relics, went to the monastery of Mariastein, where it remains today on the altar of St Pantalus. BIS

252
Barfüsserkirche

Golden figure of King David from the treasury of Basle Münster
Ca. 1280 and ca. 1320
Gold, gilt silver, translucent *basse-taille* enamel, height 21.6 cm (without wooden base 17.7 cm)
Inv. no. 1882.80.a. Alter Bestand

This miniature statuette is one of the finest and most mysterious objects from the treasury of the Münster. The three-quarters-length figure of David in embossed gold has an antique sardonyx cameo for the face. The King holds a scroll with an inscription in red niello identifying him as DAVID REX. . . . A C13 Italian cameo of a lion is set above the scroll and on that stands a Madonna and Child cast in gold. The inscription and figures of this unique creation represent the descent of Christ, the son of Mary, from his ancestor out of the tribe of Judah, from David 'the Lion of Judah'. The enamels with bust-length Prophets set on the six sides of the architectural silver-gilt base also embody Old Testament references to the birth of the Messiah. The figure of David itself should be dated to around 1280, while the Madonna and Child and the base date from a remodelling of around 1320. The crown and the carved wooden base are C15th additions. BIS

253
Barfüsserkirche

Bust reliquary of St Ursula from the treasury of Basle Münster
Basle, 1st quarter 14th century
Silver and copper, embossed, parcel-gilt, with enamel, height 36 cm
Inv. no. 1955.207. Purchase with a contribution from the Verein für das Historische Museum

The bust was made for the relics of St Ursula that had been donated before 1254 by the cathedral of Cologne, the city where the saint and her legendary company of 11,000 virgins had been martyred. After the treasure of the Münster had been auctioned in 1836, this Gothic reliquary travelled throughout Europe with stays in London, St Petersburg and Amsterdam, until it returned to Basle as the result of a dramatic purchase in 1955. The shoulders, head and hair, braided into two plaits, are made from three sections of hammered silver and are enriched with the restrained use of applied ornaments. The neckline of the saint's robe is edged with pearls and lozenges of translucent enamel, and is further decorated with a cast, star-shaped brooch. The circlet worn by the saint is also studded with decorations, but only isolated blossoms of translucent enamel segments and framing cabochons have survived. Its simplicity and the mask-like emphasis of the features give this work an almost hypnotic effect. There is a remarkable stylistic resemblance to sculpture on the west façade of the Münster.
BIS

254
Barfüsserkirche

Small processional cross from the treasury of Basle Münster
Basle, ca. 1320
Silver, engraved, parcel-gilt, with translucent *basse-taille* enamel, height 27 cm
Inv. no. 1922.261. Purchase with contribution from the Verein für das Historische Museum

The cross served as the uppermost element of a banner on a silver shaft, which would have been carried by a choirboy at the head of processions. This example was one of a pair; its identical counterpart has been missing since the C19. The four arms of the cross have bevelled edges and are extended with silver-gilt 'sleeves' ending in pointed quatrefoils. The centre of the cross is accentuated by a square casing containing a small relic, which was displayed through a round rock crystal set into the back. The elegance of the overall design is matched by the simplicity of the surface treatment and by the artistry of the workmanship. The surfaces of the arms of the cross are engraved with a recurrent pattern. The central medallion and the four terminals bear miniature-like representations in *basse-taille* enamel of red on a blue ground. On the front, the central medallion has the head of Christ shown full-face and the terminals show the four Evangelists seated and with their attributes. On the reverse the quatrefoils have the heads of two Prophets and two saints. BIS

255
Barfüsserkirche

Double cup from the convent of Seedorf
Zurich(?), ca. 1330
Silver, hammered, cast, chased, punched, engraved, gilded, handles and medallions originally enamelled, height 9.9 cm
Inv. no. 1894.265. Purchase

This double cup was part of a find unearthed in 1606 in the garden of the Benedictine convent of Seedorf near Flüelen in the canton of Uri. At the time Cysat, the town-clerk of Lucerne, noted, "... a fine, covered, silver, gilded, antique, women's drinking vessel with old coats of arms...". The cup entered the Museum in 1894 from the possession of the Lucerne goldsmith Bossard. The vessel consists of an upper cup from which one drank, and a lower part, with a ring-shaped handle, that was used for refilling. It is an ecclesiastical vessel, and has been associated with the 'Johannis-Minne', which was widespread from about 1300: by drinking consecrated wine the faithful were able to partake in Christ's love for St John Evangelist. Double cups made of hammered silver from this period are rare, though comparable examples are to be found in museums in Zurich, Amsterdam and Speyer (from the 1969 Lingenfeld find). vR

256
Barfüsserkirche

The Innocents or Apostle monstrance from the treasury of Basle Münster

Basle, ca. 1335/40

Silver, cast, embossed, gilded, with translucent *basse-taille* enamel, height 74.2 cm
Inv. no. 1933.159. Purchase

This outstanding work is the earliest of the reliquary monstrances from the treasury of Basle Münster. Its design utilises a full repertoire of architectural forms from the transition to Late Gothic typical of the Upper Rhine area. The eight-lobed foot carries an octagonal stem consisting of base, shaft and chapel-like knop. Bunches of oak leaves lead up to the main element, shaped like a miniature altarpiece, where the round relic-holder is housed beneath a graceful tracery gable with crockets and finial and flanking three-sided pinnacles. Its splendour is further enhanced by the rich use of translucent enamel in the *basse-taille* images. Those on the quatrefoil medallions of the base show events from the Infancy of Christ, including the Massacre of the Innocents, and also St Columba. The Irish monk St Columba is present because he had formerly owned the relics of one of the Innocents of Bethlehem that the reliquary once contained. The alternative name of the monstrance derives from the two series of figures of apostles, one on the knop and the other in the ring of enamel medallions around the circular ostensory. The reliquary is likely to have been remodelled as a monstrance for the Eucharistic host around 1450, when the more modest reverse was slightly modified. BIS

257
Barfüsserkirche

The Kaiserpaar monstrance from the treasury of Basle Münster

Basle, between 1347 and 1356

Silver, cast, embossed, gilded, with translucent *basse-taille* enamel, height 67 cm
Inv. no. 1933.158. Purchase with assistance from the state

On 4 November 1347 Basle received relics of the Emperor Henry II and his wife Kunigunde from Bamberg, where these former benefactors of Basle Münster are buried. The reliquary must have been made in connection with their translation or with the subsequent consecration on 2 April 1348 of the Henry and Kunigunde altar in the Münster. The form of the reliquary is a variation of the Gothic tower monstrance, extended laterally with buttressing elements. Part of its rich iconographic programme refers to the imperial couple: their slender cast figures are the most prominent feature of the monstrance. Scenes from their lives are represented on the enamelled medallions on the eight lobes of the foot. Other images in translucent *basse-taille* enamel are the heads of saints around the base of the octagonal shaft, the blossoms in the lozenges around the knop and the saints standing in front of blue backgrounds in the embrasures of the arcade beneath the spire. Amongst these last is the Annunciation, with the Virgin Mary and the angel Gabriel occupying the two central arches. BIS

258
Barfüsserkirche

Reliquary in the shape of a house from the treasury of Basle Münster

Basle, end 14th century

Silver, sheet and cast, parcel-gilt, on a wooden core, height 35 cm, width 39 cm, depth 31 cm
Inv. no. 1882.85. Alter Bestand

Reliquaries in shapes inspired by architecture were numerous in the Middle Ages and were produced in a great variety of types. This shrine in the shape of a house is characteristic in having the surfaces of walls and roofs decorated with many small silver plates stamped in the manner of bracteate coins. They are stamped with five motifs repeated in an irregular sequence over the grid-like pattern: the head of the Man of Sorrows, the head of the Virgin Mary, the Lamb of God, sprays of leaves and of lilies. The other structural elements are modelled on Gothic architectural forms: corner tabernacles with saints and crowning angels, and cornices and crockets along the ridges of the roof that define the edges of the shrine. One of the long sides is marked as the main façade by the lockable double door, and by the blue enamelled medallion with the Virgin and Child set into the surface of the roof above it. Four struck round medallions are applied to the doors: they represent the Crucifixion and Sts Catherine, John the Baptist and James. BIS

259
Barfüsserkirche

The Dorothy or Offenburg monstrance from the treasury of Basle Münster
Basle, 1430/40

Silver, cast, embossed, parcel-gilt, with paste and semi-precious stones, height 55 cm
Inv. no. 1882.81. Alter Bestand

A small door on the simple reverse reveals that the monstrance was originally a reliquary. The red niello coat of arms which is riveted to the door suggests that it was the gift of the Oberstzunftmeister (chief guild master) Henmann Offenburg of Basle. The restrained gilding on the front of this slender object creates a charming effect; the embossed figure of St Dorothy in her lavishly draped garments, hand in hand with the naked Christchild, appears to float in the mandorla. The impression of preciousness is enhanced by the paste jewels, semi-precious stones and antique gem set around the saint and, finally, by the cameo at her feet. The Gothic crockets seem to frame the almond-shaped setting like tongues of flame. In contrast the support, consisting of an eight-lobed foot, smooth shaft and a knop resembling bundled rods, is somewhat soberly treated. BIS

260
Barfüsserkirche

The Rotberg chalice from the treasury of Basle Münster
Basle, ca. 1451

Silver, embossed, cast, chased, gilded, with niello and enamel, height 21.6 cm
Inv. no. 1894.346. Gift of Frau Sarasin-Brunner

The appeal of this well proportioned communion cup does not depend upon a wealth of decoration but on its simplicity and elegance. It has an eight-lobed foot with a wide rim which has high, openwork sides. The foot rises steeply to join the octagonal stem, which develops into a knop with enamelled lozenge-shaped bosses. The smooth cupa (bowl) is rather steep-sided. The particular significance of the chalice derives from the two small nielloed plaques with coats of arms that are attached to the foot. The coat of arms of the Rotberg family (or, a fess sable) and that of the diocese of Basle (argent, charged with the Basle crosier) show the chalice to have belonged to Bishop Arnold von Rotberg and suggest a date around 1451, the year of his consecration as bishop. He bequeathed the cup to the Münster in 1458, where it took the place of the Eptingen chalice (no. 250). It is likely to be the work of the Basle goldsmith Heinrich Schwitzer, who worked for Bishop Arnold on several occasions. BIS

261
Barfüsserkirche

St Christopher from the treasury of Basle Münster

Basle, ca. 1445

Silver, embossed, parcel-gilt, height 44.2 cm
Inv. no. 1933.160. On deposit from the Eidgenössische Gottfried Keller-Stiftung

The treasury of the Münster contained many extraordinary objects, but none is more appealing than this silver statuette reliquary with its finely differentiated and lively gilding. It represents the moment when St Christopher, bearing the Christchild on his shoulder across the river, recognises the nature of his burden. The saint stands in the ankle-deep water and raises his eyes to the inexplicably heavy child, under whose weight even his staff bends. Various realistic details and sensitive observations recall the approach of the famous Basle painter Konrad Witz (died ca. 1444/46). There is delight in the careful description of details such as the binding of his hair or the purse and eating utensils tied to the saint's belt.

This masterpiece of Late Gothic silver sculpture was used as an altar decoration and has a counterpart in a *St John the Baptist* today in the Hermitage in St Petersburg. BIS

262
Barfüsserkirche

The Hallwyl reliquary from the treasury of Basle Münster
Strasbourg, ca. 1460/70
Shrine: silver, embossed, cast, gilded; Crucifixion group: gold with diamonds and a ruby; overall height (without base) 42 cm; gilded wood base (not shown), height 16.7 cm
Inv. no. 1882.83. Alter Bestand

The work was bought in 1470 by a resident of Basle, Rudolf von Hallwyl, for the treasury of the Münster and was provided with a carved wooden base by the joiner Mathias Frischmut. The shrine, conceived as the tomb of Christ and decorated with Late Gothic pinnacles and tracery, contained relics of the Holy Cross and Blood. Small plaques with nielloed coats of arms on the ridge of the roof commemorate von Hallwyl and his wife. The place of manufacture can be identified because the reliquary bears the mark of the Strasbourg guild of goldsmiths. Its Strasbourg origin is also indicated by the style of the architectural motifs, and the superb figures of the crucified Christ, Mary and St John in gold reveal stylistic affinities with the work of the sculptor Nicolaus Gerhaerts van Leyden, who was working in Strasbourg at that time. The dead Christ on the rough wood of the cross, with diamonds for the nails and a ruby for the wound in his side, is highly expressive, and this masterpiece of goldsmiths' work from the upper Rhine makes a powerful devotional image. BIS

263
Barfüsserkirche

Pax

Circle of Martin Schongauer, Basle(?)/Upper Rhine, ca. 1490/1500

Silver, beaten, engraved, parcel-gilt, diameter 12 cm
Inv. no. 1878.42. Amerbach Cabinet

Two curved, silver disks are joined together by a decorated rim to form a capsule-like medallion or pendant. Such objects were used in the Catholic mass as an *osculatorium* or *tabula pacis* (tablet of peace) for conveying the Kiss of Peace. Among the few extant late medieval examples of the same size this pax occupies a special position because of the high quality of the engraved scenes on each side. Scaled down according to the proportions of the golden section and adapted to a circular shape, the two scenes from the Passion are otherwise precise copies of Martin Schongauer's well known engravings of *The Agony in the Garden* and *The Arrest of Christ*. Their attribution to the close circle of the famous Colmar painter and engraver is justified by the fact that his brother Georg was a goldsmith and his brother Paul was in Basle between 1489 and 1491. The collector Basilius Amerbach already noted in his 1585–87 inventory that the pax was "engraved by Martin Schön". vR

264
Barfüsserkirche

Small standing cross from the treasury of Basle Münster

Basle, ca. 1493

Silver, embossed, engraved, parcel-gilt, height 26.8 cm
Inv. no. 1909.475. Purchase

Altar crosses, reliquary crosses, and processional crosses symbolizing the Redemption of mankind through the death of Christ were common in the Middle Ages. The present object is likely to have been made to be placed on an altar. The somewhat elongated sexfoil foot with high sides develops into a hexagonal stem with a compressed spherical knop. On top of this the crucifix itself is hammered work of very high quality. The effect achieved by the goldsmith's restrained engraving is particularly impressive. The front surface of the cross is decorated with an interwoven tracery-like design on a stippled ground, while the four trefoil terminals carry figurative motifs. These, the four symbols of the Evangelists, closely follow those on the so called Paten engraving by Master E. S. of 1466. As in the Hallwyl reliquary (no. 262), the wound in Christ's side is represented by a blood-red ruby. The reverse of the cross is covered with sprays of leaves with occasional blossoms, and culminates in an image of the Virgin and Child. BIS

265
Barfüsserkirche

The Münch monstrance from the treasury of Basle Münster
Basle, 1490/93
Silver, embossed, cast, height 110 cm
Inv. no. 1955.330. Gift of the Regierung des Kantons Basel-Landschaft

This monstrance, which bears the arms of the Münch family, is the most important artistically of the four tower monstrances from the treasury of Basle Münster. The curator Hans Reinhardt described it as "without doubt one of the most beautiful and perfect of the Late Gothic monstrances in existence". On grounds of style it can be attributed to the son of the famous engraver Martin Schongauer, Jörg Schongauer, who was active for a time as a goldsmith in Basle. The shrine was intended to house a relic of Emperor Henry II and is of the most lavish construction. From the sexfoil foot of embossed blind tracery develops a cantoned stem with an architectural knop. The design of the knop is based on engravings by Martin Schongauer, as are some of the cast figures in the niches. The relic was displayed in the cylindrical crystal vessel. The cylinder is framed by graceful Late Gothic architectural forms consisting of buttresses, pinnacles and gables. At the sides, level with the relic, stand cast figures of Emperor Henry II and Empress Kunigunde. In the open tabernacle above the relic-holder stands a cast figure of the Virgin and Child that is reminiscent of the work of Nicolaus Gerhaerts van Leyden, who was Jörg Schongauer's father-in-law. BIS

266
Barfüsserkirche

Beaker with cover formerly owned by Erasmus
Basle?, ca. 1490, with later additions
Silver, cast, embossed, gilded, height 14 cm
Inv. no. 1928.210. Amerbach Cabinet

The particular interest of this simple vessel made from hammered and gilt silver lies in its early ownership by three men who played significant roles in the history of Basle. The drinking vessel was a gift from the publisher Johannes Froben to Erasmus; after his death it was inherited by the jurist Bonifacius Amerbach, and from him it passed to Froben's widow. During the later part of the C16 the elegant object underwent a number of changes. Three winged angel-heads of cast silver were soldered under the lower rim to form supports. The engraved coat of arms of the Mellinger family of Basle, who had probably been the original owners of the piece in the late C15, was moved from its original position on the knob of the lid to the bottom of the beaker and was replaced by a scaled-down reproduction of the Erasmus medal of 1531, in commemoration of its famous previous owner. The reverse with the bust of Terminus, the Roman god of boundaries, Erasmus's emblem, is the side shown. BIS

267
Barfüsserkirche

Morris dancers
Basle(?), ca. 1500
Silver, cast, chased, parcel-gilt; height 2.5 cm
Inv. no. 1882.115.11–19. Amerbach Cabinet

The Historisches Museum owns a collection of goldsmiths' models that is uniquely rich in its variety. These models were originally made to facilitate the reproduction of ornamental and other elements cast in silver and applied to larger objects as decoration. The group of nine Morris dancers in the round from the Cabinet of Basilius Amerbach (of which two are illustrated) shows that such miniature models could also become collectors' items. They call to mind the ten sculpted Morris dancers in the Munich town hall carved by Erasmus Grasser in 1480. These exaggerated caricatures of foolish abandon, however, are even more distinctive. In their inventive twistings these knaves correspond still more closely to the character of the Morris dance, an exuberant interlude during social occasions and Carnival. BIS

268
Barfüsserkirche

The Hüglin monstrance from the treasury of Basle Münster
Basle, ca. 1505
Silver, cast, embossed, parcel-gilt, with enamel, height 88.7 cm
Inv. no. 1882.79. Alter Bestand

Stylistic comparison with another tower monstrance by the Basle goldsmith Simon Nachbur suggest that he also made this reliquary. An inscription on the base of the cylinder identifies it as the gift of Konrad Hüglin, master-mason of Basle Münster. The support is less elaborate than that of the Münch monstrance (no. 265) and the surface decoration is limited to an engraved tracery pattern. The lozenges on the knop bear the letters MAHIRSAI, which can be read as an anagram of MARIA and IHS. The Late Gothic, three-storeyed, spire-like structure where the relic is housed is impressive. It is peopled with cast figures gilded to make them stand out from the silver architectural forms of their setting. In the arcaded tabernacle on top of the ostensory is a Virgin and Child in a mandorla, and in the uppermost storey stands St Andrew. The figures of Sts John the Evangelist and John the Baptist in the flying buttresses to the sides of the principal level relate to the relic in the cylindrical glass, where two angels in a charming garden of paradise hold a bone from the finger of the Baptist as well as a scroll. BIS

269
Studiensammlung

The Virgin and Child
Hans Harthauser, Ravensburg, beginning 16th century
Silver, embossed, parcel-gilt, overall height 51.7 cm
Inv. no. 1896.21. Purchase

An octagonal console with engraved, patterned sides carries the mound upon which the Virgin stands. She wears a crown and has long hair. The stiff posture of body and head and the presentation of the figure as a compact drapery-covered form make her appear somewhat remote. The naked Christchild, who has an almost putto-like quality in his lively articulation and movement, nearly slips out of the Virgin's barely visible hands. The subtle use of decorative gilding and the delicate setting of jewels around the Virgin's neckline complement the restrained character of this statuette. The rather shallow and straight folds of the garment avoid the kind of virtuoso treatment of drapery that was widespread in the period around 1500. As was often the case with such statuettes, the figure probably reproduces a wooden prototype in the so called 'Schönen Madonnen' (beautiful Madonna) style. The prototype is most likely to have been carved in the Ulm-Swabia region. BIS

270
Barfüsserkirche

Double mazer (the Luther goblet)
South or middle Germany, ca. 1530
Pearwood, lathe-turned, with engraved silver-gilt mounts, height 27 cm
Inv. no. 1922.195. Gift of Hans Burckhardt-Burckhardt

The Museum owns two such drinking vessels of turned hardwood, which were widespread throughout Germany and Switzerland from the C13. Only around 50 of these cups, also called 'Doppelkopf' cups (double-head cups), have survived. They were believed to have the power of extracting poison from any drink they contained. They include cups kept in remembrance of outstanding personalities, for example the Zwingli goblet in Zurich. This is another such example, according to the Latin inscription engraved on the bottom of the tiara-shaped crown of the cover. It tells us that the vessel was presented to Luther by the Elector of Saxony John the Steadfast on 25 June 1530. On this memorable day the Augsburg Confession, the most important statement of the beliefs of the Lutheran Reformed Church, was presented to the Emperor during the imperial diet. After 1806, during the Napoleonic occupation of Wittenberg, the goblet came into the possession of the commander of an Alsatian regiment, Oberst de Graaf, and from his family it found its way to Basle by 1846. vR

271
Barfüsserkirche

Globe goblet
Jakob Stampfer, Zurich, 1539
Silver, cast, embossed, engraved, parcel-gilt, height 39.5 cm
Inv. no. 1882.103. Amerbach Cabinet

In 1555 Bonifacius Amerbach purchased this imposing piece from his friend, Thomas Blarer, the mayor of Constance. Its use as a drinking goblet, though awkward, was explained to him both in a written account and by a goldsmith. In 1579 a guest of Amerbach's son Basilius even provided a description of the use of both halves of the globe as drinking vessels. It is not certain whether the maker, the Zurich goldsmith Jakob Stampfer (1505/06–1579), had from the beginning intended the globe to be used in this fashion. In fact the scientific aspects are the dominant features of the device. A round foot with an engraved perpetual calendar and baluster stem carry the two halves of the revolving globe. It is encircled by an equatorial ring with calendar engravings and a calibrated meridian ring. A small armillary sphere sits over the north pole. The cartographical representation of the earth is of particular interest: land is gilded and the silver oceans are inhabited by sea-monsters. Engraved inscriptions provide explanations. BIS

272
Barfüsserkirche

Cup with cover
Andreas Koch, Basle, ca. 1550
Silver, cast, embossed, engraved, parcel-gilt, height 17.7 cm
Inv. no. 1962.62. Gift of the Verein für das Historische Museum

This work by Andreas Koch (1522–1572) is one of the earliest pieces of Basle goldsmiths' work to have both a hallmark and a maker's mark. The somewhat curious shape combines elements from different types of vessel, namely the beaker, the *Roemer* wineglass, and the goblet. Three soldered pomegranates carry the slightly profiled foot that leads into the cylindrical cupa (bowl). The shape of the base is repeated in the slightly domed lid, which develops into the protruding knob. It carries a small cast figure of a Roman soldier with a winged helmet, broken tournament-lance and shield. Such martial crowning elements on metal vessels were widespread in the C16; the posture of the legionary, however, half propped up and half balancing, is uncommon. While the arms and armour of the figure are gilded the exposed areas of flesh remain silver. Foot, cupa and cover are finely engraved with a frieze and a hanging pattern. The foliage sprays, arabesques and profile heads are typical motifs of Renaissance style. BIS

273
Barfüsserkirche

Fool's head beaker
Zurich(?), ca. 1556
Coconut with silver mounts embossed, engraved, parcel-gilt, height 10.5 cm
Inv. no. 1892.183. Gift of Frau Hauser-Speiser

The unknown goldsmith made use of the germination points of the coconut and the ridges between them to form a face, and this was completed as a fool or jester's head by the addition of collar, ears and rows of bells. When stood upright on the three large bells, the beaker can be opened with the face forming a lid. The rim of the cup is encircled with a lip-band with the inscribed couplet: "Der Lust zum starcken Tranck und Win macht das ich nit kan wizig sin" (The pleasure in strong drink and wine means that I cannot be witty). The inside of the cup is varnished. A single known comparable example, which is dated 1556 and stamped with the Zurich hallmark, indicates the possible place and date of origin of this beaker. For centuries the cup was in the possession of the Hauser family, who had owned the Basle inn Gasthof zur Krone from the C17. vR

274
Barfüsserkirche

Model for a pendant
South Germany, ca. 1550–70
Cast lead, height 4.9 cm, width 4.5 cm
Inv. no. 1904.1575. Amerbach Cabinet

When the plague in Basle in 1576–78 wiped out numerous artists and also caused some goldsmiths' workshops to close, the passionate collector Basilius Amerbach used the opportunity to extend his collection of models for goldsmiths' works. This insignificant lead cast, which may be the work of Erasmus Hornick from Antwerp, who was active in Augsburg, served as the model for a costly pendant in gold. The jewel is designed as miniature architecture. The niche contains a pair of intertwined, embracing naked lovers, accompanied by a cupid. Two recumbent lions flank this amorous scene. Colourful enamelling of the completed golden jewel would have resulted in a more sharply defined and three-dimensional image. Settings prepared in the cast enabled the finished pendant to be fitted with precious jewels; at the sides there are square settings for cut and polished stones and in the upper and lower parts of the niche there are recesses for cabochons. Frequently such pieces of jewellery were further enriched with hanging pearls. BIS

275
Barfüsserkirche

Model for a jewelled pendant
South Germany, ca. 1550–70
Cast lead, height 7.5 cm, width 7.5 cm
Inv. no. 1904.2190. Amerbach Cabinet

The genre character of the jewel in the preceding entry (no. 274) is entirely lacking in this piece. The pendant made from this model was designed to be a purely ornamental setting for precious stones. To cast it in gold would have demanded a high level of technical skill. Its basic shape is a triangle composed of broken scrollwork and strapwork interspersed with fruit and masks. It is likely that it would have been coated with *émail en ronde bosse* to provide colour and relief. Four rectangular settings were incorporated to hold subsidiary stones, but the eye-catching feature of the jewel was to be a group of three large gem-stones for which the mounts, including the claws and supporting fillets, were pre-cast. Considering the anticipated size of the stones, this is a model for what would have been a very valuable piece of jewellery. BIS

276
Barfüsserkirche

Model for a frieze with triglyphs and metopes
Wentzel Jamnitzer, Nuremberg, 1570
Cast lead, height 2 cm, width 8.2 cm
Inv. no. 1904.1468. Amerbach Cabinet

Goldsmiths' models of cast lead were made not only for jewellery, but also for the production of precious ornament and various kinds of setting or mount. Great effect could be achieved for small outlay by piecing together components. This frieze is a good example. Cast in silver, it was used in multiple repetition around the casing of the reliquary of St Victor, dated 1570, in the Discalced convent, the Decalzas Reales, in Madrid. It was made by the famous Nuremberg goldsmith Wentzel Jamnitzer (1508–1585), and is a miniaturised, but precise, rendition of antique architectural forms: it is a Doric entablature with triglyphs between metopes where paterae alternate with bucrania (ox-skulls). A moulding with an egg and dart enrichment forms the upper border. The Museum owns a number of other models that were used as casts for the decoration of the St Victor shrine. BIS

277
Barfüsserkirche

Model for the handle of a dagger
Jamnitzer workshop, Nuremberg, ca. 1570/80
Cast lead, height 11 cm
Inv. no. 1904.1339. Amerbach Cabinet

The two halves of the model were used to cast an octagonal handle for a dagger in bronze or silver. The model was probably designed either by the Nuremberg master Bartel Jamnitzer (1548–1596) or in the workshop of his famous father, Wentzel Jamnitzer. This delicate piece of small sculpture is an outstanding example of the refined courtly taste of the Renaissance in Germany, and is typical in its fascination with the antique, both formally and iconographically. The inspiration of the antique dictates every element of the decoration of this volute-shaped handle, and the Roman deities Minerva and Mercury and Mars and Venus occupy the niches of the upper and lower registers respectively. Further standing and reclining figures and a frieze with puttos make the handle resemble a richly populated miniature. BIS

278
Barfüsserkirche

Ostrich-egg goblet
Elias Lencker, Nuremberg, ca. 1575
Ostrich egg with silver mounts, cast, embossed, etched, gilded, height 46 cm
Inv. no. 1882.90. On deposit from the Universität Basel

The Basle ostrich-egg goblet belongs to the 24 known goldsmiths' works of the Nuremberg master craftsman Elias Lencker the Elder, whose activity is documented between 1562 and 1591, and who had been in France for seven years before that. Two further ostrich-egg goblets by him are in Cassel and Berlin. Such exotic bibelots were already sought after in the Middle Ages; another ostrich-egg beaker is recorded in Basle in 1437. It was believed that the robustness of the bird would be carried over into whatever was drunk from these eggs and so into the drinker, with beneficial effect. This goblet is superbly modelled in the Renaissance style. The cover is crowned by Minerva, the goddess of wisdom, and it was given in commemoration of its 300th anniversary to the University of Basle by the town council in 1760; nothing, however, is known about its original purchase. On the occasion of the gift an appropriate dedication was engraved on Minerva's shield. vR

279
Barfüsserkirche

Screech-owl goblet
Jakob Christoph Mentzinger, Basle, ca. 1600
Silver, cast, embossed, chased, punched, engraved, parcel-gilt, height 20.7 cm
Inv. no. 1914.597. Purchase

Among the different types of drinking vessel in the shape of an animal, silver owl or screech-owl goblets form an outstanding group. The Museum has two such cups. The oldest known wooden vessel in the shape of an owl is recorded in a Basle inventory of 1548. The representation of the bird sitting on a perch with bells tied to its feet refers to its role as a decoy in hawking and, in analogy, could be understood as a lure to drunkenness. Additionally, the special characteristics of owls gave rise to a wide range of allegorical interpretations, which were often explained in inscriptions on such vessels. The Basle goldsmith Jakob Christoph Mentzinger (1562–1637), who had been in Neuenburg am Rhein from 1587, returned to his native town in 1601. Around 1606 he entered Swedish, and later Venetian, military service, and the Museum has a portrait of 1606 showing him as an officer in the Polish army. vR

280
Barfüsserkirche

St George and the Dragon drinking vessel
Hans Bernhard Koch, Basle, ca. 1600
Silver, cast, embossed, chased, engraved, parcel-gilt, height 29.5 cm
Inv. no. 1915.241. On deposit from the Eidgenössische Gottfried Keller-Stiftung

Among figurative pieces of table decoration this disguised drinking vessel is particularly outstanding for its virtuoso design and realistic representation. The wide range of decorative techniques and motifs that are employed in the treatment of the surfaces is impressive, and especially the effective use of gilding. The group of armour-clad knight, rearing horse and winged dragon stands on a round, richly embossed pedestal. There is a mechanism concealed inside the base that moved the vessel around the table. The person in front of whom it stopped would remove the horse's head and drink the contents of the body, probably a spiced wine. One would expect to find a playful piece like this in a princely collection of rarities rather than in a bourgeois town like Basle. The Schweizerisches Landesmuseum in Zurich has a replica by the same master. BIS

281
Barfüsserkirche

Griffin drinking vessel, belonging to the Gesellschaft zum Greifen (corporation of the Griffin)
Sebastian Schilling I, Basle, 1606
Silver, cast, embossed, chased, gilded, height 32 cm, weight 1498 g, capacity 0.42 l
Inv. no. 1895.139. On deposit from E.E. Gesellschaft zum Greifen

It is already described as established practice in the 1597 'Regiment und Ordnung' (rule and order) of the city that each year the three 'honourable societies' of Kleinbasel held an armed procession and that each corporation led a living representation of its identifying emblem on a chain. The corporations' emblems were as follows: the Gesellschaft zum Rebhaus, a lion; the Gesellschaft zum Hären, a wildman; the Gesellschaft zum Greifen, a griffin (see also no. 228). This practice is still observed on 'Vogel Gryff-Tag' (griffin day). Silver-gilt drinking vessels in the shape of the corporations' emblems had also long been used, and continue to be used, in the ceremonial of corporation banquets. This striding griffin is not the customary mixture of eagle and lion, but has, in addition, horse's hooves and dog's ears: it may be inspired by Martin Schongauer's engraving of a griffin. Five medallions hung on the vessel add to its value. vR

282
Barfüsserkirche

Agate bowl and case
Johann Georg Kobenhaupt, Stuttgart, ca. 1610/20
Agate with silver-gilt and enamelled mounts, height 15.5cm; case of leather, gold stamped
Inv. no. 1882.88. Faesch Museum

This sexfoil bowl and 18 similar extant objects are the work of the Stuttgart gem-cutter Johann Georg Kobenhaupt (died 1623). They are cut from local or oriental jasper and agate and rank in quality with those produced in the imperial workshops of Rudolf II in Prague. The desirability of Kobenhaupt's work is indicated by the rank of those who collected it: comparable pieces are in the former princely collections in Copenhagen, Paris, Vienna, Munich, Dresden and Stuttgart. This example is very close to beakers in the Louvre and the Kunsthistorisches Museum in Vienna in respect of the ring below the bowl of white, green and red enamel with three dolphins and a garland of upright leaves. The bowl entered the Faesch collection probably after 1648 either as a gift or as an exchange from the French coin expert Charles Patin (1633–1693). Patin did business at the court of Duke Eberhardt III of Württemberg and was a friend of Sebastian Faesch. vR

283
Barfüsserkirche

Pail drinking vessel, of the Weinleutenzunft (vintners' guild), dated 1613
Hans Lüpold, Basle
Silver, cast, embossed, chased, engraved, parcel-gilt, height 19 cm
Inv. no. 1989.13. On deposit from E.E. Zunft zu Weinleuten

The Zunft zu Weinleuten (vintners' guild) bears a measuring pail on its coat of arms. A measuring pail, a calibrated container with a long thin spout, was used to calculate the wine tax that was one of the city's most important sources of income. Given the form of a wooden measuring pail, the silver drinking vessel evokes the different professions involved in the trade and sale of wine united in this major guild – including also clerks, notaries and city officials. It nicely illustrates the use of multiple reproduced images, whether engravings or lead castings, as sources for figurative ornament in goldsmiths' work. Thus the cast hoop around the bottom of the pail is copied from the peasant dance by Hans Holbein the Younger and one of the reliefs on the upper hoop is inspired by Peter Flötner's plaquette of Gluttony from his series of the *Seven Deadly Sins*. The lockable lid is engraved with a scene of drinking burghers. On the inside the base has the coat of arms of the guild and the inscription, "Dise Gelden wart gemachd ist war, im 1613. Iar" (This pail was made, and this is true, in the year 1613). vR

284
Barfüsserkirche

The Buxtorf cup
Melchior Trüb, Zurich, 1638
Silver, cast, embossed, chased, engraved, height 20 cm
Inv. no. 1947.273. Purchase by the Verein für das Historische Museum Basel and the Buxtorf family

In goldsmiths' work of the late Renaissance and Baroque the shell motif was very popular, whether it was a natural shell incorporated into the object, or a free, stylised representation in beaten silver, as in this case. A stand with an oval foot, a richly decorated baluster stem and scrollwork brackets carry a wide, fluted bowl. A Latin inscription at the front explains the history of the cup: it was a gift to the Hebrew scholar, theologian and librarian Johannes Buxtorf the Younger of Basle (1599–1664). It was presented to him in 1638 in thanks for his service to the city library of Zurich; a cast of the library's seal is represented in a cartouche in the curling hinge of the shell. As a precious gift of recognition this bowl reveals the high esteem in which professors from Basle were held in Switzerland. BIS

285
Barfüsserkirche

The Wettstein cup
Georg Gloner, Strasbourg, 1649
Silver, cast, embossed, chased, engraved, gilded, height 65 cm
Inv. no. 1917.18. On deposit from Jenny Burckhardt-Burckhardt

According to the inscription this splendid vessel, in the shape of a nautilus-shell cup and weighing almost 3.5 kg, was presented by seven merchants to the mayor of Basle Johann Rudolf Wettstein in recognition of his achievements during the negotiations of the Treaty of Westphalia (signed 24 October 1648). This is the subject of the decorative programme of the cup, in which a heraldic beast from the arms of Basle supports the bowl and above it a platform on which the Swiss Confederation stands united, thanks to Wettstein's negotiations. Above them the imperial eagle holding a palm of peace presents the charter of privileges granted by Emperor Ferdinand III, the document which established the independence of the Swiss Confederation from the Empire in 1648.

As a work of monumental size specially commissioned from the Strasbourg workshop the Wettstein cup is in a different class from the numerous mass-produced items made at the end of the Thirty Years War. The cup has a significance extending beyond the local interests of its donors and is effectively a Swiss national monument. vR

286
Barfüsserkirche

Salver with a scene from a bear hunt
Hans Rudolf Meyer, Basle, ca. 1680
Silver, embossed, chased, engraved; diameters 34 × 40.5 cm
Inv. no. 1941.478. Purchase

During the Renaissance and Baroque periods, apart from sacred and mythological subjects, the main themes of artistic representation were subjects taken from the immediate experience of man and his surroundings. The embossed scene of an ill-fated bear hunt in a clearing in an oak wood is of this kind. Itself savaged by a hound, a bear has attacked one of the two spear-bearing hunters. Lying on his back on the ground, his arms helplessly outstretched, he hopes for rescue by his companion. This dramatic scene in the depressed centre of the oval salver is in stark contrast to the motif on the wide rim, where an idyllic sequence of curling foliage with eight stylised blossoms forms a garland in high relief. The Basle goldsmith Hans Rudolf Meyer made the platter for an important merchant from Brig, Kaspar Jodok Stockalper (1609–1691), who had the marks of his ownership punched into the centre. BIS

287
Barfüsserkirche

Goblet with cover belonging to the Zunft zu Hausgenossen (House-companions' guild)
Sebastian Merian, Basle, 1687
Silver, cast, embossed, chased, punched, engraved, parcel-gilt, height 59 cm
Inv. no. 1895.63. On loan from E.E. Zunft zu Hausgenossen

In Basle the goldsmiths, coiners, money-changers, jewellers and foundrymen were amalgamated in the guild 'zu Hausgenossen' (house-companions). It is not surprising that the house-companions' guild's treasure is particularly rich in vessels and utensils of high quality. This mighty goblet was presented in 1687 on the election of Sebastian Merian, who made it, and of Peter Raillard as officers of the guild. The fact that a crowned bear with a halberd appears twice, as part of the stem and in place of a knob on the cover, is explained by the name of the guild house, 'zum grauen Bären' (at the grey bear), and by the charge of a crown on the guild's coat of arms. Merian demonstrated his skill as a goldsmith not only in the embossed figures, but also in the rich engraving which covers all the ungilt areas on the base, bowl and lid. The engraving includes both ornament and scenes illustrating the crafts of the goldsmith and of the other professions included in the guild. The coats of arms of the guild and of the two donors are particularly prominent. BIS

288
Barfüsserkirche

Ewer and tray for the lavabo from the Mariastein monastery
Johann Friedrich Brandmüller I, Basle, 1698
Silver, embossed, chased, engraved; ewer, height 35 cm; tray, diameters 47 × 59 cm
Ewer: inv. no. 1900.37. Gift of Dr. Alfred Geigy
Tray: inv. no. 1911.14. Purchase

The ewer was used during mass for the ritual washing (lavabo) of the priest's hands. Its size and rich decoration with coats of arms are unusual, but are explained by the fact that it was a gift from the Benedictine monastery of Murbach in Alsace to the Benedictine house in Mariastein in the canton of Solothurn, as a token of gratitude for a favourable judgement in a dispute. The escutcheon of Abbot Esso Glutz, to whom the gift was directed, is depicted in the centre of the dish. A series of 16 other coats of arms appears around the rim. The coat of arms of the main donor, Dean Amarinus Rinck von Baldenstein, is in a central position and is emphasized by shield-bearing putti. The arms of the Murbach monastery are in the same position on the opposite side. In order to maintain its special privileges the monastery could only accept members from the nobility; this is indicated by the 14 other coats of arms on the rim of the dish. Tray and ewer are lavishly decorated with embossed and engraved sprays of stylised acanthus. BIS

289
Barfüsserkirche

Master's crown of the Zunft zum Schlüssel (guild of the key)
Christian Bavier I, Basle, 1699
Silver, embossed, chased, punched, parcel-gilt, enamelled, height 26.5 cm
Inv. no. 1894.396. On deposit from E.E. Zunft zum Schlüssel

Originally it was the custom to crown the newly elected guild master with a garland of rosemary and carnations or, from the C16, with tinsel flowers. In 1663 the Zunft zu Hausgenossen, to which the goldsmiths belonged (see no. 286), was the first to introduce a permanent crown made of precious metal. By the middle of the C18 most of the other guilds and companies had followed their example. Twelve such silver crowns for masters of the Basle guilds have survived; nothing comparable in number or kind exists elsewhere. They reflect the status and importance of the guilds and corporations of Basle, not only as trades organizations but, until 1798, also as an element of civic government. The merchants', or 'Schlüssel' (key), guild, being the most prestigious, had the largest crown. The circlet resembles a coronet embossed and set with precious stones; oak and laurel leaves curve up to form the body of the crown and culminate in a key, the guild's emblem. The six enamelled medallions give the names and coats of arms of the masters. vR

290
Barfüsserkirche

Griffin goblet of the Zunft zu Webern (weavers' guild)
Philipp Jacob Drentwett IV, Augsburg, 1708–10

Silver, cast, embossed, chased, engraved, parcel-gilt; height 45.6 cm, diameters of base 30 × 24.6 cm
Inv. no. 1887.3. On deposit from E.E. Zunft zu Webern

Among the emblematic table decorations of the Basle guilds and corporations this griffin with the weavers' yardstick in its claws, the heraldic animal of the weavers' guild, is an exception, having been made in Augsburg rather than by one of the capable local Basle goldsmiths. At the time when it was made, Augsburg was the foremost centre for goldsmiths' work and had around 200 master craftsmen. It is known that one of the donors, Johann Lucas Iselin, had contacts with the Gullmann silver business there. The drinking vessel, weighing 4.688 kg, has the surprisingly small capacity of 0.35 l. The coats of arms, names and guild titles of the officers of the guild who were serving in 1710 are shown on the 16 cartouches screwed to the dome of the foot. The inscription around the rim of the base commemorates the donor of the goblet, "Einer Ehren Zunft zu den Leinwättern und Wäbern haben disz Geschirr verehrt Iohann Heinrich Sarasin, Hansz Lux Iselin and Niklaus Heueszler als die drey iungst erwehlte Sechsere Anno 1710" (This drinking vessel was given to the honourable guild of linen-weavers and wool-weavers by Johann Heinrich Sarasin, Hans Lux Iselin, and Niklaus Heusler as newly elected officers of the guild in the year 1710.) vR

291
Haus zum Kirschgarten

Teapot
Hans Jacob d'Annone, Basle, ca. 1720

Silver, embossed, cast, height 15.3 cm
Inv. no. 1983.925. On deposit from a private collection

Basle's affluent upper class had a predilection for costly plate and tableware, which a flourishing goldsmiths' trade was able to satisfy with quality products in the latest fashion. The collection in the Haus zum Kirschgarten affords a profound insight into the precious world of Basle's pleasure at the table. From the beginning of the C18 silver teapots, *chocolatières* and coffee-pots, each with its own characteristic shape, came into use. This teapot by Hans Jacob d'Annone (1684–1744) is typical in form with a fat body on a slender base, a carved wooden handle and a dainty lid. Variations were possible in the decoration – here the body and lid have ribbed bands – and in the design of the spout. The curved neck of the spout of this teapot ends in a naturalistic dog's head with its tongue hanging out, an example of the Baroque pleasure in the comical. BIS

292
Barfüsserkirche

Oval box
Johann Ulrich Fechter II, Basle, ca. 1720
Silver, embossed, cast, chased, punched, parcel-gilt; height 7.4 cm, width 9.3 cm, length 11.5 cm
Inv. no. 1991.256. Gift of Prof. Rudolf and Marie-Jenny Stamm-Lotz

The gilded box stands on a protruding wavy-edged rim that is repeated on the lid. The embossed sides are patterned with interwoven bands interspersed with flowers against a punched ground. The focus of the box is the relief on the lid framed by an engrailed and gadrooned rim. The representation of *Abraham and the three angels* (Genesis 18) was based on an etching by Matthäus Merian the Elder (1593–1650) in the so called Merian Bible (1625, reprint 1704). The goldsmith, however, made very free use of the century-old model and his late Baroque interpretation has the character of an elegant genre scene. He made skilful use of all levels of relief, working from the finest of punching in the cloudy sky through to the almost fully three-dimensional figures worked *à jour* in the foreground. Johann Ulrich Fechter II was one of the most important Basle goldsmiths of the C18, but his works scarcely ever achieved the virtuosity of this relief, and the question arises whether it could have been produced in collaboration with another artist. BIS

293
Haus zum Kirschgarten

Kettle and stand with burner
Johannes Fechter, Basle, ca. 1750
Silver, embossed, cast; height 36.3 cm
Inv. no. 1987.709. Gift of the E. Zünfte und E. Gesellschaften der Stadt Basel

Bourgeois silverware of the C18 is dominated by the various types of pot used for the preparation and enjoyment of the fashionable beverages of tea, coffee and chocolate. The tea-kettle for the infusion of the tea, resting on a stand that contained glowing coals or a spirit burner, was one of these. Such devices, of brass, were already used in the Late Gothic period as chafing dishes, and the characteristic wooden handle was added to the design in the C17. This kettle does not have the simple round shape repeatedly found in Basle, but curved, fluted grooves curling over the whole body from stand to lid. It is a splendid, unusual piece indebted to the Louis XV style. Johannes Fechter (active 1735–55) was a member of one of Basle's best known dynasties of goldsmiths. The family flourished from the end of the C17 to the end of the C18 and twelve masters of the name of Fechter were registered in the guild. vR

294
Haus zum Kirschgarten

Travelling tableware set with case
Fork and spoon: Edmée-Pierre Balzac, Paris, 1768; plate and covered dish: Robert Josephe Auguste, Paris, 1772–73
Silver, cast and turned, gilded; plate: diameter 25.3 cm; bowl: diameter 16.2 cm (without handles); combined weight 1905 g
Inv. no. 1974.221.a.-f. Purchase

Due to the division of labour, specialisation and stock holding that was already common in the C18, this set was not made at one time by a single goldsmith. The parts have the marks of two different craftsmen, and the letters denoting the years of manufacture make a difference of date of up to five years possible. The sexfoil shape of the plate is typical for the C18, while the edges of both the plate and the dish cover are set with fasces, a characteristic ornament of French Neoclassicism. The travelling service belonged to Daniel Frischmann (1728–1808), who, after serving in the British East India Company, returned in 1770 via London and Paris to his home town of Basle, where he married Sybilla Heitz in 1773. vR

295
Barfüsserkirche

Coffee service of the Zunft zu Webern
Tray (with two salvers, not shown): Jacques Henri Alberti, Strasbourg, 1774; coffee-pot, milk jug, sugar bowl: Johann Ulrich Fechter III, Basle, 1764
Silver, embossed, cast, chased, engraved; lengths 71, 28 and 28 cm; silver, embossed, cast, chased, engraved; heights 36 cm and 21.5 cm and length 17.1 cm
Inv. nos. 1894.499.1.–5. On deposit from E.E. Zunft zu Webern

The masters' crowns and the drinking vessels used on ceremonial occasions were intended to express and display the prestige of the Basle guilds. However, they also reveal their members' inclination towards the pleasures of the table – evident in this coffee service of the weavers' guild as in many other examples. The Basle goldsmith Johann Ulrich Fechter III made the vessels in 1764. Another Basle goldsmith, Johann Rudolf Wolleb III (1709–1785), arranged for the trays to be purchased from the Strasbourg master Jacques Henri Alberti (1730–1795). Two other masters engraved the coats of arms of the guild in 1766 and 1774 respectively. The splendid set is of an elegant Rococo design. The three-legged coffee pot with two openwork volute handles is especially notable. Coffee flowed through the three dolphin-shaped taps into cups of Meissen porcelain that had been purchased in 1774. BIS

296
Barfüsserkirche

Goblet with cover
Johann Jakob Handmann II, Basle, ca. 1790
Silver, cast, embossed, chased, punched, engraved; height 34 cm
Inv. no. 1882.186. On deposit from E.E. Zunft zu Spinnwettern

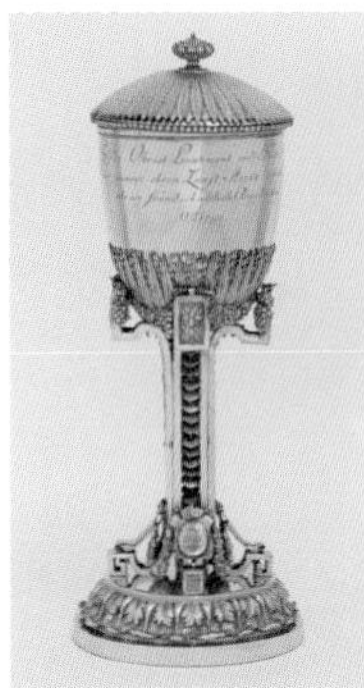

On New Year's day 1790 Hans Rudolf Gessler, formerly Lieutenant Colonel of the royal French infantry, offered 25 gold pieces to his guild, the Zunft zu Spinnwettern (building trade workers' guild), for the manufacture of a silver guild cup. The result of his gift was an unconventional covered cup in the severe style of the transition from Louis XVI to Directoire. According to the hallmarks, it was made by Johann Jakob Handmann II (1758–1793) of Basle; the design, however, is undoubtedly by a contemporary French designer. The round foot has a garland of acanthus leaves and it carries a stem composed of four flat strips ending in volutes decorated with scales and hanging festoons. The tall cupa is decorated with lanceolate leaves that cup the bowl and cover the lid. An engraved inscription by Johann Ulrich Samson refers to both the donor and the recipient, whose coats of arms are engraved on the foot of the cup. BIS

297
Barfüsserkirche

Cup with cover, dated 1844
Johann Jakob Handmann III after a design by Melchior Berri, Basle
Silver, cast, embossed, stamped, chased, parcel-gilt; height 38 cm
Inv. no. 1981.112. Gift of the Christoph Merian Stiftung

With the spread of banquets held by clubs and societies during the period of the Restoration a new market opened up for goldsmiths and the gold trade. The 'Gabentempel' (tower of prizes) at festivals of singers, gymnasts and marksmen needed to be supplied with trophies, objects of applied art which were increasingly supplied by the manufacturing industries. With this development came the division of design from production. This trophy presented by the officers' corps of the city of Basle for the Swiss shooting contest in Basle in 1844 was designed by the architect Melchior Berri (1801–1854). Like his contemporary Karl Friedrich Schinkel or the designer-architects of today he was responsible not only for a number of important buildings and architectural designs but also for everyday objects, such as a letter-box, tableware, or this neo-Gothic cup with battle iconography typical of the period. The elaborate fabrication using the most diverse techniques was left to the goldsmith Johann Jakob Handmann III (1789–1868). The stamped openwork neo-Gothic tracery overlaid on both bowl and lid is particularly remarkable. BIS

298
Study collection

Table decoration in the form of a fountain

Ulrich Sauter, Basle, beginning 20th century
Silver, cast, embossed, punched, chased; overall height 21 cm, maximum diameter 42.2 cm
Inv. no. 1934.76. Ulrich Sauter bequest

This miniature silver rendition of a neo-Baroque fountain shows the birth of Venus from the waves of the sea. It was not copied from a real monumental fountain, either planned or executed, but is a small-scale transposition from a mural of 1868 by Arnold Böcklin entitled 'Magna Mater' which decorates the staircase of the first important purpose-built museum in Basle (the present Ethnology Museum), which opened in 1849. It was in this mural that the tritons supporting the shell, as they appear on the table fountain, first appeared as themes in Böcklin's work. The goldsmith also used motifs from other works by Böcklin and quoted three of the four masks from the famous keystones of the Basle Kunsthalle. The table decoration, which is not functional, is typical of historicist products in being a compilation of several features from different sources. The years from 1884, when Ulrich Sauter and his enormously productive workshop specialised in figurative works and fulfilled numerous commissions from the guilds and townspeople, mark a sustained period of excellence in Basle goldsmiths' work. vR

Clocks and scientific instruments

The collection of clocks, watches and scientific instruments in the Historisches Museum, consisting of around 1200 objects, is one of the largest and most important in Switzerland. It is comparable to those in La Chaux-de-Fonds and Geneva, and enjoys an international reputation. It derives from four private collections that entered the Museum in 1919 and the 1980s, as well as from donations and purchases that have taken place regularly since 1870. Additionally there are permanent deposits from the University of Basle of two groups of scientific instruments (Astronomical Institute, 1960, and Physics Institute, 1986).

The collection bequeathed in 1919 by Marie Bachofen-Vischer of Basle included 250 watches of various origins dating from the C16 to the C19. With the bequest of Carl and Lini Nathan-Rupp of Binningen in 1982, 242 clocks of similar date entered the Museum, among them 22 coach clocks. In the same year the Museum received on permanent deposit the collection of Emanuel George Sarasin-Grossmann of Basle, including notably non-mechanical clocks (sundials) and a total of 200 scientific instruments. Finally in 1983 an extremely important private collection was added to that of the Museum, the 208 clocks and watches of the Dr. Eugen Gschwind-Stiftung. They originate from German, French, Dutch and English-speaking countries, and date from between the C15 and the C19. Amongst them is a very large number of enamelled gold watches by the enamellers Huaud of Geneva. The heyday of clockmaking in Basle, from the C16 to the C18, is documented with about 80 examples. VG

299
Haus zum Kirschgarten

Weight-driven wall clock
Unsigned, France(?), mid–15th century
Foliot iron; height (front) 29 cm, depth 13.5 cm, diameter of chapter-ring 12.5 cm
Inv. no. 1983.1162. Dr. Eugen Geschwind-Stiftung

This early example of a clock of frame construction was used as a watchman's clock and originally had a bell or alarum attached to the side. The bell was sounded by a spigot catching in a hole in the count-wheel, which is fitted inside the dial-ring. It signalled to the bell-ringer that it was time to toll the bell of the tower. The front with the dial terminates in a fleur-de-lys above and below, and is painted. The hours, numbered I to XII in Roman numerals, are indicated by a single hand. The clock is driven by pointed oval weights. VG

300
Haus zum Kirschgarten

Double quadrant
Unsigned, 1552
Silver, parcel-gilt, engraved with inscriptions, numbers and lines; height 4.6 cm, diameter 6.1 cm
Inv. no. 1905.367. Alter Bestand

Within the quadrant, with a gilded scale of twice 90°, is a shadow square, also gilt. The tips of the two rules, gilt side to the front, silver on the back, which are mounted at the centre of the diameter, terminate flush with the edge of the quadrant. Shadow squares were originally a feature of the back of astrolabes, but since the Middle Ages had been used independently, and as such were very common in the C16. They were used for measuring angles and distances, or for telling the time. However, on this instrument the lines necessary for the former are lacking; its small size and precious material indicate rather that it was used simply for telling the hours of the day. VG

301
Haus zum Kirschgarten

Table clock
Jeremias Metzker, Augsburg, 1570

Case: fire-gilt bronze; applied silver figures; hands blued steel and gilt brass; wooden base, going-train and striking train modern additions; height (without base) 29.5 cm, width 19.4 cm, depth 12.9 cm
Inv. no. 1982.1190. Carl and Lini Nathan-Rupp bequest

Jeremias Metzker (1530–1592) was active in Augsburg, where he was granted the right to practise as a metalsmith in 1555. His signature is to be found on the base, IEREMIAS METZKER / VRMACHER / 1570 / MITBURGER ZVO AUGSPVRG (Jeremias Metzker, clockmaker, 1570, citizen of Augsburg). The exquisite decoration of the casing, using motifs deriving from engravings, the applied silver figures, the hunting scenes on the top and the crowning statuette of a female figure on a ball, are evidence of Metzker's skill. On the corners are female herms, who, together with silver figures representing the Virtues, are set on high plinths. The front side (not shown) has the pointers for the hours, minutes, the cardinal points, the signs of the zodiac, the position of the sun in the zodiac and the date; the reverse (shown) bears an astrolabe (rete with 22 stars, sun and moon pointers) and underneath a dial showing the days of the week. On the side of the case are six levers for setting the clock. VG

302
Haus zum Kirschgarten

Sundial
Unsigned, Germany(?), 1572

Brass, gilt, engraved; height 5.6 cm, width 9 cm, depth 9.2 cm; folding gnomon height 4.5 cm, width 9 cm, depth 9.2 cm; compass diameter 1.8 cm
Inv. no. 1982.564. On deposit from Emanuel George Sarasin-Grossmann

The base-plate is scalloped on the sides and rests on four feet. It has ornamental engraving in the angles and at the front, on either side of the compass, the date 1572 (15 on the left and 72 on the right). The sundial in the middle is marked for a day of 16 hours (from the fourth to the twelfth and from the first to the eighth). The gnomon, in the shape of a right-angled triangle, is mounted on the noon line. When set up, it casts shadows on the dial, and from the lines on which they fall the time can be told. Among the non-mechanical clocks of the Museum's collection the sundials from the C16 to the C18 occupy an important position. Apart from a few garden sundials they consist mainly of small, portable examples. Of these, 93 sundials, more than half the entire holdings, are from the Sarasin collection, seven from the Nathan-Rupp collection and 61 from elsewhere. VG

303
Haus zum Kirschgarten

Box sundial in the form of a pendant
Christoph Schissler the Elder, Augsburg, 1580
Three parts (lid, plate, base); bronze, gilt; diameter 4.4 cm, height 1.2 cm; compass: diameter 1.5 cm
Inv. no. 1982.522. On deposit from Emanuel George Sarasin-Grossmann

Christoph Schissler (Augsburg ca. 1530–1608 Augsburg) was one of the outstanding instrument-makers of his period. The engraved signature is to be found on the outside of the rim, CHRISTOPHORVS SCHISSLER .S[enior]: FACIEBAT AVG ANNO 1580. On the outside of the lid is a figure representing Vanitas in a columned hall; on the inside is a windrose. On the upper side of the plate is an engraved sundial with Roman numerals for a day of 16 hours (IV-XII-VIII). The plate has a narrow opening for the foldable gnomon and a round opening for the compass fitted into the bottom part of the box. In the lower part there is an equinoctial sundial with a folding gnomon and a concave sunken dial with engraved lines for the hours (9–24), the tropics and equator, and the latitude at 45°. On the outside underneath are punched arabesque designs. VG

304
Barfüsserkirche

Astrolabium planisphericum
Germany(?), after 1582
Brass, engraved, diameter 16.4 cm, thickness 0.6 cm
Inv. no. 1892.28. Gift of Fritz Burckhardt

The principle of this versatile instrument of medieval astronomy is the projection of the fixed stars on a flat surface, in this case a pendant disc. The oldest extant astrolabes come from mid-C10th Persia; the first European ones date from the C13 or C14. The instrument consists of a round disc, the 'mater', with a raised rim, the 'limb', housing the plates, 'tabulae', which are set with their lines aligning with the latitudes and the horizon-zenith co-ordinates. Above lies the 'rete' with the zodiac and 23 star pointers (13 outer, 10 inner) in the shape of little flames, as well as the pointer, the 'index'. On the reverse is a rule with two upright sights, the 'alidade', with which to make astronomical estimations. The reading can be obtained on the basis of the month and the day and the numbers of days in the month, the zodiac position, division by 30°, and the shadow scale. VG

305
Haus zum Kirschgarten

Pendant oval watch

Isaac Forfait I, Sedan, ca. 1600

Bronze, gilt; casing: silver, parcel-gilt, engraved, pierced; lid: cut rock crystal; spring with gut-line on fusee; hands: blued steel; height 6.4 cm, width 3.4 cm, thickness 2.6 cm

Inv. no. 1982.1061. Carl and Lini Nathan-Rupp bequest

Isaac Forfait I lived from 1586 to 1648. His signature, "Jsaac Forfait / Sedan", is engraved on the back-plate in italics. The watch, which was worn round the neck, is furnished on both sides with a lid of cut rock crystal and so exposes the back-plate to view. The dial-plate is decorated with engraved and pierced foliage. A silver band with engraved foliage and fluttering putti runs round the sides of the case. The single hand indicates the hours on the silver chapter-ring with engraved Roman numerals. VG

306
Haus zum Kirschgarten

Automaton clock (seated monkey)

Carol Schmidt, Augsburg, 1st quarter 17th century

Hour-striking train; figure: bronze, fire-gilt; base: wood painted black, glass and iron; mechanism: brass and iron; plates gilt; spring with gut-line on a fusee; bell: bronze; dial: silver, enamelled on the inside; hands: blued steel; height 32 cm, width 18 cm, depth 15.8 cm

Inv. no. 1982.1195. Carl and Lini Nathan-Rupp bequest

Carol Schmidt, born probably in 1586 in Augsburg, became a master in 1614 and died in 1635/36. His signature, "Carll Schmidt", is engraved on the back-plate. The dial has Roman (I-XII) and Arabic (13–24) numerals for the hours. The monkey sits on the gilded, engraved brass plate which closes the hexagonal case. Its right shoulder-joint, jaw and eyes move. In its left hand it holds a mirror, in its right an apple which it raises to its open mouth when the hour strikes, as if to bite into it. The rolling eyes are connected to the going-train. On its head it wears a fool's cap and a crown. VG

307
Haus zum Kirschgarten

Quadruple hour-glass of the bell-ringer of St. Thomas, Leipzig
Leipzig(?), 17th century
Spruce frame with pasted engravings, four glasses, overall height 69 cm, width 23 cm, depth 10.5 cm
Inv. no. 1880.190. Gift of the Universitätsbibliothek Basel

According to the inscription, CHRISTIANUS HEINING THÜRM: ZU ST. THOM. IN LEIPZIG., this is the hour-glass of the bell-ringer of St. Thomas in Leipzig, the church made famous by the music of Johann Sebastian Bach. Represented on the engravings above the hour-glasses are two 'Turmmusiker' with trumpet and cornet. The dial in the middle (diameter 9.6 cm) is held by two rampant lions and has in its centre a view of the city of Leipzig ("Lipsia") and, below, a Vanitas allegory with skull, hour-glass and plants. The hand to mark the hours is wooden. Beneath the glasses there is another view of Leipzig in the centre of a round calendar with indications of the day and the month, marked by a pointer (missing) and a pin (missing). Each glass carries top and bottom the indications 1/4, 2/4, 3/4 and 4/4 painted in red. VG

308
Haus zum Kirschgarten

Pendant or pocket watch with outer case
Hans Mettler, Basle, ca. 1640
Case and dial silver, rim of gold; mechanism: gilt bronze and brass; hands: blued steel; outer case: black sharkskin with silver *piqué* ornament; watch: diameter 4.1 cm, thickness 1.8 cm; outer case: diameter 4.9 cm
Inv. no. 1954.38. Purchase

The exact dates of Hans Mettler's life are unknown. He came from Riehen bei Basel and was granted citizenship of Basle in 1634. From a receipt for the repair of the mechanism of the Münster clock in 1643 it emerges that he dealt not only with watches but also with large clocks. This watch has an engraved signature in italic script on the back-plate, "Jean Metler / ABasle", and is the oldest extant pocket watch from Basle. It has a burnished silver case and an engraved silver dial on which the hours are indicated in Roman numerals and which is decorated with flowers. VG

309
Haus zum Kirschgarten

Astronomical coach clock with outer case
Jean Le Senne, Paris, ca. 1650

Alarum and hour-striking train; case: silver, cast, pierced, engraved; dials: parcel-gilt; cover with inserted glass; hands: blued steel; outer case: copper, beaten, covered with shagreen leather; mechanism: brass and iron plates gilded; spring with gut-line and fusee; diameter 12.6 cm; with outer case 13.7 cm; thickness (with glass) 6.3 cm
Inv. no. 1982.1161. Carl and Lini Nathan-Rupp bequest

The engraved signature in italic script on the back-plate reads, "A Paris Jean le Senne". On the dial are (left) the indications of the day of the week (in Spanish) and the planet of the day and (right) of the month (in Spanish), the number of days in the month and the ruling sign of the zodiac. Above on two concentric dial rings are the solar calendar (1–30, gilt) and the lunar calendar (1–29); in the centre on the right is an aperture for the phases of the moon. Below on the smaller dial there are a gilt chapter-ring with Roman numerals for the hours and an alarum-disc with Arabic numerals. The bell is screwed to the base. Coach clocks were the equivalent of later pendant and pocket watches. They were furnished with a ring for hanging up and were used for telling the time on journeys. VG

310
Haus zum Kirschgarten

Table clock
Samuel Berckmann, Augsburg, ca. 1670

Hour-chime and alarum; decagonal casing of bronze, fire-gilt; spring with chain and fusee; hands of blued steel; height 12 cm, diameter 14 cm; enamel chapter-ring, diameter 9.5 cm, width 2.1 cm; alarum-disc, gilt, diameter 5.2 cm
Inv. no. 1983.1154. Dr. Eugen Gschwind-Stiftung

Samuel Berckmann, born in Reichenstein in Silesia, was granted the right to practise as a smith in Augsburg in 1667. Many of his decagonal clocks are extant. The engraved signature, "Samuel / Berckmann / Augusta", is situated on the lower inside of the back-plate. The engraved and punched case rests on four turned feet, between which hang circular stabilisers. Each side allows a view through small apertures on to the mechanism which is mounted on spiral pillars. On the chapter-ring the full hours are indicated with Roman numerals (I–XII) and there are pointers also for the half and quarter hours (innermost). The alarum-disc has Arabic numerals (1–12); the bell is mounted on the bottom of the casing. VG

311
Haus zum Kirschgarten

Astronomical table clock

Niklaus d'Annone, Basle, end 17th century

Case: gilt copper with silver inlay; hands: blued steel; overall height 66 cm, width 30.3 cm, depth 26.3 cm

Inv. no. 1889.70. Purchase

This late example of a clock in the form of a tower is probably the most precious extant Basle clock. The engraved signature, "Nicolas / Annone / A / Basle", is situated in the front in the middle between the two small dial-rings. D'Annone was a member of the guild from 1678 and died in Basle in 1703. The case rests on a stepped base with four hemispherical feet and is flanked by four spiral columns which bear a balustrade; it is crowned by a figure of Atlas, whose globe shows (on a $29\frac{1}{2}$-day calendar) the age and phases of the moon. On the upper part of the case are two portrait medallions, on the front the Sun King Louis XIV and on the rear the Dauphin. On two small dials on the front the clock indicates the planetary time with the rulers of the hours (left) and the signs of the zodiac (right), while in the chapter-ring the hour-hand indicates the hours in Roman numerals in silver, and the minute-hand indicates the minutes in Arabic numerals in gold. On the back the constellations, the month and the saint's feast-day can be read, and the quarter and hourly strike can be adjusted. VG

312
Haus zum Kirschgarten

Pocket watch
Casing: Huaud brothers, Geneva, ca. 1720; movement and enamel dial: Abraham Colomby, Geneva, ca. 1740
Enamelled gold, hands silver; diameter 3.15 cm, thickness 2 cm
Inv. no. 1983.1155. Dr. Eugen Gschwind-Stiftung

The case of this smallest known watch by the Huaud brothers bears a delicately painted representation of the Holy Family. The signature, "Les deux freres / Huaut Les / Jeunes", is inscribed in a yellow cartouche on the painted border beneath the Christchild. The mechanism, dating from some 20 years later, is signed in black on the white enamel dial, "Abraham / Colomby". Two hands indicate the hours in Roman numerals (I-XII) and the minutes are represented by division-lines and by Arabic numerals for every five minutes. The different dates of case and movement suggest that a certain number of their cases remained and became available after the Huauds' deaths. VG

313
Haus zum Kirschgarten

Cartel clock
Movement: Jean-Philippe Gosselin; casing: Dumont; Paris, mid–18th century
Half-hour striking train (bell); case: bronze, fire-gilt, chased and punched; putto: painted porcelain; hands: gilt brass; height 52.5 cm, width 31.5 cm, depth 12.5 cm; enamel dial diameter 13 cm
Inv. no. 1982.1182. Carl and Lini Nathan-Rupp bequest

Jean- Philippe Gosselin became a master in 1717 in Paris; he died in 1776. One of the signatures, GOSSELIN / A PARIS, is placed on the dial (below XII and above VI), the other is engraved in italic script on the back-plate, "Gosselin / A / Paris". The Rococo casing in the form of a cartouche carries the mark DUMONT on the upper left side of the back. Its various decorative elements are characteristic of the Louis XV style – the waves, the wings, the volutes, the posture of the painted porcelain putto seated under a trellis-like canopy. These create an anti-clockwise motion in strong contrast to the functional part of the clock. Two hands indicate on a white dial the hours in Roman numerals, every five minutes in Arabic numerals, and the single minutes marked by lines. VG

314
Haus zum Kirschgarten

Armillary sphere (geocentric)
Unsigned, Italy(?), 18th century

Brass, partially engraved, wood; height 33 cm, diameter of meridian 17 cm, sphere 14.5 cm, earth 3 cm
Inv. no. 1982.661. On deposit from Emanuel George Sarasin-Grossmann

A horizon ring is attached to a stand with three arms on a square base. Within it a movable meridian ring which bears the sphere is fixed on the vertical axis; its diameter is the axis of the ecliptic with the wooden globe of the earth in the middle. A band of brass engraved with the signs of the zodiac, the equator ring, the two tropics and the polar circles, as well as the poles, both real and magnetic, together with two of the seven planets then known (probably sun and moon) complete the armillary sphere. It is a late example of the 'Ptolomaic' geocentric view of the universe challenged by Copernicus but favoured by astrologers up until the C18. Such spherical models of the heavens had been used for astronomical calculations since antiquity. In this case the representation of the paths of the planets with rings of brass wire ('armillae') had the advantage of transparency, by contrast to solid celestial globes. VG

315
Haus zum Kirschgarten

Chronometer
Thomas Mudge, London, 1755

Mechanism: polished brass; dial: silver-plated and engraved; hands: blued steel; winding time: ten days; height 15.2 cm, width 15.2 cm, depth 10.4 cm
Inv. no. 1960.20. On deposit from the Astronomisch-meteorologische Anstalt der Universität Basel

This earliest known clock with a 'constant force escapement' was made by the London clockmaker Thomas Mudge (1715–1792) between 9 June and 31 October 1755. He followed the instructions and design of the Basle mathematician and astronomer Johann Jakob Huber (1733–1798), a pupil of Johann II and Daniel Bernoulli, who was in London during the summer of 1755. Huber had acquainted the renowned astronomer James Bradley with his proposals and following his recommendation had commissioned Mudge to build the clockwork. Huber brought the chronometer back with him to Basle. It was left to the scientific 'cabinet' of the University in 1829 by his son, the mathematician Daniel Huber. VG

316
Haus zum Kirschgarten

Horse-shoe magnet in six layers
Johann Dietrich, Basle, 1755
Iron; height of four outer layers 14.5 cm, width 10.5 cm, depth of two outer layers 0.95 cm; of two inner layers 15.9 cm, width 10.5 cm, depth 9.5 cm; sleeves of brass, partially engraved
Physikal. Sammlung Nr. 3/2. On deposit from the Physikalisches Institut der Universität Basel

The invention of the horse-shoe magnet should perhaps be credited to the Basle citizen Johann Dietrich, who produced this example. On both sides of the bend and the ends it is furnished with brass sleeves; on the front of one end is the engraved signature, "Johan / Dietrich/ Inv[enit] et Fe[cit] / 1755", and on the reverse SUD; on the front of the other a Basle crosier and on the reverse NORD. The two middle layers, which are about 1 cm longer, project beyond the sleeves, in order to serve as the magnet. Attached is a piece of iron with moveable hooks on which weights can be hung to demonstrate the strength of the magnet and at the same time to measure it. The magnet is suspended on a special cross-beam by a leather strap. VG

317
Haus zum Kirschgarten

Organ clock
Pierre Jaquet-Droz, La Chaux-de-Fonds, ca. 1760
Hour and quarter-hour striking train with three bells without repetition; organ with 13 metal pipes and eight tunes; wood casing with Boulle marquetry, stained horn and tortoiseshell inlaid on brass; mounts: bronze, fire-gilt, chased and punched; hands: brass, gilt, perforated; height 103 cm, width 54 cm, depth 27 cm; diameter of white enamel dial 30 cm
Inv. no. 1951.14. Gift of the heirs of Dr. Albert Zellweger, Basle

Pierre Jaquet-Droz (La Chaux-de-Fonds 1721–1790 Biel) became famous above all for the mechanical perfection of his automata and clocks. The engraved signature is located on the cover of the upper mounting of the pipes, "P Jaquet Droz à la / Chauxde fonds en Suisse". The case, with its coloured floral inlay and gilt bronze, its wind-blown foliage and, beneath the dial, the representation of a deer and a hound, is a sumptuous example of the style transitional between Louis XV and Louis XVI. The hours are indicated by Roman numerals, the five minutes by Arabic numerals, the single minutes by division lines. VG

318
Haus zum Kirschgarten

Astronomical longcase clock
Philipp Matthäus Hahn and assistants, Kornwestheim, 1775
Case: solid walnut; painted dials screwed on to brass disc; weights lead (ca. 25 kg); height 209.6 cm, width 46 cm, depth 29 cm
Inv. no. 1913.94. Purchase

Only two clocks by Philipp Matthäus Hahn (see no. 193) with such a comprehensive system of dials are extant. The main dial in the middle has the minutes of mean time with two subsidiary dials for the minutes (below) and seconds (above) of real time; on the left are the hours (below) and the phases of the moon with a movable horizon (above); above, in the middle, are the constellations over a fixed horizon; on the right, the positions of the sun with a movable horizon (above) and calendar with the days of the month and week (below). The engraved signature is situated above the main dial: "erfunden / von M. Hahn / in Kornwestheim / und verfertigt / durch / seine Arbeiter / 1775" (devised by M. Hahn in Kornwestheim and produced by his workers 1775). The clock was made for the Basle silk manufacturer Wilhelm Brenner. The mechanism was carried on his back to Basle by Mauritius Steiner, one of Hahn's apprentices; the weights were cast in Basle, and the casing was commissioned by Hahn from a Basle joiner. VG

319
Haus zum Kirschgarten

Night-and-day clock
Georg David Polykarp Hahn,
Kornwestheim, 1776

Case: iron; front and chapter-ring: brass; dial: enamel, with black numbers; hands: perforated brass; height 37.8 cm, width 28.9 cm, depth 16 cm; diameter of chapter-ring 21 cm, dial 11 cm
Inv. no. 1982.1207. Carl and Lini Nathan-Rupp bequest

David Georg Polykarp Hahn (1747–1814), younger brother of Philipp Matthäus (see nos. 318, 320), was a professional surgeon but worked occasionally in his brother's workshop. The engraved signature is situated in a cartouche in the middle below the chapter-ring, "Georg David Hahn / in Kornwestheim / 1776". The Roman numerals on the chapter-ring and the pointing hand above are cut through the brass face and backed with red silk so that when a burning candle is placed behind them they are visible at night. The ring rotates anti-clockwise and the pointing finger indicates the time. For the daytime the hours are indicated on the enamel dial in Roman numerals and the five minutes in Arabic numerals. The *mouvementé* outline and engraved decoration of the front are manifestly in Rococo style. VG

320
Haus zum Kirschgarten

Equatorial sundial
Philipp Matthäus Hahn, Echterdingen
(Baden-Württemberg), 1782

Wood, brass, iron; height with base 38 cm, length of axis 21 cm, diameter of enamel dial 4 cm; brass box 13.2 × 14.5 cm
Inv. no. 1960.23. On deposit from the Universität Basel (Physicalische Sammlung Nr. 133)

Philipp Matthäus Hahn (1739–1790) invented this particular type of table sundial in 1763. The disc at the socket has a wind rose; from the socket an iron arc rises on which a brass ring calibrated for setting the latitude for the location is suspended. Two signatures, "Hahn 1782" and "Hahn / Echterdingen / 1782", are engraved on the disc and on the brass ring. An open brass box moves round on the diameter of the ring and engages through a gear with the dial on the inside bottom of the box. Hahn's invention consists in the fact that instead of a shadow cast by a gnomon the rays of sunlight themselves, passing through two tiny holes in the wall parallel to the axis, strike the time scale on the inside of the box. Thus either the mean time or the real local time can be read off the dial. Two hands indicate the hours in Roman (I–XII) and the five minutes in Arabic numerals. VG

321
Haus zum Kirschgarten

Pocket watch with outer case
George Charle, London, ca. 1800
Gilt bronze, brass; case: gold, embossed and pierced; dial: enamel; hands: blued steel; spring with chain and fusee; height 6 cm, width 4 cm, thickness 2.3 cm; diameter of outer case 4.7 cm
Inv. no. 1919.203. Bequest of Marie Bachofen-Vischer, Basle

The signature, "Charle in London", is engraved in italic script on the back-plate. Its author was almost certainly George Charle, who is recorded in London from shortly before the end of the C18 until 1842. The two hands indicate the hours in Roman numerals (I-XII) and the minutes in division lines. The back of the richly embossed outer case shows a boisterous company of musicians with (from right to left) viola da gamba, harpsichord, lute, together with a singer and two drinking companions. The image surely derives from the engraved frontispieces typical of musical publications of the late C17 and the C18.
VG

322
Haus zum Kirschgarten

Pocket watch with automaton in shape of a lyre
Mechanism: Piguet & Capt(?), Geneva, ca. 1800
Gold enamel inset with pearls; hands: blued steel; height 7.2 cm, width 3.3 cm, thickness 1.3 cm
Inv. no. 1982.1007. Carl and Lini Nathan-Rupp bequest

The arms of the lyre terminate in the heads of two eagles. Small inlaid pearls on the edges, on the foot and around the neck of the eagles accentuate the shape. The front shown here has an almond shape cut into it and glazed. Behind the glass are (at the top) the seconds dial in Arabic numerals with a hand for the seconds and quarter minutes, the balance wheel and the hour dial with Arabic numerals and division lines for the minutes with two hands. Beneath on a folding cover three putti play musical instruments. Hidden behind the cover is an automaton with six movements representing a pastoral scene with a shepherdess, two sheep, a drinking dog, a millwheel and water. The painting on the rear of the lyre depicts two lovers. VG

Ceramics

Stoneware, faience or porcelain has never been made in the town of Basle or its surrounding area. Earthenware was produced but confined to simply decorated crockery for everyday use and for cooking. A few pieces of Zurich faience were acquired in the C19, intended for the Historisches Museum when it should open, and a little later 155 items of 'peasant' pottery made mainly at the Heimberg and Langnau factories were purchased. These were handed over to the Schweizerisches Museum für Volkskunde Basel (Swiss Folklore Museum) in 1954. The Historisches Museum's ceramics collection, consisting of some 2400 pieces in all (excluding services), is based on gifts and bequests from old Basle families, the first dating from an early stage in the Museum's development. As some of the great Basle merchants had invested in the Zurich/Schooren factory in the C18, items from there, tea services in particular but pieces from other series and several figures as well, found their way into the Museum via bequests. The Hans Burckhardt-Burckhardt bequest in 1923 enlarged the collection by 62 pieces made in various factories. An extensive and very well documented private collection was bequeathed to the Museum by Dr. Emanuel Hindermann in 1948, consisting of porcelain plates from the Compagnie des Indes of the type prized in C18 Basle and parts of services made in French factories. Many items of everyday crockery from the former Burckhardt residence and later museum of domestic life, the Segerhof, came to the Haus zum Kirschgarten in 1951 with the rest of that collection.

Five hundred and 14 items, approximately one fifth of the total collection, are grouped according to the factories that produced them in the basement of the Haus zum Kirschgarten; the remainder is distributed through the other rooms or stored as a study collection. The Strasbourg faience made by Charles-François, Paul and Joseph Hannong in the period 1721–81 is both the focal point of the display and one of the strongest aspects of the collection. Blue faience from the early period and Joseph Hannong's flower services were used in Basle as tableware for special occasions. Soon a tradition of private collecting also developed in this field. Thanks to the gift in 1992 of more than 80 items from Jacques Voltz and his heirs Théodore and Mathilde Voltz-Vogel, supplemented with other gifts and deposits of outstanding single items – as well as selective purchase – a collection has been assembled that is regarded today as the most important collection of Strasbourg faience in Swiss public ownership. The quality of several outstanding pieces in the collection such as the shaving bowl painted and signed by Christian Wilhelm von Löwenfinck (no. 333) is comparable with any of those held by the Musée des Arts Décoratifs in Strasbourg.

With the incorporation in 1976 of some 500 porcelain figures from the Pauls-Eisenbeiss-Stiftung, established by Rosemarie Pauls Wilz – formerly the private collection of her parents Dr. Emil Pauls and Dr. Erika Pauls-Eisenbeiss – which are on display on the ground floor of the Haus zum Kirschgarten, the ceramic collection of the Historisches Museum Basel has achieved international importance. The emphasis in this collection, which is restricted to the Meissen, Höchst, Frankenthal and Ludwigsburg factories, is on groups of figures and single figures made by Meissen modellers, with figures by Johann Joachim Kändler occupying pride of place. As well as choice pieces from all four factories decorated by outstanding painters, the tableware in the collection includes a few items from famous services, such as a plate from the coronation service of King Augustus III of Poland (no. 327).

Between 1987 and 1993 more than 400 items in the very heterogeneous ceramics collection of the Basle Gewerbemuseum (arts and crafts museum) were taken over by the Historisches Museum, so that more modern work is now also represented. It includes groups of vessels in Art Nouveau and early Art Deco style made by the factories of Zsolnay/Pécs (Hungary), Richard Mutz, Altona (Hamburg) and Amstelhoek (Amsterdam), also pieces from the Copenhagen porcelain factory, the Grand-ducal factory in Darmstadt and by the ceramicist Max Laeuger (Kandern and Karlsruhe). Such leading Swiss artists as Mario Mascarin, Edouard Chapallaz, Arnold Zahner father and son, and others are represented by single items, without forgetting ceramicists from the Basle region such as Horst Kerstan and Hermann Messerschmidt (Kandern). IPM

323
Study collection

Dish on low foot
Pesaro, ca. 1540
Maiolica, painting in 'high-temperature' pigments, diameter 26 cm, height ca. 5 cm
Inv. no. 1882.150. Alter Bestand

The maiolica plate with a scene representing Gaius and Octavius was acquired before the foundation of the Museum and may have been purchased in the hope that the Swiss National Museum, which was established in Zurich in 1898, would be founded in Basle. An inscription on the underside of the dish, "gaio co / lanio / fato in / pesaro", still the subject of scholarly debate, places the dish among a small group that are all inscribed "fato in Pesaro". The painter of these *istoriato* plates is named the 'Argus painter' after a dish showing Mercury freeing Io from Argus in the British Museum. He was one of the circle of ceramic painters in Urbino, of which the leading figures were Nicolò da Urbino and Francesco Xanto Avelli da Rovigo. IPM

324
Study collection

Bellarmine (jug in the form of a bearded man)
Frechen, 3rd quarter 16th century
Stoneware, height 24 cm
Inv. no. 1898.81. Purchase

The "Bartmannkrüge aus rheinischem Steinzeug" (bearded men jugs of Rhenish stoneware), known in English as bellarmines, developed from the anthropomorphic vessels made in the Middle Ages in the area around Cologne. These early pieces, which probably had an apotropaic significance, had a modelled face and arms applied across the belly. They evolved in the C16 into a round-bodied vessel with a stylised mask on the spout. The face and the other decorations were made from applied relief-stamped pieces of clay. The decoration consists of formalised leaf-shapes and round medallions with profile heads and a damaged inscription encircling the jug that repeats the words, "Des Herren Wort bleibt in Ewigkeit" (the word of the Lord is everlasting). The brown ground colour that is typical of these jugs was produced by a thin coating of slip containing iron that combined with salt thrown into the kiln when the temperature was at its highest. The resulting oxidization gives an orange-skinned glaze. The touches of blue were produced by a smalt, similar to a glass flux, containing cobalt. IPM

325
Haus zum Kirschgarten

Dish
Hanau (no mark), ca. 1700
Faience, painting in 'high-temperature' pigments, diameter 37.8 cm
Inv. no. 1928.709. Rudolf Nötzlin-Werthemann bequest

This dish from the early period of the Hanau factory gives no hint of the decoration and shapes that would be characteristic of its later products. The floral decoration of this dish can be parallelled with that of two other pieces, a dish with the arms of Bavaria in the Museen der Stadt Hanau and a jar with a narrow neck in the Landesmuseum Cassel. An identical set of stencils was used on all three. The flowers, known as 'woodcut-flowers' or 'Barockblumen' (baroque flowers) are derived from German engraved patterns, for example those by Johannes Tünckel (1642–1683). They perpetuate the Asian *fleurs des Indes* motifs; together with a Chinese crane, these are most strikingly reproduced on the Cassel jar the shape of which is reminiscent of an East Asian covered vase. IPM

326
Haus zum Kirschgarten

Covered tureen
Meissen, painter probably Johann David Kretszschmar, swords mark in underglaze blue, ca. 1730/35
Porcelain, underglaze blue, on-glaze painting and gilding, diameter of tureen without handles 25 cm, height with cover 21 cm
On deposit from Pauls-Eisenbeiss-Stiftung Basel

The culture of eating at table had reached a peak in the C18 and had a lasting impact on the manufacture of tableware. The forms that still adorn our tables today were designed then. While the lids of some tureens had a notch for a ladle and were intended for punch or other fairly liquid foods, tureens such as this, with a closed cover, were usually used for serving cold pies or pâtés. Since the handles are shaped like little fish – gudgeons or gobies – this example would have been used for fish dishes. The painted decoration is based on Japanese Imari ware, which in its turn drew upon Chinese porcelain of around 1600: the brocade-like lambrequin is decorated with Chinese 'imperial flowers' and Buddhist symbols. The stand – a rare survival – completes the effect; the pattern of the cover and the lambrequin are repeated as decorative elements around the border. IPM

327
Haus zum Kirschgarten

Plate from the coronation service of Augustus III, King of Poland and Elector of Saxony
Meissen, painting of Höroldt period, swords mark in underglaze blue, incised Johanneus number N = 147 over W, 1733
Porcelain, on-glaze painting and gilding, diameter 22.8 cm
On deposit from the Pauls-Eisenbeiss-Stiftung Basel

The service that was used on the coronation day of Augustus III in Cracow (18 January 1734) has the arms of Saxony and Poland in a gilt cartouche. This use of the owner's coat of arms may be a reference to the silver tableware with armorial decoration belonging to his predecessor, Augustus the Strong. The rim of the plate is decorated with delicate gold scrollwork, similar to that in Chinese scenes designed by Höroldt in the 1730s. Two small sheaves of rice in the depressed centre and the scattered 'Indian' flowers are based on East Asian patterns. Höroldt preferred simple shapes for tableware since his painting showed to special advantage on the smooth surfaces. In the case of the coronation service, the elegant forms are emphasized most effectively by the subtly applied gilt lace-work and the restrained colour. IPM

328
Barfüsserkirche

Jug, dated 1737
Oberwil bei Basel
Earthenware with *sgraffito*, height 40 cm
Inv. no. 1878.31. Purchase

The city of Basle is surrounded by valleys with rich clay deposits: to the south lies the Leimental (*Lehm-Tal* – clay valley) with blue clay, and the Kandertal in the north with red clay. However, neither faience nor porcelain were manufactured there and these wares had to be imported. In the city, as in the valleys, potters produced glazed earthenware. In order to be accepted as masters of their craft, Basle potters were required to submit, as a masterpiece, a jug such as the one illustrated here: "... a jug capable of containing ten measures with a narrow neck thrown in a single piece...". The inscription on the present jug reads, "1737 de 6 dag meyen von Johannes p gemacht in Oberwill" (made on the 6 day of May 1737 by Johannes p in Oberwil). It refers to the potter Johannes Parnier (or Bannier, baptized 1697, died 1751) from Oberwil near Basle in the Leimental. IPM

329
Haus zum Kirschgarten

The queen's pet dog, dated 1739
Meissen, modeller Johann Joachim Kändler, no mark, 1738
Porcelain, on-glaze painting and gilding, height 11 cm
On deposit from the Pauls-Eisenbeiss-Stiftung Basel

Miniature and lightweight decorative dogs of various breeds had been depicted on the portraits of high-ranking women and children from the C16. They were bred from long-legged hunting dogs and kept these proportions. The little drawing-room pet with clipped ears that is shown here is not a classic pug, such as appears in other Meissen figures, for it does not have a flattened nose. The little animal seems to have been asleep, as is indicated by the relaxed position of the turned-in paw. Now it has been disturbed and looks up attentively towards the person approaching. In fact the dog belonged to Queen Maria Josepha of Poland, and was modelled by Kändler from a painted likeness. The initials R(egina) P(oloniae) M(aria) J(osepha) and the year 1739 are marked on the collar. In his workbook Kändler commented on his successful rendering of the fabric of the cushioned seat on the "dainty" stool of ornate design. IPM

330
Haus zum Kirschgarten

Spice and egg stand
Strasbourg, Paul Hannong, no mark, ca. 1735/48
Faience with mixed technique of painting, 'high-temperature' pigments and on-glaze with enamel colours, height 16 cm
Inv. no. 1986.310. Purchase

This piece of hors d'œuvre tableware, which has no known parallel, may have been part of a table decoration. If the lower bowls were intended for boiled eggs, the upper ones could have been used for salt, or for nutmeg, pepper or mustard, which last had been in use from the C14. The upper part is detachable and could be used on its own as a spice dish. The painted decoration combines *fleurs des Indes*, the fantastic flowers and insects evolved by Paul Hannong between 1735 and 1748, with realistic garlands of fruits and flowers. This is a first venture, still with a restricted range of colours, towards the European style of flower decoration in enamel colours. IPM

331
Haus zum Kirschgarten

The indiscreet Harlequin, Beltramo and Colombine
Meissen, modeller Johann Joachim Kändler, no mark, ca. 1740
Porcelain, on-glaze painting and gilding, height 16 cm
On deposit from the Pauls-Eisenbeiss-Stiftung Basel

In 1567 a troupe of professional actors in Mantua broke away from the rules of the classical theatre, and started to improvise in a broader context as the *Commedia dell'arte*. Their success contributed to a standardisation of the costumes and the actors always played characters of a certain type and origin. The plays were burlesque, and vulgar *lazzi*, or farces, connected the loosely linked scenes. Their coarse eroticism and bright colours fascinated courtly society beyond the frontiers of Italy. Thus in 1737 Augustus III arranged for a troupe of his own to be assembled in Venice and to be brought in 1738 to the court at Dresden. Painters such as Watteau portrayed the *comici*, and the rewarding subjects these characters afforded were also appropriated for the applied arts, too. Virtually every porcelain factory production-line featured them, and they often occurred on painted wallpapers in upper-class houses (for example in the dining room of the Haus zum Kirschgarten). The reform of the Italian theatre introduced by Goldoni brought their colourful activities to an end: burlesque comedy ceased to be popular towards the mid-C18. IPM

332
Haus zum Kirschgarten

The happy family
Meissen, modeller Johann Joachim Kändler, no mark, 1744
Porcelain, on-glaze painting and gilding, height 16.7 cm
On deposit from a private collection with the Pauls-Eisenbeiss-Stiftung Basel

According to Erika Pauls-Eisenbeiss only one other version of this crinoline group was made. It is not mentioned in Kändler's workbook, but in the sales catalogue or 'Taxa' it appears as a group consisting of a "well dressed lady sitting on a chair, with a child on her lap wearing a 'Fell hütgen' and a long dress, and a young man in attendance on the lady"; at 18 thalers it was one of the most expensive pieces. Because of the intimacy of the scene, emphasized by details such as the arms forming an embracing circle and the lady demurely offering her cheek to be kissed, the group was somewhat over-hastily named *The happy family*. The child – quite the lady – is correctly offering her left hand to be kissed. The "Fell hütgen" is in fact a 'Fallhütchen' or padded forehead band to protect the head from injuries caused by falling (see no. 422). This accessory for small children was used in middle-class circles, too, and several examples survive in the costume collection of the Museum. IPM

333
Haus zum Kirschgarten

Shaving bowl
Strasbourg, Paul Hannong, painter Christian Wilhelm von Löwenfinck, 1748–53
Faience, on-glaze painting and gilding, length 33.5 cm, width 17.8 cm, height 8 cm
Inv. no. 1895.78. Gift of Adelheid and Elisabeth Buxtorf

Because of its decoration and the signature in gold on the underside, "v.Löwenf.peint", this object is one of the most valuable surviving ceramics from Strasbourg. The signature is that of Christian Wilhelm von Löwenfinck, who had trained in Meissen and then worked in Strasbourg from 1748. The flower spray in the centre of the bowl and the decoration on the rim are painted with the utmost delicacy and reflect von Löwenfinck's absolute mastery of his art. Nonetheless, he did not work without patterns: the outlines of the flowers are produced from stencils following various prints by Jacques Bailly (Graçay ca. 1629–1679 Paris), Jean-Baptiste Monnoyer (Lille 1636–1699 London), and Jacques Vauquier (Blois 1621–1686 Blois). Once the design was transferred on to the glazed surface of the dish it was painted with enamel colours. The shaving bowl carries the coat of arms of the Buxtorf family, scholars and merchants who were resident in Basle. This particular shape was not only used by barbers for shaving, but also served as the shop-sign of their trade. It is not known why it was chosen for a costly faience present. IPM

334
Haus zum Kirschgarten

Pair of duck tureens
Strasbourg, Paul Hannong, numbered on-glaze 1 and 2, 1748–54
Faience with painting on-glaze in enamel colours, height 32.5 and 36.5 cm
Inv. no. 1973.76. Purchase

The Paul Hannong factory owed its success to its policy of employing potters, painters and modellers from the best faience and porcelain centres of Germany. There is a solid sensuality to the table decorations that the factory was famous for: covered vessels in the shape of boars' heads, wild and domesticated fowl accompanied by white cabbage and salad, and plates with all kinds of decorative foodstuffs. The painting of this ware was exceptionally refined and exploited every nuance of the technique of painting in enamel colours to define the robust forms of the dishes. Tureens such as these, on a table or sideboard, would hardly have been convenient for serving warm food as the complex shapes of the covers made their removal and replacement difficult. More often, smaller dishes, perhaps containing duck or boar pâté, would have been placed inside until they were due to be served. IPM

335
Haus zum Kirschgarten

Miners
Meissen, modellers Johann Joachim Kändler and Peter Reinicke, small swords mark in underglaze blue, ca. 1750
Porcelain, on-glaze painting and gilding, height 22 cm
On deposit from the Pauls-Eisenbeiss-Stiftung Basel

The profitable mining of silver around Dresden led to miners' processions being held on feast-days in the presence of the court and its guests in nearby Freiberg. The daintily modelled figures contrast with the real circumstances outlined by one miner in a poem he presented to the prince on the occasion of such a parade: "I work yet I am poor". A mining academy was founded in Freiberg in 1765 and in 1768 the official dress of the miners was regulated. On his shoulder the figure on the left carries the ornamental, broad axe reserved for the higher grades. The middle figure can be recognised as belonging to the rich tradition of 'mining musicians': he accompanies his singing on the triangle. The figure on the right – identifiable by reference to an engraving by Christoph Weigel as an 'Untersteiger', a kind of overseer for underground workings and the workforce – has a silver pan on his shoulder; he holds a pointed trowel, and his unsheathed sword indicates his noble birth. All three are wearing caps decorated with a hammer and chisel, padded jackets, boots with knee-guards, and leather aprons – indispensable for their work – known as 'bum-leathers'. The overseer is more finely worked than the others; his face is modelled in the same way as that of the chief of the mine, also in the collection, who has the features of Augustus the Strong. IPM

336
Haus zum Kirschgarten

Covered vase
Hoechst, wheel mark in underglaze blue, ca. 1755
Porcelain, on-glaze painting and gilding, height 35.3 cm
Inv. no. 1948.710. Dr. Emanuel Hindermann bequest

A comparable vase in the Historisches Museum in Frankfurt-am-Main has two merry putti sitting on the shoulders of the vessel and the reserved area round the landscape decoration richly adorned with applied roses. The Frankfurt piece shows the influence of still more lavishly decorated display ornaments which could be up to 40 cm tall. The present example is more modest and, from the numerous perforations, can be identified as a container for pot-pourri, a form produced in several variants by Hoechst. Such vessels were used to contain aromatic wood, dried petals, etc, substances with a scent that would be diffused through the openings in the shoulder and the lid. The two iron-red dragons are stock *chinoiserie* motifs, giving the lid a more pagoda-like appearance. IPM

337
Haus zum Kirschgarten

Merchant's wife*, companion piece to a *Merchant
Frankenthal, modeller Johann Friedrich Lück, crowned CT mark in underglaze blue, after 1765/70
Porcelain, on-glaze painting and gilding, height 15 cm, width 16 cm
On deposit from the Pauls-Eisenbeiss-Stiftung Basel

Porcelain figures depicting domestic or family scenes give an intimate insight into everyday life. The merchant's wife is carefully shown in informal dress; over her frilled bodice and long floral skirt she wears an open robe or jacket of the same pattern with a wide, turned collar, the *caraco* popular with the middle classes. Her dainty shoes are decorated with buckles. On her fashionably powdered hair she wears a simple mob-cap. Though she is alert, her pose is relaxed as she enters items with her goose-quill, copying from the account book held in her other hand. The invoice in front of her lists the goods spread on the floor around her, along with their prices and the name of the town, Frankfurt: "(Zucker)hut" (sugar loaf), "[?...]back" (... cake) and "Liceur" (drink). The simple little Rococo table also holds ceramic writing materials including an ink-pot, a sander and an open box. This piece was modelled after the Meissen group of ca. 1755 by Johann Joachim Kändler that is also in the collection. IPM

338
Haus zum Kirschgarten

Casque ewer with bowl
Hoechst, wheel mark in gold, ca. 1755
Porcelain, on-glaze painting and gilding; ewer height 22 cm; bowl, length 38 cm, width 27 cm
On deposit from the Pauls-Eisenbeiss-Stiftung Basel

Ewers and bowls had been used for hand washing since antiquity. In the C18 they were made from porcelain or faience as part of table services and were handed around by servants. The wide spout provided the most efficient stream of water for hand washing. The first Hoechst tableware was made of faience; it was after 1750, when the factory manufactured porcelain, that it achieved the outstanding quality of which this set – one of two in the collection – is an example. The elegant painting with 'German flowers' – roses, auriculas, buttercups, scillas and others – is skilfully applied over the fine background relief moulding that was then in fashion. IPM

339
Haus zum Kirschgarten

Ballerina and male dancer bowing to applause
Ludwigsburg, modeller Joseph Nees, probably with collaboration of G. F. Riedel, CC mark in underglaze blue, painter's mark, scratch marks, ca. 1760/62
Porcelain, on-glaze painting and gilding; height 15.5 cm, base length 11 cm, depth 8 cm
On deposit from the Pauls-Eisenbeiss-Stiftung Basel

Duke Karl Eugen von Württemberg (1728–1793), who began his reign at the age of 16, turned his court into one of the most magnificent in Europe. He had been brought up at the court of Frederick II of Prussia and took the French way of life cultivated there as his model. After the influx of actors from Dresden resulting from the Seven Years' War the Württemberg opera became the finest in Europe. Its ballet employing more than 100 male and female dancers and soloists under the direction of Jean-Georges Noverre was world famous. Noverre wrote a comprehensive theoretical work and the illustrated part of it must have been a source of inspiration for the ballet scenes reproduced at the Ludwigsburg factory. These dancers, bowing to applause, are dressed in the costumes then customary for ballet. In contrast to women singers who appeared in large crinolines, the female dancer is dressed in a short, bobbing crinoline with side panniers which does not hide the movement of her legs. Her partner also wears a crinoline skirt over his knee-breeches. Nees emphasized the gestures of his dancers by modelling over-long arms. IPM

340
Haus zum Kirschgarten

Dish
Strasbourg, Joseph Hannong, IH mark, mould number 96, painter's mark 90, ca. 1764/70

Faience, on-glaze painting in enamel colours, diameter 29 cm
Inv. no. 1983.397. Gift of Théodore and Mathilde Voltz-Vogel in 1992

The renewed prosperity of the faience manufactory in Strasbourg from 1762 under Joseph Hannong accompanied a streamlining of the methods of production. This is apparent in the wares decorated with fine flower painting where the palette of enamels used is restricted to a few, typical colour combinations – in expensive decorations, the purple used for the main blooms is dominant. The painter's brush flew fast and fluently over the glaze; nevertheless, even in the case of fine flower painting, stencils were used to provide the outlines. The wilting tulip on the present dish follows a print by Jean-Baptiste Monnoyer (Lille 1636–1699 London). Joseph Hannong had probably brought the stencil with him from the Frankenthal porcelain factory that his father had founded: a more elaborate version of the same flower appears on an oval dish from Frankenthal. IPM

341
Haus zum Kirschgarten

Plate
Strasbourg, Joseph Hannong, IH mark, mould number 43, ca. 1764/70

Faience, on-glaze painting and gilding, diameter 24 cm
Inv. no. 1991.250. Purchase

Around 1765 the Paul Hannong factory produced a service for Cardinal Louis-César-Constantin de Rohan (1697–1779), Bishop of Strasbourg, and his nephew, Cardinal Louis-René-Eduard de Rohan (1734–1803). The pieces were in shallow relief and had rich flower painting in decorated borders of cobalt blue with a golden rim. Of the entire service, scarcely more than a dish and a plate in the Musée des Arts Décoratifs, Strasbourg, and a plate in a private collection survive. After Joseph Hannong, son of Paul Hannong, had taken over the Strasbourg factory in 1762, he would have come across either the moulds for this service or unpainted white ware, which moved him to produce some individual pieces including this plate. It is painted, in a manner that was unusual for Strasbourg ware, with purple *camaieu* landscapes based on stencils. These scenes are in the style of François-Antoine Anstett, although no evidence exists for his employment at the Strasbourg factory at this time. IPM

342
Haus zum Kirschgarten

***Violin-plucker*, from the *Solo musicians* series**

Ludwigsburg, attributed to the modeller Johann Christian Wilhelm Beyer, no mark, incised Elbs, ca. 1765/66

Porcelain, on-glaze painting and gilding, height 20 cm, length 12 cm, depth 9.2 cm
On deposit from the Pauls-Eisenbeiss-Stiftung Basel

The Pauls-Eisenbeiss Foundation owns all the soloist figures from the Ludwigsburg concert set except the woman singer: they are the French horn player, the cellist, the violinist, the violin-plucker, the female spinet-player and the guitarist. The violin-plucker is modelled with the expressive twist of body and casual clothing typical of all these figures. They were probably made as a table decoration for use at the Württemberg court. The artist took the opportunity to make the most of the figures' varied poses and drapery, and was very probably also a distinguished sculptor of large-scale works. IPM

343
Haus zum Kirschgarten

The sleeping shepherdess

Hoechst, modeller Johann Peter Melchior, no mark, ca. 1760 or earlier

Porcelain, on-glaze painting and gilding, height 22.5 cm, width 32 cm
On deposit from the Pauls-Eisenbeiss-Stiftung Basel

Court life in the Rococo period, which sought refuge from reality in a constantly re-created, imaginary world – a *paradis artificiel* – compensated for such elaborate presentation by glorifying country life, which was perceived as natural and sweet. Thus Queen Marie-Antoinette would go dressed as a shepherdess with her attendants to her *hameau* on one of her estates and while away the time drinking milk from expensive porcelain cups. In this piece the shepherdess, wearing an unusually short dress, has lain down to sleep beside her beribboned lamb. The shepherd, boy and dog form an apparently protective arch over her. But an erotic element is present (although compared with the French engraving on which it was based it has been greatly toned down for the German market): the shepherd has just taken a rose which had been covering her breast. The group derives from the engraving *Les Amours pastorales* by Claude-Augustin Duflos (1752) after François Boucher. Another example of the same group, unpainted and with the blue Hoechst wheel mark, is also owned by the Pauls-Eisenbeiss-Stiftung. IPM

344
Haus zum Kirschgarten

The sultan's children
Hoechst, modeller Johann Peter Melchior, wheel mark with electoral crown in underglaze blue, ca. 1770
Porcelain, on-glaze painting and gilding, height 18.5 cm
On deposit from the Pauls-Eisenbeiss-Stiftung Basel

The girl and boy are portrayed in costly oriental clothing made of silk and edged with gold. The modelling concentrates particularly on the fabric: the eye dwells on the swathes of drapery, by which the movement of the figures seems virtually smothered. One can appreciate the weight of the lined cloaks and admire the contrast between the undersleeves of fine, transparent material and the firmer texture of the other garments. The fairytale, decorative aspect of the Orient that was conveyed by prints such as that of the *Recueil Ferriol* (1712–15, 1719/22, Weigel, Nuremberg) was particularly appealing to C18 taste. More pompous than *chinoiserie*, the fashion for things Turkish – a final response to the Turkish wars of the C18 – found its way into court portraiture: thus the Marquise de Pompadour was painted three times as a Sultana. Almost all the great porcelain factories produced Turkish series after engravings, but those made in Hoechst do not follow the printed models exactly, and that makes them particularly attractive. IPM

345
Haus zum Kirschgarten

With the hairdresser
Ludwigsburg, modeller Karl Gottlieb Lück, CT mark with crown in underglaze blue, year number 72, 1772
Porcelain, on-glaze painting and gilding, height 18.5 cm, length 22 cm, depth ca. 14.5 cm
On deposit from the Pauls-Eisenbeiss-Stiftung Basel

This group shows a wig-maker doing the hair of a splendidly clad gentleman in the presence of his uncoiffed and informally attired lady and a little spaniel. Wigs for men came into fashion at the French court at the end of the 1660s in spite of Louis XIV's initial rejection of them. Originally they were bulky and heavy but at the time when this group was made they were more lightly constructed, with the hair raised high above the forehead. The hair was always powdered. For practical reasons, the French Regent, Philippe d'Orléans, introduced the use of a hair bag made of black, rubberised taffeta to the French army. It restrained the plait or knot of the wig at the neck and prevented powder soiling the jacket. Soon the hair bag, forming a pretty contrast with the white hair, became an indispensable fashion accessory. In the C18 hairdressing scenes were a popular theme in graphic art, providing glimpses of intimate domestic life. The high wigs which were fashionable between 1764 and 1778 were also a theme for caricature. This scene depicting the hoisting up of an excessively large hair bag should also be understood as such. IPM

346
Haus zum Kirschgarten

'Veilleuse' or nightlight
Durlach, no mark, ca. 1770–75
Faience, painting in 'high-temperature' pigments, height 22.2 cm
Inv. no. 1922.17. Purchase

In Basle, where many objects of the applied arts are known by French names, this object is called a 'Veilleuse', or nightlight. Originally it would have included a small oil-lamp to keep warm the liquid or broth in the container on top. The faience factory in Durlach, Baden, also supplied Basle, though it was less important than Strasbourg. Like most ceramics manufacturers in the C18, Durlach offered, besides a range of traditional and genre European decorations, *chinoiseries* with painting in 'high-temperature' colours in blue/black and light green/manganese – the latter was particularly striking and typical of Durlach. The source for such subjects was mainly the engravings of Elias Baeck (1679–1747), the favourite painter and engraver of the Durlach painters in the Chinese manner. IPM

347
Haus zum Kirschgarten

Maid
Zurich/Schooren, Z mark with 2 points in underglaze blue, scratchmarks, ca. 1773
Porcelain, on-glaze painting and gilding, height 14 cm
Inv. no. 1894.269. Gift of F. Weitnauer

One response to the ideas of the philosopher Jean-Jacques Rousseau (Geneva 1712–1778 Ermenonville) was the fashion at court for pursuing 'innocent country life'. These pastoral games were reflected in porcelain figures. This little maid of Zurich holding her hymnbook is at once a particularly appealing variation of German court pastoral groups and a document of fashion history. Though it is coloured gold, purple and red her light summer clothing remains modest. The small yellow bonnet is probably a 'Schwefelhütchen' (a sulphur cap); such a hat made of straw coated with a sulphur-dyed substance was an element of several Swiss costumes. IPM

348
Haus zum Kirschgarten

Plate
Zurich/Schooren, Z mark with 3 points in underglaze blue, ca. 1775
Porcelain, on-glaze painting and gilding, diameter 23 cm
Inv. no. 1932.312. Purchase

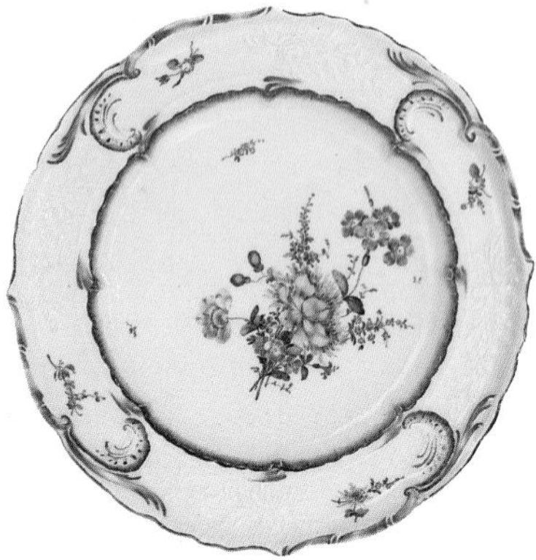

During a dispute over the use of the Zürichsee, delegates from Zurich had lodged in the monastery of Einsiedeln. To compensate for the high costs they had incurred, the council of Zurich had a table service of nearly 500 pieces made for the monastery by the Zurich/Schooren factory. One artist is believed to have been occupied for more than a year in painting the floral decoration. This plate could be one of the group of "plate(s) with a golden rim and a rose garland, magnificent, diameter 23 cm" mentioned in the inventory of 1883. The white moulded pattern of roses, which runs in relief around the plate, augments and enhances the painted decoration. The delicately shaped border was based on prototypes from the Meissen and Ludwigsburg factories, including a form of relief decoration for the rim of a cup from Ludwigsburg. The flourishes that curl from the edge of the plate over the border are, however, original inventions of the Zurich/Schooren factory. IPM

349
Haus zum Kirschgarten

The town of Mannheim in mourning
Frankenthal, modeller Konrad Link, no mark, after 1778
Porcelain, on-glaze painting and gilding, height 22.5 cm, width 32 cm
On deposit from the Pauls-Eisenbeiss-Stiftung Basel

In 1720 after a chequered history the town of Mannheim was chosen by Karl Philipp, Elector of the Palatinate, as his official residence, and it developed into a centre of court culture. It was further embellished in the reign of his successor Karl Theodor, whose initials CT appear on the pieces manufactured by the Frankenthal porcelain factory which he supported. In 1778 Karl Theodor left Mannheim, transferring his court to Munich. The mourning over the departure of such a great patron of the arts is represented in this group of figures. The town, in the person of a beautiful young woman, is overwhelmed by grief. She is still wearing the royal ermine, but has already laid aside the crown and sceptre, placing them on a cushion. The Elector's sword is lying at her feet near an urn, and a distressed putto is pointing to the helmet among the pieces of armour left behind. A second putto is trying to comfort her while sharing her grief. A woman dressed in bourgeois clothes is weeping into her handkerchief – no doubt indicating that it was not only in court circles that the departure of the popular Elector was regretted. IPM

350
Study collection

Dish
Les Islettes, no mark, after 1785

Faience, on-glaze painting, length 31.5 cm, width 21.8 cm

Inv. no. 1983.980. Gift of Théodore and Mathilde Voltz-Vogel in 1992

As the taste for *chinoiserie* spread in the C18, most large ceramics factories came to offer wares decorated in this manner alongside their range of products with traditional European decorations. Bizarre and exotic vehicles, such as the one on the dish illustrated here, became a popular motif after the publication of Arnoldus Montanus's work on the embassies of the emperor of Japan (Amsterdam, 1669). His book had included an illustration of a Japanese lady riding in a two-wheeled vehicle pushed by a servant, and the same rickshaw-like conveyance reappears in an engraving by Johann Christoph Weigel of ca. 1720. The cheerful, richly coloured *décor au chinois* of the eastern French factories, however, depended more upon variations based on engravings by Jean Pillement. The vehicle that is pulled and pushed by two men on this dish was reproduced from a similar stencil on a fish platter by the same factory that is also in the Museum. It also appears on numerous faience pieces from the Lunéville region, as well as some from Trouche/Raon L'Etape, and on a faience dish from Lyons. IPM

351
Study collection

Potpourri vase
Gérardmer, studio Joseph Vincent, no mark, 1834

Earthenware, marbled clay, transparent glaze, height 40 cm.

Inv. no. 1992.62. Christiane Seiler bequest

Archival research on minor French faience manufacturers has brought to light previously little known wares with unusual decoration. The technique of marbling clay was practised in China during the T'ang dynasty (C8) and first appeared in Europe, in Staffordshire, England, as 'agate-ware' ca. 1730–40. Clay that was in part naturally marbled was combined with oxide-coloured clay in such a way that the separation of the colours was maintained and vessels thrown from the integrated mass had a marbled appearance. This vase is designed to hold potpourri, or aromatic organic substances, and is also documented as a pouring vessel, a *fontaine*. In the factory it was recorded as a 'Medici-vase', next to all sorts of everyday items. IPM

352
Haus zum Kirschgarten

Mayeux as a painter with his model
Zizenhausen, Anton Sohn, after 1835
Clay, made in a mould, fired and painted, height 16 cm, length of base 16 cm
Inv. no. 1983.130. Dr. Charles Morel-Plievier bequest

Painted terracotta Zizenhausen figures, of which the Museum owns numerous groups and single pieces, were made in the workshop of the Sohn family in Kümmerazhofen or, after 1799, in Zizenhausen near Stockach on Lake Constance. Typical Zizenhausen figures, which were used as everyday ornaments in bourgeois, Biedermeier living rooms, feature a wide range of subjects. Under the influence of the Basle art dealer Johann Rudolf Brenner, who supplied Anton Sohn with models, these included groups of the famous Basle *Dance of Death* after Merian the Elder and further Basle characters and genre scenes after Hieronymus Hess (1799–1850). An important group is concerned with political caricatures from the satirical journal *La Caricature* (1830–35) by, among others, Daumier, Grandville and Traviès. Traviès devised the group copied here, the comical hunchback Mayeux, who is shown as the portraitist of a society lady. The inscription on the base, which does not survive, read, "Il n'y a qu'une bonne école, madame, c'est l'école de *la bosse*" (There is only one good school, Madame, that is the school of 'la bosse'), where *bosse* meant both hunchback and also *bosser*, hard work. IPM

353
Haus zum Kirschgarten

Decorative plate
Sarreguemines, stamp in brown CHINA SARREGUEMINES, ca. 1880/90
Fine stoneware, transfer printing, on-glaze painting and gilding, diameter 39.8 cm
Inv. no. 1991.66. Purchase

The rise of trade and industry fairs and world exhibitions that were such a characteristic feature of the C19 encouraged ceramics manufacturers to ever higher technical achievement. Splendid vases and wall-plates decorated with portraits were particularly suitable vehicles for the historicising taste of the period. The circulation of prints and the application of transfer-printing to ceramics facilitated an eclectic mixing of styles. This decorative plate from the firm of Utzschneider & Cie portrays against a rich gold ground the Basle mayor Jakob Meyer zum Hazen, following a drawing made by Hans Holbein the Younger around 1516 in connection with the painted double portrait of the mayor and his wife now in the Öffentliche Kunstsammlung Basel. The decoration around the borders of such portrait dishes was by preference derived from Italian Renaissance ceramics, in this case Deruta. This 'Holbeinplatte' is unique; it is not known who commissioned it, and it was probably an experimental piece intended for an exhibition. IPM

Glass

The glass collection of the Historisches Museum comprises about 1100 items, most of which are in store though available for study. About 150 glass objects from the collection are shown in limited-period exhibitions in the garden pavilion of the Haus zum Kirschgarten.

The collection has not been built up typologically but has been accumulated as a result of gifts and bequests from private Basle collectors. However, it has a good range and offers the connoisseur some interesting examples of international manufacture – for instance, a very early example of cut glass from Nuremberg (no. 357), or three diamond-cut glasses of historical importance, or the bottle once owned by the mayor of Basle Johann Rudolf Wettstein (no. 359). The earliest glass, from the C13 or C14, has come from excavations in Basle. The range extends forward to large crystal-glass services from the first half of the C20. Quantitatively German and Bohemian cut glass of the C18 and C19, of varying quality, predominates. The collection includes simple beakers and goblets incised with the coats of arms of old Basle families or of the guilds, which were probably sold by itinerant glass-cutters. Swiss glass manufactories of the C18 and C19, for example the Entlebucher factory, producing enamelled, coloured and cut glass with folkloristic motifs, are also represented.

In 1993 more than 500 glasses passed to the Historisches Museum from the former, very varied, collection of the Gewerbemuseum, now the Museum für Gestaltung. As a result the collection extends to industrial design and to historicising glasses, such as a group of glasses from the Rheinische Glasshütten AG of Ehrenfeld near Cologne, which in the C19 specialised in copies of antique and historic glass. IPM

354
Barfüsserkirche

Millefiori ball
Venice, after 1500
Glass embedded with coloured glass and gold, diameter 3.25 cm
Inv. no. 1917.824. Amerbach Cabinet

With the development of glass manufacturing an inlaying technique had already been evolved in antiquity, based on the ability to draw fine threads from the molten lump of glass, the paraison. However, it required the particular skills of Venetian glassmakers to develop the refined technique that this glass ball exemplifies. Fine glass rods of various colours were fused together and the resulting fragile and colourful skein of glass was sliced across to produce cross-sections in the form of tiny stars and rosettes. These components were combined with spirals twisted from fine ribbons of glass and gold foil and were fused into the clear glass of the ball. In 1495 this type of decoration was described as *millefiori* (thousand flowers) by the Venetian Marcantonio Sabellico. The technique has continued to be used through the centuries and is still found today, although of coarser execution, in glass paperweights. This rare, early example is listed in Amerbach's inventory of 1578 as "1 venedische Kugelen" (1 Venetian ball). It was included more as a curiosity than for its value and its presence illustrates the diversity of a Renaissance 'Wunderkammer'. IPM

355
Barfüsserkirche

Flute glass with raspberry prunts
South Germany or Bohemia, 1st quarter 16th century
Blue-green glass with applied raspberry prunts, engraved, height 28.8 cm
Inv. no. 1922.194. Gift of Hans Burckhardt-Burckhardt

This glass was owned by the Schaffhausen alderman Hans Stockar-Peyer (1490–1556). He is known to have made three pilgrimages, in 1517 to Santiago di Compostela, in 1518 to Rome, and in 1519 to Jerusalem. He became a Knight of the Holy Sepulchre during his last pilgrimage and the fact that crosses of Jerusalem appear next to his engraved initials and its style suggests that the glass should be dated around 1519. The main decoration of such glasses, the rich application of raspberry prunts, was explained by the Lutheran preacher Johannes Mathesius in 1562 as a response to German drinking customs: "... but finally art had to adjust itself to the country, so that glasses became stronger and more durable and could be more easily held by drunk and clumsy people, therefore the strong, knotted or knobbed glasses came into use". With a capacity of almost 2.5 litres a glass as heavy as this would indeed have needed a firm grip. IPM

356
Barfüsserkirche

'Humpen' with the coat of arms of the abbey of St. Blasien, Germany, dated 1626
South Germany
Green glass with enamel painting, height 34 cm, diameter 13 cm
Inv. no. 1893.320. Purchase

The 'Humpen', a large cylindrical beaker, is a German, or rather Bohemian, form of drinking vessel. The one illustrated here can hold about 3 litres of beer and reflects the heavy drinking customary in some male circles. The three-dimensional prunts that formerly decorated the sides of narrow flute glasses and afforded a firm grip gave way at the end of the C16 to a smooth form that could be decorated with enamel painting. The arms of the Benedictine abbey of St. Blasien (St Blaise) are set within a scrollwork cartouche; they are not, however, entirely correct heraldically. The reverse carries the coat of arms of the abbot. On the basis of its date, the glass is assumed to have belonged to Blasius Münzer II, abbot of St. Blasien 1625–38, who would have used it as a 'Willkomm', a beaker for offering a welcoming drink. The abbot fled from the warfare raging first in the Basle region, then spreading to the Black Forest in 1632, by going into exile in Switzerland, where he died in 1638 in Wislikofen in the canton of Aargau. IPM

357
Haus zum Kirschgarten

Beaker
Nuremberg, 17th century
Intaglio engraved glass, height 9 cm, diameter 9 cm
Inv. no. 1890.31. Purchase

From the C16 South German glass-houses sought to raise the technical skill and quality of their glass to the standard of Venetian products, and, at the same time, to develop particular forms of decoration for German glasses. At the turn of the C17, stone and glass cutting flourished in Prague at the court of Rudolf II. In 1609, during Rudolf's reign, Caspar Lehmann from the Principality of Liechtenstein both was raised to the nobility and received the privilege of cutting glass. After his death in 1660 Lehmann was succeeded by his highly talented assistant Georg Schwandhardt, who moved to Nuremberg and, with the goldsmith and glass cutter Hans Wessler, founded the great tradition of glass cutting and polishing there. Though lacking the usual small ball-feet, the beaker has a shape characteristic for Nuremberg, one which lent itself to glass cutting, diamond-point engraving or 'Schwarzlotmalerei' (enamelling in black or sepia). Such very early engraved decoration with flowers and insects executed in the stiff manner of woodcuts is extremely rare. IPM

358
Haus zum Kirschgarten

Wing glass 'à la façon de Venise'
Netherlands, 1st half 17th century
Smoke-tinted glass, worked at the lamp, height 16.8 cm, diameter of bowl 11 cm
Inv. no. 1908.124. Purchase

This glass is an extremely thin and graceful *calice ad alatte* (goblet with small wings) with a wide bowl supported on a winged stem and broad, attached foot. The transparent *cristallo* has a delicate tint that reflects the blue of the wings. Only a few glasses with bowls of this shape are known, although soon afterwards other Mannerist glasses with snake-like and lyre-shaped winged stems were being produced by glass-houses working *à la façon de Venise*, for example in Brussels, Liège and Hessen-Kassel. Compared to authentic Venetian examples, the austere style of the undecorated parts and the flat, pinched wings indicate a transalpine workshop working to emulate Venetian ware. IPM

359
Barfüsserkirche

Flask, dated 1664
Cobalt-blue glass, with diamond-point engraving, height 31.3 cm, diameter 29.8 cm
Inv. no. 1908. Gift of A. La Roche-Burckhardt

This flask was owned by Johann Rudolf Wettstein (1594–1666), who was mayor of Basle in 1645 and in 1648 at the peace conference of Westphalia at Münster achieved the separation of the Swiss Confederation from the Holy Roman Empire. The engraved decoration of the bottle was incised with a diamond point, a technique that was developed in various centres of glass production from the end of the C16 and was especially popular during the C17. The coat of arms of Wettstein, with griffins as supporters, is on the front of the flask while on the back there are three medallions in a frame: in two of them the Basle crosier appears – pointing to the right in one, to the left in the other – and in the third the nimbed, crowned, double-headed eagle that was the emblem of the Holy Roman Empire. The eagle occasionally appeared as a decorative element on Swiss applied arts even after 1648. The place of production of this flask and a similar one in cobalt-blue in the Kunstmuseum, Düsseldorf, has yet to be identified. IPM

360
Haus zum Kirschgarten

Beaker
Bohemia, 2nd quarter 18th century
Double-walled glass with inserted gold leaf decoration, height 8.8 cm, diameter 7.3 cm
Inv. no. 1970.3463. Purchase

In his 15th sermon, on glass-making, of 1562, Johannes Mathesius declared, "When the wine stands beautifully in a glass, hence particularly if one pours a clear red wine into a gold or well gilt cup or bowl it appears like a ruby within it, so that one covets it for oneself". The Bohemian 'Zwischengold' beakers and cups of the first half of the C18 seem a manifestation of this vision. The stag-hunt depicted around this beaker is engraved in gold leaf on the smooth outer side of the inner layer of glass. The lip of this layer overlaps the facetted outer layer that encases it, and the join is also cemented, so the protective colourless lubricant between the two glasses will not escape. The inserted base is decorated with a small basket of flowers in the same technique, but heightened with red lacquer.
IPM

361
Haus zum Kirschgarten

Goblet with the coats of arms of the 13 'Alte Orte'
Probably Switzerland, 18th century
Glass with enamel painting, height 19 cm, opening 9.2 cm
Inv. no. 1917.153. Purchase

This goblet was made with the simplest of techniques and in a form that has served as a type of wine glass throughout Europe from the C16 to the present. Nevertheless, in comparison with similar glasses from important centres of glass making, it appears rustic and is likely to have been made in a minor glass-works. It is a product of folk art, which continued the stylistic characteristics of the leading centres of glass making after they had been superseded in their places of origin. As only the 13 cantons of the pre-Napoleonic Federation, the 'Alte Orte', are displayed the goblet can be dated before 1798. A date in the C18 is confirmed by the small, white cross in the upper left corner of the coat of arms of "Schweitz", the canton of Schwyz: from the formation of the Swiss Federation until the C17, Schwyz had only a plain red coat of arms, but during the C18 a small, white cross was used somewhere in the upper part of the shield, and from 1815, in the Federal seal of the 22 cantons, the cross gained its permanent position in the upper right corner. Similarly the heraldic position of the 'Baselstab', the crosier of Basle, was not established until the C19.
IPM

362
Haus zum Kirschgarten

Goblet
Bohemia, ca. 1830/40
Double-layer or flashed glass, height 19.3 cm, diameter 7.6 cm
Inv. no. 1930.213. Purchase

After decorative techniques on colourless, transparent glass had reached their peak towards the end of the C18, the old coloured glass techniques were revived and were put to fresh use on pieces conforming to contemporary taste. Here, a transparent, pink layer of light 'gold-ruby' glass is fused on to a colourless glass body. By polishing (as opposed to glass-cutting, which involves fine incisions) the surfaces were decorated at the same time as areas of the coloured layer were removed. In this way the effect of slender neo-Gothic tracery was achieved on the goblet. Without its stem the glass would resemble the much more common beaker shape of the period. Later double-layer techniques were limited to the cheaper application of red or yellow stain fired in a 'muffle' kiln and the authentic technique of flashing was not revived until the Art Nouveau period. IPM

363
Study collection

***Asymmetrical cat*, glass object**
Designer Walter Bodmer, Basle; Centro Studio Pittori Arte Vetro, Murano, 1955
Transparent coloured glass, opaque enamelled decoration, height 30 cm
Inv. no. 1955.8. Purchase

After taking over the glass collection of the former Gewerbemuseum in 1987 the holdings of the Historisches Museum were extended to include glass art objects of the C20. Following the 1955 exhibition *Glaskunst aus Murano* (art glass from Murano) in the Gewerbemuseum (now Museum für Gestaltung), four glass pieces were purchased: *Goat* by Pablo Picasso, *Rays* by Gio Ponti of Milan, *Rocket* by Gino Krayer of Venice, and *Asymmetrical cat* by Walter Bodmer of Basle. A document of 25 November 1955 confirms that these objects were made in the Centro Studio Pittori Arte Vetro Murano "from original designs and according to the specifications of the artist". Walter Bodmer (Basle 1903–1973 Basle) is one of the most important modern artists to come from Basle. His abstract wire pictures and sculptures first came to public attention in 1936 and soon found international recognition. The material and technique of the glass cat do not do justice to the abstraction of Bodmer's design and, for this reason, he was unhappy with the project. IPM

Furniture and woodwork

The Historisches Museum has approximately 1400 pieces of furniture. More than one third (520) of the total stock is permanently exhibited. The larger part (ca. 350) is displayed in the 25 rooms devoted to domestic life in the Haus zum Kirschgarten; the five so called 'historical rooms' in the Barfüsserkirche are furnished with the smaller part (ca. 170). Other important individual pieces are integrated in the itinerary through the history of Basle in the Barfüsserkirche and elsewhere. Generally the furniture of the C15 to the early C18 can be found in the Barfüsserkirche, while the furniture of the period after about 1720 is set out in the Haus zum Kirschgarten.

The Late Gothic, Renaissance and Baroque periods are represented in the Museum by a range of chests, cupboards, tables, sideboards and beds of international importance. Certain pieces of furniture have particular weight from the point of view not only of typology and craftsmanship but also of provenance. The churches and monasteries, the town councils, guilds and wealthy citizens that formerly commissioned or owned them are known. Several pieces of furniture are associated with famous personalities such as Erasmus of Rotterdam, Basilius Amerbach or Jacob Burckhardt. The largest part of the collection consists of everyday bourgeois furniture of the C18 and C19. The emphasis has been placed on furniture from Basle; however, it has not been limited to objects produced in Basle, but extends to furniture used in Basle, and thus to pieces imported from Paris in the C18 and Milan and Mainz in the C19.

The Museum's holdings of furniture as a whole may be divided into two large groups: the general collection, which has about 600 pieces of furniture of all typological categories, and the special collection of 800 chairs. The latter includes the collection of chairs from the former Gewerbemuseum Basel (arts and crafts museum), which dates up to very recent times and is available for research purposes.

The selection from the furniture collection presented here is complemented by that of fixtures such as panels and portals, and also by architectural elements made of wood. This testimony to the art of joinery, usually originating from houses that have been torn down, has been built into the Museum or has been preserved as fragments to serve as sources for the history of architecture. vR

364
Barfüsserkirche

Cupboard for the treasure of the Basle Münster
Basle, 2nd quarter 15th century

Wood carcase, with limewood carvings, iron hinges, tin-coated; height 356 cm, width 268 cm
Inv. no. 1904.375. Alter Bestand

According to an inventory of 1477 the two-stage four-doored cupboard was donated to the Münster by the chaplain Johannes Hanffstengel, who died in 1452. It was fitted into an upper bay of the vault of the Romanesque sacristy in the Münster, and this situation was reconstructed for its installation in the 'Schatzkammer' (treasure chamber) of the Barfüsserkirche in 1906. The frame of the Late Gothic cupboard consists of an openwork frieze of leafy tendrils running through birds, flowers and grapes and crowned on top by merlons. The panels of the doors are decorated with openwork tracery on red and blue backgrounds. The iron hinges develop at each end into stylized garlands, which blossom into Basle crosiers in three places. This gives an indication of the important function of the cupboard: it contained the liturgical instruments and vessels of the Basle Münster treasury. vR

365
Barfüsserkirche

Marriage chest
Zurich(?), ca. 1490

Oak carcase and carving, height 57 cm, width 177 cm, depth 64 cm
Inv. no. 1870.505. Purchase

Chests from the Late Gothic period that declare their secular function in the programme of their imagery are rare. The front of this chest is decorated with six round arches with ogee tracery carved in low relief: the two outer arches are filled with sprays of flowers and leaves; the two innermost ones display the coats of arms of the Eastern Swiss house of the von Brandis (on the left) and of the Zurich family of the von Ottikon (on the right), making its production for a wedding probable. In the arches in between are represented Delilah cutting Samson's hair, from the Old Testament, and St Jerome taming the lion; as the nearby scrolls once must have explained, these two scenes probably allude to married life. Stylistic comparison with the carvings on the choir-stalls in the church of St. Peter in Basle has led recently to the suggestion that the woodcarver Ulrich Bruder, who had immigrated from Otwyl on Lake Constance in 1495, was responsible for the chest (see also no. 150). The chest was published with an illustration as early as 1868. Its purchase by the Museum prevented its imminent disposal on the Paris art market. vR

366
Barfüsserkirche

Wainscotting from the Haus zum Cardinalshut, Freie Strasse 36
Basle, ca. 1500
Pinewood, height on wall 302 cm
Inv. no. 1893.93. Gift of the Aktiengesellschaft der Brauerei zum Cardinal

Hans Bär, who died a hero's death in 1515 in the battle of Marignano as the Basle standard-bearer, and whose colossal image decorates the tower of Basle town hall, is recorded as the owner of the property zum Cardinalshut from 1490, and it can legitimately be supposed that he commissioned this Late Gothic panelling. Its installation in the Museum in 1894 made some changes to the proportions necessary, with the rearrangement of doors and windows and even the restoration of whole sections of the wainscotting. Comparison to reception rooms of the same period remaining *in situ*, such as the episcopal bedchamber or so called Rotbergstube in the Bishop's Palace dating from the middle of the C15, or the Zscheckenbürlinzimmer in the Charterhouse of 1509 (see no. 367) illustrate the more modest character of this wainscotting from a bourgeois house. Elements of its decoration include a frieze of blind ogee arches running along the top of the long sides of the room, and carved heads, rosettes and ornamental motifs on the beams of the ceiling. Coloured wall-hangings made in the Upper Rhine area in the C15 provided decoration for the rest of the wall, and the wainscotting was unpainted. The room is illuminated by two windows, each of three lights, with a stone column between them. AN

367
Barfüsserkirche

Bed from the Basle Charterhouse
Basle, 1510 or 1512
Carcase: oak, beech; carving: pinewood, limewood; height 291.5 cm, width 194 cm, length 241 cm
Inv. no. 1906.3504. On deposit from the Inspektion des Waisenhauses

The buildings of the Carthusian monastery at St. Margarethenthal in Kleinbasel, founded in 1401, were extended and splendidly refurbished by Hieronymus Zscheckenbürlin, prior 1501–36. This splendid bedstead with its 'Halbverdeck' (half-canopy) protruding 140 cm came to the Museum from the so called 'Zscheckenbürlinzimmer', a richly panelled room in the guesthouse which had been redecorated under Prior Zscheckenbürlin. In fact the donation of a large bed worth six guilders by Morand von Brun and his wife Maria for the visitors' chamber in the "great house" is documented in 1510, together with a white 'Catalan' ceiling, as well as in 1512 the donation of a second bedstead by the merchant Lienhard Fuchs from Neuenburg. Characteristic elements of the extant bed are the parts of the frame carved in a shallow relief pattern, the 'cheeks' beside the headboard with openwork tracery, and the canopy crowned by little merlons. vR

368
Barfüsserkirche

The Erasmus chest, dated 1539
Jakob Steiner(?), Basle
Carcase: limewood; veneer and carving: Hungarian ash, walnut; height 113 cm, width 197 cm, depth 69 cm
Inv. no. 1870.911. Amerbach Cabinet

As an early example of a piece of Renaissance furniture from north of the Alps, as a secular reliquary for the effects of the famous humanist Erasmus of Rotterdam, who died in Basle in 1536, and symbolically as the nucleus of the collecting and museum tradition in Basle, the Erasmus chest occupies a prime place amongst the objects of the Historisches Museum. The programme of carving on the chest conceived by Erasmus's heir, the jurist Bonifacius Amerbach, refers to the chest's function and raises it to the status of a cenotaph: "For myself and in remembrance of the greatest among the circle of scholars have I had this made", reads the Latin dedication on the feet at the front. The heads in the medallions are those of Solomon, Aristotle and Virgil, to be interpreted as representatives of Hebrew, Greek and Latin literature, and that of Erasmus himself, the leading scholar of his time and their match and equal. Erasmus's effects, consisting of household goods, ornaments and cutlery of precious metal, are partially preserved and displayed in the Museum next to the chest. vR

369
Barfüsserkirche

Coin cabinet of Basilius Amerbach
Mathys Giger(?), Basle, 1576/79
Walnut, oak, pine, limewood, beech, maple, height 45.7 cm, width 73.3 cm, depth 55.8 cm
Inv. no. 1908.16. Gift of the Universitätsbibliothek Basel

This display cabinet is formally and technically without precedent and is striking in its simple elegance, its functionality and its quality of craftsmanship. Its cuboid shape has no unused interior cavity and is accessible on all four sides. On the front side are three niches, in which statuettes of the ancient gods Jupiter, Venus (no. 154) and Mercury stood like tutelary deities of the chest's treasure, which consisted mostly of antique coins, and of about 3,780 pieces altogether. The drawers on the right contained Greek and Roman coins in 803 pouches, those at the back held the collection of medals, including the medal of Erasmus, and on the left were kept pieces of particular value, such as gold coins, works in mother of pearl, gems, cameos and uncut precious stones. The cabinet's refinement illustrates the importance given by Basilius Amerbach (1533–1591) to the collection of coins and medals within his collection as a whole. It is the only extant piece of furniture from the annex to his residence in the Rheingasse that he constructed for his collection between 1578 and 1582. vR

370
Barfüsserkirche

The Wettstein bed
France(?), 2nd half 16th century, with alterations made about 1650
Solid walnut, height 157 cm, length 299 cm, width 162.5 cm
Inv. no. 1873.17. Gift of Margarethe Burckhardt-Heusler

According to family tradition the splendid bed which entered the collection in 1873 came from the household of the mayor of Basle Johann Rudolf Wettstein (1594–1666) (see no. 285). It is an example of a bed without posts, for which the canopy had to be attached to the ceiling or to the wall. Characteristic elements are the dominating motif of godroons on the frame and the front legs and that of feathers on the sides of the bedhead frame. Both motifs are typical of the repertoire of the French Renaissance during the reign of Henri II; the royal deathbed, as depicted in an engraving of 1570, makes a good comparison. Thus the frame of the Wettstein bed suggests that it was made before the time of its presumed owner. Only the top part of the bedhead, consisting of carved scrollwork with masks and a cartouche with a male bust, with which the bed was fashionably refitted for Basle's prominent citizen, can be securely dated to the C17. vR

371
Barfüsserkirche

Dropfront cabinet of Andreas Ryff: detail of the marquetry on the inside of the dropfront, dated 1592
Basle
Walnut and various woods, some stained and smoked; height of panel 49.5 cm, width 70.3 cm
Inv. no. 1906.1120.a. Purchase

Cabinets with rich marquetry inlay were extremely popular during the C16. In this example from Basle, a cabinet entirely plain on the outside, the luxury is limited to the inside and reserved to the owner when handling the objects of his collection. The owner is known: he was the Basle cloth merchant Andreas Ryff, whose initials AR with the date 1592 are inlaid on the rear of the upper part of the cabinet, and on the inside of the dropfront shown here the combined coats of arms of the Ryff and Brunner families appear in the central ring of foliage. Von Ryff's collection – he was involved in excavations at Augst – is unfortunately not preserved. There is evidence for his particular knowledge of music from early youth (see no. 466) and the instruments portrayed in the marquetry are a further reflection of his ownership, even though musical instruments were a common subject of still lifes in general. Nine instruments and various other utensils are represented: transverse flute, eye-glasses, cornet, case for the flute, harp, lute, trumpet, score, viola da gamba, transverse flute, drum and recorder. vR

372
Barfüsserkirche

Door from the guildhall of the Zunft zu Spinnwettern (building trade workers' guild), dated 1593
Basle
Oak and walnut, height 336 cm, width 236 cm
Inv. no. 1879. On deposit from E.E. Zunft zu Spinnwettern

In the late C16 the interior of the house of the Basle guild 'zu Spinnwettern' (building trade workers) in the Eisengasse was refurbished. The main room on the first floor was supplied with a splendid door and corresponding panelling in 1593. Straightening of the street in 1839 made it necessary to tear the guild's house down. Only the door with its carvings and inlay was preserved; it is the only evidence of the room's interior decoration and an outstanding example of the art of woodworking in Basle during the late Renaissance. Corinthian columns and carved volutes resembling herms flank the door and carry the complicated lintel or attic. In the middle is a cartouche with an inscription which carries details of the redecoration of the guildhall and the names of the officials and master of the guild in office in 1593. The arms of the guild and the coats of arms of the officials mentioned decorate the broken pediment over the attic; there is also, hidden behind the left-hand capital, an unidentified coat of arms, which should be interpreted as the signature of the master carpenter who executed the work. AN

373
Barfüsserkirche

Cabinet
Basle, ca. 1593
Carcase: oak, walnut; veneer: oak, walnut, ash, maple; height 254 cm, width 225 cm, depth 109 cm
Inv. no. 1882.187. On deposit from E.E. Zunft zu Spinnwettern

From 1589, in order to qualify as a master craftsman in Basle, a cabinetmaker had to make a four-doored cabinet (or in exceptional cases alternatively an extending table). For the exterior decoration he was required to use the five orders of columns and to show his knowledge of the laws of proportion, for architectural theory was regarded as the basis of his art. For the purpose, he would use the printed model books that were available. Those following the trades of joiners, cabinetmakers, makers of tables, woodworkers and carvers were all members in Basle of the guild 'zu Spinnwettern'. Shortly after the new ordinance came into effect the guildhall was redecorated in 1593 (see no. 372) and supplied with "its first masterpiece" (as the qualification piece was called), presumably this mighty cabinet. The design is articulated in full accord with the classical rules: the lower part is in the Tuscan order, the upper part in Ionic. Characteristic of this type of cabinet in southern Germany around 1600 is the linking of the two 'storeys' by a projecting entablature supported by flanking columns in the Corinthian order. vR

374
Barfüsserkirche

'Häuptergestühl' (stall of the council and magistrates) **from the Basle Münster,** dated 1598
Hans Walter, Conrad Giger, Franz Pergo, Basle
Solid oak, height 814 cm, width 850 cm, depth 196 cm
Inv. no. 1914.626. Gift of the Baudepartement Basel-Stadt

In appearance this monumental masterpiece of the art of woodworking in late Renaissance Basle follows the tradition of choir-stalls. Functionally, however, it derives from household and council seats or thrones. It is the earliest and largest such work created in the aftermath of the Reformation in Switzerland, overshadowing the choir-stalls in Wettlingen, Beromünster and Lucerne. The inscription on the top of the middle section bears a dedication honouring the Basle government as the protector of the true religion and defender of the law and of justice. On the 18 seats of the 'cathedra magistratus' or 'Häuptergestühl' sat the mayor or 'Bürgermeister' and the chief of the guild masters ('Oberstzünftmeister'), flanked by their predecessors in office and the town council and court clerks. Members of the inner council ('Kleiner Rat') and the servants of the council ('Ratsdiener') divided amongst themselves the rest of the seats. The 'Häuptergestühl' stood on the left side of the nave of the Münster near the main entrance until 1854 (see no. 186). Its installation in the church in 1598 had provoked controversy, as the clergy feared that with its overwhelming sculptural decoration with purely secular motifs dominated by grotesques, there would be a pagan idol publicly displayed in their church. vR

375
Barfüsserkirche

Panelling and sideboard from the Haus zur Isenburg, Martinsgasse 18, dated 1607
Franz Pergo, Basle
Oak, walnut, ash, maple; wall-panelling, height 305 cm; sideboard, height 279 cm, width 184 cm, depth 63 cm
Inv. no. 1879.105. Purchase
Inv. no. 1914.200. Gift of A. Refardt-Bischoff

The merchant Johann Lucas Iselin, trading in spices and arms, also called 'reiche Iselin' (rich Iselin), bought the Haus zur Isenburg on the corner of Martinsgasse and Stapfelberg in 1594. The rich panelling which Iselin had made in 1607 for a corner room of almost square plan is testimony to the modernity of his taste and his high pretensions. The architectural articulation with three-quarter columns in the Tuscan order, the window-like infill elements and the marquetry resembling ironwork in the friezes characterize the wall-panelling. In the deeply cut centrepiece of the richly moulded, symmetrical coffering the combined coats of arms of Iselin and his wife, Anna d'Annone, are resplendent, followed by the date. The buffet or sideboard, which belonged to the room originally and formally harmonizes with the decoration of the walls, is one of the oldest extant examples of this type of furniture in Basle. Both panelling and sideboard can be attributed on grounds of style to the master joiner Franz Pergo, who had worked in Basle since 1593. AN

376
Barfüsserkirche

Portal of the Haus zum Schwarzen Rad, Steinvorstadt 6, dated 1615
Basle
Oak, sandstone, height 319 cm, width 265 cm
Inv. no. 1882.207. Gift of the Borgognon brothers

During its extensive refurbishment in 1615 the Haus zum Schwarzen Rad in Steinvorstadt was supplied with a magnificent Renaissance portal, which came into the possession of the Historisches Museum in 1882, when the property was converted into a pharmacy. Both elements, the wooden door and the stone portal, were executed at the same time and formally harmonize with each other, but were not necessarily from the hand of the same craftsman. On the basis of certain stylistic peculiarities the wooden part may be regarded as the work of the Burgundian master joiner Franz Pergo, who had made a name for himself in the town of his adoption with the splendid portal of the hall of the governing council in 1595. The imposing stone arch with strapwork relief decoration encloses a richly carved oak door, of which the surface is articulated by architectural motifs. Framing pilasters and built-in tabernacles create an illusion of space and disguise the opening of the door proper. A 'green man' mask, a characteristic element of Renaissance decoration, crowns this illusionistic architecture. AN

377
Barfüsserkirche

Cabinet, dated 1619
Franz Pergo, Basle
Walnut, height 241 cm, width 170 cm, depth 68 cm
Inv. no. 1905.278. Faesch Museum

This 'Kunstkammer' cabinet, which is to be associated with the collection of the Basle jurist Remigius Faesch, follows in the tradition of the South German 'Kunstschrank' (ornamental cupboard) of the C16, but owes its appearance and design entirely to court-influenced Burgundian furniture in the style of Hugues Sambin. The woodworker and joiner Franz Pergo had emigrated to Basle from Burgundy in 1590. With its lavish exterior this piece of furniture, which has numerous interior drawers to contain the precious items of the owner's collection, itself is a work of art. Its repertoire of decorative motifs and its programme of imagery flattered the owner's taste and culture. Additionally, the cabinet claims attention through a series of Mannerist devices, such as the precocious use of winding columns which seem to be giving way to the force of the exploding bombs above them on the cornice, or its cunningly shaped keyholes, or its large but disguised notice of the year of its making. vR

378
Barfüsserkirche

Panelling and buffet from Schloss Gross-Gundelfingen, dated 1674, 1677, 1741
Basle
Painted pinewood; height of wall-panelling 234 cm; height of sideboard 285 cm, width 181 cm, depth 58 cm
Inv. no. 1895.172. Purchase

The series of historical interiors installed in the Barfüsserkirche concludes with a painted panelled room with matching sideboard from Schloss Gross-Gundelfingen. This largest of the four moated castles situated south of Basle at the foot of the Bruderholz came into the possession of the Platter family in the middle of the C17. The doctor Felix Platter III was responsible for decorating the room in the north-west corner of the first floor with panelling on the walls and fictive marble painting and figures on the ceiling. The coffers of the ceiling are decorated with scenes from Greek mythology. The twelve rectangular panels on the walls feature the female personifications of the months. Allegories of the Virtues on the buffet, dated 1674, and allegories of the Senses on the C18th doors complete the programme, a reflection of the humanistic culture of the owner. The painted ceiling from the Haus zum Hasen, today in the chancery of the Basle town hall, is a further work by the same unidentified painter. AN

379
Barfüsserkirche

Table of the Basle town council
Johann Christian Frisch, Basle, 1675
Solid walnut, inlaid with mother of pearl, ivory, ebony and tin; height 85 cm, width 116 cm, length 184 cm, 348 cm extended
Inv. no. 1894.490. Alter Bestand

Described as a "mensa artificiosa", an ingenious table, this lavish piece of furniture was immediately installed as a showpiece in the Haus zur Mücke together with the rarities of the Amerbach Cabinet in the year of its presentation to the council of Basle. It was never actually used as the table of the council of Basle, or as an element of the town hall's furniture, in despite of the intentions of its maker. The table is remarkable for the mastery of its carving and its lavish marquetry; it was the masterpiece of the Linz-born J. C. Frisch, who presented it to the city of Basle in 1675. In return he was remitted the fee of 100 guilders for the right of citizenship. The deeply carved feet of the table represent pairs of lions, basilisks, putti and wildmen bearing coats of arms. The inlaid frieze on the table top carries depictions of the 12 months and of the 12 cantons joined with Basle in the Confederation, also an inscription praising Basle as the most fortunate republic in Helvetia. A copy of the table, made in 1878–82, has stood in the town hall since 1964, and a second, still later copy also exists. vR

380
Study collection

Bay window from the Domprobstei (residence of the provost) **of the Münster, Rittergasse 18**
Basle, 2nd half 17th century
Oak, height 96 cm, width 72 cm, depth 53 cm
Inv. no. 1886.134. Gift of Carl Bachofen-Burckhardt

'Guggehyrli' ('see and hearies') was the name given in Basle to the carved oak bay windows that in the C17 and C18 were installed on numerous house fronts and enriched the city's streets. Travellers' accounts confirm the multitude of 'Guggehyrlis' in Basle, but only three examples have been preserved in the collection of the Historisches Museum. These wooden window extensions, decorated with flower and leaf ornaments, have a peephole on each of their three sides. They enabled the inhabitants inside, principally the female ones, to watch what was going on in the street, while being both concealed and protected from the wind and rain. The 'Guggehyrli' of the house in Rittergasse 18 is representative of an earlier type: in contrast to later examples its peepholes are not glazed and are held in openwork panels resembling grills. A small opening in the floor made it possible to see vertically downwards, but probably was mainly used to throw alms to beggars. AN

381
Barfüsserkirche

The Meyer zum Pfeil wardrobe
Basle, ca. 1700
Carcase: pine; veneer: walnut; height 256 cm, width 230 cm
Inv. no. 1937.20. Caroline Meyer-Seiler bequest

This magnificent wardrobe, along with other pieces of Baroque furniture, forms part of the Meyer zum Pfeil room, a room in the Historisches Museum dedicated to the memory of this prominent Basle family. The twin-doored wardrobe is in general typical of southern and south-western German furniture of its period, in which such spiral columns were fashionable. However, its three turned finials above the columns are unusual, and columns like these, which were carved by hand – unlike diagonally fluted examples, which were produced on a lathe – were a particularly frequent feature of cupboards and sideboards made in Basle between about 1664 and 1710. In this respect the joiner and 'ornemaniste' Johann Heinrich Keller (guild member 1657), who published a model book on columns and decoration in 1680, was particularly influential, not only in Basle but also further afield. Wardrobes like this with spiral columns, consoles in the shape of angels' heads and motifs of fruit on the cornice, yet otherwise restrained in the use of decoration, are therefore in Switzerland often called 'Basle' cupboards. vR

382
Haus zum Kirschgarten

Painted door from the Haus zum Lautengarten, Malzgasse 28/30
Basle, ca. 1700
Painted oak, height 206 cm, width 97 cm
Inv. no. 1919.61. Gift of Peter Sarasin-Alioth

Ceilings and wall-panellings painted with ornaments or figures had been an element of fashionable interiors in numerous houses of Basle's citizens since the C17. This door painted on both sides comes from the Haus zum Lautengarten in the Malzgasse, belonging to the Sarasin family. The rear side (not shown) represents a cooper with a hammer and a glass of wine under an arch; the front depicts a gardener with a glass of wine and a pruning-knife standing between plants. A small Seville-orange tree in a tub indicates the predilection of the period for exotic plants – as in a well known full-length portrait of the Basle town doctor Felix Platter by Hans Bock the Elder, dated 1584. Probably the door belonged to the 'Trinkstube' (parlour) of the summerhouse which is known to have been in the garden, or marked the entrance to the wine-cellar or wine-press of the house. AN

383
Barfüsserkirche

Great sideboard of the Gartnerzunft
(gardeners' and grocers' guild)
Matthias Müller, Basle, 1710
Carcase: softwood; veneer: walnut; height 344 cm, width 230 cm, depth 72.5 cm
Inv. no. 1901.54. On loan from the E.E. Zunft zu Gartnern

This magnificent example of Baroque display furniture, measuring almost 3.5 m in height, was the centrepiece of the large guildhall of the Basle guild 'zu Gartnern' (gardeners and grocers), which was newly decorated in 1710. The carved crown is decorated with the arms of the guild, as well as the coat of arms of the old and new masters of the guild, Philipp Dienast and Leonhard Felber; the latter was the donor of the sideboard. Found in bourgeois households in Basle from about 1530, the so called 'Italian' buffet or sideboard was used to contain and exhibit precious tableware and as a dresser. The architectural articulation with broken-forward double columns of a classical order, not spiral columns, the heavily moulded motifs of the panels, reminiscent of Baroque bastions, and the deep carving are characteristic features of this late example. The buffet of the Basle Safranzunft (merchants' guild) of 1664 in Berlin/Köpenick is an early counterpart. vR

384
Haus zum Kirschgarten

Panelled alcove from a house in the Hebelstrasse
Basle, ca. 1750

Oak, height 298 cm, width 431 cm
Inv. no. 1903.316. Gift of the Pflegeamt des Bürgerspitals

Usually an alcove is a small, windowless niche functioning as a bedroom, connecting to the living room through a large opening. In the middle of the C17 this feature of interior design, originating, as the name recalls, from Arabia, came to Europe via Spain, and became widespread particularly in France. From the C18 it became a typical part of the interior decoration of bourgeois houses in Basle. This alcove with carved oak boiserie in Louis XV style from a house in the former Neue Vorstadt in Basle is firmly symmetrical: the opening in the middle, supplied with a curtain, behind which the bed chamber can be concealed, is flanked by two doors leading to a dressing-room and a toilet respectively. The curvacious profile of the central opening, the relief-carved cartouches in the spandrels of the arch, the frisky lines of the side panelling, the glazed windows and the marquetry panels of the side doors, all these are characteristic features of the Rococo style. AN

385
Haus zum Kirschgarten

Dresser
Johann Gottfried Leuchte(?), Dresden, ca. 1750

Carcase: oak and pine; veneer: rosewood; gilt bronze mounts; height 220 cm, width 124.5 cm, depth 66 cm
Inv. no. 1974.133. Hans Peter His-Miescher bequest

This prestigious piece of courtly furniture reached Basle from the Saxon royal palace in Dresden, following the sale of effects of the Saxon crown around 1880/90 on the Berlin art market, and thence from the collection of the Berlin banker Prof. Werner Weisbach who left Germany for Basle in 1935. The Berlin cabinetmaker J.G. Leuchte (guild member 1747, died 1759), whose signed masterpiece is a very similar cabinet, has been proposed as its maker. On top of an elegantly waisted commode, raised by one level of drawers, rises a cupboard with two doors, originally fitted with mirrors. At the top there are still three bases on which one can imagine three porcelain vases. The migration of this piece of furniture from Dresden to Basle is an occasion to recall that in 1688 Johann Jacob Gothier, a citizen of Basle, travelled in the opposite direction to become a citizen of Dresden and to work there as court joiner and cabinetmaker. vR

386
Haus zum Kirschgarten

Small encoignure (corner cabinet), one of a pair
Paris, ca. 1750
Carcase: oak; veneers: jacaranda, mahogany and other woods; gilt bronze mounts; marble top; height 91 cm, width 86 cm, depth 55.5 cm
Inv. no. 1923.95. Hans Burckhardt-Burckhardt bequest

This elegant piece of Louis XV furniture, together with its pendant, illustrates the inclination of the upper strata of society in Basle during the Ancien régime to French courtly taste. French luxury goods were often imported. The two cabinets stood in the 'Gartensaal' (rear drawing room) of the house at Leonhardsgraben 38, together with a matching commode bearing the mark of the Migeon family of Paris *ébenistes*. From 1771 the house was the residence of Colonel Daniel Frischmann-Heitz (see no. 294), who had returned home after a career with the English East India Company. The convex front of the two-doored encoignure or corner-piece features an asymmetrical rocaille cartouche, decorated with stylised flowers, while the four corners are filled by small cartouches with a cube pattern. vR

387
Haus zum Kirschgarten

Cupboard, dated 1751
Joseph Labhardt, Constance
Carcase: softwood; veneer and carving: walnut; height 234 cm, width 210 cm, depth 87 cm
Inv. no. 1986.217. Gift of Violette Volderauer

Amongst the many anonymous works of furniture documented masterpieces such as this are rare. The carpenter left his name, Joseph Labhardt, the place, Constance, and the date he qualified, 9 December 1751, on a slip of paper hidden behind the base of the central pilaster, where it was discovered during restoration. Further, the coat of arms of the Constance patrician family of Leiner on the keys informs us of the original owners. This type of two-doored cupboard was the standard 'masterpiece' required by guild regulations in South Germany from the middle of the C17 (in Basle from 1664) for aspiring master cabinetmakers. By contrast to Basle examples, this wardrobe achieves a more monumental effect by eschewing double columns and using single pilasters: this is characteristic of Baroque cupboards from the Lake Constance area, as is the light-hearted decoration of the marquetry and the rocaille ornament of the capitals. vR

388
Haus zum Kirschgarten

Console table and upright mirror
France(?), 1768/82
Carved and gilt limewood, marble top; table, height 81.5 cm, width 88.5 cm; mirror, height 293 cm
Inv. no. 1934.82. Purchase

The slenderly proportioned ensemble in the style transitional between Louis XV and Louis XVI comes from the Wendelstörferhof in Basle, also known as the White House, the former town residence of the silk ribbon manufacturer Jakob Sarasin. For the sophisticated decoration of the new house built for him between 1763 and 1770 by the architect Samuel von Werenfels, paintings, textiles, tapestries, wallpaper, furniture and lighting mounts were ordered directly from Amsterdam, Frankfurt, Coblenz, Colmar, Constance, Innsbruck, Berne, Besançon and Nancy, or from dealers. An inscription on the underside of the mirror informs us of its provenance: "J.B. Dubost de Luneville en Lorene près Nancy". The frame of the mirror is decorated with pelicans and climbing roses, which were symbols used in freemasonry and must have directly to do with Jacob Sarasin himself. Similar symbols are found again on the documents and seal of the "grande loge mère égyptienne des pays helvétiques", of which Sarasin was the 'Maître de Chef'. The society was founded in 1781–82 by Count Cagliostro (see no. 172) and existed side by side with the regular masons' lodges that came into being in Basle between 1768 and 1783. vR

389
Haus zum Kirschgarten

Panelling of the Rose Boudoir from the Haus zum Kirschgarten, Elisabethenstrasse 27, dated 1780
Painted by Matthias Klotz, Basle
Painted oak, height 365 cm
Inv. no. 1923.303. Gift of the Regierung Basel-Stadt

The Louis XVI panelling, which from 1923 to 1951 was installed in the Barfüsserkirche, originally belonged to the Haus zum Kirschgarten, where it has now been returned. Its date of 1780 is also the date of the whole suite of living rooms of which it forms a part. Taking its name from the roses with which it is decorated, it was designed as a lady's private room and was given by Johann Rudolf Burckhardt-de Bary to his wife Anna Maria as a kind of moving-in present. It is the last of the suite of rooms on the second floor on the street side of the house, and gives on to a terrace. According to a hidden signature, the painted decoration of roses, forget-me-nots and lilies-of-the-valley bound into hanging bouquets by blue ribbon was the work of the Strasbourg-born court scene-painter of the Bavarian Palatinate, Matthias Klotz, whom Goethe praised in his book on the theory of colour. Klotz was influenced by the art of the Stuttgart court and by his teacher Nicolas Guibal: he followed the French taste in a South-west German variation.AN

390
Haus zum Kirschgarten

Dinner table
France(?), ca. 1780
Walnut and oak, with brass rollers, height 75 cm, diameter 147 cm
Inv. no. 1925.55. Purchase

As the ten legs and the divided top indicate, the table can be converted according to need from a semicircular console to be pushed against a wall to a round dinner table or to a long table, extending nearly 4.8 m. Though so modern in its practicality, the table originally belonged, according to unconfirmed tradition, to a refurnishing of the Haus zum Kirschgarten in 1780 of which very little else remains. The dining room was then one floor below the dining room presently fitted out in the piano nobile. The simple Louis XVI style of the table, round which runs a frieze of carved rosettes punctuated by attachments for the legs decorated with laurel, harmonizes completely with the Neoclassical dignity of the architecture of the Haus zum Kirschgarten. vR

391
Study collection

Part of a window casement, from the Segerhof, Blumenrain 17/19
Basle, ca. 1790
Oak, partially gilded, later painted grey, height 229 cm, width 110 cm
Inv. no. 1990.480. Alter Bestand

The panel fragment with a mirror below and a picture above originally was set above a console table as cladding on a window pillar. It probably belonged to the interior decoration of the Segerhof carried out by the architect Christoph Burckhardt-Merian between 1788 and 1790. Above the mirror, which is set off with rosettes, the corners of the rectangular field around the oval picture are filled with finely carved foliage. The picture is a mezzotint – a printing technique perfected in England in the C18 – of an Old Testament scene as represented in Benjamin West's 1776 painting *The Golden Age*. The work of Benjamin West, an American artist who became the royal History Painter at the English court in 1772, was widely disseminated in such prints. Entitled L'AGE D'OR, the picture also recalls Basle's 'Golden Age' and its affluent merchant patriciate. The gilded carving would have glittered in the light cast by the candles that were originally held by mounts on either side of the mirror. AN

392
Haus zum Kirschgarten

Armchair
Basle, ca. 1790
Oak, with Aubusson coverings, height 95 cm, width 62.5 cm, depth 63 cm
Inv. no. 1923.320.c. Marie Burckhardt bequest

The Louis XVI armchair belongs to a set consisting of a sofa, four armchairs, six upholstered chairs and four stools or *tabourets* together with matching wall-tapestries (no. 246). The whole ensemble was purchased by the Burckhardt family of merchants for the 'Visitenstube' (reception room) of the Segerhof, built 1787–90, one of their residences in Basle. The sturdy but elegant oak frames of the chairs were surely made by a Basle craftsman, but the woven coverings were obtained from Elias Grellet in Aubusson in France. Animals, partly after La Fontaine's fables, are depicted on the seats, while genre scenes appear on the backs. The complete decoration of the Burckhardt 'Visitenstube', which was transferred to the Haus zum Kirschgarten in 1951, consists not only of the set of chairs and the accompanying tapestries, but also of oak panelling and carved overdoors, which were once partially gilded. It is a testament to the influence of the French style of living over the leading citizens of Basle in the years of Reform. vR

393
Haus zum Kirschgarten

The Landammann's chair, 1806
Basle
Frame: beech; carving: limewood(?), gilt; height 122 cm, width 83.5 cm, depth 76 cm
Inv. no. 1884.70. Gift of the Staatskanzlei Kanton Basel-Stadt

During the so called 'Mediation period' (1803–13), when Switzerland was effectively controlled by Napoleon, the head of the government of the cantons of Basle, Berne, Fribourg, Lucerne, Solothurn and Zurich each held the office of 'Landammann' in turn for one year. The office had no executive power and was held by conservatives still devoted to the Ancien régime. The mayor of Basle and Landammann for 1806, Andreas Merian (1742–1811), was no exception. In Basle, in contrast to Berne, where there was a suitable 'Schultheissen' or mayoral throne already in existence, a suitable throne of office for "His Excellency" had to be made. The result was an over-sized upholstered armchair with the gilt ornament of a throne but no insignia. Both its construction and its decoration show the persistence of a rather clumsy Louis XVI style influenced to some degree by the Empire – especially in the way the ornament is applied over a mahogony-coloured ground. vR

394
Study collection

Jacob Burckhardt's desk
Basle, about 1850
Softwood, oilcloth; height 73.5 cm, width 140 cm, depth 96 cm (top, in two parts, 56 cm high, 107 cm wide, 29 cm deep)
Inv. no. 1990.497. Alter Bestand

The desk stood in the private study of the great historian of culture and art Jacob Burckhardt (1818–1897) in his home at am Aeschgraben 6, where he lived from 1892; a photograph shows it in position there. The desk was probably transferred from the house in St. Alban-Vorstadt 64 where he had lived from 1866 until that time. Burckhardt had taken his degree at the university of his native city in 1844 and taught at Basle from 1848 to 1893 as Professor of History and the History of Art. Much of his comprehensive historical work must have been written at this desk. The plain Biedermeier design of the desk with a top with fifteen drawers combines comfort with functionality; despite its formal elegance the desk is not veneered and is surface covered only with black oilcloth. It reflects the rigid discipline and Spartan spirit of its owner. vR

395
Haus zum Kirschgarten

Sitting room furniture of Christoph Merian
Mainz(?), before 1855
Chairs: stained walnut, with velvet coverings; table: jacaranda, solid and veneered; cabinet: mahogany veneered over oak
Inv. no. 1986.123.–127. On deposit from the Christoph Merian Stiftung

This set of furniture for a living room has been preserved from the estate of Christoph Merian (1800–1858), the wealthiest citizen of Basle and probably also the richest man in Switzerland of his time. It consists of a settee, two armchairs, four upholstered chairs, one table and a cabinet. Other items from the possession of Christoph Merian are also preserved and are displayed with these. Two monumental portraits, which show Merian and his wife seated in these armchairs in 1855, demonstrate the value given to the furniture by its owners. It is characteristically historicist in returning to the Louis XV style and, more generally, to the taste of courtly society in the C18. In its homogeneity the suite corresponds to the ideal of bourgeois furniture propagated in the world exhibition of 1851 – a total harmony of all the elements of interior decoration. Mainz was a centre for the production of such furniture, influenced by French taste. Christoph Merian's father had already in 1837/38 ordered large consignments of lamps in Paris and furniture in Mainz for the family's town residence, the Ernauerhof. vR

396
Study collection

'Quinta' armchair, 1985
Designed by Mario Botta, Milan
Steel tubing, perforated steel panels, height 95 cm, width 45 cm, depth 57 cm
Inv. no. GM 1987.74.

Until the C19 a knowledge of architecture was essential for the cabinetmaker or joiner, but in the C20 it is a basic challenge for many important architects and designers to come to terms with the chair. With this a change of material has much to do: metal, instead of wood. An example is the 'Quinta' armchair, designed by the contemporary Ticino architect Mario Botta, and produced by Alias Srl in Milan. This chair both reflects the internationality of production and distribution of contemporary furniture, and holds local interest, since Botta has also designed architecture in Basle. Further important examples, regarded as classics of our century, are represented in the study collection, formerly the chair collection of the Gewerbemuseum Basel (the arts and crafts museum), among them chairs designed by Marcel Breuer (1926), Mies van der Rohe (1926), Le Corbusier (1928), Alvar Aalto (1933), Charles Eames (1944), Max Bill (1950), Eero Saarinnen (1956), M. Pélard (1960) and Don Allinson (1965). vR

Stoves

From the Middle Ages and into modern times tile-clad stoves were the usual form of heating in Basle and its region, as elsewhere. Although Basle has never been a significant centre of the production of such stoves, the collection of the Historisches Museum is outstandingly well endowed.

An early example is the Gothic tower-stove reconstructed in the Barfüsserkirche, with tiles with animal motifs in relief. In the historical rooms of the Barfüsserkirche there are four Winterthur faience stoves with painted or green-glazed relief tiles, of the kind that in the C16 and C17 were an essential feature of the reception and living rooms of the more well-to-do citizens of eastern Switzerland. Though not originating in Basle, these monumental stoves were acquired as suitable ornaments for the still infant Museum in the 1880s and 1890s from the Basle collector and dealer in iron August Scheuchzer-Dür. At the same time Scheuchzer-Dür also supplied the Gewerbemuseum in Basle and the Schweizerisches Landesmuseum in Zurich with stoves, stove tiles and other such objects.

In the Haus zum Kirschgarten 25 tile stoves dating from the C18 to the early C20 are displayed. The tower-stoves and other great stoves of the C18 are richly decorated with paintings and reliefs. Basle had no faience manufactory of its own, so monumental stoves were ordered mostly from Berne and Zurich, although by far the most elegant came from Strasbourg. The Strasbourg faience manufactory of Paul Hannong and the stove-maker François-Paul Acker are represented in the Museum by three singular and splendid painted examples.

Together with the tile-stoves 13 models of stoves are exhibited in a case, including three unique pieces from the Hannong factory, making a well documented, coherent group.

In 1990 more than a thousand tiles were transferred to the Historisches Museum from the former Gewerbemuseum. This study collection, which derives again predominantly from Scheuchzer-Dür, comprises relief and painted examples from Switzerland and Germany dating from the C16 to the C20.

Further disassembled Swiss stoves, including for instance a chest stove from Locher (Zurich), one from Steckborn and a tower-stove made by Andreas Dolder (Beromünster), and other stove parts, account for the remainder of the study collection. IPM

397
Barfüsserkirche

Mould for a stove tile found in the Haus zum Blauen Stein, Rheingasse 11
Basle, 15th century
Coarse clay (grog), design impressed and reworked, height 26.5 cm, width 19 cm, depth 7.5 cm
Inv. no. 1928.36. Gift of Philipp Labhardt

The unicorn, like the basilisk, is one of the fabulous beasts that feature in the imagery of medieval Basle: it is included among a range of mythical creatures shown on tapestries, where its ambiguous powers are subdued by virtuous virgins. The significance of its appearance has been the subject of much scholarly interpretation. The beast figured on this pattern for a stove tile reappears in a modified form on the stove from Augustinergasse reconstructed in the Barfüsserkirche (no. 398). There the animal is transformed into a rearing stag, whose antlers can be better accommodated in the rectangular surface of the tile than the unicorn's horn, which had to be bent round in order to fit. IPM

398
Barfüsserkirche

Stove tile
Basle(?), Peter Hartlieb, 15th century
Relief tile, light slip coating, transparent green glaze, height 24.5 cm, width 25 cm; height of image 24.5 cm, width 16 cm
Inv. no. 1963.260. Gift of the Museum für Völkerkunde Basel

When lift shafts were being dug in the Museum für Völkerkunde in the Augustinergasse tiles and fragments of tiles from a stove were discovered. They were of two types: small, square filler-tiles decorated with griffins and large tiles decorated with powerful, yet delicately worked heraldic animals. In 1981 these rather few surviving pieces were combined with copies and contemporary tiles already in the possession of the Museum so as to reconstruct a Gothic tower-stove for the Historisches Museum's reopening in the Barfüsserkirche. The diameter of 140–150 cm for the stove was determined by the fragments of tiles. A huge and impressive stove was reconstructed, conveying an idea of the one that must originally have stood in the refectory of the Augustinian monastery. One of the original tiles of the stove tower is illustrated here. IPM

399
Study collection

Stove tile, from a series, dated 1552
Lake Constance(?)
Faience with painting in 'high-temperature' pigments, height ca. 29 cm, width 33 cm
Inv. no. GM 1894.1.ff. Purchase

Winterthur, the regions around Schaffhausen and Lake Constance in north-eastern Switzerland, and the bordering parts of southern Germany were early centres for the production of faience tableware and stoves. This group of seven tiles, including three from the holdings of the Gewerbemuseum, is from an early example of a faience stove. The tile illustrated here carries the date 1552. The design, in which the various scenes are set within a Renaissance arcade, was painted with swift yet sure brushstrokes in 'high-temperature' pigments on the unfired tin-glaze, in an early version of the distinctive Winterthur style of painting. The initials "hk" on the tile showing a cooper have resulted in the series being attributed to the well known stove-potter Hans Kraut of Villingen in Swabia. More recently these letters have been interpreted as the monogram of the person depicted rather than of the artist. The tiles came from a stove in Bottigkofen near Kreuzlingen on Lake Constance. IPM

400
Barfüsserkirche

Tiled stove, from Thiengen near Waldshut, dated 1682(7?)
Winterthur, Abraham Pfau
Faience with painting in 'high-temperature' pigments, height 285 cm
Inv. no. 1895.13. Purchase

The majority of the large faience tower-stoves made in Switzerland for upper-middle-class homes and guild and council chambers in the C16 to C18 were produced in Winterthur, mostly at the Pfau and Graf factories. The wide-ranging subject-matter painted on the stoves included allegories, historical scenes and spectacular scenes from the Old and New Testaments. In this case the stove is decorated with scenes from Greek mythology combined with representations of the Seven Wonders of the World. Such stoves, with a thematic programme accompanied by explanatory inscriptions, were conversation pieces that illustrated the culture as well as the wealth of their owners. Five splendid examples from various periods are on permanent display in the Museum, although none of them came from Basle houses. Stoves produced in Winterthur were shipped to eastern Switzerland, the Lake Constance area, and the region round Zurich as far as Brugg. In the 1880s and 1890s the opportunity arose to acquire stoves of this kind for the Gewerbemuseum and Historisches Museum; with a view to the Museum soon to be founded, they were purchased with the help of Federal funds. IPM

401
Haus zum Kirschgarten

Model of a stove, dated 1712
Basle
Earthenware, coated in slip, *sgraffito* decoration, transparent green glaze, height 29 cm, base 16 × 13.5 cm
Inv. no. 1928.291. Purchase

This small tower-stove is a miniature version of the type of stove required by the guild of stove potters as a masterpiece in 1737: "... a round stove for a room with an oval 'head' with good clean glass (glazing)". Such a stove had to "be erected clean and true" by the potter who also had to supply a pitcher with a narrow neck and a pot with a capacity of 11.47 litres. The model stove is decorated with *sgraffito* which is rarely used on real stoves and serves here as an indication of the intended shape of the tiles and the floral decoration. The date 1712 is inscribed on the back of the stove seat and a bird perched on a flower is drawn on its side. The motifs are scratched into the pale coating that covers the model so that the exposed red clay base appears dark under the transparent green lead-glaze. IPM

402
Haus zum Kirschgarten

Model of a stove
Basle, 1st half 18th century
Earthenware, stencilled pattern, height 20 cm, length 29 cm, depth 12.6 cm
Inv. no. 1928.108. Gift of the heirs of Valerie Huber

This model represents the simple type of tiled stove that was used for heating smaller rooms in townhouses and, above all, houses in the countryside around Basle. This shape of stove is also common in the Zurich area. One of these stoves was installed in the maid's room on the upper floor of the Haus zum Kirschgarten. The decoration of the tiles with a stencilled pattern was widespread in the area during the C16 and again from the C18 to C20. Before firing the tile was covered with a stencil of perforated leather and white slip was applied over it. Once the stencil was removed the pattern stood out against the dark ground. A transparent green lead glaze enhanced the contrast of light and dark and gave strength and gloss to the pattern. The knobs and feet were turned on the wheel, and further modelled as necessary. The pilasters on the back carry the inscription "Got gib Gnad" (God give mercy). IPM

403
Haus zum Kirschgarten

Tiled stove
Elgg (canton of Zurich), potter Hans Othmar Vogler(?), painter David Sulzer I(?), ca. 1735(?)
Faience with painting in 'high-temperature' pigments, height 329 cm, width 101 cm, depth 132 cm
Inv. no. 1895.14. Purchase

The stove comes from Zurich, from the Burghof at no. 5 Froschaugasse. Although its painted decoration is in the Winterthur style, its shape, with elegantly articulated forms and contracted tower, is a departure from the classic Winterthur stove. It is attributed to two craftsmen who, having wearied of the rigid Winterthur tradition, built up a rival stove-making company: Hans Othmar Vogler, who had trained in Winterthur but founded a workshop in Elgg in 1717, and the outstanding stove-painter David Sulzer I, who worked in later years with his son David II. For the scenes that he painted on the firebox Sulzer used as a source a series of illustrations to the New Testament by Christoph Weigel that had been published in Nuremberg in 1712. The saints on the pilasters are after Matthäus Merian the Elder; his illustrations in the so called 'Merian Bible' published by Christoph Murer in 1625 were the source for many of the scenes on traditional Winterthur stoves. The tower is decorated with allegories of the Virtues from an unidentified source. IPM

404
Haus zum Kirschgarten

Model of a stove
Strasbourg, Paul Hannong, ca. 1748–50
Faience with on-glaze painting in enamel colours, height 25 cm, base 16.5 × 11 cm
Inv. no. 1991.203. Gift of the Verein für das Historische Museum Basel

Like all the model stoves from Strasbourg in the collection this is a unique piece. The lower part is in the form of a fireplace with the top of a tiled stove curving out on top of it. The missing crowning element was already broken off before the model was glazed. This stove resembles other Strasbourg stoves in the collection not only in the shape of the upper part but also in the delicate painting of *rosé-faux-marbre* and the sketchily applied flower sprays. IPM

405
Haus zum Kirschgarten

Tiled stove

Strasbourg, probably workshop of François-Paul Acker, decorated in the Paul Hannong factory, 1748–53

Faience with on-glaze painting in enamel colours and cold gilding, height 316 cm, width 115 cm, depth 162 cm

Inv. no. 1932.359. Gift of the heirs Valérie Burckhardt-Thurneysen

This Rococo stove from Strasbourg is a unique combination of a simple box shape with magnificent decoration. It was originally in the Würtemberger Hof, one of the great city residences, which was demolished for the building of the Kunstmuseum. The stove now dominates the Louis XV room in the Haus zum Kirschgarten. The models for the exquisite flower paintings were engravings by Jacques Bailly (Graçay ca. 1629–1679 Paris) and Jean-Baptiste Monnoyer (Lille 1636–1699 London), from which single blooms were traced and recombined to form new bouquets. After undergoing pantographic enlargement and further embellishment the outlines of the design were pricked, the cartoon was placed on the white tin-glazed surfaces of the stove and the outlines of the decoration were transferred by means of pouncing powder through the perforations. The completion of the painting in this case was undertaken by a master: on the basis of comparison with a signed shaving basin, also in the Haus zum Kirschgarten (no. 333), the decoration of this stove can be attributed to Christian Wilhelm von Löwenfinck. IPM

406
Haus zum Kirschgarten

Model of a stove
Strasbourg, Paul Hannong, painter probably François-Antoine Anstett, mid–18th century
Faience with on-glaze painting in enamel colours and cold gilding, height 33 cm, base 13 × 17.7 × 13 cm
Inv. no. 1975.96. Purchase

This peculiar hybrid is more of a corner fireplace than a tiled stove, as it is heated from an open hearth and the warmth is accumulated in the tiled casing above. The triangular ground-plan, which would make it possible for the stove to be placed in a corner against an outside wall, demonstrates that these miniature faience stoves were not made for dolls' houses, but as models for envisaged projects. The only known stove of comparable shape is installed in the Augustusburg in Brühl, south of Cologne: it was made in Strasbourg, as this model must have been. The landscape, with a feather-leafed tree arching high over travellers, and the seascapes painted on the model are attributed to François-Antoine Anstett, who worked with Paul Hannong in Strasbourg until 1754. IPM

407
Haus zum Kirschgarten

Model of a stove
Paul Hannong factory, painter probably François-Antoine Anstett, mid–18th century
Faience with on-glaze painting in enamel colours, height 32.5 cm, width 12.5 cm
Inv. no. 1949.357. Purchase

The model shows a type of stove that was most commonly built in German regions and Vienna. They are known as 'Überschlagofen' ('thrown-over stoves') after the method of construction. The free, sculptural shape, in this case including a curling, flowing Rococo tower, was not assembled from standardised tiles but manufactured in a way that made great demands on the skills of the craftsman, known as an 'Erdpoussier' or clay-former. The main body of the stove was first modelled as a single piece from clay 'thrown over' an armature. After being left to dry this piece was cut into sections and fired, together with additional architectural elements that had been modelled separately. These components were then glazed and painted on-glaze with enamel colours. The pieces were then assembled so that the architectural parts concealed the joins. It appears that the stove represented by this model would have been stoked from the front. The lower opening was for the tray for ash. The painting of the model, with motifs similar to those of no. 406, can also be attributed to François-Antoine Anstett. IPM

408
Haus zum Kirschgarten

Tiled stove
Strasbourg, probably workshop of François-Paul Acker, probably decorated in the workshop of Paul Hannong, mid–18th century
Faience with on-glaze camaieu painting in enamel colours, height 290 cm, width 96 cm, depth to wall ca. 118 cm
Inv. no. 1971.316. Purchase

This splendid stove from the Reinacherhof at St. Johanns-Vorstadt 3 in Basle, belonging to mayor Johannes Ryhiner, is among the most beautiful of all surviving Strasbourg stoves. Its attribution to the Acker/ Hannong factories is based on its similarities to the larger stove of comparable design in the Residenz in Würzburg that was made in Strasbourg in 1764. The tiles with painted scenes that make up the body of the stove are large and the architectural elements cover the joins so effectively that the stove seems to have been made in a single piece. The painting in precious *pourpre de Cassius*, obtained from a solution of gold and tin, is masterly, though the artist has not been identified. The scenes painted on the tiles of the tower – pastoral idylls and so on, and personifications of the seasons (at the top) – were derived from engravings by Jacques-Philippe Lebas, Joseph Parrocel and others. The firebox is decorated with landscapes in the broad cartouches and pastoral scenes and children's games in the more rectangular panels above them. These are based on engravings by Nicolas de Larmessin IV (after Nicolas Lancret) and Pierre Avelin (after François Boucher). Similar motifs were also used for a stove made in Berne for the Wildtsches Haus on Petersplatz. IPM

409
Haus zum Kirschgarten

Tiled stove
Strasbourg, probably workshop of François-Paul Acker, putti probably by Johann Wilhelm Lanz, probably decorated in the workshop of Paul Hannong, ca. 1755–60
Faience with on-glaze painting in enamel colours and gilding, height 310 cm, width 117 cm, depth 65 cm
Inv. no. 1921.267. Purchase

This tiled stove from the estate of the mayor of Basle Johannes Ryhiner, who lived at the Reinackerhof at St. Johanns-Vorstadt 3, is designed like a piece of fine furniture. It is particularly unusual in having an opening at the front with small, pierced brass doors. Generally tiled stoves were stoked from behind, either from the kitchen or from a corridor. Presumably this stove stood against an outer wall and the fire could only be tended from the front. This cannot be proven, however, as the working parts of the firebox do not survive. Similar flower sprays in Rococo cartouches, freely painted with swift brushstrokes, can be found on a service made in 1754–60 for Cardinal Rohan and on another stove, both now in the Musée des Arts Décoratifs, Strasbourg. The painter has yet to be identified, although there are similarities in style with the flower painting of Emanuel Jakob Frisching who worked at the Berne factory from 1760 to 1776. Comparable figures of putti are found on a Strasbourg stove in the Residenz in Würzburg, made during the time that Johann Wilhelm Lanz was chief modeller at the Paul Hannong factory. IPM

410
Haus zum Kirschgarten

Tiled stove, signed and dated 1759
Zurich, Leonhard Locher
Faience with painting in 'high-temperature' pigments, height 315 cm, width 93 cm, depth 144 cm
Inv. no. 1909.296. Gift of the Verein für das Historische Museum

Leonhard Locher (1695–1766), president of the Zurich potters' guild, delivered several stoves to Basle in the 1750s. His speciality was *camaieu* painting of brilliant cobalt blue on a white ground. This style provided an alternative to the gayer colours of the Strasbourg stoves, or to those of stoves from the Frisching factory in Berne. In this case the tiles forming the main body of the stove are painted with Rococo views that are somewhat monotonous and meagrely figured, but the garlands of flowers on the pilasters provide a more characteristic example, from Locher's own hand. The stove came from the living room of the Grosser Rollerhof at the corner of Münsterplatz and Augustinergasse. Both this house and the Kleiner Rollerhof were owned by the wealthy silk ribbon manufacturer Martin Bachofen-Heitz (1727–1824). His country estate was the Schloss Ebenrain. His widespread contacts and his knowledge of art led to his founding the Bachofensche Gemälde- und Kunstsammlung, his own art collection. IPM

411
Haus zum Kirschgarten

Tiled stove, signed and dated 1773
Muri, potter Michael Leontius Küchler, painter Caspar Wold
Faience with painting in 'high-temperature' pigments, height (without vase) 320 cm, length 210 cm, width 117 cm
Inv. no. 1895.15. Purchase

This mighty stove once occupied the hall of the powerful Benedictine abbey at Muri, whence it entered the Museum in 1895 thanks to the iron and stove dealer August Scheuchzer-Dür. Michael Leontius Küchler, who signed and dated the stove, came from a family of stove potters. He settled in Muri in the 1750s and, supported by the prince-abbot, supplied stoves to the monastery in Muri, to the abbey in Wettingen, and to distinguished private households in central Switzerland. A similar stove, dated 1770, in the council chamber of the town hall of Stans was purchased for 321 guilders and 3 pounds – a sizeable sum, if one considers that the inn in Muri was sold for 3225 guilders in 1747. The tiles of this stove are exceptionally small; they are decorated in a simple pictorial sequence, like an unfolded picture book, and may have catered to a different taste from that for large-format architectural tiles, portraying more pretentious subjects. The monastery of Muri and some of its estates in Thurgau are depicted in a stiff and linear manner. The remaining tiles show broadly painted fantastic landscapes with figures within narrow curling Rococo frames. IPM

412
Haus zum Kirschgarten

Tiled stove
Strasbourg, workshop of Luc (Lukas) Walter II, ca. 1810–15
Faience, height 230 cm, width 90 cm, depth without junction 97.5 cm
Inv. no. 1930.238. Gift of Eugen Seiler-Mager

This elegant architectural stove formerly stood on the first floor of a private house at Totentanz 10, Basle. It is the work of Luc Walter II, one of the last great Strasbourg stove-makers (signed with a heart and the initials LW scratched into the tiled 'neck'). Pilasters, architraves, and gables form a classicising structure that is decorated with applied gold mounts. By the early C19 a wide and rich range of printed models for ornaments and figured reliefs was available, and so called *ornements d'architecture* were pre-cast in a synthetic material that was like a harder version of stucco. In 1805 Joseph Beunat had founded a Manufacture de Pâtes et de Décors in Sarrebourg (Lorraine) that sold such decorative, semi-finished products internationally. In 1825, the factory moved to Scharrachbergheim in Alsace and its head office to Strasbourg. Hitherto it has been assumed that the applied golden ornaments on this stove were from the Beunat factory, but in fact they are moulded in clay on the tile and were fired, glazed and cold-gilt as an integral part of the structure. For reasons of economy the acanthus frieze on the back of the stove is not gilded. IPM

413
Haus zum Kirschgarten

Model of a stove
Basle, attributed to Walter Böcklin-Müller, ca. 1850
Faience, height 33.5 cm (of cladding 28.5 cm), diameter of top 20.3 cm
Inv. no. 1966.7. Gift of Clara Fischer-Müller

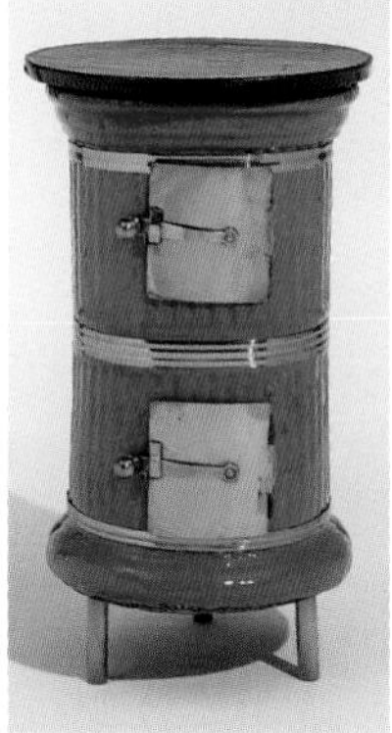

Stoves for private houses in the Biedermeier period were typically cylindrical, fluted and made of white or ivory-coloured faience bound by brass rings. This ceramic quality led to their being called, inaccurately, 'Wedgwood' stoves. Cylindrical stoves of sea-green or turquoise in fact produced in Switzerland matched the often strong shades of the self-coloured Biedermeier wall-coverings (as opposed to the striped wallpaper of the same period that was a revival of a Louis XVI style). This model is attributed to the Kleinbasel stove potter Walter Böcklin-Müller. The ceramic exterior is made of two vertical sections. The interior is constructed of sheet-iron and brass and comprises a lower chamber for the fire, with a flue at the back, and an upper chamber for keeping water or food warm. IPM

414
Haus zum Kirschgarten

Stove tile
Basle, Tonwarenfabric Allschwil, ca. 1884
Faience with painting in 'high-temperature' pigments, height 51.7 cm, width 42 cm, depth 7 cm
Inv. no. 1986.140. Purchase

The Winterthur type of tower-stove did not become established in Basle and its surroundings. However, its characteristic shape made a late and splendid appearance in the guildhouses of the guilds 'zu Schmieden' (smiths) and 'zum Schlüssel' (merchants). On 3 December 1884 the latter ordered from the Allschwil ceramic factory, owned by the Passavant brothers, a mighty tower-stove in the Winterthur style, to be erected on the ground floor of their guildhall in Freiestrasse. Beforehand, however, the decorative painter Ludwig Schwehr-Müller had been required to produce a number of sample tiles for the varied historical programme. The Historisches Museum acquired three large pictorial tiles from the factory that are probably some of these trial pieces. Among them is one, painted in strict Winterthur style, that represents the handing over of the city of Basle to Rudolf of Hapsburg in 1273, in reverse after an illustration by Johann Senn (Liestal 1780–1861 Liestal). The stove itself can still be seen in its original setting in the Zunfthaus zum Schlüssel, which is now a restaurant. IPM

415
Study collection

Stove tiles
Elgg, Mantel Keramik AG, 1943(?)
Coarse clay (grog), underglaze drawing, height 23.5 cm, width 23.5 cm, depth 6 cm
Inv. no. 1992.8. Gift of Rudolf Fritsche

When the Swiss secured their borders in 1943, although it led to grave difficulties, especially for small companies and in agriculture, many a soldier was happy to be granted leave and to put aside his pack having earned his laurels – as is represented on this pair of tiles. The bag shown is the traditional hide-covered, Swiss infantryman's knapsack. Only the pack used by the Basle regiment differed from this design and material (being made of sailcloth). The helmet on top of the mess tin, known as a 'Gamelle' (porringer), could be worn with the neckshield either in front or behind. The hide knapsack represented here is not packed in the prescribed manner; the gas-mask, which was obligatory even during leave, is missing. On top is the detachable haversack, under which the nailed boots are attached by a strap tied through the loop on the heels. The correct rolling of the greatcoat, the 'Kaputt', needed extensive practice. The Mantel Keramik AG in Elgg allowed individuals to decorate their own stove tiles, which may have been the case here, for the handling is more draughtsmanlike than is appropriate to ceramics. IPM

Dress

If one understands by dress everything that human beings like to have around their body, including for example fans, walking sticks, gloves and fashion ornaments, then the Museum's dress collection contains about 5000 objects. It is primarily a collection of bourgeois dress in Basle; workers' clothing is missing altogether and there are only a few examples of professional, official and casual clothing. Uniforms are included in the 'Militaria' section or as part of the 'State and Law' section.

The collection of dress from the second half of the C18 is modest – the clothes were thrown out or ended up in the costumes chests for amateur theatricals or in the old-clothes cupboard for dressing-up for the Basle Carnival. The collection is concentrated more on gentlemen's and ladies' clothes and accessories from the second half of the C19, and has, for example, some 1500 items from both the earlier and later C20 that came from the wardrobe of one Basle lady. Representative of local *haute couture* are several dresses from the estate of the Basle couturier Fred Spillmann (died 1986), and of international *couture* a few clothes and hats for women. Baby clothes and children's clothes of the late C19 and early C20, especially children's carnival costumes, are comprehensively represented.

Since the Museum has no suitable facilities for the permanent exhibition of these highly light-sensitive textiles, small, temporary exhibitions are held in a room of the Haus zum Kirschgarten, showing either new acquisitions or a selection from the existing holdings. IPM

416
Barfüsserkirche

Cap
Basle, ca. 1460
Wool yarn, knitted and felted, circumference of crown 62 cm
Inv. no. 1981.10. Alter Bestand

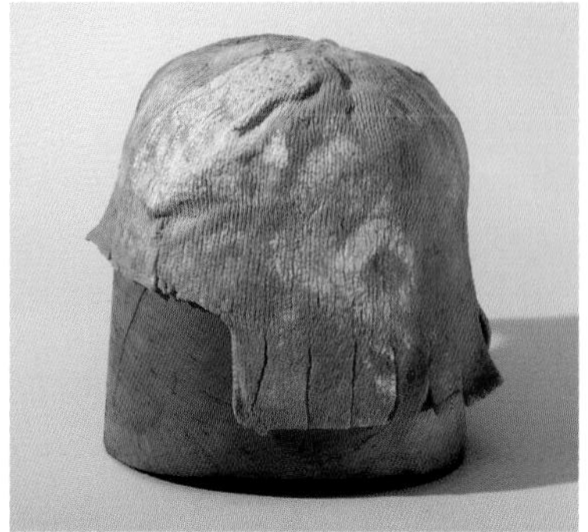

Unfortunately everyday clothes and working clothes from the distant past have rarely survived. There is scant interest for them in museums unless they coincide with a special focus, such as folklore. This cap was found during restoration work under the wooden floor of the choir screen, in a hollow of a cross vault, in the church of St. Leonhard, Basle. It had probably belonged to a stonemason: a contemporary carving of a mason on a keystone in the vault of the chancel of the Berne Münster depicts a similar red cap. These caps, like the berets of the time, were made by the 'Barettlimacher' who, like the 'Lismer' (knitters), were members of the Herrenzunft zu Safran. They were made in the same way as the North African skull-shaped *chechias* of today. They were loosely knitted from woollen yarn, overlarge, and then shrunk and felted to their desired shape by washing in lye and mechanical milling. The fringe was cut later by the cap's owner. IPM

417
Study collection

Bag
England(?), 17th century
Silk fabric with gold and silver thread, silk ribbons, height 9.5cm, width 16cm
Inv. no. 1969.449. Alter Bestand

Women were already by the Middle Ages keeping items for everyday use with them by attaching them to their belts, and a bag for the purpose became a fashionable accessory. It was used to contain coins and personal effects such as keys, small scissors and, when required, a personal set of cutlery. This bag was made in two halves of tabby woven with gold and silver thread on a linen warp. The pattern, of a monogram under a crown between rampant lions, is interwoven in dark brown silk. The draw-strings and the ruched frills are made from silk ribbons, trimmed with silver lace. Two tassels of gold thread with knobs of Turkish braid over a wooden core complete the decoration of this pretty lady's or child's bag. IPM

418
Study collection

Bodice of the costume of the 'Mägd'
Basle, 1st half 18th century
Silk, quilted and embroidered, length 67 cm
Inv. no. 1901.223. Gift of the E.E. Vorstadt-Gesellschaft zur Mägd

With the growth of the city in the C16 the Basle 'Vorstadtgesellschaften' (suburbs societies) were formed. They had a role similar to that of the guilds in the town proper and watched over the rights and duties of the inhabitants of their quarters. In parades and 'Schützenfeste' (shooting contests) they demonstrated their communal spirit and solidarity. In 1706 the 'Gesellschaft zur Mägd' (society of the maid), which was chiefly responsible for the St. Johanns-Vorstadt, a district inhabited by fishermen, boatmen and bakers, paraded about 400 strong in the Münsterplatz in Basle. The corporation took its name from its meeting house, the Haus zu den Megten, which it had purchased in 1517. A silver beaker of 1722 made by Johann Ulrich Fechter II (guild member in 1720) shows the 'Mägd' (maid) as an elegant woman, dressed in a bodice similar to the one pictured here. It is likely that the present small, embroidered garment was worn by a young woman personifying the 'Mägd' during the society's festival processions. IPM

419
Barfüsserkirche

Necklace
Basle, Hans Georg Lindenmeyer (guild member in 1738); clasp: Augsburg, 1st half 18th century
22-carat gold, clasp enamelled, height 4.5 cm, width 5 cm
Inv. no. 1950.90. Gift of the Verein für das Historische Museum

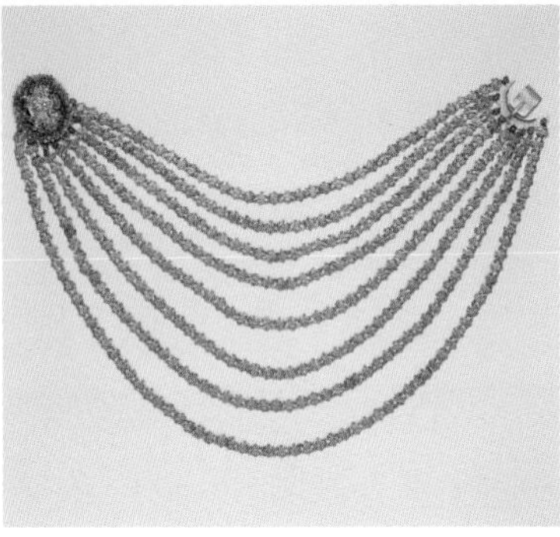

The chain came from the estate of the Basle art historian, keeper of the Öffentliche Kunstsammlung and city historian, Daniel Burckhardt-Werthemann (1863–1949). It is a particularly precious variant of the traditional marriage necklace, popularly called 'Bätti'. The regulation of the strictly Protestant town forbade the wearing of heavy golden jewellery. Weighing 239.5 g the chain exceeded the provisions of the sumptuary law by 37.5 g, but this is not immediately apparent because although the chain is extensive, its structure has a light, delicate appearance. The eight strands of the necklace consist of 387 elements with rosettes, flowers and pomegranates, these last clasped by cockle-shells; the pomegranates were believed to bring wealth and good fortune. The clasp was made in Augsburg and shows Minerva enthroned under a baldachin, surrounded by cornucopias, birds and flowers. A garland with forget-me-nots, symbolizing fidelity, surrounds the image. The coloured enamelling was a response to a further regulation that the "clasp should not be decorated with any precious stone". IPM

420
Study collection

Shoe buckles in a leather case
Paris, mid–18th century
Silver, strass, height 4.5 cm × width 5 cm; morocco case length 11 cm, breadth 5.8 cm, depth 2.5 cm
Inv. no. 1961.213. Gift of Hans A. Burckhardt

These shoe buckles, which were once owned by a wealthy Basle family, are made of cast silver; the fasteners are gilt. The buckles are studded with imitation diamonds, which did not, however, have cheap associations; they are made of strass, a special form of brilliant lead crystal with a high constituent of quartz. This paste is now believed to have been the invention of the Strasbourg chemist and jeweller Georges Frédéric Stras (1710–1773); it is no longer to be associated with the Viennese jeweller Strasser. Paris was a centre of production for such imitation gemstones; in 1767 around 300 people are documented as involved in the processing of 'pierres de Stras'. The strass stones were cut like gemstones and to enhance their brilliance facetted on the rear and set into silver foil cuffs. The careful presentation of these buckles in a morocco case identifies them as prized pieces of jewellery. IPM

421
Study collection

Two smelling bottles
Left: Basle(?), dated 1760; right: Basle(?), 2nd third 18th century
Silver, cast, engraved, height 10.5 cm; silver, cast, engraved, enamelled, height 8.2 cm
Inv. no. 1887.7. Purchase
Inv. no. 1926.39. Purchase

Bottles made to contain aromatic essences come in a great variety of shapes and materials. From the C18 the more precious examples were goldsmiths' work, cast in moulds and then finely worked. They served as love-tokens and as remembrances. The most prevalent type in the Basle collection is pear-shaped, made of silver, sometimes gilt, or, more rarely, made of gold. The top unscrews to reveal the bung; it has an air-hole which makes it easier to open, but also tightens against the bung to close the bottle firmly. Often, as in the bottle on the right, the base also unscrews to reveal a tiny compartment containing a beauty spot or 'mouche'. The bottle on the left is lavishly decorated with masks and animal forms, and with two inlaid plaques with engraved initials, and bears on the reverse the date 1760. Enamel portraits of a lady and a gentleman enliven the front and back of the bottle on the right, which is decorated with scrolling leaf-shapes. Both smelling bottles came from the estate of an old Basle family. IPM

422
Study collection

'Fallhaube' (fall cap)
Eastern Switzerland(?), 2nd half 18th century
Silk, with embroidery, height 13.5 cm
Inv. no. 1899.187. Purchase

The 'Fallhaube' (fall cap) was a very practical garment for small children. It consisted of a padded, more or less bulky, headband, sometimes extended to resemble an open helmet, that encircled the child's forehead to protect it from bumps and falls. Contemporary paintings show that these caps were common and were not only worn by children with disabilities such as 'falling sickness' (epilepsy). The caps were mostly made from self-coloured or printed cloth, but more rarely might be made of leather or, as in this case, from padded, embroidered silk. IPM

423
Haus zum Kirschgarten

Fan
France(?), 2nd half 18th century
Leaf: paper, hand-coloured etching; sticks: rosewood; length 27 cm
Inv. no. 1888.48. Gift of Hans Burckhardt-Burckhardt

The Museum has a collection of around 170 fans, including some with precious fittings or decoration. This one is a curiosity that has a special link with Basle. The portraits in the medallions represent Giuseppe Balsamo, alias Count Alexander Cagliostro (Palermo 1743–1795 Urbino) and his wife Seraphina Feliciani (see also no. 172). Cagliostro was an exceptionally charismatic charlatan. During an apprenticeship as an apothecary, he had acquired sufficient knowledge to present himself as a gifted doctor. His scandalous life-style forced him to flee Europe after 1768. The scene on the left shows his departure for Asia, while the illustration on the right shows him as a doctor, whose miraculous deeds are praised in the inscription. In the course of his adventurous life, not least as the dubious founder of a freemason's lodge, he had established links with the highest circles; these also led him to Basle. Between 1781 and 1788 he lived some of the time in Riehen bei Basel and then, on the basis of his reputation as a miracle healer, in the Weisses Haus, the city mansion of the silk ribbon manufacturer Jakob Sarasin. IPM

424
Study collection

Gentleman's formal dress
Ca. 1760/70
Silk velvet, applied embroidery; coat: length 117 cm; waistcoat: length 79 cm
Inv. no. 1974.472. Alter Bestand

This suit, of coat, waistcoat and knee-breeches, is alleged to have belonged to the clerk to the Basle council, Peter Ochs-Fischer (1723–1821). From 1798 he was a member of the directorate of the Helvetic Republic. A shirt with cuffs and a lace cravat would have completed his 'habit à la française'. Richly decorated silver or silver-gilt buckles sparkled at the knees of the breeches. The obligatory wig was carefully dressed and powdered white. From the watch chain in front of the waistcoat would have hung not only a watch but also a seal or signet ring and other decorative items. The coat and waistcoat are made of fine velvet that had already been decorated and embroidered before the garment was tailored; the decoration consists of appliquéd blue and clear cut-glass stones and gilt spangles and lavish gold threads such as purl and braid. There are matching buttons on the coat, the pockets, the cuffs and at the waist. This fashion was not regarded as effeminate in high society: it was a playful Rococo variation of the opulence that had come in with the Louis XIV style. For a short time, the 'habit à la française' survived the French Revolution as the appropriate dress, alongside full-dress uniform, at formal diplomatic occasions. IPM

425
Study collection

Cashmere shawl (detail)
France(?), ca. 1825
Wool and silk; Jacquard woven, twill 2/2: length 333 cm, width 142 cm, fringe 8 cm
Inv. no. 1954.88. Gift of I. Borel-Legrand

The original Indian Kashmir shawl was woven from the wool of the Tibetan goat and the pattern was often embroidered. The garment was introduced to France and made fashionable by the Empress Josephine, wife of Napoleon I. The subsequent demand led to shawls being woven in more and more variations of the classical palmette pattern in India and shortly afterwards in Europe as well. Here the weft is in four colours and the pattern weft consists of eight further colours woven into it, exemplifying the high quality of the early production. Only later were cashmere shawls draped like capes or cloaks. In the second half of the C19 the shawls might be much larger and were also made into dresses. In Basle they have survived most often after being used as covers for grand pianos. IPM

426
Haus zum Kirschgarten

Lady's ring
Basle(?), 19th century
Gold, diamond chips, enamel, diameter 2.4 cm
Inv. no. 1950.491. Gift of Gertrud Preiswerk

To this ring there is a story attached. It is supposed to have its origin in a present given by Tsar Alexander I to a noblewoman of Basle. After the collapse of his empire in 1813 Napoleon was pursued by enemy troops to the Basle borders, and the city had to billet the officers passing through. In 1814 Tsar Alexander I lodged in the Segerhof, a mansion which in 1926 became the predecessor of the Haus zum Kirschgarten as a museum of domestic life and is now demolished. During his stay there he developed a personal friendship with the aged lady of the house, Dorothea Burckhardt-Merian (1744–1821). According to tradition, on his departure in the same year Alexander presented her with a rectangular brooch with a topaz set in its centre. Her descendants are presumed to have had the brooch reworked into several pieces of jewellery, one of which is possibly this ring. IPM

427
Study collection

Cameo brooch
Cameo: Italy; setting: Vienna, 2nd half 19th century
Lavastone set in gold, height 4.5 cm, width 3.5 cm
Inv. no. 1970.183. Gift of Esther and Ruth Thurneysen

Cameo jewellery, usually made from large seashells with banded layers of different colours, is still a popular souvenir from Naples. From 1830 cameos were carved by Italians in London and Paris and those made with a view to the World Exhibition were particularly extravagantly designed. The same technique of carving in high relief was also used on sardonyx, coloured agate, black and white onyx, malachite, tortoiseshell, coral and ivory. Cameos cut from the lava of Vesuvius are less well known. Typically they were sold as souvenirs in Pompeii and Naples. Pieces of good quality often feature subject matter from antiquity shown in high relief, as in this detailed and highly finished brooch. The portrait may represent a helmeted goddess or Omphale, the Queen of Lydia from the legend of Hercules, since a lion is lying next to the plume on her helmet. IPM

428
Study collection

Evening bag
Vienna(?), 1st third 20th century
Leather, glass, synthetic mother of pearl, height 16.2 cm, width 22.5 cm
Inv. no. 1992.48. Hilde Born bequest

This evening bag was purchased from a quality leather goods shop, B. Leuthold & Schuchmans, in Lucerne, where its elegant Basle owner was a frequent customer. Fashionable shops in Basle also offered high quality leather goods, but they showed a certain resistance to the flamboyance of the 'Liberty' style with its element of *japonisme* or to similar advanced fashions. This product, probably of a Viennese bag maker, is made of the finest chamois leather. The dragonflies are made of appliquéd coloured leather heightened with gold paint. The moons in front of the black glass eyes of the dragonflies are an enchanting, eye-catching feature. IPM

Household utensils

In 1882, the director of the Medieval Collection, Moritz Heyne, published a series of illustrations of household utensils from the Collection under the title 'Art in the Home' (Kunst im Haus). The objects presented included a pan holder, a bird-cage and a jewellery case – simple but richly embellished utility objects which were valued as models for the arts and crafts of the time. Since then, the area of the collection relating to everyday living has grown considerably. The holdings of the Historisches Museum Basel have been built up mainly from the contents of dissolved households, but also in certain cases, such as the comprehensive collection of lighting mounts, by purchase.

The kitchen from the Segerhof, an intact ensemble with stove, furniture and kitchen utensils from the late C18, is a special centre of attraction. In 1982 a complete Basle household was taken over by the Museum by bequest of Dr. Edith Stocker-Nolte: it comprises several thousand objects from the early C19 and C20, and very adequately illustrates household utensils of this period. The special collection of about 200 clay and wooden baking moulds from the C17 to the C19 is also important. It includes many examples of good technical quality and a rich repertoire of motifs.

The transfer to the Historisches Museum of the collection of the Gewerbemuseum (Museum für Gestaltung) in 1993 supplemented the Museum's holdings with more than 500 objects from the C19 and C20. IPM

429
Barfüsserkirche

Aquamanile
Found among fire debris in the cellar of Gerbergasse 28, Basle; 14th century(?)
Earthenware, glazed; height 19 cm, length 22.5 cm
Inv. no. 1935.222. Gift of Albert Löhrer

The term aquamanile originally referred to the vessels used for ritual hand-washing during sacred moments in the Catholic service, in particular the ewer and bowl for pouring and catching the water, which were usually made of precious metal. Later the term was used for the ewer alone, which often would take on figurative form: animals embodying strength such as lions and rams, or, less frequently, an anthropomorphic body. Such decorative vessels were also suitable table ornaments, and, especially in the C13 and C14, were passed round at noble banquets so that guests might rinse their hands. The aquamanile in the shape of a ram illustrated is of this kind. The body and neck of the earthenware ram were turned. The rectangular filling hole, which is also the air hole, is in the neck. Imprints with a four-pronged implement indicate the fur of the animal. A light honey-coloured glaze prevents the liquid from evaporating through the pores of the vessel, which was fired at low temperature. IPM

430
Barfüsserkirche

Cooking-pot
Found at Unterer Petersberg, Basle; 15th century
Earthenware, partly glazed; height 19 cm
Inv. no. 1939.642. Gift of the Baudepartement Basel

The well preserved fragments of this pot from an excavation in the centre of Basle show traces of fire. The heating of the food over a small fire hole or on embers had to be done gradually, owing to the low resistance of the pot. The vessel was shaped on the wheel by eye, while the legs were drawn from a lump of clay, attached with a visible thumbprint and bent over at the foot. Since the earthenware was not fired at high temperature, so that its sides remained porous, it was coated on the inside with a yellow, transparent lead glaze, which today would be regarded as a danger to health. Three legs provide a better base than four if the surface the vessel rests on is likely to be uneven; three legs are commonly found on modern utensils as well. However, for stability, the supports must always form a triangle lying outside the contour of the vessel. IPM

431
Barfüsserkirche

Wooden casket
South Germany(?), end 15th century
Beech, painted; length 13.5 cm, width 7.5 cm, height 4 cm
Inv. no. 1885.99. Gift of Prof. Jacob Burckhardt

Small caskets that have come down from the C15 are usually carved. The motifs suggest that they were used as bridal gifts and since the C19, with its idealised view of the Middle Ages, they have been called 'Minnekästchen' (courtly love caskets). Painted caskets and boxes from the C15 are rare, but in South Germany and Switzerland examples from the C16 and C17 are numerous and they lived on in the popular and souvenir art of the C18 and C19. A special group had paintings in tempera on a smooth, polished bismuth ground. This metal was mixed to a paste with a binding agent, applied over a chalk ground and usually lacquered in 'golden' yellow to protect it from oxidisation. Here bismuth is used in the foliage decoration in the background of the motif. IPM

432
Barfüsserkirche

'Leuchterweibchen' (chandelier lady)
Switzerland(?), ca. 1500
Stag antlers, wood with polychromy; length 100 cm, height 48 cm
Inv. no. 1874.6. Gift of the E.E. Zunft zu Gartnern

Antlers have always been imposing collectors' items and in many instances served an apotropaic function. Wall-mounted candelabra with the antlers of a stag, an elk or an ibex surrounding, for example, a figure of a saint or the Madonna are documented as early as the C15. In the C16 antlers combined with half-length figures were widely used in the German-speaking area as ceiling candelabra. Even Albrecht Dürer took an interest in their construction and for his friend Pirckheimer drew a design for one in 1513. The light they provided was limited. Rather, their display function was predominant, and was underlined by mounting a coat of arms on the underside or front. The Basle 'Leuchterweibchen' (chandelier lady) shows the coat of arms of the Zunft zu Gartnern (gardeners' and grocers' guild), a three-pronged fork. The fittings, with chains and an iron strut with four candle-holders, are modest. Compared to examples from court or high bourgeois circles the figure seems rather crude, coming close to folk art. IPM

433
Study collection

Hand warmer
16th century
Brass, sawn through; diameter 11 cm
Inv. no. 1877.6. Gift of Herr Merian-Bischoff

Hand warmers in the form of two perforated hemispheres forming a 'Wärmeapfel' (warming apple) are known since the end of the C12. The earliest description known to date, of a "silver apple for warming the hands", is found in the 1214 inventory of Salisbury Cathedral. The use of hand warmers whether in church or elsewhere peters out around the C18. These two hemispheres, pierced with simple star and wave patterns, are joined by a hinge and are closed with a hook and eye. The container inside held a liquid combustible material, which was drawn up for burning by a wick through the spout. However the sphere is turned, the container always remains horizontal, to avoid spilling the contents. This mechanism, the so called Cardan suspension, is found in all hand warmers and is illustrated for use in an "échaufaude de mains" in the mason's workshop book of Villard de Honnecourt about 1235. At least two rings (here three) enclose the container concentrically. Each ring is attached by a free-turning pin at two opposite but offset points both to the outer wall and to the burner. These elements, swinging freely on their axes, keep the fuel container upright in all positions. IPM

434
Barfüsserkirche

Toilet box
Mathias Wallbaum, Augsburg, ca. 1595–1600
Walnut with ebony veneer, silver parcel-gilt; height 12.5 cm, width 37 cm, depth 16.5 cm
Inv. no. 1920.150. Purchase

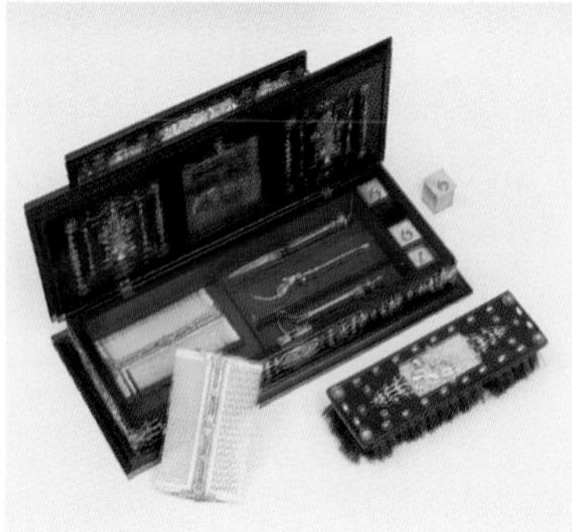

Cases for jewellery and toilet articles were prestigious gifts, often love gifts, and as such were richly decorated. Since the Renaissance the implements contained in them have also been formed to match the outer appearance of the case, giving an ensemble character to the whole. The small box of stained walnut veneered with ebony is faced with silver and parcel-gilt plaquettes, of which the imagery is incomplete or mixed up: allegories of the seasons and the elements, mythological and biblical scenes. They are accompanied by rosettes and inlaid silver filigree. The compartment set into the hinged top, with a sliding lid, is a container for the brush; the lower compartment is lined with satin and houses two ivory combs, four small engraved ointment boxes and three toilet implements decorated with silver-gilt grotesques in the round: knife, ear spoon with toothpick, tongue scraper. A mirror is let into the underside of the triple-coffered lid. IPM

435
Study collection

Waffle iron, dated 1606
Upper Rhine
Cast iron; diameter 15 cm, length 83 cm
Inv. no. 1901.19. Purchase

A thin pastry with images on both sides is formed by the two plates of this waffle iron, constructed like a pair of tongs. Slightly sweetened dough in a creamy consistency is poured on to the heated plates with their recessed designs and heated briefly until it forms a flat cake. Often one plate has a honeycomb grid of grooves ('waffles'), enabling the steam from the viscous mass to escape easily. Such 'iron cakes' were distributed by families and monasteries on feast days. Numerous waffle irons in the collection of the Historisches Museum come from the Alsace region. This example shows on its left plate the Annunciation to the Virgin, in an image like that on the Basle Julius banner (no. 238), and the Basle crosier; St Catherine of Alexandria and her instrument of martyrdom, the wheel, appear on the other plate. The waffle iron was owned by the family of Jakobus and Catharina Enderlin-Keifler from the Alsatian village of Sierentz (between Mulhouse and Basle). IPM

436
Barfüsserkirche

Savings box
Basle, 17th century
Earthenware, coated with slip, partly glazed; height 7.5 cm
Inv. no. 1977.A.5136. Excavation find

A group of finds dating from the C16 and C17 brought to light in the latrine of the Reischacherhof mansion on the Münsterplatz, Basle, included this small savings box ('Sparhafen') among other well preserved ceramic pieces. The German term 'Hafen' or pot designates it the product of a potter: indeed the same manipulation that turns a lump of clay into a pot shaped this little vessel. Once the clay had reached a leathery consistency it could be marked with grooves. The finishing is plain: a thin layer of light-coloured slip and over that a honey-coloured transparent glaze. To get at the coins the full savings box had to be broken. Thrift was taught to children at an early age; they kept their own money in the savings box. They also learnt that one had money but one did not show it. IPM

437
Barfüsserkirche

Iron, dated 1699
Iron, brass decoration, pierced, engraved; height 15 cm, length 16.5 cm, width 8.2 cm
Inv. no. 1890.54. Gift of Antiquar Jecker

Irons are used both for smoothing out and for producing creases, or, as Corvin's lexicon for ladies recommended in 1739: "smoothness and creases should be brought into a pleasing relationship". With the emergence of close-fitting clothes, the seams had to be ironed flat even when they were being made, yet only bone or glass blocks for smoothing, pressing and rubbing cold have survived from the Middle Ages. The dress of the Renaissance, with its heavy materials, probably only needed light smoothing after it was made, but neck ruffs could have been given their shape only by means of special frilling and ruching irons. The shape of the iron, essentially unchanged today, was developed in the C17; only the means of heating has evolved. The type of iron shown here, which was heated by inserting a plug taken from the fire, was used together with more modern shapes up until the 1920s. IPM

438
Study collection

Baking pattern
Signed WF, Basle, 17th century
Cherrywood; height 26 cm, width 33.5 cm
Inv. no. 1894.371. Gift of Albert Grossmann

Basle's heraldic emblem, the Basle crosier, is based formally and no doubt historically on the bishop's staff. It achieved its classic form, with crook, knob and three spines, in the third quarter of the C14. Lions appeared as supporters about 1400, notably on the outer side of the Spalentor; wild men supporters appear on the escutcheon of a 'Bannwart' (field warden) of about 1470/80, and angels or putti were also used. Since the end of the C15 the basilisk has accompanied the Basle coat of arms, as on this baking form pattern. Why is not known; the similarity of the names Basle/basilisk may have played a part. There was no very clear conception of the monster, witness the fact that in 1474 the Basle executioner put to death a cock pregnant with an egg which otherwise would have brought forth a basilisk! Copies after this pattern, with its Baroque fruit and blossoms promising happiness and wealth, were used by Basle pastrycooks to produce the marzipan covering of gingerbread, and are still used today to make the traditional white 'Anisbrot' (aniseed bread). IPM

439
Study collection

Baking pattern
GIS carved on the back, Switzerland (?), 17th century
Pearwood; height 16 cm, width 8 cm
Inv. no. 1892.110. Purchase

In the C17 pairs of lovers were frequently depicted standing stiffly side by side in rich clothing against a flat background and holding each other at the waist and shoulder. It seems likely that sweetmeats bearing such images were used as love or wedding gifts. The smooth, 'lacquered', honey gingerbread, with figures heightened with white icing, or marzipan cakes with coloured markings, were well suited to this treatment. Depictions of single people in festive dress are less common. This example has a costume image based on an engraving from the series *Noblesse* by Jacques Callot of Nancy (1592–1635). The tightly laced bodice with a long hanging train has a deep *décolleté* and is framed by a stiff lace collar. The long sleeves have slit puffs and lace cuffs folded back. The under-skirt is richly embroidered while the over-skirt is gathered up at the back, as the fashion of the 1630s allowed. As accessories the lady wears a feathered hat, a necklace, a pair of gloves and a feather fan. The woodcarver's technique, limited to a few forms but subtly applied, gives the image a poster-like force. IPM

440
Study collection

Baking pattern
HWD burnt on the back, Switzerland(?), 17th century
Pearwood, diameter 18 cm
Inv. no. 1894.475. Purchase

The fool, the playful personification of folly, is shown here in the costume traditional since the C15: donkey-eared cap with bells and a cape with bells over his gaudy coat. His attribute is the cudgel or fool's sceptre, known as a 'marotte', tipped with a carved fool's head. Today, quirky forms of behaviour are known as 'Marotten' in German. The jug, glass and loaf point to the intemperance of the fool, to whom any idea of abstinence or fasting is alien. The broken glasses and the gesture of looking through his fingers' indicate his simple-mindedness, bereft of 'insight' behind appearances. With its round shape, the pattern resembles a round mirror held up to the carouser: hence the inscription, "Unser sind drei" (there are three of us) – the fool in the picture, his image on the marotte, and the beholder himself. IPM

441
Haus zum Kirschgarten

Inkwell in the form of a model stove
Winterthur, end 17th century
Faience with painting in 'high temperature' pigments, height 27.5 cm, width 22 cm, depth 22.7 cm
Inv. no. 1923.42. Hans Burckhardt-Burckhardt bequest

The ceramics factories at Winterthur, in which table and oven ceramics were produced from about 1550 until about 1730, were famous for their sumptuous tower-stoves for use in luxuriously equipped rooms in eastern Switzerland (see no. 400). Stove models were generally used to illustrate the factory's products or as three-dimensional maquettes of stoves to be made. But two models are also known from the Winterthur factories that were intended to be used as receptacles for ink and writing sand: one, dated 1641, is in the Schweizerisches Landesmuseum in Zurich; the other, shown here, represents a later type with blossoms, hanging fruit, allegorical figures and genre images. On two of its pilasters its function is humorously alluded to in words and pictures: "Vor Mittag will/ geistlich sein./ Nach Mittag gehn/ sy zum Wein" (before midday you're fond of thinking/ after midday you're off to drinking); and "Trinken macht oft/ dass man schreiben/ und/ studieren/ lasset bleiben" (drinking oft has the effect/ that script and study you neglect). IPM

442
Study collection

Cutlery and case
Jakob d'Annone, Basle, ca. 1717/44
Silver gilt, engraved; worked morocco case; length of case 12.5 cm, width 5.5 cm, height 3.5 cm
Inv. no. 1912.626. Purchase

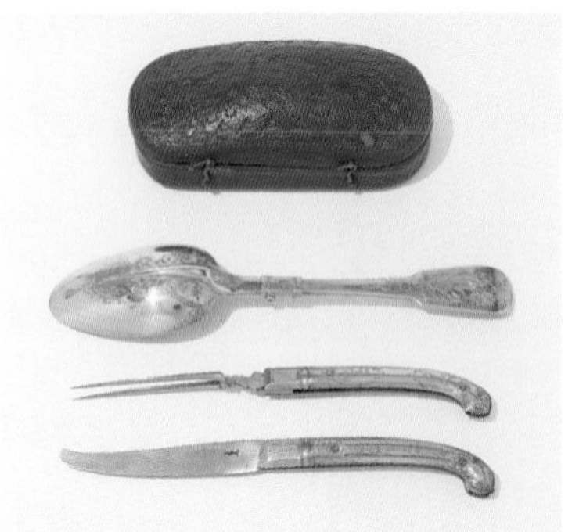

According to Amaranthe's *Nutzbares... Frauenzimmer-Lexicon* (Useful lexicon for ladies), published in Leipzig in 1715, a set of cutlery consists of "knife and spoon case or étui, which is a container covered in gold and red leather and hollowed out, and in which lie a silver or ornately gilt spoon with matching knife and fork...". As late as the C18 one often took one's personal cutlery to a banquet, and certainly on one's travels. In view of the hunting scene with dogs, hares and foxes in morocco work on the lid of the case, the set might have been hunting cutlery. It was the personal property of a member of the Basle Bernoulli family, whose coat of arms is engraved on the gilt-silver spoon. The knife blade was produced in an unidentified Basle factory; it is engraved with a Basle crosier. IPM

443
Haus zum Kirschgarten

Coffee mill
France(?), 1st half 18th century
Cherrywood, brass; height 20 cm, base plate 10.7 × 10.7 cm
Inv. no. 1968.54. Gift of Esther Thurneysen

When coffee reached Europe via the Middle East just over 300 years ago, the roasted beans were ground with a mortar and pestle and kept in a bag sealed with wax or grease. Pulverisation took place either by further grinding in the mortar or in a suitable spice mill. Mills with a mechanism specifically for grinding coffee, produced by smiths in precious metals, were undoubtedly invented in different places; for example, the German town of Remscheid was exporting them all over the world from more than 20 workshops at the end of the C18. The body housing the axial grinding mechanism is made of a single, finely worked piece of cherrywood and is embellished with rich Bérain decoration of engraved brass. The neck is bevelled to allow a good grip while grinding. The lid of engraved brass is rivetted to the body; one half of the lid opens, and is secured by a hook and eye. The drawer for the coffee powder is grooved and pegged and reinforced with wood dowels and wire. A simple catch prevents the container from sliding out during grinding. IPM

444
Haus zum Kirschgarten and Study Collection

Two sugar casters
Left: Strasbourg, Paul Hannong, ca. 1750; right: Emanuel J. Streckeisen, Basle, ca. 1800
Faience, overglaze painting, height 20.7 cm; pewter, height 18.8 cm
Inv. no. 1988.211. Purchase
Inv. no. 1895.66. Gift of Dr. Rudolf Wackernagel

In times of shortage traditional utensils of silver or vermeil were replaced by cheaper material, but always in the established precious metal shape. Numerous instances of this can be found in the Historisches Museum. With the change in eating customs and the emergence of the sugar bowl in the C18, the caster for showering fruit and sweet foods abundantly with sugar was superseded by the more economical perforated spoon sprinkler. A traditional sugar caster, a container standing on a narrow foot and with a screwed, perforated dome, is shown on the left – made of costly painted faience from the heyday of the Paul Hannong manufactory in Strasbourg. The pewter caster looks distinctly more compact beside it, although it differs only in details from the faience caster; both imitate silver examples. IPM

445
Haus zum Kirschgarten

Spittoon
Zurich/Schooren, mid–18th century
Faience, overglaze painting; length 19.5 cm, diameter ca. 13.5 cm, height 5.8 cm
Inv. no. 1896.76. Purchase

Little has been written on the history of hygienic utensils. At the time they were used they were no doubt taken for granted, and later discussion of them was prevented by decorum. In the field of ceramics this applies to the 'Bourdalou' (small transportable chamber pot) and the spittoon. Two "Speihmulten" (spittoons) are listed under crockery in the inventory of the Zurich/Schooren manufactory of 1800–01, but their shape is not described. Parallels to the present example are found in the Strasbourg faience of Paul Hannong, with blue decoration, but Hannong's catalogue does not list any *crachoirs*. In later French publications further turned spittoons are illustrated, together with other sorts of shapes for the same purpose. They are classified with tableware, and one wonders at what point in the meal, by whom and to whom these vessels, joined to their shaft handles by a screw-thread or socket and filled probably with sawdust or ash, were passed for spitting. IPM

446
Haus zum Kirschgarten

Sewing box
Copenhagen(?), 18th century
Silver; length 15.5 cm
Inv. no. 1896.22. Gift of Frau Simmoth-Schneider

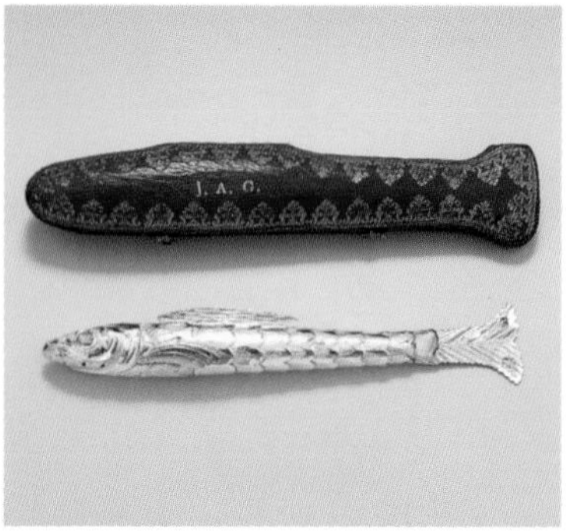

Eight sections, building up from the smallest, overlap with enough free play to allow wriggling movements of the fish body. The head section is pushed under the fin on the fish's back and contains a thimble which fits over a screw-cap doubling as a cotton spool. The compartment for needles has another small compartment half its width at the top, the function of which is as yet unknown. The case is said to have been won by an ancestor of the donor at a Swabian shooting contest. In that event the outer case in fine morocco leather must have been made later, or the initials J.A.G., showing the fine gift to be the very personal property of a lady, added afterwards. Such silver fishes are documented as smelling salts containers and in popular use as talismans; in the C19 they are found as pendants and are now again available from India as small enamelled ornaments. IPM

447
Haus zum Kirschgarten

Baking mould
18th century(?)
Copper, zinc plated; length 17 cm, height 7 cm, width 18.3 cm
Inv. no. 1898.11. Gift of J.G. Mende-Sandreuter

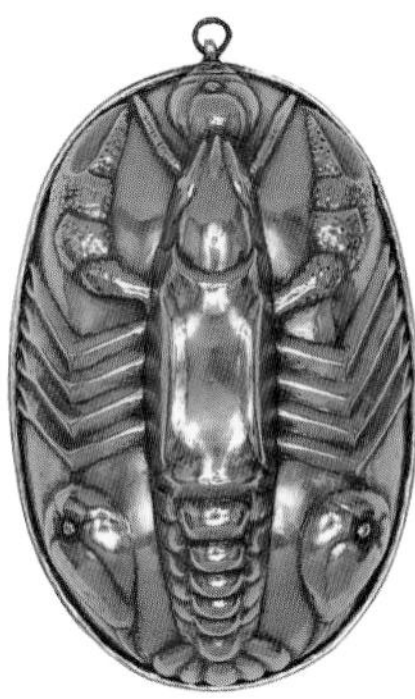

"Crayfish tart. Make a crayfish dough, spread it well on a dish, put in a filling of veal titbits, young chicken or whatever other good things you wish, pike liver, chicken liver, turtle and other fish parts, bake it in a cake tin, but not too long, so that it does not become greasy, and serve it hot" (Josepha Hirt's C18 cookery book). Such cake tins were not only used for baking. Even in upper-middle-class households economy was practised in the kitchen, and many recipes were devoted to using up left-overs. Especially in summer jellied meat or fish was produced from decoratively layered and prettily shaped moulds. For solid sweets such as charlottes and frozen foods, more ornamental moulds were used. IPM

448
Study collection

Baking pattern
Nikolaus Wilhelm Götz, Basle, 1st third 19th century
Pearwood; height 15 cm, width 23 cm
Inv. no. 1896.190.d. Purchase

The quadripartite pattern, stamped *GOETZ * GRAVEUR * IN BASEL*, shows scenes that will charm the historian of dress and culture. At top left the first shepherd comes to worship the Christchild, beckoning the two others who are outside the picture. The kneeling Virgin is dressed in the style of the Empire period in a long garment of fine material. The scene below is the Flight into Egypt: Joseph carries his carpenter's tools on his back. At top right a gunner has just fired a cannon with a fuse. His uniform with three-cornered hat, long-tailed jacket, short waistcoat and knee breeches can be dated to the early C19. The scene below is a winter excursion in elegant swan-necked sledges, while the horse has a caparison with bells. The craftsman responsible, Nikolaus Wilhelm Götz, who is documented about 1835 as a "device maker" resident in "lesser Basle", also engraved patterns for moulds for table decorations made of 'Tragant' (comparable to present-day salt dough). These tiny decorations often also had written 'devices' or mottoes. IPM

449
Study collection

Sewing case
Paris, ca. 1840
Ivory; length 12 cm, width 6 cm, height 1.9 cm
Inv. no. 1986.233. Gift of Beatrix Hoffmann-Burckhardt

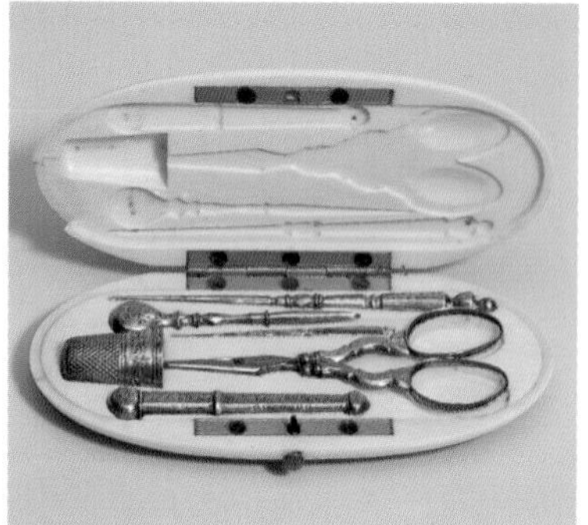

Both the lid and the tray of this elegant case from an aristocratic Basle house are made of ivory. The contents comprise a fine hook for crochet or embroidery work, a pricker, a needle for pulling through coarse thread or elastic, a thimble, embroidery scissors and a needle box. All the fittings, like the hinge and push-button catch, are made of partially polished steel and engraved gilt silver. The simple, elegant shape of the case makes it look outwardly like a modern product of C20th 'Neue Sachlichkeit'. It bears witness to a functional sense of style distinct from the eclectic historicism of the time. However, the contents are decorated in a neo-Rococo style. IPM

450
Study collection

Coffee machine
France(?), 1st quarter 20th century
Porcelain, glass, copper, brass; height 29 cm, base plate 17.5 × 8 cm
Inv. no. 1992.142. Gift of Dr. Irmgard Peter-Müller

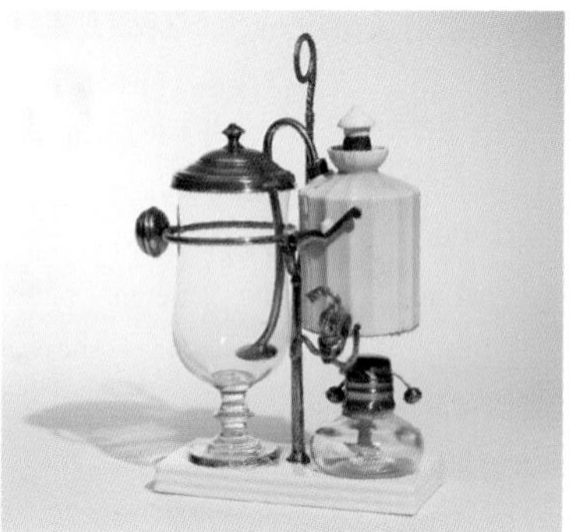

This type of coffee machine was sold under the name 'Balance' by the Paris department store Samaritaine in the 1920s. It was meant to be an appliance for two people. This example was bought in Basle and was in use up to the 1960s. The coffee-pot filled with water is first lowered on to the burner, the lid of which is thus held open. Once the water has reached boiling point, it flows through the jet into the glass vessel holding the ground coffee, and the now empty pot rises, shutting the lid and extinguishing the flame. As the pot cools, a vacuum is created that now draws the hot coffee through the filter at the end of the jet and back into the pot, which is lowered to its original position over the now closed burner. The coffee is ready to serve. IPM

Games and toys

Unlike the Spielzeugmuseum (toy museum) in Riehen bei Basel, which is international in scope, the Historisches Museum Basel has specialised in documenting games and toys as a part of domestic life in Basle. The first donations of toys by Basle families were made about 1880, to the Museum's predecessor, the Medieval Collection. The years between 1920 and 1970 brought the largest increase in the number of objects. Since then fewer pieces have come into the collection, nor have objects been purchased.

The present display of toys was set up in the Haus zum Kirschgarten by the Basle architect Hans-Peter His-Miescher in collaboration with the later director of the Museum, Hans-Christoph Ackermann, in 1972, when His-Miescher donated part of his well kept collection of dioramas and toys to the Museum. The exhibition includes every kind of object from this miniature world, in a display using showcases laid out like dioramas. Two rooms are reserved for the twelve dolls' houses and rooms, which form a centrepiece of the collection. The oldest, dated about 1680, is a prototype of the dolls' house in a lockable cupboard, the Basle 'Doggetekänschterli', that children were only allowed to play with on certain occasions. Another example was made by the Basle painter Ludwig Adam Kelterborn about 1840 for his daughter; however, its furniture was made up largely of mass-produced items. The most recent examples are two houses in 'Deauville' style.

Several hundred objects are preserved in the study collection, classified by category. Here the main emphasis is on dolls with their wardrobes, and on table services. At present there is no possibility of an extended display or thematic exhibition of these items. Among the games for adults the card games and tarots deserve mention; this collection is arranged typologically. A group of seven 'Poch' boards includes an early example dated 1749, and four from the early C19. Numerous wooden board-game pieces with allegorical figures, portraits and scenes – some after Callot, for example – are included in the area of the collection devoted to small sculptures, and some are exhibited in the Barfüsserkirche. IPM

451
Barfüsserkirche

Game-board piece
England(?), 12th century
Carving in bone (tusk), remnants of red paint, diameter 6.5 cm, height 1.45 cm, weight 69.9 g
Inv. no. 1871.51. Gift of Pfarrer Carl Stückelberg-Preiswerk

The origin of the piece is unknown: it was donated to the Medieval Collection, which preceded the Historisches Museum. These pieces, usually associated with the board game 'trictrac' (now backgammon), are mostly found in castles and early urban centres, for example the similar piece with a basilisk, dated ca. 1020/70, found in Burg Altenberg near Füllinsdorf not far from Basle. The game itself consists of a set of 2 × 15 pieces. Like chess, it can be traced in antiquity, and was taken up again in the Middle Ages. The scene, carved in fine detail, shows a fight between two horsemen, one of whom is falling backwards to the ground. The armour comprises helmet, tunic and hose, while the weapons are lance, sword and shield. In view of their similar format, the encircling string of beads and the deeply cut carving, this piece is assigned to a group of five, and the scene has been interpreted as Achilles killing Cyprus (two other pieces also show scenes from Greek mythology). In the current state of knowledge the question of where the piece was produced – Cologne, northern France or England – must be left open. IPM

452
Study collection

Playing cards
South Germany or Alsace, last quarter 15th century
Woodcut, hand coloured, diameter ca. 4.5 cm
Inv. no. 1975.48. Gift of the Christkatholische Gemeinde Basel

In 1377 a Dominican named Johannes of Freiburg praised card-playing as a mirror of the divine world order. But by 1367 strife among players and losses of worldly goods had led to a ban on the 'devil's stuff' in Berne. All the more intriguing, therefore, is the discovery of these cards, cut to a round shape, underneath the medallions of a Gothic crucifix owned by the Christ-katholische Gemeinde (Catholic community). In view of the figures' clothing and by comparison with the earliest depiction of a card game in Switzerland, on a needle-woven tapestry in the Museum of 1471, the cards should be dated in the last quarter of the C15. About 1440 the Basle councillor and merchant Heinrich Halbysen the Elder set up a paper mill, probably with an eye for an increased demand for paper during the Council of Basle in 1431–48; thereafter it supplied paper for playing cards. For more than 200 years Basle manufacturers supplied the Confederation with cards. The suits were shields, bells, acorns and roses. However, Basle card games from that early period are not represented in the collection of the Historisches Museum. IPM

453
Study collection

Child's rattle
17th century
Silver, engraved, length 13 cm
Inv. no. 1881.168. Purchase

When the infant has grown out of the purely receptive phase, he shows an early desire to grasp the world by touch. The little body begins to serve the senses in a purposeful way. Soon the young child feels the pains of teething. The child's rattle was made for this stage, and was often lavishly equipped: teething rings of coral, ivory and agate were held by silver-gilt handles and embellished with bells. This silver rattle in the form of a trumpet is a variant without teething rings. Although it is closed at the front, the mouthpiece is formed as a whistle and can produce sounds. Rattles were not only objects for a child to hold and make a noise with, but were also regarded as talismans that could keep evil spirits away with their clatter and whistling. IPM

454
Haus zum Kirschgarten

Cupboard with built-in doll's house
Basle(?); furnished with objects dating from 17th to 19th century
Walnut, height 152 cm, breadth 160 cm, depth 57 cm
Inv. no. 1945.63. Gift of Herr and Frau Dr. Chiedera-Haegler from the bequest of Dr. Haegler-à Wengen

Dolls' rooms like those shown here are called 'Doggetekänschterli' (dolls' boxes) in Basle. They are built into a lockable cupboard, because traditionally children were only allowed to play with these expensively furnished dolls' rooms under supervision, and not every day. Such dolls' rooms often survived for generations and were re-furnished as needed, as is clearly the case in this example, since only the kitchen shows the original furnishings. On the table stands a silver dish with a lid with an engraved inscription on the bottom: "Von H: Pet: Bierman – verehrt–17:09-" (presented by Peter Biermann, 1709); Peter Biermann (1641–1728) was a Basle goldsmith who became a member of the guild in 1669. The former kitchen stove, dated 1829 (no. 456), has been replaced by an older ceramic stove from the toy collection. IPM

455
Haus zum Kirschgarten

Part of a doll's table service
Niderviller(?), Claude F. Lanfrey, 1st quarter 19th century
Porcelain, on-glaze painting and gilding; pot: height 11 cm
Inv. no. 1923.354. Gift of Dr. Rudolf F. Burckhardt

Children's services, dolls' services and doll's house services are usually distinguished when smaller versions of china services are discussed in monographs on toys. Studies on their attribution and function within the manufactory's output exist most abundantly for English factories, which after 1800 decorated children's table sets with 'educationally valuable' motifs applied by transfer. Some examples were no more than occasional by-products of tableware manufacturers, for example miniature chinaware by the Durlach faience factory. But often doll's service assortments were meant to give an idea of the maker's real products, and as such were advertising models, though they could later be used as toys. About the turn of the C19 assortments of china intended only for dolls, with motifs suited to children, were brought out. In the first half of the C20 doll's table services were popular as prizes given in exchange for coupons or stamps given out when certain goods were sold. The porcelain service illustrated here, however, is probably a special set made to order. IPM

456
Haus zum Kirschgarten

Doll's stove
Basle(?), dated 1829
Wood, painted, height 44 cm, base board 21 × 15.5 cm
Inv. no. 1945.63.a.

An engraving by Daniel N. Chodowiecki from the second half of the C18 shows two little girls playing with a stove. The stove, placed on a table, with its accompanying chairs and stools in the same scale, is about 60 cm high, so that it could be manipulated quite easily. This is early evidence that kitchens were isolated from the dolls' house as separate entities. They evidently had enough educational potential in themselves. In the 1803 edition of the Nuremberg toy catalogue of Georg Hieronimus Bestelmeier, three differently furnished toy kitchens in wooden boxes were offered; their equipment exactly reflected the vessels and utensils of contemporary kitchens, including those for cooking over an open fire on a solid hotplate under a smoke hood. This small stove, selected, because it is dated, from the many examples in the toy collection, originally stood in a dolls' house cupboard that has also been preserved (no. 454). IPM

457
Study collection

Joke object
Erzgebirge(?), 1st half 19th century
Bone and horn, height of box 7.5 cm, diameter 3 cm
Inv. no. 1948.493. Gift of Dr. Hans Schneider-Christ

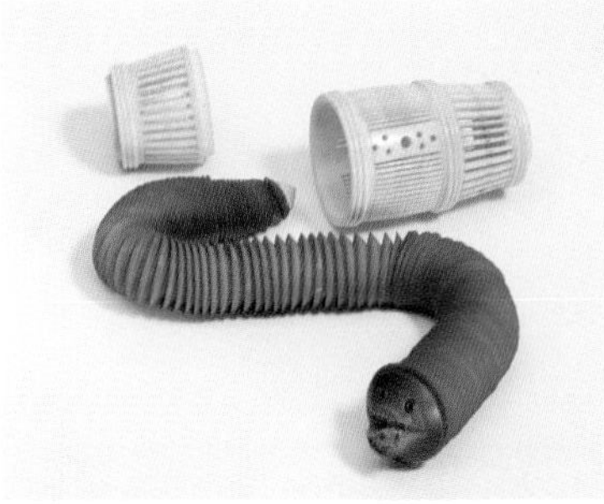

A good joke object always causes a blissful moment of terror or revulsion. The thing looks innocent enough at first – an openwork bone screw-top box, of the kind made as boxes for smelling salts, flea traps, needle containers and such like. But when the box is opened a little monster with a gaping mouth shoots out, twisting in all directions. The worm has a real aggressive vitality that is bound to cause a start. It is a fine piece of turning: the body is a spiral from end to end cut barely 0.5 mm thick. IPM

458
Haus zum Kirschgarten

Doll
Hilburghausen (Thüringen), Andreas Voit factory, mid–19th century
Leather body and limbs, papier mâché, real hair, height 57 cm
Inv. no. 1900.79. Gift of Frau Oberst Merian-Iselin

A child's unselfconscious, unsupervised play with a baby doll as a partner and object for identification is a phenomenon of the late C19. The child now had a world of its own to experience. C19 dolls usually embody adults who, with soft bodies and a tranquil expression, promise motherly protection and could be used for teaching purposes. They therefore have a wardrobe of ordinary clothes, unlike fashion dolls or mannikin dolls with rich appurtenances. However, changing their clothes was always an important part of play with dolls, making them specifically toys for girls. The wide range of historic mannikin and character dolls has found a new public in collectors, including many who, in these charmingly displayed figures, seek a substitute for a childhood not fully lived. IPM

459
Haus zum Kirschgarten

Coach
Biedermeier, 19th century
Wood and metal, painted, length 49 cm, height 20 cm
Inv. no. 1914.411. Purchase

The toy coach, said to have come from Schloss Maienfeld (Grisons), is a so called 'Jagdwurst' (hunter's sausage), modelled on the type in widespread use from the end of the C18 in central Europe, especially Germany and Austria. Its nickname derives from the seat, placed longways above the central spar of the vehicle and covered with drill or leather upholstery. The passengers sat astride the seat, their number depending on the vehicle's length. Such 'Wurstwagen' or 'sausage waggons', called 'vourste' in French, had forerunners in the German court 'sausage' sleigh of the C17 and C18, which carried drummers and trumpeters at parades, and in the Russian 'promenade chaise'. This vehicle, of wood, is rather clumsily made, unlike the accompanying horses, inspired by elegant English engravings, and the figures in Biedermeier dress. The piece is an interesting 'marriage' of a carriage home-made with hand tools and bought manufactured figures. IPM/EJB

460
Barfüsserkirche and Study collection

Picture strip for a magic lantern
Basle, ca. 1850
From a series of 13 pieces; oil painting on glass, height 10 cm, length 37 cm
Inv. no. 1976.186. Acquired by exchange

The principle of projecting images by means of a light source and lens goes back to an invention of the C16. The so called magic lantern, the earliest optical toy, was first used to entertain the public at markets. In the C19 it was produced industrially and came into domestic use, providing entertainment and instruction on Sundays or family occasions. The subject-matter was correspondingly diverse. The images were at first hand-painted on glass strips or transparencies, later giving way to transfers and photographic reproductions. The scene shown here includes the dance of the honorary sumbols of the three societies of Kleinbasel, 'zur Hären' (wildman), 'zum Rebhaus' (lion) and 'zum Greifen' (griffin) (see nos. 228 and 281). The communal processions, which since 1797 have been held regularly in January on the anniversary days of each of the societies, are unique to Kleinbasel. They are still held today, following an exact ritual, before the societies' members meet to eat and drink together. IPM

461
Haus zum Kirschgarten

Toy shop
Germany or Switzerland, mid–19th century; formerly owned by the Zellweger family in Trogen (canton of Appenzell Ausserrhoden)
Wood, painted, height 44 cm, width 70 cm, depth 47 cm
Inv. no. 1916.210.1–44. Gift of A. and F. Roth

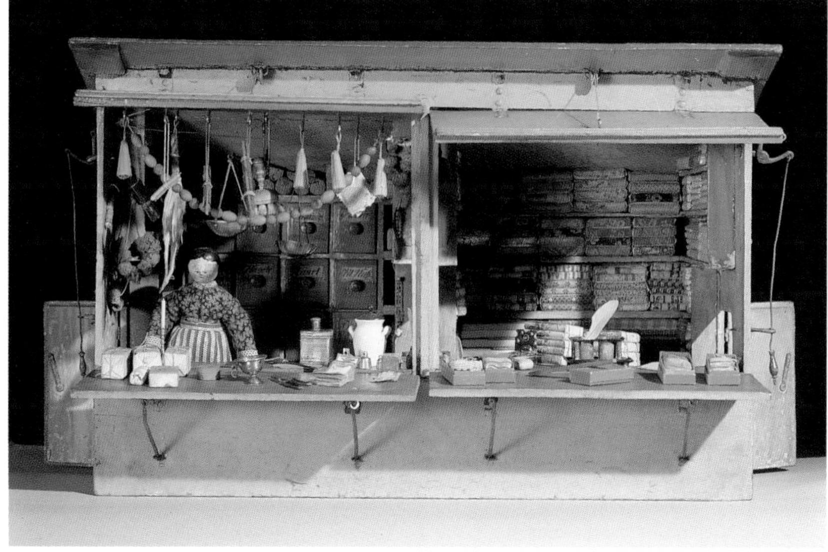

Playing at buying and selling has always been fun for children of pre-school age, with its variety of activities and objects. When toy money comes into play, and even a cash register complete with bell, the stage of getting used to weights, measures and money, and forming an idea of generally accepted values, is not far off. For adults this very large shop is a rich source of information on cultural history, with its diversity of groceries and commodities, some of which are scarcely seen any more, such as sugar sticks, gum mastic, gum arabic, whalebone, sulphur soap, tinder, flints, etc. In the drapery section 44 bales of material are on sale: printed indienne cotton, 'Kölsch' (linen material from Cologne with a cube pattern), silk, brocade, damask, silk ribbon.
IPM

462
Haus zum Kirschgarten

Noah's ark
Erzgebirge, 19th century
Wood, animals lathe-turned, painted; ark height 24 cm, width 55 cm, depth 15.5 cm
Inv. no 1954.139. Gift of the heirs of Frau M. Christ-Merian

One of the most powerful stories in the religious education of young children is that of the Flood, and the wooden ark built to save the animals and the family of the 300-year-old Noah – the only humans allowed to survive – provided material for a whole range of models. The emergence of the toy industry in Nuremberg and the Erzgebirge and the rapid production of wooden animal figures by mechanised lathes gave rise to a rich variety of figure groups, among which Noah's Ark proved especially saleable. It encouraged movement, taking things in and out, naming the animals and making choices between them. IPM

463
Haus zum Kirschgarten

'The Lady of Sonneberg'
Thuringia, 2nd half 19th century
Head of waxed papier mâché, real hair, height 47 cm
Inv. no. 1928.85. Gift of the heirs of Valerie Huber

Lady dolls are elegant toys not intended for rough playing. Among court circles, isolated examples are recorded in princes' account books from the late C14. From the C18 they became envoys of Parisian fashion to haute-bourgeoise ladies elsewhere, and were sought after in other countries up to the end of the C19. French lady dolls were expensively worked and came equipped with a rich trousseau. Both giver and recipient of such dolls would be well informed and fairly wealthy. Copies after such dolls made in Thuringia were less lavish, but still splendidly dressed. The salon furniture reflects the style of about 1875–80, with ebonised, delicately turned or bent wood and luxurious upholstery with deep buttoned padding. IPM

464
Haus zum Kirschgarten

Model warship
Bing brothers, Nuremberg, ca. 1910
Metal with steam engine; height with trolley 17.2 cm, length without flag 60 cm
Inv. no. 1972.178. Gift of Verena Mast

The warship is one of those mechanical toys, like trains and cars, that presuppose technical understanding. Fathers are always eager to pass on such expertise. Such objects can be regarded as toys for both adults and children. The ship is a vedette with a low deck and various superstructures: free-standing bridge, hatches, two anchors, two mortars and two torpedo tubes. There is clearly no room for crew's quarters in this little propeller-driven steamer. The mast flies a flag of the German Empire with an iron cross, and similar flags adorn the bow and stern. Propulsion is by a steam engine below deck. A trolley supports the model, made by the famous Bing brothers' metal-toy factory in Nuremberg. IPM

465
Haus zum Kirschgarten

Kasperl and a ghost
Carlo Böcklin, Basle, after 1911
Wood, painted; Kasperl: height 57 cm; ghost: height 55 cm
Inv. no. 1951.936. Gift of Frau N. Böcklin, Florence

In the age of electronic media the popularity of Kasperl has declined. Kasperl was first created as a figure on the real stage by the actor Johann Joseph Laroche (Pressburg 1745–1806 Vienna), as a variant of the jester Hanswurst. Kasperl was soon making public appearances in hand-puppet shows at markets, amusement parks and on special family occasions. As a fool – first for adults and then for children – Kasperl was permitted everything: to engage in political satire and pranks, use foul language, eat Bratwurst and drink a lot, and above all deal out blows. He did this to settle quarrels according to his own peculiar standards of good and evil, giving the spectators occasion for cathartic laughter and shrieks. He could get away with anything. Carlo Böcklin (1870–1937), son of the painter Arnold Böcklin, was an architect and painter. He made these hand puppets of Kasperl and a ghost as toys for his children, then sold them through the Dürerbund until about 1920; he was a pioneer of 'art' puppets. IPM

Musical instruments

At the end of 1992 the Musikinstrumenten-Sammlung (musical instrument collection) of the Historisches Museum contained more than 1900 items, produced between the C16 and the C20. It is by far the largest of its kind in Switzerland and the equal of similar collections in European museums.

Its history goes back more than 130 years; the first instrument, an organ in table form (inv. no. 1870.886.), came into the Medieval Collection, as it then was, as early as 1862. In 1878 a room was set aside solely for musical exhibits, with about 40 instruments. When the Historisches Museum Basel occupied the Barfüsserkirche in 1894, the collection, by now swollen to about 70 instruments, was given its own area. But in 1905 it was removed for space reasons and housed in a room in the administrative building at Steinenberg 4. The musical instruments were subsequently moved and stored several times. In 1943 they found a new home at Leonhardskirchplatz 5, under the same roof as the Musikwissenschaftliches Institut of Basle University.

In 1956 the opportunity arose to rent the rooms still used today, close to the Basle music academy, on the ground floor and first floor of the late Neoclassical Vorderer Rosengarten building at Leonhardsstrasse 8. The newly prepared museum was opened in 1957. Its arrangement remained practically unchanged until 1984. Then in 1985–86 the exhibition rooms were renovated, and the Museum was re-opened in re-organized form with new interior lighting on 1 March 1986. Although the rooms seem tasteful, and at first sight to harmonise very well with the musical instruments displayed, from a technical point of view they are, sadly, unsatisfactory and the space is insufficient for the collection, which in the meantime has much enlarged, so that about three quarters of the exhibits have to be stored.

The musical instrument collection has repeatedly received special donations, but without four especially generous and important gifts and legacies it would not have attained its present significance. In 1927 it received the legacy of Maurice Bedot-Diodati (Geneva) with 48 instruments. In 1956 the especially large and diverse collection of Otto Lobeck (Herisau), comprising 350 instruments, was acquired by Dr. h.c. Paul Sacher and donated to the Museum. This was followed in 1957 by the legacy of the Zurich violin-maker Albert Riemeyer (1860–1938) with 25 bowed string instruments, including special forms of the violin family in use in the C19. Finally, in 1980, the collection of historic brass instruments and drums of Pfarrer Dr. h.c. Wilhelm Bernoulli-Preiswerk (1905–1980) at Greifensee was bequeathed to Basle; with over 900 instruments and appurtenances it doubled the Museum's holdings as they then were.

The display of the instruments is determined largely by the confined space available; in order to offer the visitor the fullest cross-section possible, it follows the Curt Sachs system. In the corridor and the three ground-floor rooms are the aerophones (with air as the primary vibrating material), and those membraphones which have been particularly associated with certain wind instruments in the course of history, such as flute and drum or trumpets and kettle drums. Among the flutes and double-reed instruments, those by the Basle instrument-maker Christian Schlegel and his son Jeremias are outstanding – they include recorder, flute, shawm, oboe and bassoon. The harmonium, positive and regal organs and mechanical pianos share the somewhat cramped second room. The diverse Bernoulli collection is represented by a number of selected brass instruments. Most notably in this part of the exhibition unusual trumpets and horns by famous Nuremberg and Viennese makers are represented.

In the stairway area a number of idiophones – instruments with a solid body as the primary vibrating material, such as Jew's harp, rattle, castanets, Turkish crescent – are displayed, while the rooms on the first floor contain stringed instruments or chordophones. The stringed instruments for bowing and plucking include rarer types like the trumpet marine, hurdy-gurdy and chitarra battente. Harps of various origins from the C17 to the early C19, dulcimers and stringed keyboard instruments by well known makers over four centuries (virginal, spinet, harpsichord, clavichord, fortepiano), are other main centres of interest. In the corridor two showcases are reserved for small temporary exhibitions.

Some instruments are included among the exhibits in the Barfüsserkirche (the Ab Yberg positive organ, various drums), and in the Haus zum Kirschgarten (various stringed keyboard instruments and two positive organs). VG

466
Musikinstrumenten-Sammlung

Virginal

Unsigned, Flanders, 1572

Fifth or octave instrument, compass 41 keys, C/E-a2 (without g#2) with short bass octave; case poplar with tempera painting: sound-board pinewood; key facings bone (white keys) and dark oak (black keys); strings brass and steel; height 17.9 cm, width 92.5 cm, depth 33 cm (closed); keyboard length (F-e2): 48.5 cm Inv. no. 1990.426. Gift of the heirs of Benedikt Vischer-(Koechlin)/Staehelin and Verein für das Historische Museum Basel

The instrument is painted uniformly green on the outside with a pomegranate at the front, left, and two apples at the front, right. On the inside are depictions from the legend of Orpheus, with isolated fruit and flower decoration on the sound-board. The jack bar carries the inscription * SIC TRANSIT GLORIA MUNDI * 1572 *. The painting and instrument type indicate a Flemish origin. The Basle merchant Andreas Ryff (1550–1603) may have bought the instrument in Antwerp as a gift to his bride; this is suggested by the Ryff family coat of arms on the lid of the compartment to the left of the keyboard and the date, 1594, the year of his wedding. VG

467
Barfüsserkirche

Drum
Unsigned, Basle, 1575

Body: wood painted in tempera; seven concentrically arranged sound holes at the side; two stretching hoops of wood; cord strung between iron hooks, eight each at top and bottom; cord straps in knotted leather; calf or goat skin; height 64 cm, diameter of head 51 cm

Inv. no. 1874.120. On deposit from the Zeughaus Basel

The Museum's collection, which includes over 130 drums, holds the two oldest dated drums surviving, from 1571 and 1575. On both the stretching cord runs over hooks on the stretching hoop and not, as later, through holes in the hoops. This instrument has never been cut down in height, and makes clear how large drums were in the C16. Accordingly it was carried at the side and not in front of the body, and the rhythms played on it were simpler than today's. The depiction of two basilisks, each carrying a coat of arms arranged around the date, 1575, with the Basle crosier, are evidence that the drums were used in Basle. Drums were used either on their own or with a fife at municipal ceremonies and in infantry manœuvers. VG

468
Musikinstrumenten-Sammlung

Two fanfare trumpets in E♭
Jacob Steiger, Basle, 1578

Coiled clockwise; silver-coated copper; pommel, bell rim and ferrule gilt; overall length 231 cm, mouthpiece diameter 1.2 cm, bell 10.4 cm; each with its own mouthpiece

Inv. no. 1874.121. On deposit from the Zeughaus Basel

Inv. no. 1880.206. Gift of the Regierung Basel-Landschaft

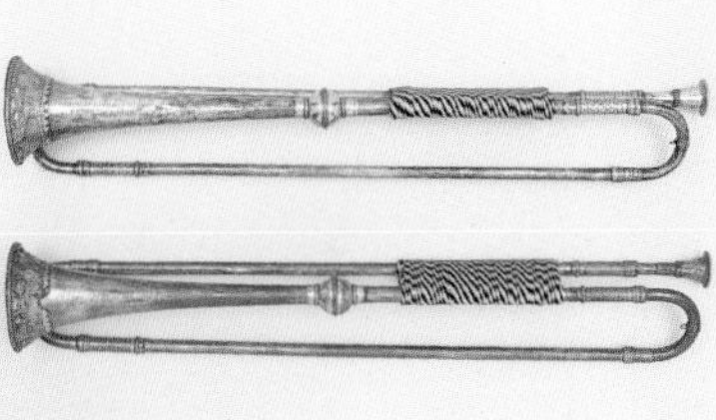

No other information on Jacob Steiger is available. The signature IACOB S is engraved on each of the bell ferrules and on one of the mouthpieces; on the rims of both instruments is the engraved inscription ALS REGIERT HER BONAVENTURA VON BRUN 15 / 78 and a coat of arms with the Basle crosier. Bonaventura von Brunn was mayor of Basle from 1570 until his death in 1591. The two instruments are the oldest surviving dated trumpets in stirrup form. The sound compass comprises the notes in the natural tone series above E♭; only in the fourth octave above the pedal note is a diatonic row (with restrictions) possible. In keeping with the custom of using trumpets at ceremonies at that time, often together with kettle drums, these two instruments are likely to have been blown on special occasions in the city of Basle. VG

469
Barfüsserkirche

The Ab Yberg table organ
Unsigned, South Germany(?), end 16th century, altered in 18th century

Compass 38 keys, F-a2 (without F♯, G♯ and g♯2); four stops: 4′ stopped, principal 2′ (at front), quint $1\frac{1}{3}'$, cymbal simple $\frac{1}{2}'$ (from f rep. in 1′; from a1 in 2′); all pipes metal; pitch a1 = 445 Hz; tuning mean tone; case height 82.5 cm, width 68.5 cm, depth 34 cm; keyboard (A-g) length 50.5 cm
Inv. no. 1927.258. Purchase

The three-part front is surmounted by gilt carving. At the sides and back the case has grisaille painting in the Renaissance style. It shows clear traces of alteration in the C18; when this was done the original reed stop is likely to have been replaced by the quint $1\frac{1}{3}'$. The two bellows lie horizontally behind the instrument. An inscription below the keyboard refers to Psalm 150: LAUDATE DOM[INUM] IN CHORDIS ET ORGANA (*sic*) PS[ALMUS] CL. The instrument comes from the family chapel of St Sebastian 'Im Grund' of the Ab Yberg family in Schwyz (built 1566–78), and was probably used for private services. Before it was offered for sale it was part of the private collection of Heinrich Schumacher in Lucerne (died 1921). VG

470
Musikinstrumenten-Sammlung

Positive organ in table form
Unsigned, Switzerland(?), 1st half 17th century

Compass 48 keys, C-c3 (without C♯); three stops: 8′ regal (reconstruction), 4′ stopped, octave 2′; all pipes wood; pitch a1 = 466 Hz; tuning heavily moderated mean tone; table top with ornamental walnut, mapleroot and oak veneer; case height 98.4 cm, width 158.5 cm, depth 114.7 cm; keyboard length (F-e2) 50.2 cm
Inv. no. 1870.886. Gift of the E.E. Bann der St. Leonhardsgemeinde

The pipes lie in the case behind the keyboard. Mounted above the keys and on the side of the instrument are brass strips with openwork foliate decoration and engravings; at the front they carry an inscription not yet interpreted: D.B./BA,/ 1505. The two horizontal wedge bellows incorporated in the base of the table are actuated from the back. The wind is fed to the pipes through the front legs. The organ was used by the Reformed parish of St. Leonhard in the Winterkapelle (winter chapel) of the Leonhardskirche until 1858. When it was replaced by a harmonium, it became a part of the Medieval Collection in 1862; together with a drum it initiated the musical instrument collection. VG

471
Musikinstrumenten-Sammlung

Chitarra battente
Giorgio Sellas, Venice, 1641

Five double course strings; front softwood, sides and back rosewood with ivory veins; inlaid with ivory, mother of pearl and ebony; sound hole with painted rosette of parchment and paper; overall length 89 cm, length of body 46 cm
Inv. no. 1927.271. Maurice Bedot-Diodati bequest

Giorgio Sellas, whose original name was Georg Seelos, was born in Füssen im Allgäu between 1574 and 1596. Like many makers of plucked and stringed instruments of his time he emigrated to Italy, to make a livelihood in one of the centres of instrument production there. His activity in Venice is documented from 1624 to 1648. The signature and workshop mark GIORGIO SE / LLAS ALLA / STELLA IN VEN / ETIA 1641 are scratched on a mother-of-pearl plate on the tuning board. The five sets of two strings are like those of the Baroque guitar common at that time, but are here of metal and are plucked with a plectrum. The back of the instrument is not flat as in a guitar, but is convex and formed of splints. VG

472
Musikinstrumenten-Sammlung

French flageolet
Master's sign D, Nuremberg, 2nd half 17th century

Six finger holes (four at front, two at back); ivory, block of fruit-tree wood; overall length 13.3 cm
Inv. no. 1956.361. Lobeck collection

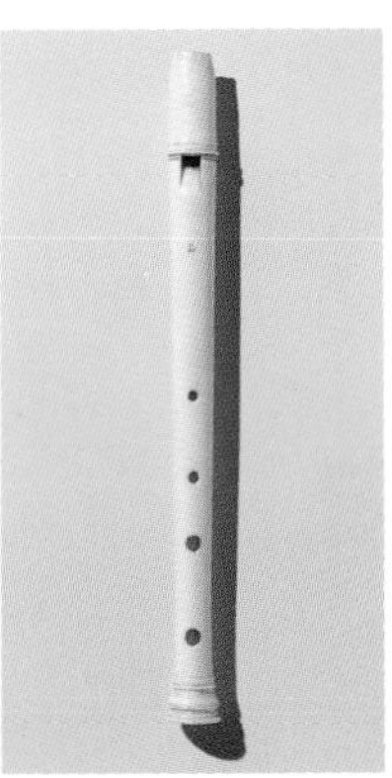

The master's sign "D" (stamped) is to be attributed to the 'Wildruf-und Horndreher' (hunting-horn and horn turners) of Nuremberg. From the surviving lists of surnames the producer can be assumed to be 'Denner', the father of Johann Christoph Denner, later a leading wind instrument maker, who attained the right to use his own mark in 1697. The valuable materials suggest the instrument was used in elevated society. As opposed to the flageolets usual in the C18, these small instruments were not intended for practical music-making, but to teach tunes to tame birds such as starlings. VG

473
Musikinstrumenten-Sammlung

Harpsichord, dated 1696
Giovanni Andrea Menegoni, Venice

Compass 45 keys, C/E–c3 with short bass octave; two 8′ stops; case and sound-board of cypresswood; key facings boxwood (white keys) and ebony (black keys); outer case in the shape of the instrument covered with leather and painted inside; height (body sides) 19 cm, width 70 cm, length 170 cm; keyboard length (c–b2) 49 cm
Inv. no. 1879.123. Gift of Signor Barzaghi-Cattaneo, Milan

Giovanni Andrea Menegoni is documented in Venice from 1690 to 1715. Only a few instruments by him have survived. The signature is burnt into the board above the keys: IOANNIS ANDREA MENEGONI VENETI MDCXCVI. The instrument is a relatively late example of an Italian harpsichord of the kind usual from the C16, with thin walls and a decorated case shaped around the instrument. To be played it could be either left in the case or taken out and placed on a table. The harpsichord is an illustration of the excellent holdings in the Museum of stringed keyboard instruments of the C17 and C18 (harpsichord, spinet and clavichord). VG

474
Musikinstrumenten-Sammlung

Bass viola da gamba
Joachim Tielke, Hamburg, ca. 1708

Six strings; front spruce, sides and back maple, edges reinforced with ivory; two C-shaped sound holes; fingerboard and string holder with tortoiseshell and ivory inlay; overall length 119.4 cm, length of body 68.4 cm
Inv. no. 1872.65. Purchase

Joachim Tielke, who was born in Königsberg in 1641 and died in Hamburg in 1719, is one of the most important North German stringed-instrument makers. His instruments are of exceptional quality and are usually decorated with much artistry. Here, for example, the neck ends with a finely carved female head. A number of such distinctive features suggest that this unsigned instrument can be attributed to Tielke. A burnt stamp inside on the back records a repair by the Basle violin-maker Simoutre (mid-C19). It might have been done with a view to using the instrument at one of the first concerts with early music played on old instruments held in Basle about that time. During Tielke's lifetime the bass viola da gamba was the preferred chamber-music and solo instrument, especially in France and Germany. VG

475
Musikinstrumenten-Sammlung

Hurdy-gurdy with lute-shaped body,
dated 1746
François Feury, Paris

Two melody and four drone strings of gut, four steel sympathetic strings; front fir, body of maple and mahogany splints; two C-shaped sound holes; keys and edge of lid faced or inlaid with ivory and ebony; overall length 64 cm
Inv. no. 1882.27. Purchase

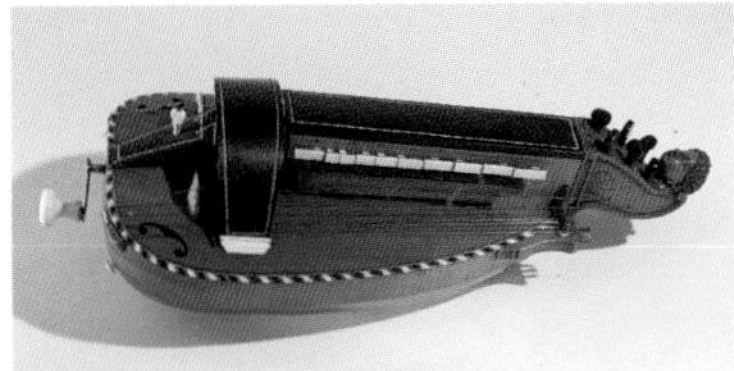

The signature of François Feury (Paris ca. 1711 – after 1772) is found on the inside of the openable lid, above the tangent mechanism: "F. Feury, rue des Fossez St. Germain de l'Auxerrois proche la Rue de l'Arbre sec. A Paris 1746". The strings are played by a wheel connected to a handle; the melody strings are shortened by a keyboard mechanism with tangents. One of the four drone strings ('la trompette') runs over a snare bridge. This is engaged by a tailpiece inserted in the peg and produces a timbre reminiscent of the braying of a trumpet. These luxurious instruments were used for pastoral music-making in elevated society in France in the C18. VG

476
Musikinstrumenten-Sammlung

Bassoon
Jeremias Schlegel, Basle, second half 18th century

Boxwood, six keys, crook brass; height with crook 128.5 cm, diameter 1.4–3.6 cm
Inv. no. 1976.179. Acquired by exchange from Willi Burger, Zurich

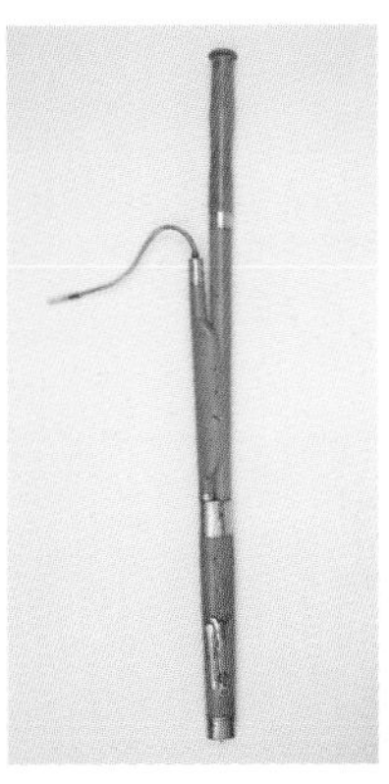

Jeremias Schlegel lived in Basle from 1742 to 1792 and, like Johann Jacob Brosy, is one of the important Basle instrument-makers of the C18. He probably learned his craft from his father Christian, whose workshop he took over in 1746. In 1752 he was appointed as a "musicus" to the post of "civis academicus" and produced woodwind instruments for the city's Collegium musicum. The total of 13 instruments made by the two Schlegels in the Museum is represented here by this bassoon, which is outstanding especially for its costly material. The signature SCHLEGEL / A BALE (stamped) is found on all parts of the instrument. The six-keyed instrument represents the type used in orchestras and in chamber music in the late C18. It is quite conceivable that the instrument was played in the Basle Collegium musicum at that time. VG

477
Musikinstrumenten-Sammlung

Single-action harp
Unsigned; attributed to Georges Cousineau, Paris, 1775–85

Compass 38 strings (E1–g3); seven pedals (left A, G, F, E, right D, C, B); sound box pine and maple, painted black; tuning pegs, pedals and mechanism iron; strings, gut; overall height 161.5 cm, width 40 cm, depth 79.5 cm
Inv. no. 1956.542. Lobeck collection

Many details of the construction, of the execution of the carved neck spiral and of the painting of the post and sound box indicate that the harp was built between 1775 and 1785 by the important Parisian harp-maker Georges Cousineau (1733–1800). At that time Paris was a centre of harp playing. In a single-action pedal harp only one position is provided for each pedal, not two as in the more recent double-action pedal harp or in modern concert harps. The same notes in the different octaves are each assigned to one pedal, and are mechanically interconnected. By pressing down the pedal the string concerned is raised by a semitone, enlarging the range of the instrument to the chromatics. VG

478
Musikinstrumenten-Sammlung

Square piano
Johann Jacob Brosy, Basle, 1790

Compass 5 octaves, F1–f4; simple action without release; two knee levers for stop damper lifting (treble and bass) and hand pull for moderator; case in walnut, inlaid above keyboard; sound-board spruce; key facing ebony (diatonics) and ivory (chromatics); strings brass and steel, all double; height of body 18.3 cm, width 164.4 cm, depth 54.9 cm; keyboard length (c–b2) 47.5 cm
Inv. no. 1908.416. Purchase

Johann Jacob Brosy lived in Basle from 1748 to 1816. His signature is found on a label stuck to the sound-board: "Johann Jacob Brosy Instrument und Orgelmacher in Basel" (printed) "137 1790" (added by hand). He took over his father's workshop after his death in 1764. From ca. 1770 until the end of the century he maintained, repaired and built various organs in the Basle region, as well as clavichords, harpsichords, spinets and square pianos. These stringed keyboard instruments were very popular for domestic music-making in middle-class houses at that time, especially square pianos from the late C18 onwards. VG

479
Musikinstrumenten-Sammlung

Turkish crescent
Unsigned, Switzerland(?), early 19th century
Brass, iron, wood; overall length 169.2 cm, width 39.1 cm
Inv. no. 1980. 2058. Dr. h.c. Wilhelm Bernoulli-Preiswerk bequest

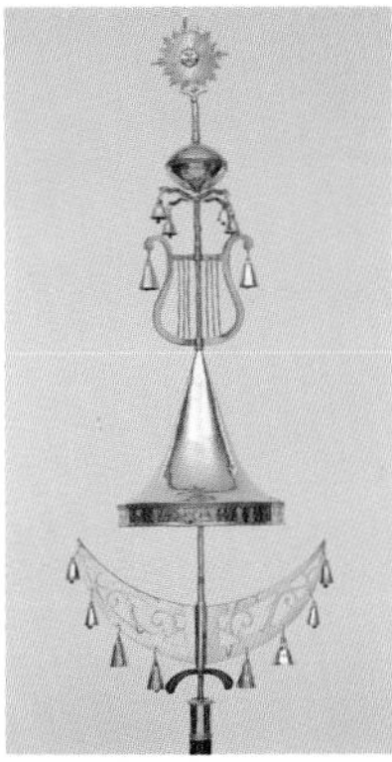

Variously shaped brass elements are fixed to an iron post: from the bottom upwards, a crescent-shaped frame with eight small bells, a helmet with perforated rim, a lyre with two small bells and a cross with four, and a hollow sphere probably symbolizing the world; the top is formed by a sun with a face and separate projecting rays. The post fits loosely into a wooden tube and rests on a spring. This causes it to move when marching so that the bells ring to the rhythm of the march. Its appearance in military bands from the late C18 onwards was due to the prevailing fashion for things Turkish. Its 'Turkishness' is apparent in the fondness for crescent-shaped elements and musically in the desire for rattles and jingles to accentuate the march rhythm. VG

480
Musikinstrumenten-Sammlung

Keyed trumpet in G
Alois Doke, Linz, 1823
Coiled clockwise; five keys; brass; overall length 160 cm, mouthpiece diameter 1.1 cm, bell diameter 11.8 cm
Inv. no. 1980. 2369. Dr. h. c. Wilhelm Bernoulli-Preiswerk bequest

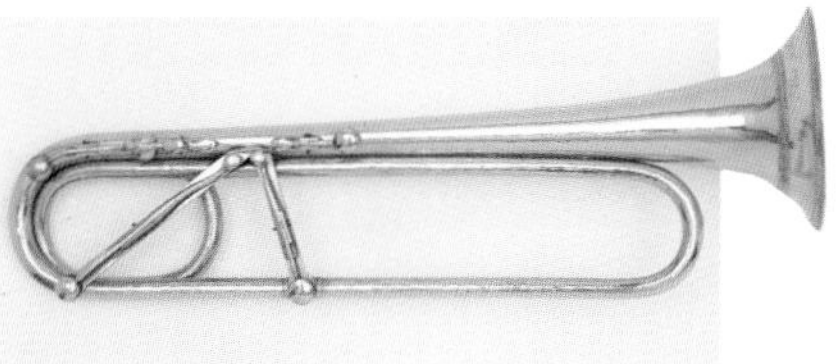

All that is known about Alois Doke is that he became a member of the Linzer Gesellschaft der Musikfreunde (Linz society of music-lovers) in 1823. The engraved signature in italics on the rim is to be read from the outside: "Aluis Doke in Linz". The five keys are arranged radially. They allow a greater chromatic range than that of the natural trumpet, in that the fourth between the 3rd and 4th harmonics can be filled in. Experiments with keyed trumpets go back to the 1770s and, with the less common stopped and 'invention' trumpets, form an intermediate stage between the natural or fanfare trumpet and the valve trumpet patented in 1818 in Berlin. The enlarged tone compass is clear, for example, in the concertos for keyed trumpet written by Joseph Haydn (1732–1809) and Johann Nepomuk Hummel (1778–1837). VG

481
Musikinstrumenten-Sammlung

Post horn in B$^{\flat}$

Unsigned, Germany, 19th century

Coiled clockwise; four keys; brass; diameter of mouthpiece 1.0 cm, of bell 11.1 cm, of coil 16 cm
Inv. no. 1980.2001. Dr. h.c. Wilhelm Bernoulli Preiswerk bequest

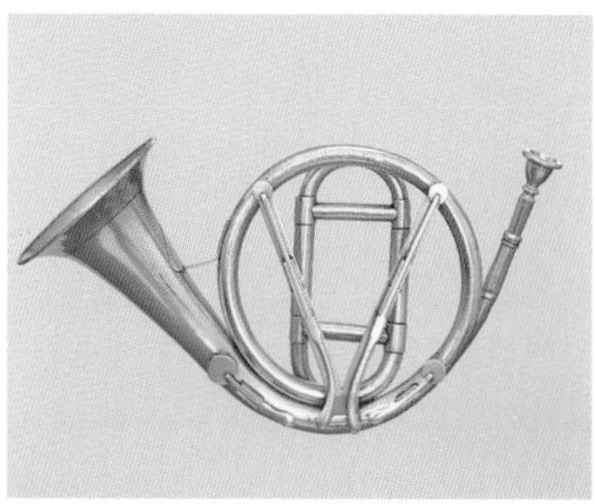

The post horn was used by the Thurn und Taxis postal service from the C16 to signal the arrival or departure of the mail coach or courier. To distinguish the calls further, different rhythms were played. The modest original tone range, limited to a few notes of the harmonic series, was enlarged first by an open fingering hole and in the C19 by means of keys. This instrument is also of special importance in respect of the Bernoulli collection itself, since it was the very first instrument acquired by Dr. h.c. Wilhelm Bernoulli, in 1926 in Frankfurt, thereby laying the 'foundation stone' of his comprehensive brass instrument collection. VG

482
Musikinstrumenten-Sammlung

Lyre piano

Johann Christian Schleip, Berlin, ca. 1830

Compass 6 octaves, F1–f4; upright English piano action with release; three knee levers for una corda, fagotto stop (F1-f1) and damper lifting; case of mahogany with veneer and fillet inlay; upper frame open, filled with stretched green silk; key facings ivory (white keys) and ebony (black keys); strings brass and steel, all double; overall height 207 cm (without legs 152.8 cm), width 111.6 cm, depth 59 cm; keyboard length (F-e2) 48.0 cm
Inv. no. 1989.31. Gift of the Verein für das Historische Museum Basel

In 1816 Schleip moved from Gotha to Berlin, where his work is documented until 1844. The signature is on a porcelain plaque above the keyboard: "J.C. Schleip in Berlin". The lyre-shaped upright pianoforte is a Berlin speciality closely linked to the name of Schleip; cupboard-shaped versions are found as early as the 1790s, while other variants such as pyramid and giraffe pianos appeared in the C19. They were all intended for music-making on a small domestic scale. Other important items of interest in the Museum's piano collection are several Viennese grand pianos (from 1792) and French grand and square pianos by the firm of Erard. VG

483
Musikinstrumenten-Sammlung

Bass horn (basson russe) with dragon's head

Dubois & Couturier, Lyons, 1835–37

Maple; two keys, crook and mouthpiece brass; head in sheet iron, painted; height 100 cm; diameter 3.15.4 cm
Inv. no. 1956.413. Lobeck collection

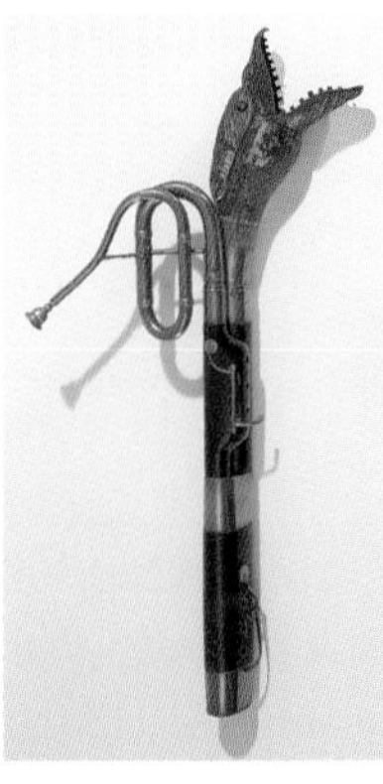

This bass horn has the signature Dubois & Couturier, which was used for only a short time, in two places: "DUBOIS / COUTURIER Lyon" (stamped). Outwardly the bass horn, favoured by military bands, resembles the bassoon; it is likewise made of wood and conically bored. However, the sound is not produced by a double reed as in the bassoon, but by a hemispherical mouthpiece as in trumpets. The bell, also deviating from the bassoon, is made of metal. It often had the shape of a frightening dragon's head, no doubt to add a decorative touch to parades. VG

484
Musikinstrumenten-Sammlung

Signal horn in C

Henry Distin, London, 1860

Coiled twice anti-clockwise; silver, engraved; overall length 112.5 cm, diameter of mouthpiece 1.25 cm, bell 9.8 cm
Inv. no. 1980.2519. Dr. h.c. Wilhelm Bernoulli-Preiswerk bequest

Henry Distin was born in London in 1819. With his father and his three brothers he played in the 'Distin Family Quintet' brass ensemble. In 1849 he took over the family firm. In 1882 he moved to Philadelphia where he founded another firm in 1886. He died in Philadelphia in 1903. The signature is engraved on the bell: H^{Y}. DISTIN . MAKER . LONDON . The instrument, made of costly material in comparison to other horns, and preciously fashioned, has engraved foliage and flowers and a dedicatory text on the bell. The inscription indicates that it was a gift of the ladies of Wells to a voluntary company of riflemen formed in 1860, when an invasion by Napoleon III was threatened: "Presented / to the / 10th SOMERSET. / RIFLE VOLUNTEER COMPANY / by the Ladies of / Wells and its Vicinity / Octr. 19th. / 1860". VG

Coaches and Sledges

Fine horses, coaches and sledges were highly prized in wealthy Basle households from early times until the C20. Before the advent of the railway the Basle silk manufacturers and merchants used coaches for their many long business journeys. In the age of the railway coaches were used only for short-distance travel and sporting entertainment by the ladies and gentlemen of Basle's wealthy upper class. Although increasing numbers of motor cars were bought after the turn of the century, the decisive turning point came with the First World War, when most private horses were commandeered for the army. The rapid social change during and after the War saw the disappearance of most luxury horse teams in Basle. The imposing aristocratic villas with parks, stables and coach-houses on the St. Alban estate, in the Gellert quarter, on the Lange Gasse and in other parts of the city near the centre were replaced by apartment blocks and commercial buildings. Today there is little architectural evidence left in the city of Basle's great enthusiasm for horses.

The hackney cab firms of Basle also operated the hotel omnibuses, horse-drawn trams, ambulances and so on. The two largest cab firms, Gebrüder Keller and Gebrüder Settelen, also enjoyed an excellent reputation outside Basle. From 1881 until 1895 the Centralbahnhof and the Badische Bahnhof in Basle were linked by a rail-less horse-drawn tram. This was replaced in 1895 by an electric tramway. The last horse-drawn hackney cab ran in 1936, and in 1955 the post office stopped delivering parcels by horse-drawn waggon.

By the end of the C19 a few old sledges from the C17 and C18 had been donated to the Historisches Museum. They were exhibited for a time in the Barfüsserkirche, and later in the basement of the Haus zum Kirschgarten. Their number was increased by isolated purchases. After 1930 they were joined by an increasing number of coaches, though for reasons of space most of these were stored. For the Schweizerische Gartenbauausstellung (Swiss horticultural show) held in 1980 the former cow-shed on the Merian country estate at Brüglingen was converted into an exhibition building. After the show the Christoph Merian Stiftung, on the Historisches Museum's initiative, agreed to make the ground floor of the building available gratis as an exhibition space for the coach and sledge collection. In 1981 the Kutschen und Schlittensammlung (coach and sledge collection), Brüglingen, was opened as the fourth building of the Historisches Museum Basel. Since then the number of exhibits has increased steadily, though lack of space has meant that they have had to be restricted to typical objects relating to Basle. Presently exhibited are two mail coaches, a horse-drawn hackney cab, about 20 luxury coaches, about 10 sledges, roughly 10 children's coaches and sledges and about 15 commercial carts, as well as harness and numerous small items such as pattern sheets from coachwork firms, sledge furs, coachmen's liveries, etc. The collection is located in the middle of the Brüglingen Botanical Garden, in a popular recreation area near Basle. EJB

485
Brüglingen

Diana sleigh
Mannheim(?), perhaps by the court sculptor Gabriel Grupello, ca. 1700
Wood, carved, with bronze fittings, height 185 cm, width 108 cm, length 235 cm
Inv. no. 1922.360. Purchase

'Carousel' sleigh-rides, in which the sleighs performed various figures to music, were a popular winter recreation among the nobility in the Baroque period. The order in which they drove was decided by rank, and also determined which figures were performed. The sleighs were drawn usually by a single horse harnessed directly to the long runners, the harness consisting only of a collar, bridle and lead rope. Richly embroidered sleigh bells and plumes on the horses contributed to the cheerful, festive appearance of such sleigh teams. The historian Rudolf H. Wackernagel wrote of the Diana sleigh, which came from the Court of Elector Johann Wilhelm of the Palatinate (1690–1716), "The single-seat body represents an opulent chariot 'alla romana', i.e. a two-wheeled war chariot of antiquity. However, the body seems to be mounted the wrong way round on the sledge runners. It is supported at the front by a pair of tritons, above whom Diana is enthroned. The victorious arrival of the goddess of hunting preceding a high-born lady sitting in the car is announced by a Fortuna on her turning sphere at the front apex of the runners." EJB

486
Brüglingen

Biedermeier barouche
North Switzerland, ca. 1810
Height 220 cm, width 144 cm, length 255 cm
Inv. no. 1982.88. Purchase

This oldest coach in the collection can, as a 'voiture multiple', be converted in a few minutes, by fitting front and side windows and the front roof section, from an open barouche for town use into a closed travelling carriage. The body is suspended by leather straps from C-springs, the most sophisticated suspension available at the time. The front and back axles are joined by a longitudinal beam. The vehicle is braked by a wheel-shoe that can be applied or released from the coachman's box by means of a leather strap. The half-chaise body contains two seats and an emergency seat at the front. Below the back seat is a removable travelling case, to the left and right of which are secret compartments. The compartment for personal effects behind the back-rest, which projects from the body at the back, is called the 'drum' or 'wig bag'. The coach was completely restored in 1982. The lacquerwork was reconstructed from the carefully exposed remains of the original paint by Basle's last trained coachwork painter, Rudolf Meier-Börlin (1913–1991). EJB

487
Brüglingen

Children's coaches: vis-à-vis (left); **barouche** (right)
Zurich, ca. 1820/30; Basle, ca. 1820/30
Vis-à-vis: height 82 cm, width 75 cm, length 150 cm; Barouche: height 115 cm, width 77 cm, length 132 cm
Inv. no. 1920.176. Purchase
Inv. no. 1915.22. Gift of L. Thurneysen-Mende

Such vehicles, produced either as toys for children or as working prams, were pulled by the children themselves or by a nursemaid or houseboy. Sometimes dogs, goats or sheep were harnessed to them. The vehicle on the left is a C-sprung vis-à-vis of the Biedermeier period scaled down but with every detail present. The wooden parts of the vehicle on the right reveal the hand of the best coachbuilders; this is especially clear from the chassis, of which the front part is beautifully made. The whole vehicle is a miniature of a Biedermeier barouche, correct in all its coachbuilding details. The box is fully suspended on C-springs and leather straps. Restraining straps between the body and the central beam of the chassis prevent violent pitching of the body. The old velvet upholstery with white porcelain buttons is also well preserved. EJB

488
Brüglingen

Char-de-côté, mail coach of the Berne Federal postal service
Ca. 1850

Height 210 cm, width 137 cm, length 340 cm
Inv. no. 1971.3066. On loan from the Schweizerisches Museum für Volkskunde

The char-de-côté was in widespread use in the first half of the C19, above all in western Switzerland and the neighbouring regions of France. The Swiss postal service owned only a few vehicles of this type. The design of the char-de-côté, with the body turned anti-clockwise through 90° and its unsophisticated chassis with straight wooden bearers, made possible a light, narrow and inexpensive vehicle. The unreinforced bearers supporting the cabin, made of tough, flexible ash, contributed to the soft, pleasant springing of the coach. Its disadvantage was that the passengers had to face sideways to the direction of travel. This was found uncomfortable, and made it impossible to look out on to the right side of the road. The bearers are supported on the axles by simple transverse springs. One longitudinal beam joins the two axles. The first chars-de-côté were completely open at the top: the body consisted of a simple seat with a footboard. With the improvement of roads in rural districts and the rising demand for comfort, the char-de-côté was superseded by other types of carriage. EJB

489
Brüglingen

Basle 'sausage' sledge
Basle, 2nd half 19th century

Height 187 cm, width 135 cm, length 270 cm
Inv. no. 1982.164. Gift of Maja Sacher, A. and H. Keller

In the C18 and C19 and in the early C20 young people from wealthy families regularly went out on sledge rides together, with a night-time meal and dancing. In this the middle class took over the tradition of the aristocratic 'carousel' rides of the Baroque age (see no. 485) in a form adapted to the time. These Basle sledge parties often crossed into neighbouring Baden and Alsace. Those who did not have sleighs of their own travelled on a so called 'sausage', a hired sledge with several seats and driven by a coachman. The acquaintanceships made in this way not uncommonly led to marriage. The sausage sledge exhibited belonged to the Basle hackney cab firm of Gebrüder Keller and was used until about 1930. However, this type of sledge, with the seat bench running round the inside of the body, was not usually called a 'sausage' in Basle. Generally a 'sausage' was a long, narrow sledge having a chest-like body with a sausage-shaped leather-upholstered seat on which the passengers sat astride. EJB

490
Brüglingen

Two children's sledges
Sledge (left), formerly owned by the Sarasin family of Basle, 2nd third of C19; sledge (right) made by Wagner Hungerbühler, Kreuzlingen (Thurgau), formerly owned by the Basle family of Burckhardt-Jacker, 1871
Sledge (left): height 57 cm, width 54 cm, length 90 cm; sledge (right): height 80 cm, width 50 cm, length 144 cm
Inv. no. 1947.138. Gift of Philis von Salis-Sarasin
Inv. no. 1947.206. Gift of J. Liechti-Burckhardt

Such sledges, pulled or pushed by hand, were used as prams in winter. Children of rich families, wrapped in warm furs, were taken to school in them by a housemaid or valet. When school finished the various servants waited outside to take the children home. The children were also taken to the skating rink in such sledges pushed by servants. The single-seat sledge on the left is modelled on an elegant horse-drawn sleigh and fitted with a draw-bar. The two-seat sledge on the right is designed for pushing. With its sideways-facing seat and backrest made of lathe-turned struts, this type of sledge was known as a 'Sackschlitten' (sack or bag sledge). EJB

491
Brüglingen

'French' postillion's livery
Formerly owned by the Paravicini-Engel family, ca. 1890
Inv. no. 1934.121d. Gift of Emil Paravicini-Engel

The 'French' postillion's livery formed part of the post harness in pure French style of the Paravicini-Engel household, the rest of which is also in the Brüglingen collection. The harness, with heavy breast collars, badger hair-trimmed bridles, supporting halters, neck rolls and fox tails, was used on the break de chasse et de promenade (no. 495). The postillion's livery in fresh moss green and red, edged with red galloons and golden braid, with brass buttons and a brass plate with a monogram on the arm band, made a very colourful effect. However, it was no less elegant for all that than the more restrained 'English' liveries. Another noteworthy feature is the coachman's tapering top hat, made of waterproof felt impregnated with shellac. Riding breeches of white leather were usually worn when the horses were driven from the saddle, but, as the Basle post-chaise was driven from the box, the livery included long coachman's breeches of green cloth. The trousers were worn over the boots and were held by straps running under the soles in front of the heel. EJB

492
Brüglingen

Pattern sheet for the coachwork of a mail omnibus
Basle, Carrosserie Heimburger, ca. 1890
Height 20 cm, width 31 cm
Inv. no. 1981.211. Gift of Alfred Heimburger

Coachwork guides made up of sheets of this kind with accompanying text booklets were used by coachbuilders to keep up with the latest fashions in carriage design. This is from *Le Guide du Carrossier*, published by Brice Thomas, 135, Boulevard Haussmann, Paris, no. 54, série A. As coaches were not usually mass-produced in Europe, but were built one by one, the customer was often advised personally when making the order. He could state his wishes regarding lacquerwork, upholstery, etc. The function of these pattern sheets is entirely comparable to that of the illustrations in present-day fashion magazines. The *Guides du Carrossier* by well known publishers, such as Louis Dupont and Brice Thomas, both of Paris, could be obtained on subscription. They often reported on exhibitions and the coaches and sledges shown at them. For Basle coachbuilders it was usual to spend a certain period of apprenticeship in Paris. Many vehicles in the Brüglingen collection illustrate that they worked closely with Paris firms and were familiar with the *dernier cri* of Parisian coachwork fashion. EJB

493
Brüglingen

Minerva sleigh
Basle, Carrosserie Kauffmann, ca. 1890
Height 188 cm, width 117 cm, length 206 cm
Inv. no. 1933.223. Gift of Georges Fürstenberger-Vonder Mühll

The unusually lavish sleigh, furnished in the Louis XV style, came to the Museum from the estate of Johann Jakob Bachofen-Petersen of Basle (1865–1904). The signature of the maker, "Carrosserie Eugène Kauffmann, Bâle", appears inside the lamps. The sleigh bears the head of the Roman goddess Minerva on its runners; the neck of the figure merges below into a fabulous creature resembling a dolphin or a lion. The arm rests of the front seat are adorned with lions' heads. The gentleman drove the sleigh himself. A footman was carried on the groom's seat at the back. The richly decorated silver-plated gala lamps provided illumination on night journeys. At an exhibition in Amsterdam in 1877, the Munich court coachbuilder F.P. Gmelch showed a sleigh remarkably similar to the Basle example. The similarity suggests that when Johann Jakob Bachofen-Petersen ordered his Minerva sleigh from the Basle coachbuilder Kauffmann he used an illustration from the exhibition report in the *Guide du Carrossier* by Brice Thomas, Paris, as his pattern. The sleigh passed to the Fürstenberger family, whose arms appear on the body, in 1904. EJB

494
Brüglingen

Coupé
Basle, Carrosserie Kauffmann, Reinbolt & Christé, Successeurs, formerly owned by the La Roche family ca. 1895
Height 189 cm, width 177 cm, length 332 cm
Inv. no. 1931.489. Gift of Adèle La Roche

Coupés are elegant town carriages driven by a coachman with one or two horses in English harness. They were favoured for evening trips in cool or bad weather, on social occasions such as concerts, theatre outings and the like. For use in fine, warm weather, a 'mylord' or a half-enclosed victoria probably stood waiting in the coach-house. The bodywork of this coupé is fitted, in the latest Paris carriage fashion, with narrow panels outlined in red, small leather mud-flaps in front of the door handles and large flaps, also vertical, in front of the side windows. The interior furnishings are covered in beige woollen material and include a small folding emergency or child's seat, arm straps and a device for signalling to the coachman with a whistle and rubber bulb (the bulb and tube are missing). The doors bear the coat of arms of the La Roche family. Long, soft springs, solid rubber tyres and sealed, oil-lubricated, Collings patented axles ensured a comfortable ride. The carriage was in regular use until 1930. EJB

495
Brüglingen

Break de chasse et de promenade
(hunting and driving break)
Basle, Carrosserie Kauffmann, Reinbolt & Christé, Successeurs, ca. 1890
Height 212 cm, width 178 cm, length 340 cm
Inv. No. 1934.121. Gift of Emil Paravicini-Engel

Such hunting and driving carriages were usually driven by the owner himself. The Paravicini-Engel family used the vehicle for sporting excursions. At the horse races at the Schützenmatte and later at the Schänzli, such carriages belonging to rich Basle families were driven on to reserved spaces opposite the spectators' stand. There they provided their owners and their guests with an exclusive private grandstand. To quote the historian the historian Philipp Sarasin, "Horse races, especially on Monday afternoons, were one of the best means of demonstrating status in high society for reasons that are self-evident. The arrangements were made accordingly. Spectators who were unwilling to alight from their open carriages paid 20 francs for a place on the inside of the track, opposite the grandstand". Herr Paravicini-Engel owned four elegant carriage horses to pull his break, as well as a four-in-hand in English harness and a French post-chaise also with four horses. On the rearmost seat of the carriage rode a coachman and a footman in English or French livery (see no. 491) to match the harness. EJB

496
Brüglingen

Phaeton
Basle, Carrosserie Kauffmann, Reinbolt & Christé, Successeurs, ca. 1900
Height 180 cm (roof folded down), width 159 cm, length 258 cm
Inv. no. 1981.177. On loan from the Einwohnergemeinde Riehen

A phaeton is a sporting, four-wheeled carriage which has a comfortable bench seat at the front for the ladies and gentlemen and another seat at the back for one or two footmen. The name goes back to Phaeton, the son of the Greek sun-god Helios and Klymene. Depending on its construction and weight, this type of vehicle might be driven by the gentleman himself, or the lady, with one, two or even four horses. The Clavel-Respinger family's carriage can be drawn by one or two horses. Alexander and Fanny Clavel used it for excursions into the country around Basle, as well as for several major journeys through Switzerland which took them over Alpine passes. The phaeton was well suited to these journeys thanks to the protection of its leather roof and the stowage space in the carriage body. Noteworthy features are the patent French brake-lever mounted inside the seat and roof area, and the mudguards fixed to the front canopy bow. EJB

497
Brüglingen

Dog cart
Basle, Carrosserie Kauffmann, Reinbolt & Christé, Successeurs, ca. 1900

Height 180 cm, width 175 cm, length 192 cm (without shafts)
Inv. no. 1981.178. On loan from the Einwohnergemeinde Riehen

Dog carts were light sporting carriages driven by the lady or gentleman. They were used for excursions and shopping trips in town. Originally, dog carts were used to transport hunting dogs in a dog box under the seat, fitted with suitable ventilation slots at the sides. Later versions, like this dog cart formerly belonging to the Clavel family, were mostly built purely as sporting vehicles without the dog box. The carriage was often driven by Frau and Herr Clavel with a tandem team, i.e. two horses harnessed one behind the other. Two-wheeled carriages have to be in balance, so that they run smoothly without pitching motion. Balance was achieved by moving the seats longitudinally, by means of a crank handle on the body. A noteworthy detail is the brass bulb horn. The dummies on the cart are dressed as Fanny Clavel and a coachman of the Clavel household about 1920. The horse wears English harness with the coat of arms of the Clavel family. EJB

498
Brüglingen

Landau (the last Basle hackney carriage)
Basle, Carrosserie Kauffmann, Reinbolt & Christé, Successeurs, ca. 1900

Height 203 cm, width 173 cm, length 373 cm
Inv. no. 1982.167. On loan from Settelen AG

As an all-weather town and touring carriage, the four-seat landau was formerly an indispensable occupant of any large upper-class coach-house. The roof, in two halves, offered good protection in rain and snow, but could be fully opened in fine, warm weather. Thanks to its low door the landau could be entered decorously even by ladies dressed in the fashion of former times. A practical, comfortable but prestigious vehicle, the landau was driven by a coachman with two horses. Thanks to its versatility it was also popular with the postal service, hotels, waggon yards and hackney cab firms. Landaus were produced by all good coachbuilders in large numbers and in many versions. The example exhibited was used by the Basle hackney carriage company Gebrüder Settelen until 1937. It was equipped with a large, cast-iron Berlin taxi meter, of the kind introduced in Basle in 1897. In service as a cab this landau, despite its size, was drawn by only one horse. EJB

499
Brüglingen

Painter's handcart
Ca. 1920
Inscribed "E. Nachbur, Maler, Tel. 22 117"; height 140 cm, width 112 cm, length 260 cm
Inv. no. 1985.306. Gift of Ernst Nachbuhr, Binningen

Such handcarts, used by all kinds of tradesmen and craftsmen, once played an important part in the street-scene in any town or village. Their superstructure was adapted to the needs of the particular trade. Bakers' carts, for example, had an enclosed body with slots for air. These handcarts were used essentially for transporting tools and materials. They could also serve as an advertising medium for the traders or craftsmen. This handcart, with a box-like body for the painter's equipment and iron frames to carry his ladders, is a typical example of a commercial hand-pulled cart. The long, soft leaf springs and the relatively large wheels prevented the goods in the cart from being too violently shaken in the unmade or cobbled streets. The light brown or beige paintwork with metal parts painted black and silver, and the dark-red lettering, give the cart a certain elegance. EJB

500
Brüglingen

Name plate of the Basle coachbuilder Julius Kölz
Basle, Max Hindermann, ca. 1920
Height 129 cm, width 94 cm
Inv. no. 1982.400. Gift of Rudolf Kölz

The firm of Julius Kölz built primarily mail coaches, mail waggons and commercial vehicles. They built hardly any luxury coaches, although Kölz supplied other coachbuilders with parts for luxury coaches. One wagonette, of the luxury vehicles built by Kölz, is preserved in the collection at Brüglingen. The Swiss postal service ordered its vehicles as a rule from small and medium-sized firms, and sometimes even from rural smiths and cartwrights. The plans and exact specifications were laid down by the post office. The name plate shows how important the custom of the post office was to Kölz, since a motor-driven parcels van is shown. The name plate is particularly important in illustrating the transition from coachbuilding to motor vehicle body construction. Until well into the 1930s the motor car producer often supplied only the chassis, on which the bodywork-maker erected a piece of traditional coachbuilding. The frame of the body was made of ashwood and covered in sheet steel, or later aluminium. EJB

Bibliography

The following bibliography is organized by section, and within the section in chronological order of publication. It does not claim to be a complete bibliography of all scholarly contributions relating to the Museum's collections. Some of the more recent titles are available for sale at the Museum.

Introduction

Führer durch die mittelalterliche Sammlung zu Basel. Basle 1880. – **Festbuch zur Eröffnung des Historischen Museums Basel**. Basle 1894. – **Führer durch das Historische Museum in Basel**. Hrsg. Verwaltung des Museums. Basle 1899. – **Burckhardt-Finsler, Albert**: Zweck und Ziele des Historischen Museums. In: Basler Jahrbuch 1902, p.226–256. – **Reinhardt, Hans**: Historische Schätze Basels. Basle o. J. [1942]. – **Major, Emil**: Das Fäschische Museum und die Fäschischen Inventare. In: Jahresbericht der Öffentlichen Kunstsammlung Basel 1908, p.1–69. – **Major, Emil**: Fünfzig Jahre Historisches Museum Basel 1894–1944. Basle 1945. – **Alioth, Martin; Barth, Ulrich; Huber, Dorothee:** Basler Stadtgeschichte 2: vom Brückenschlag 1225 bis zur Gegenwart. Basle 1981. – **Oeri, Hans-Georg et al. (Red.)**: Erasmus von Rotterdam: Vorkämpfer für Frieden und Toleranz. Ausstellung zum 450. Todestag von Erasmus von Rotterdam veranstaltet vom Historischen Museum Basel. Basle 1986. – **Huber-Greub, Barbara (Red.)**: Johann Jakob Bachofen (1815–1887). Begleitpublikation zur Ausstellung im Historischen Museum Basel 1987. Basle 1987. – **Landolt, Elisabeth; Ackermann, Felix**: Die Objekte im Historischen Museum Basel. Band 4 der Publikationen zur Ausstellung "Sammeln in der Renaissance: Das Amerbach-Kabinett". Basle 1991. – **Historisches Museum Basel, Jahresberichte und Rechnungen** [vorher: Verein für die Mittelalterliche Sammlung und für Erhaltung Baslerischer Altertümer, Jahresberichte und Rechnungen 1891–1907] Basel 1908–1963, Jahresberichte 1964 ff. – **Basler Zeitschrift für Geschichte und Altertumskunde**, Basel 1902 ff. [Vormals Beiträge zur vaterländischen Geschichte, Basel 1939–1901]. Hrsg. Historische und Antiquarische Gesellschaft Basel, 1902 ff.

Archaeology

Berger, Ludwig: Die Ausgrabungen am Petersberg in Basel. Basle 1963. – **Berger, Ludwig**: Archäologischer Rundgang durch Basel. Basle 1981. – **Fellmann, Rudolf**: Das römische Basel (Führer durch das Historische Museum Basel 2). Basle 1981. – **Furger-Gunti, Andres**: Das keltische Basel (Führer durch das Historische Museum Basel 1). Basle 1981. – **Moosbrugger-Leu, Rudolf**: Die frühmittelalterlichen Gräberfelder von Basel. (Führer durch das Historische Museum Basel 3). Basle 1982. – **Furger-Gunti, Andres**: Frühchristliche Grabfunde. Basle 1983. – **Rippmann, Dorothea; Kaufmann, Bruno; Schibler, Jörg; Stopp, Barbara**: Basel, Barfüsserkirche, Grabungen 1975–1977. Ein Beitrag zur Archäologie und Geschichte der mittelalterlichen Stadt. Olten; Freiburg in Breisgau. 1987. – **Archäologie in Basel: Fundstellenregister und Literaturverzeichnis**: Jubiläumsheft zum 25.jährigen Bestehen der Archäologischen Bodenforschung Basel-Stadt. Basle 1988. – **Basler Beiträge zur Ur- und Frühgeschichte.** Hrsg. Amt für Museen und Archäologie des Kantons Basel Landschaft et al. Derendingen-Solothurn 1976 ff. – **Basler Stadtbuch** [seit 1971 regelmässige archäologische Fundberichte von R. Moosbrugger und R. d'Aujourd'hui]. Basle 1971 ff. – **Jahresberichte der Archäologischen Bodenforschung des Kantons Basel-Stadt** [1962–1987 in Basler Zeitschrift für Geschichte und Altertumskunde; seit 1988 als selbständige Publikation]. Basle 1962 ff. – **Materialhefte zur Archäologie in Basel**. Hrsg. Archäologische Bodenforschung des Kantons Basel-Stadt. Basle 1985 ff.

Coins and medals

Geigy, Alfred: Katalog der Basler Münzen und Medaillen der im Historischen Museum deponierten Ewig'schen Sammlung. Basle 1899.

– **Reinhardt, Hans**: Basler Münzsammler. In: Historisches Museum, Jahresberichte und Rechnungen 1945. Basle 1946, p.33–44. – **Lindau, Johann Karl**: Das Medaillenkabinett des Postmeisters Johann Schorndorff zu Basel. Seine Geschichte bis zur Erwerbung durch das Historische Museum Basel. Basle 1947. – **Cahn, Erich B.**: Schöne Münzen der Stadt Basel. Basle 1975. – **Schärli, Beatrice; Weder, Marcus**: XI. Die Fundmünzen. In: Helmig, Guido und Jaggi, Bernhard: Archäologische und baugeschichtliche Untersuchungen in der Deutschritterkapelle in Basel, Jahresberichte der Archäologischen Bodenforschung Basel-Stadt 1988, p.167–187. – **Schärli, Beatrice; Jungck, Christoph**: Das Basler "Schulgeldlein". Die Schulprämien des Gymnasiums von Basel, Ausstellung zum Jubiläum 400 Jahre Humanistisches Gymnasium, 1589–1989 Basle 1989. – **Weder, Marcus R.**: Der "Bachofensche Münzschatz" (Augst 1884). Mit einem Exkurs über die unter Aureolus in Mailand geprägten Postumusmünzen. In: Jahresberichte aus Augst und Kaiseraugst 11, 1990 p.53–72. – **Fellmann Brogli, Regine**: Die Gemmensammlung im Münzkabinett des Historischen Museums Basel – Entstehung, Zusammensetzung und ausgewählte Beispiele. In: Historisches Museum Basel, Jahresberichte 1986–1990. Basle n.d.. [1992], p.77–84. – **Schärli, Beatrice**: Die Inventarisation der Gemmen im Münzkabinett des Historischen Museums Basel. In: Historisches Museum Basel, Jahresberichte 1986–1990. Basle n.d. [1992], p.85–90.

State and law

Wackernagel, Rudolf: Geschichte der Stadt Basel (3 Bände und Registerband). Basle 1907–1954. – **Baer, C. H.**: Die Kunstdenkmäler des Kantons Basel-Stadt Bd. 1 [François Maurer: Die Kunstdenkmäler des Kantons Basel-Stadt Bd. 1, Nachträge. Basle 1971]. Basle 1932. – **Burckhardt, Paul**: Geschichte der Stadt Basel. Basle 1942. – **Heitz, August**: Grenzen und Grenzzeichen der Kantone Baselstadt und Baselland. Liestal 1964. – **Teuteberg, René**: Basler Geschichte. Basel 1986. – **Egger, Franz**: Das Szepter der Universität Basel. Basle 1992.

Crafts and trades

Koelner, Paul: Basler Zunftherrlichkeit. Basle 1942.

Metals

Gysin, Fritz: Katalog der eisernen Ofenplatten im Historischen Museum Basel. In: Oberrheinische Kunst, Jahrbuch der oberrheinischen Museen, Jg. V, 1932, p.219–230.

Militaria

Schneewind, Wolfgang: Historisches Museum Basel: Die Waffensammlung (Schriften des Historischen Museums Basel III) Basle 1958. – **Kopp, Peter F.**: Valentin Sauerbrey in Basel 1846–1881. Katalog zur Ausstellung im Historischen Museum Basel. Basle 1972.

Sculpture

Kaufmann-Hagenbach, Annie: Die Basler Plastik des 15. und frühen 16. Jahrhunderts. Basle 1952. – **Landolt, Elisabeth**: Der Holbeinbrunnen. Basle 1984. – **Häusel, Bruno**: Die Restaurierung des Altars aus Sta. Maria im Calancatal. In: Jahresberichte des Historischen Museums Basel 1980. Basle 1985, p.40–55. – **Fuchs, Monique**: La sculpture en Haute-Alsace à la fin du Moyen-Age 1456–1521. Colmar 1985. – **Streeter, Colin**: Two Carved Reliefs by Aubert Parent. In: The Getty Museum Journal, Vol. 13, 1985, p.53–66. – **Zimmermann, Eva**: Zur Rekonstruktion des ehemaligen Hochaltares der Kippenheimer St. Mauritiuskirche. In: Festschrift für Peter Bloch zum 11. Juli 1990, hrsg. von Hartmut Krohm und Christian Theuerkauff. Mainz 1990, p.121–133. – **Roda, Burkard von**: Die kirchlichen Holzbildwerke im Historischen Museum Basel. Zwischenbericht einer Bestandesaufnahme. In: Unsere Kunstdenkmäler 41. Jg. 1990, p.161–192. – **Landolt, Elisabeth; Ackermann, Felix**: Die Objekte im Historischen Museum Basel. Band 4 der Publikationen zur Ausstellung "Sammeln in der Renaissance: Das Amerbach-Kabinett". Basle 1991.

Painting and graphic art

Wollmann, Therese: Scheich Ibrahim. Die Reisen des Johann Ludwig Burckhardt 1784–1817. Basle 1984. – **Roda, Burkard von**: Der Peter Rot-Altar. Basle 1986. – **Egger, Franz**: Basler Totentanz. Basle 1990. – **Zehnder, Franz Günther (Hrsg.)**: Stefan Lochner Meister zu Köln. Herkunft–Werke–Wirkung. Wallraf-Richartz-Museum. Cologne 1993.

Stained glass

Ganz, Paul L.: Katalog der Glasgemälde [Historisches Museum Basel Katalog III]. Basle 1901. – **Ganz, Paul L.**: Die Basler Glasmaler der Spätrenaissance und der Barockzeit. Basle; Stuttgart 1966. – **Landolt, Elisabeth**: Die Webern-Scheibe. Basle 1982. – **Gut, Johannes**: Die Farbfenster der frühklassizistischen Klosterkirche St. Blasien. In: Jahrbuch der Staatlichen Kunstsammlungen in Baden-Württemberg 25. Band 1988. p.198–259. – **Hoegger, Peter**: Standesscheibenzyklus aus dem Tagsatzungssaal Baden. In: Zeichen der Freiheit. Das Bild der Republik in der Kunst des 16. bis 20. Jahrhundert. Ausstellung im Bernischen Historischen Museum und Kunstmuseum Bern 1991. Berne 1991, p.131–136.

Textiles

Boser, Renée; Müller, Irmgard: Stickerei: Systematik der Stichformen. Zur Sonderausstellung Orientalische Stickereien vom 20. Februar 1968 bis 16. Februar 1969 Museum für Völkerkunde Basel. Basle 1968. – **Schneider, Jenny**: Textilien: Katalog der Sammlung des Schweizerischen Landesmuseums. Ausgewählte Stücke. Zurich 1975. – **Peter-Müller, Irmgard:** Ein rätselhaftes Bischofsgrab [Münstergrabung 1974 Grab 104]. In: Historisches Museum Basel Jahresbericht 1978. Basle 1978, p. 33–57. – **Peter-Müller, Irmgard:** Seidenband in Basel. Basle 1983. – **Lanz, Hans:** Die alten Bildteppiche im Historischen Museum Basel. Basle 1985. – **Peter-Müller, Irmgard:** La rubanerie bâloise. In: La soie – art et tradition du façonné lyonnais, 23 mai–5 oct. 1986, Musée d'Art et d'Histoire Neuchâtel. Neuchâtel 1986. p. 119–126. – **Peter-Müller, Irmgard:** Roses (vol. 1); Kaleidoscope (vol. 2); Fragrance Flowers (vol. 3); Modern Times (vol. 4) of the Series: Silk ribbons from The Basle Historical Museum. Suita (Japan) 1987–1989. – **Rapp, Annas; Stucky, Monica:** Der Flachslandteppich. Basle 1989. – **Rapp, Anna; Stucky, Monica:** Zahm und Wild: Basler und Strassburger Bildteppiche des 15. Jahrhunderts. Mainz 1990.

Goldsmiths' work

Burckhardt, Rudolf F.: Die Kunstdenkmäler des Kantons Basel-Stadt Band II: Der Basler Münsterschatz. Basle 1933. – **Reinhardt, Hans**: Der Basler Münsterschatz [Katalog der Ausstellung in der Barfüsserkirche zu Basel September – Oktober 1956]. Basle 1956. – **Barth, Ulrich**: Das alte Zunftsilber im Historischen Museum Basel. In: Schweizerische Kunst- und Antiquitätenmesse Basel. Basle 1974, p.10–20. – **Barth, Ulrich**: Altes Silbergerät im Hause zum "Kirschgarten". Basle 1976. – **Ackermann, Hans Christoph**: Das goldene Davidsbild. Basle 1981. – **Barth, Ulrich**: Schätze der Basler Goldschmiedekunst 1400–1989 / 700 Jahre E. E. Zunft zu Hausgenossen. Katalog der Ausstellung im Historischen Museum Basel, Barfüsserkirche 20.5.–2.10.1989. Basle 1989. – **Roda, Burkard von**: Das Stammbuch des Basler Goldschmieds Johann Heinrich Schrotberger (1670–1748). Basle 1989. – **Barth, Ulrich**: Auserlesenes aus dem Basler Münsterschatz. Basle 1990. – **Landolt, Elisabeth; Ackermann, Felix**: Die Objekte im Historischen Museum Basel. Band 4 der Publikationen zur Ausstellung "Sammeln in der Renaissance: Das Amerbach-Kabinett". Basle 1991.

Clocks and scientific instruments

Reindl, Peter: Wissenschaftliche Instrumente. Basle 1978. – **Gschwind, Eugen**: Montres de Genève 1630–1720. Basle 1978. – **Gschwind, Eugen**: Stackfreed 1540–1680. Basle 1979. – **Gschwind, Eugen**: Montres Françaises 1580–1680. Basle 1983. – **Ackermann, Hans Christoph**: Die Uhrensammlung Nathan-Rupp im Historischen Museum Basel. Basle 1984. – **Ackermann, Hans Christoph**: Uhrmacher im alten Basel. Basle 1986.

Ceramics

Meister, Peter Wilhelm: Porzellan des 18. Jahrhunderts: Meissen, Höchst, Frankenthal, Ludwigsburg. Frankfurt am Main 1967. – **Peter-Müller, Irmgard**: Geschirr des 18. Jahrhunderts im "Kirschgarten". Basle 1978. – **Bastian, Jacques**: La faïence et la porcelaine de Strasbourg. Rennes 1982. – **Peter-Müller, Irmgard; Bastian, Jacques**: Strassburger Keramik. Basle 1986. – **Lanz, Hans**: Porzellan des 18. Jahrhunderts im "Kirschgarten". Basle 1986 [2.ed.]. – **Bastian, Jacques**: Les Hannong: Etude des décors peints sur les faïences et porcelaines de Strasbourg et de Haguenau

(1721–1784) [Thèse de Doctorat]. Strasbourg 1986. – **Menzhausen, Ingelore**: In Porzellan verzaubert. Die Figuren Johann Joachim Kändlers in Meißen aus der Sammlung Pauls-Eisenbeiss Basel. Basle 1993.

Glass

Peter-Müller, Irmgard: 10 Gläser 10 Techniken. Basle 1982. – **Baumgartner, Erwin; Krueger, Irmgard**: Phönix aus Sand und Asche: Glas des Mittelalters [Rheinisches Landesmuseum Bonn 3. Mai–24. Juli 1988, Historisches Museum Basel 26. August–28. November 1988]. Munich 1988.

Furniture and woodwork

Burckhardt, Rudolf F.: Das Basler Büffet der Renaissance- und Barockzeit. In: Historisches Museum zu Basel Jahresberichte und Rechnungen Jahr 1914. Basle 1915, p.35–65. – **Kölner, Paul**: Geschichte der Spinnwetternzunft zu Basel und ihrer Handwerke. Basle 1931. – **Lanz, Hans**: Basler Wohnkunst und Lebensart im 18. Jahrhundert. Basle 1959. – **Reindl, Peter**: Basler Frührenaissance am Beispiel der Rathaus-Kanzlei. In: Historisches Museum Basel Jahresberichte 1974. Basle n.d. [1978], p.35–60. – **Pfister, Dieter**: Franz Pergo – Zur Nordwestschweizerischen Möbelkunst um 1600. Basle 1984. – **Roda, Burkard von**: Wohnstuben der Biedermeierzeit: Bilder zur Geschichte der bürgerlichen Einrichtung in und um Basel 1809–1849. In: Kunst und Antiquitäten 1/1989, p.64–73. – **Landolt, Elisabeth; Ackermann, Felix**: Die Objekte im Historischen Museum Basel. Band 4 der Publikationen zur Ausstellung "Sammeln in der Renaissance: Das Amerbach-Kabinett". Basle 1991. – **Ackermann, Felix**: Der Münzkasten des Basler Sammlers Basilius Amerbach. In: Schweizerische Münzblätter 42, 1992, p.47–56.

Stoves

Ackermann, Hans Christoph: Ein Strassburger Fayence-Ofen aus dem "Reinacher Hof". In: Historisches Museum Basel Jahresberichte 1971. Basle 1976, p.21–31. – **Bastian, Jacques**: Faïences de Strasbourg et de Hagenau: Les décors des Löwenfinck. In: L'Estampille No. 121, Mai 1980, p.42–57. – **Minne, Jean Paul**: Strassburger Fayence-Öfen im "Haus zum Kirschgarten" des Historischen Museums Basel. Bemerkungen zur Geschichte der Strassburger Ofenfabrikation. In: Peter-Müller, I.; Bastian, J.: Strassburger Keramik. Basle 1986. – **Peter-Müller, Irmgard; Bastian, Jacques**: Der Strassburger Blumenofen. Basle 1988.

Household utensils

Heyne, Moritz: Kunst im Hause. Abbildungen von Gegenständen aus der Mittelalterlichen Sammlung in Basel. Teil 1 und 2. Basle 1880 und 1882. – **Jauslin, Manfred**: Das Walbaum-Kästchen. Basle 1985.

Games and toys

His, Hans Peter: Altes Spielzeug in Basel. Basle 1973. – **Kopp, Peter F.**: Die frühesten Spielkarten in der Schweiz. In: Zeitschrift für schweizerische Archäologie und Kunstgeschichte, Band 30, 1973, p.130–145. – **Kopp, Peter F.**: Basler Spielkartenfunde. In: Basler Zeitschrift für Geschichte und Altertumskunde, Band 77, 1977, p.37–44. – **Kalt, Irène**: Die Spielzeugsammlung im "Haus zum Kirschgarten". In: Historisches Museum Basel Jahresbericht 1992. Basle 1993, p.39–41.

Musical instruments

Nef, Walter: Alte Musikinstrumente in Basel. Basle 1974. – **Gutmann, Veronika**: Mit Pauken und Trompeten. Ausstellung ausgewählter Instrumente aus der Sammlung historischer Blechblasinstrumente von Dr. h.c. Wilhelm Bernoulli. Basle 1982. – **Gutmann, Veronika**: Trommeln und Tambourstöcke in der Sammlung alter Musikinstrumente des Historischen Museums Basel. Basle 1983. – **Orgeln aus vier Jahrhunderten**. Schallplatte mit Begleittext. Orgel: Jean-Claude Zehnder. Basle 1985. – **Gutmann, Veronika**: Faltblatt mit Abbildungen als Führer durch die Ausstellung. Basle 1987. – **Gutmann, Veronika**: Das Virginal des Andreas Ryff (1572). Basle 1991. – **Gutmann, Veronika**: Katalog der Kleinorgeln. In: Historisches Museum Basel Jahresbericht 1992. Basle 1993, p.4–20. – **Kirnbauer, Martin**: Verzeichnis der Flöteninstrumente in der Musikinstrumenten-Sammlung des Historischen Museums Basel. In: Historisches Museum Basel Jahresbericht 1992. Basle 1993, p.21–30.

Coaches and sledges

Furger-Gunti Andres: Kutschen und Schlitten im alten Basel. Basle 1982. – **Belser, Eduard J.**: Der Minerva-Schlitten. Basle 1993.

Index

Numbers in **bold** characters are catalogue numbers. Those in roman are page numbers.